The
Vegetable
Gardener's
BIBLE

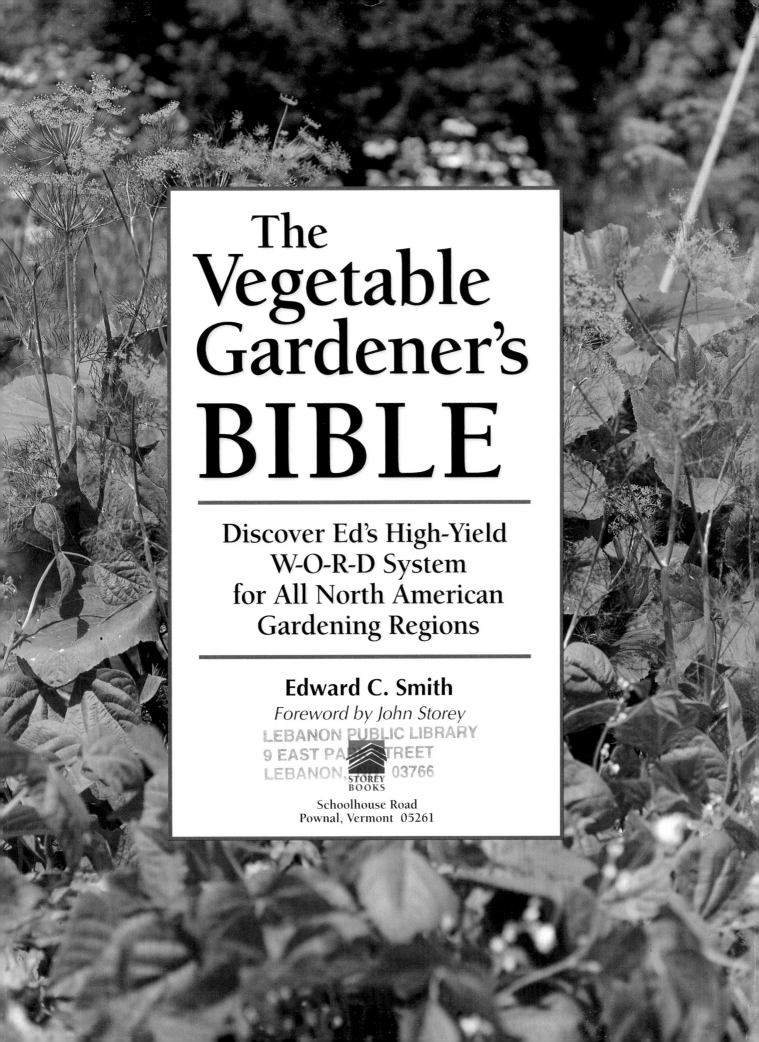

The Vegetable Gardener's BIBLE

Discover Ed's High-Yield
W-O-R-D System
for All North American
Gardening Regions

Edward C. Smith

Foreword by John Storey

STOREY
BOOKS

Schoolhouse Road
Pownal, Vermont 05261

The mission of Storey Communications is to serve our customers by publishing practical information that encourages personal independence in harmony with the environment.

Edited by Gwen W. Steege

Horticultural Editor: Charles W. G. Smith

Cover design by Meredith Maker

Cover photographs by Walter Chandoha and Giles Prett

Text design by Betty Kodela and Susan Bernier

Text production by Susan Bernier and Jennifer Jepson Smith

Interior photographs by Giles Prett, except for those noted below.

©Sylvia Ferry Smith: pages 33, 52, 59 (bottom right), 62 (bottom right), 76 (bottom right), 87, 100 (bottom left), 102, 103 (middle), 109, 145 (top left and right, and bottom left), 150, 152 (top right and left), 153, 155, 156 (bottom right), 159, 161 (top left), 195 (top left), 219 (top right and bottom left), 246, 251, 252, 254, 257, 258 (bottom), 259, 264, 266, 267, 268 (top right), 269, 270, 272, 277, 278, 295 (top right), 296 (top left and right), 303, and back cover (third one down); ©David Cavagnaro: pages 245 and 274; ©Christine DuPuis: pages 54, 114, 226, and 243; Bruce Curtis: page 233; ©Artville/Jeff Burke and Lorraine Triolo: pages 34, 90, 124, and 138

Illustrations by Beverly Duncan, except for those on pages 158, 159, 162, 166 (leaf miner, mite, snail), 167 (whitefly), and 221 by Brigita Fuhrmann; and pages 164, 165, 166 (flea beetles, Mexican bean beetle, slug), and 167 (squash bug, squash vine borer, tomato hornworm) by Kurt Musfeldt

Indexed by Northwind Editorial Services

Copyright © 2000 by Edward C. Smith

The information in this book is true and complete to the best of our knowledge. All recommendations are made without guarantee on the part of the author or Storey Books. The author and publisher disclaim any liability in connection with the use of this information. For additional information please contact Storey Books, Schoolhouse Road, Pownal, Vermont 05261.

Storey books are available for special premium and promotional uses and for customized editions. For further information, please call Storey's Custom Publishing Department at 1-800-793-9396.

Printed in the United States by R.R. Donnelley

10 9 8 7 6 5 4 3 2 1

Library of Congress Cataloging-in-Publication Data

Smith, Edward C. (Edward Clarke), 1941-
    The vegetable gardener's bible: discover Ed's high-yield W-O-R-D system for all North American gardening regions / Edward C. Smith; foreword by John Storey.
      p.   cm.
    ISBN 1-58017-213-X (alk. paper) ISBN 1-58107-212-1 (pbk.:alk. paper)
    1. Vegetable gardening.   2. Organic gardening.   I. Title.
SB324.3.S62   2000
635—dc21   99-052610

Dedication

To my darling Sylvia, with whom
I have gardened joyously for more than twenty years

Acknowledgments

Books are often mostly the work of the author and an editor, but not a book like this one. Many people did a lot of work to make this book a reality, not just the one who got his name on the cover.

Sylvia Ferry Smith has gardened with me through all the summers of our marriage. The ideas in this work are ones we've discovered, discussed, and tested together. Sylvia is also a photographer. Not only are some of the images in this book hers, but it was she who designed the garden this year so it would be accessible to the camera.

Lindsey and Nathaniel, daughter and son, who have gardened with us every year of their lives, spent a lot of extra time this year to keep the garden "photo-ready" and served as photographers' assistants all summer long.

Giles Prett, Storey Photographer, had the primary responsibility for the photographs and spent a total of more than two weeks with us in the garden this year. He made the effort to learn about gardening and about us, and his images capture not only the garden but the joy we experience there.

Charles W. G. Smith, Horticultural Editor at Storey, garden writer, and my brother, spent hours discussing garden problems and helping me get beyond what all the other garden books say. He also directed the photo shoots with a firm but gentle hand, and got us all through long, hot days with smiles on our faces.

Deborah E. Burns, Acquisitions Editor, saw that I had the seeds for a special book and helped me grow it to fruition.

Maggie Lydic, Editorial Director, was what every writer most wants and many never get, a reader. She identified the virtues of this book and made sure they survived the difficult journey from manuscript to finished book.

Gwen W. Steege, Editor, had the biggest and hardest job of all, fitting text and image together and keeping everybody on task and on time. This book is a tribute to her skill and patience, and to her continual good humor.

contents

Some Thoughts about Vegetable Gardening

Once in a long time, a truly fresh gardening personality emerges. Over the past 30 years, I've had the privilege of working with a few of these — Jim Crockett in the 1960s, Dick Raymond and Bob Thomson in the '70s, Louise Riotte in the '80s, Lewis and Nancy Hill in the '90s.

Ed Smith, vegetable gardener, Cabot, Vermont, is the latest of these amazing personalities. He and his family tend a richly fertile garden of over 1,500 square feet filled with raspberries, blueberries, flowers, herbs, and nearly 100 varieties of vegetables, including some Vermont heirlooms. His garden looks like what I envision as the "vegetable garden of Eden."

I never would have learned of, nor met, Ed but for his brother Charly, a Storey staff editor and horticultural expert in his own right. When we were looking for someone who was doing new and exciting things in the vegetable garden, he suggested that we meet his brother Ed.

When we learned that Ed lived in the Northeast Kingdom of Vermont (where gardening is only slightly easier than in Siberia!), we were skeptical. That is, until we saw his vegetable gardens. They are beautiful, the result of a high-yield system of gardening that Ed has been refining for over three decades. "If I can do it here in northern Vermont, it can be done just about anywhere," said Ed.

The proof was before our eyes, and as we talked, we realized how logical and easy his approach was. To underscore a point, he took us to the richest compost pile I've ever seen. With mock seriousness he instructed, "The path to a high-yield garden leads straight through the middle of a compost pile." Clearly, Ed's no stick-in-the-mud when it comes to gardening.

Wherever we walked, Ed had gardening wisdom to share. At the corn patch he said, "Corn has the highest sugar content early in the morning. So pick it then, before it's warmed by the sun, and refrigerate it in the husk until dinnertime. You'll get the best-tasting corn with the morning harvest." It's true.

When we saw him dusting his seed potatoes with sulfur, he explained that sulfur is a fungicide, but that wasn't the reason he did it. "Treat seed potatoes with sulfur, and Colorado potato beetles will be much less of a problem." I followed his advice, and my new red potatoes were the best I've ever had.

In the pages that follow, you'll see the results of his gardening system with your own eyes. We've come to refer to this system as the "W-O-R-D," to remind us of the wide rows, organic methods, raised beds, and deeply dug soil that underlie everything Ed does. You'll discover these, along with the trellises that allow beans to grow to the sky, knowledgeable companion planting, and basic crop rotation, all leading to remarkable harvests — a vegetable gardening paradise.

We spent the past year with Ed in Vermont, photographing his gardens from the first day of soil preparation to the last days of putting the garden to bed. These year-round photos will be very helpful to you in planning and planting your own vegetable garden, as will the numerous charts, tables, and garden plans.

We think that this is the most comprehensive and exciting new system of gardening that has come along in a very long time. Through the dozens of illustrated gardening lessons, and hundreds of tips, insights, and suggestions that Ed shares, you'll quickly become a more skilled gardener. This book will help you do it, and have the best vegetable garden ever. That's why we call it "the bible."

And please, if ever you have a suggestion or question, don't hesitate to call (802-823-5810).

M. John Storey
Pownal, Vermont

▲ This healthy garden demonstrates W-O-R-D in action.

PART 1

From Seed *to* Harvest
Higher Yields with Less Work

CHAPTER 1

A New Way to Garden: Wide, Deep, Raised Beds

My first vegetable garden, when I was 8, was very traditional: The vegetables were arranged in narrow rows separated by wider paths. That was the way my parents gardened, and every year we gathered what looked like a pretty good harvest. When I moved to Vermont, my address changed, but the way I gardened stayed the same. It hadn't yet occurred to me that gardening could be, or needed to be, improved.

The more I gardened, the more I learned. I tried wide rows and liked the results. It wasn't just that I grew more in less space; the plants actually grew better in wide rows than they did in narrow ones. From wide rows I tried wide raised beds, and again there was a noticeable improvement. After more investigation, I began using wide, deep, raised beds and growing my best gardens ever. I noticed that whenever a plant's growing space gets wider or deeper or both, its growth improves. I asked why. The answer led me to a new system of gardening. It has to do with roots.

A Radical View of Roots

There's a saying here in the Northeast Kingdom of Vermont that the worst part of ignorance isn't what we don't know; it's that so much of what we do know just isn't so. The truth of that adage has, as we put it in this part of the country, hit me right up side of my head a number of times in my life. But it was never more true than it was in my garden. For a lot of my gardening life, my decisions about how best to grow plants were informed by some ideas about plant root systems that just weren't so.

▲ **Give 'em stretching room.** This wide, deeply dug bed of carrots thrives because its roots have room to stretch and find the nutrients and moisture they need.

WHAT I KNEW ABOUT CARROT ROOTS

The box on the next page shows two drawings of carrots. The one on the left represents what I thought I knew about carrot roots; and it's what guided my decisions about how best to grow carrots. The root system, of which there isn't a whole lot, extends outward a few inches and downward about the same amount. It covers about the same area below ground as the foliage does above ground. I rather suspect that I'm not the only gardener to see things more or less this way. I've often seen drawings very much like this in books.

With this narrow view of roots to guide me, it made perfect sense to grow carrots in narrow, shallow beds. I believed that all the carrot really needed was a band of loosened soil about 8 inches (20 cm) wide and about the same depth, just what it gets in the traditional garden.

I further assumed that what was true for carrots was also true for the other vegetable plants. If they had a band of loose soil about as wide as the reach of their foliage and as deep as my tiller could till, vegetable plants had all the space they really needed. That's the space they get in a traditional row-based garden, so it made good sense to garden that way.

BUT IT JUST ISN'T SO

I remember the moment I first really *saw* a drawing similar to the one on the right in the box. I'd looked at it before, but I hadn't really seen it. I felt that a bulb lit up in my head, illuminating the reason my plants preferred those wider rows and deeper beds.

The drawing on the right, rather than that on the left, shows the way carrot roots really grow, or more precisely, how carrot roots *can* grow if they get enough loose soil to grow in. Carrot roots can extend as much as 1½ feet (45 cm) on all sides and as much as 3 feet (90 cm) downward. In other words, the roots extend outward much farther than the foliage does.

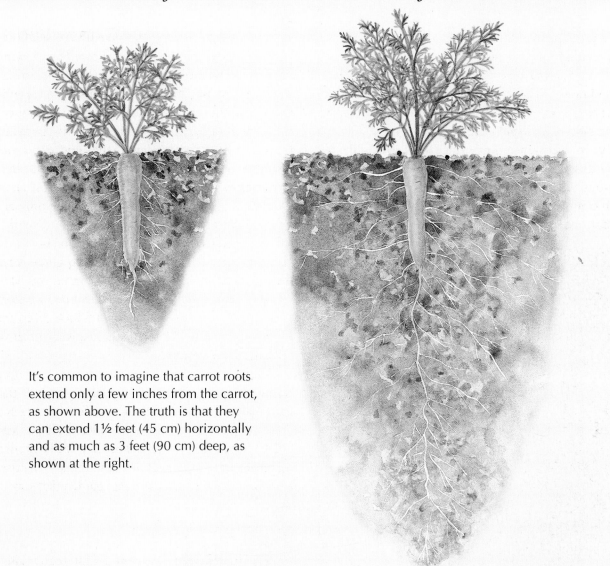

It's common to imagine that carrot roots extend only a few inches from the carrot, as shown above. The truth is that they can extend 1½ feet (45 cm) horizontally and as much as 3 feet (90 cm) deep, as shown at the right.

What is true for carrots is also true for all the other vegetable plants in the garden. Even so-called shallow-rooted sorts like celery or onions can grow much more extensive root systems than we usually imagine, and all of them grow better with a lot more room than they get in a traditional narrow, shallow row.

From that moment, I set about designing a garden bed that gives plant roots substantially more room to grow and at the same time can be easily built and maintained. Unlike the traditional garden, in which each foot (30 cm) of row provides plant roots with about ⅔ of a cubic foot (.02 m³) of growing space, a wide, deep, raised bed provides over 5 cubic feet (.14 m³) per row foot, almost 8 times more space. This is why the vegetables I grow in my wide, deep, raised beds are the most vigorous, healthy, and productive I've ever grown.

Why Wide, Raised Beds Outshine Traditional Rows

A garden contains two kinds of space — space for plants to grow, and space for a gardener to walk while tending the plants. Walking on garden soil exerts pressures of as much as 10 pounds per square inch (4.5 kg per 2.5 cm^2), quite enough to force soil particles together and compress the spaces between them. The result is compacted soil, which, although it still contains all the nutrients and moisture it did before, can no longer support abundant root growth. Roots, particularly the tiny, delicate root hairs that absorb moisture and nutrients, grow in the spaces between soil particles. They grow poorly or not at all where such spaces are absent or not sufficiently numerous.

In a typical narrow-row garden, over half the soil is compacted into walkways for the gardener. If the gardener favors power tilling and cultivating machines, as much as three-quarters of the garden becomes inhospitable to plants.

In a garden with wide, deep, raised beds like the ones I use, plants get the lion's share of the space, and they get the lion's share of the soil. In my garden, about three-quarters of the garden space is used to grow plants, and only about a quarter is used for walkways.

A traditional garden puts the needs of the cultivator first. A garden based on wide, deep, raised beds puts the needs of the cultivar first.

▲ **Spring: after the coverup.** These wide beds received their winter blankets of straw mulch in October. Now, in early spring, they've been uncovered so that the strengthening sun can warm the soil. The first peas are even sprouting beneath the trellis.

Midsummer: weed-free, plant-friendly soil. As the long days of summer spur the garden into full growth, wide, deep, raised beds provide good drainage, closely planted crops shade out weeds and keep moisture from evaporating, and mulched paths provide walking and working areas, while protecting the soil from compaction.

Late summer: the path to a successful harvest. The abundant harvest from efficiently planted wide, deep, raised beds will convince even skeptical gardeners that this is the path to gardening success.

Getting the Size Right

When you plan your garden beds, one of your first questions should be, How wide and deep does this wide bed have to be for the plants to grow their best and simultaneously allow me to enjoy the garden? The rule here is pretty easy to remember: The width of the bed is determined by your own comfort, while its depth reflects the plants' needs.

HOW WIDE A BED IS WIDE ENOUGH?

How wide you make a bed depends on how wide a bed you can comfortably tend. You need to be able to reach easily to its center to weed, cultivate, prune, and harvest. For me, that's about 18 inches (45 cm), so a bed width of about 3 feet (90 cm) is just right. For trellised or staked plants, I like a slightly narrower bed of about 30 inches (75 cm). Applying this "rule of comfort," different gardeners are likely to come up with different answers. I know gardeners who like beds 4 or even 5 feet (1.2 to 1.5 m) wide, while others prefer narrower ones. Whatever width you come up with for your beds, remember that they are now reserved for your plants and shouldn't be walked on.

▲ **Keep off the beds.** Easy to tend, these 3-foot-wide (90 cm) garlic beds never get compacted because I don't have to step into them to weed or harvest.

HOW DEEP IS DEEP ENOUGH?

Bed depth is determined not by what's comfortable for the gardener but what is best for plants. Increasing the depth more than the standard 8 inches (20 cm) requires some work. Sometimes it also means additional materials and money. But once you do it, you'll have amazing results and much less work in following years. Using the designs and techniques in this book, I combine deep tilling with raising the soil level to achieve beds with about 18 inches (45 cm) of loosened soil. The plants might like even more, but they don't really need it. I'm quite satisfied with the results I get.

HOW LONG SHOULD THE BED BE?

Bed length is pretty much arbitrary and depends on how much space you have. For me, though, I prefer beds that are 15 feet (4.6 m) long. One reason for this is purely psychological. I usually assign myself garden work "by the bed," and I become overwhelmed at the prospect of coping with a bed longer than about 15 feet (4.6 m). I have another, more practical reason, too. I build trellises for many of my crops, and the lumber I use for them comes in 8-foot (2.4 m) lengths. If my beds are 15 feet (4.6 m), the trellises are easy to construct, using two boards with some overlap (see pages 72–73).

No rule says that all the beds need to be lined up next to one another, or even that they have to be all squares or rectangles. A garden made of wide, raised, deep beds allows you to go beyond the traditional grid system of so many vegetable gardens.

▶ Scatter beds around your yard, wherever optimum growing conditions exist. Or, like flower beds, let them be part of your landscape plan, their shapes and locations determined in part by aesthetic considerations.

▶ If you like squares or circles, go for it. I sometimes wonder why flowers get most of us thinking in free-form designs for beds, while vegetables confine us to straight lines and right angles.

▲ **What an angle!** Garden beds can be any shape your imagination dreams up, even triangles.

▲ **Good things come in small packages.** Raised beds can be unsupported, or supported by planks, plastic wood, stones, cement blocks, or other materials. This commercially made 3' x 6' (0.9 x 1.8 m) untreated cedar bed is ideal for gardeners in the city or country, young and old. It is easy to care for and produced quantities of vegetables, flowers, and herbs on this brick patio for months.

Grow More in Less Space with Less Work

Wide, deep, raised-bed planting has many practical advantages in addition to offering a better growing environment. Because of the high ratio of bed space to walking space, you can grow substantially more vegetables in substantially less space. Switching from "gardener-centered" to "plant-centered" spacing results in dramatic savings. Raised beds are also less work, because they're easier to weed, water, and fertilize. And after the first year, weeding is almost a thing of the past.

SPACE SAVERS

Walkways are narrower in a bed-based garden because they are used just for walking, not for wide cultivating machines. They are also fewer, because they do not occur between every row. In a traditional garden, the recommended spacing between rows is determined more by the needs of the cultivator than it is by the needs of the cultivar. In beds, most vegetables can be grown much closer together, resulting in a further saving of space.

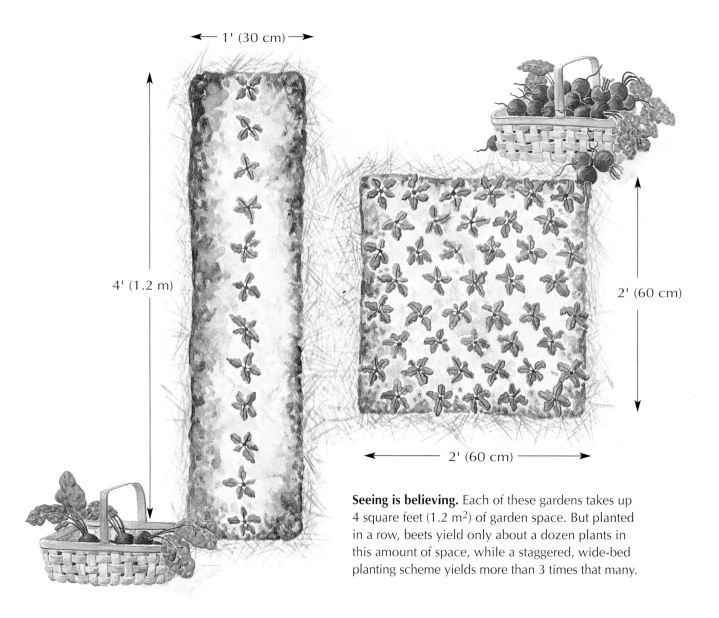

Seeing is believing. Each of these gardens takes up 4 square feet (1.2 m²) of garden space. But planted in a row, beets yield only about a dozen plants in this amount of space, while a staggered, wide-bed planting scheme yields more than 3 times that many.

WORK SAVERS

Because wide beds are permanent, you will no longer waste time, labor, and materials adding compost, fertilizers, and minerals to what will be walkways. Watering, too, can be concentrated where it will do the most good. Efficient systems, such as soaker hoses or drip irrigators, are easy to install in wide beds and allow you to direct the water right to the plants, not to the walkways. Fewer walkways also means less of a very tedious form of weeding: digging weeds out of the hard-packed soil of walkways. And when you grow plants in beds so that their leaves just barely touch when the plants are mature, you create a microclimate that not only saves water because there's less evaporation, but also inhibits weeds because soil is shaded.

Just as wide beds make watering more convenient, you'll also find that you use less compost and fewer fertilizers and other soil builders, because you dig them into the beds only, not into areas where plants won't be growing.

▲ **Don't waste the walkways.** Narrow, straw-mulched walkways need little care, and more space is left for growing plants.

◄ **A built-in umbrella.** As the plants grow, their foliage shades the ground beneath so that it stays moist; and with little sun to encourage growth, any weeds are thin, spindly, and easily removed.

Recognizing the Right Site

With enough time, work, and materials, you can probably create a productive garden almost any-where, but most people are not looking for more work to do in their garden. They want more joy when working their garden. A good start toward this goal comes when you select the site for your garden. You can save a lot of work and expense if you start with a site that already has most of what your garden will need.

LET THE SUN SHINE IN

If there is a "most important" consideration in planning a garden, it is sunshine. Some plants do thrive in deep shade, but none of them are vegetable plants. Although some vegetable plants (usually those grown for their leaves) can tolerate partial shade, most need full, unobstructed sunlight for at least six hours a day to produce the best yields. Morning sun is particularly helpful because it dries the dew from leaves and hinders certain diseases.

Observe your potential garden spot in spring every hour or so, marking the areas of shadow with stakes and recording the times. If you don't end up with at least six hours of sun over the whole garden-to-be, consider the following:

▶ **Clear the decks.** Remove whatever causes the extra shade, if possible.
▶ **Change its shape.** Consider changing the shape of your garden to match the full-sun area. One of the advantages of gardening in beds is that you aren't limited to the traditional straight lines of a narrow-row garden. You can vary the arrangement of your beds and even their shapes to match different situations.
▶ **Smaller can be better.** Create several smaller gardens instead of one large one. Put as much of the garden as you can in the largest sunny area and, if possible, scatter two or three others where they can take advantage of other small sunny spots.

▲ **By dawn's early light.** Throughout the season, observe patterns of light and shadow in your garden. Here, in late August, beds are sunlit by 10 A.M. For best results, you need six hours of direct sun.

▲ **As shadows lengthen.** In June, the time of year when the sun is most directly overhead, you can see shadows from neighboring trees beginning to creep toward the beds about 4 o'clock in the afternoon.

JUDGING WHICH WAY THE WIND BLOWS

Just as it's important to observe the patterns of sun on your garden, you can also improve your chance for success by learning which way the breeze blows. Gentle, consistent movement of the air benefits a garden by mixing different pockets of air together. This helps prevent extremes of hot and cold and modifies very humid or dry air. On the other hand, frequent high winds can quickly steal moisture from the leaves and damage plants by breaking stems, tearing leaves, or damaging trellises. It is sometimes difficult to know if winds will be a problem, but here are some clues. If your garden has a beautiful long-range view, it may also be windy. Other windy sites include those in coastal areas, as well as those with western or northern exposures, especially when weather fronts or storms pass through. In windy sites place the garden where there is already a windbreak, or plan on creating one.

Effects of Air Movement and Sun on Sloping Gardens

Air movement. Cold air moves downhill and will collect in low areas or where fences, buildings, or dense plant growth block its movement. Frosts will be less of a problem in gardens on slopes where cold air can move over and past the garden rather than settling in it.

Sun. In northern regions, a site that slopes to the south will warm more quickly in spring and stay warm longer in fall. In milder regions, a gentle northern slope will be less likely to overheat in summer.

▼ **Fruits of protection.** Situated on a beautiful hillside, this vegetable garden is protected from strong westerly winds by a row of raspberry bushes. This barrier not only blocks the wind, but it provides a bonus crop of delicious berries as well.

NOBODY LIKES WET FEET

You can't grow vegetables in a swamp, but in the spring or after a rainy spell swamps can look dry compared to some folks' gardens. If you have no choice but to garden in a too-wet site, you may be able to correct the problem (or have it corrected) with drainage ditches or subsoil piping. But most people's swampy garden problems come from putting their gardens in a site that looks dry most of the time but whose natural preference is being wet.

If you suspect your garden is too wet, look for these two clear signs of a site with poor drainage:

▶ **Slow drying.** The soil takes much longer to dry out after a rain than nearby soil. After drying, the soil often cracks or forms a crust.
▶ **Puddle-forming.** Rather than drying up and draining away, puddles remain for hours after rain. Standing water in early spring, shortly after the snow is gone, is okay, but if it's still there in late spring after the soil has completely thawed and it's time to start working in the garden, then the site is too wet.

▲ **Dry up!** There are many types of garden soils, and each drains a little differently. Sandy soils drain and dry quickly. Loam drains well, forming puddles that quickly disappear after it stops raining. Silt and clay soils are most often associated with wet places and often harbor puddles hours after a storm.

Bigger Isn't Necessarily Better

Here's a good rule that helps keep vegetable gardening enjoyable: How large a garden you need should match how large a garden you want. Many people vegetable garden to grow food for their families. That's what I do, and it's a serious undertaking. But how do you know how large your garden should be? When I started gardening, I consulted many different charts on plant yield and family size for guidance. I didn't find any of these practical. So instead I started with the size garden that felt manageable. There's no quicker way to extinguish the spark that ignites the joy of gardening than by taking on too much too soon. If you find that you're running out of green beans before the season is over, or you're longing to work in the garden but there doesn't seem to be anything to do, then it's probably time to expand. If this is your family's first vegetable garden, however, make it of a size that you think you can take care of, and remember that whatever size you choose, a wide, deep, raised-bed garden will give you more food than will a row-style garden. So you'll grow more in less space anyway.

"A BIRD IN THE HAND . . ."

After you've determined which sites meet the criteria for light, slope, and moisture, it's time to decide how close the garden will be to the house. Why this is important is easy to see. Lettuce is more likely to become a salad if its fetching does not involve a hike. Watering is easier to do when the garden is near the spigot, and general garden care is more enjoyable when your time is spent actually caring for the garden and not walking back and forth from the garden to the house. A garden that is close to your house is also likely to be close to your heart.

We have more than one garden, and each is sited with an eye to what is growing in it. The large storage garden is a short walk from the house, while the smaller kitchen garden is only a few steps from the front door. Both gardens are visible from the house, and this is a nice plus. For me the vegetable garden is as much a part of our home's attractive landscape as the flowers and trees. One of vegetable gardening's subtle pleasures is contemplating the garden from inside the house, particularly on a rainy summer day, or imagining the garden-to-be while gazing at the snow that covers it in winter. When you view a garden through a window, regardless of the season, it keeps that garden in your thoughts, and that makes gardening more fun.

▼ **A room with a view.** I enjoy my garden from inside the house, even when I can't be outdoors working in it.

The Joy of Garden Tools

"One feels so kindly towards the thing which allows the hand to obey the brain." These words, written by the garden author Gertrude Jekyll (1843–1932) about her gardening tools, capture for me a very important part of the enjoyment I experience in the garden. A good tool allows me to do exactly — not approximately, but exactly — what I want to do, and it allows me to do it comfortably. It was created by a tool designer and craftsman who were striving, as I am, to do the best they could. And if form dictated by function is part of what makes something beautiful, then a good tool is also a worthy object of contemplation.

A garden tool is your partner in the garden. It should be a good partner.

This isn't to say that you can't enjoy your garden unless you have lots of expensive tools. It means that you should acquire the tools you need to do the tasks you wish to do, and that the tools should be of sufficient quality to help you in the garden, not frustrate you. While it's true that some of the best gardening tools are expensive, it's also true that many are not. Learning to recognize quality, scrutinizing garage sales, and buying tools out-of-season can stock your garden shed with excellent tools at little expense.

Tools for Bed Building

If your garden is small — a single bed or just a few beds — you may choose to dig it by hand. In this case, you will be best served by a spade and a stout garden fork. A crowbar will be handy if you encounter rocks. Although both spades and shovels are used for digging and the words are often used interchangeably, the terms actually refer to quite different tools.

SPADE. With its flat, rectangular blade, a spade allows you to cut a straight edge around a bed or to cut out neat squares of sod and peel them off evenly at the root line.

SHOVEL. The convex, pointed blade of a shovel makes it a good tool for moving soil — from walkway to bed, for instance.

STEEL RAKE. The rake head should attach to its handle by a hoop. Steel rakes are useful for drawing soil from walkways into beds and for moving soil within beds. If you flip it over and use the flat side, it's an excellent tool for smoothing the bed surface.

GARDEN FORK. Useful for tilling the soil, a well-made garden fork has thick, somewhat narrow tines. Thick tines are strong and won't bend when working in the soil or when they encounter a large rock. The tines should be also be narrow so they easily move through the soil when loosening clods of dirt.

YOU GET WHAT YOU PAY FOR

I don't buy cheap tools because I've found that, in the long run, they always end up costing more than the expensive ones. The trouble is that at first glance a lot of cheap tools can look like expensive ones. On more careful inspection you can see that some cheap tools are made from inferior materials or put together poorly. They break. By the time you've bought a second cheap tool to replace the broken one, you'll probably have spent more than one good tool would have cost.

Cheap tools are often poorly designed, sacrificing utility in favor of a lower sales price. At best, such tools make gardening more work. At worst, they don't do the job right or they end up hurting you. They make your back ache, they make your muscles sore, or they give you blisters.

Sometimes I can tell that I will like a tool just by looking at it or seeing a picture of it, but usually I need to hold it. Check to see if the fit is comfortable: Is there room for your hands within enclosed handles? Is the surface smooth and welcoming to your skin? Does the handle fill, but not overfill, your hand? Next, observe how it balances. It should be easiest to hold in just the way you'll hold it when at work. At the same time, notice its weight. You obviously don't want a tool that's too heavy, but it can also be too light. For digging tools in particular, you may want a slightly heavier tool to provide some of its own inertia to get the job done.

Judging a Shovel's Merits

The forged steel shovel on the right is much stronger than the pressed steel shovel on the left. Forged steel is thicker and must be heated in order to shape it by hammering; pressed steel is simply bent to shape. Note that on the shovel on the right, the socket is forged as part of the tool head and then welded closed. Tools with a pressed socket loosen after use. Look for this construction when you purchase a shovel, spade, or garden fork.

Comfort for the gardener. This sturdy trowel has a number of good points. Its stainless-steel head will not rust, and although it's harder to sharpen than softer metals, stainless steel keeps its edge longer. I also like the wooden handle. It's not only pleasing to the eye and hand, but it doesn't feel freezing in chilly spring weather nor hot when it's been left in the summer sun.

Poor: pressed steel

Good: forged steel

Tool Buyer's Criteria

▶ Forged steel

▶ Good balance

▶ Comfortable grip

▶ Appropriate weight

▶ Smooth surfaces

The Search for a Perfect Rectangle

Regardless of what style garden you prefer, from tight and formal to loose and free-form, there are some skills that you need to know so you can plan and create the garden of your dreams. The first steps in creating a wide, deep, raised-bed garden are the same as those you'd take when starting any garden.

Laying out beds is something I'm fussy about. Once I've decided on rectangular beds, I want rectangles, not parallelograms. You don't have to be this particular, but making accurate rectangular beds is really pretty easy, and it's fun. All you need are five stakes, some twine, a steel tape, and the only thing I remember from geometry class: Magic triangles (see the box below).

Before you begin, mow the garden area, leaving the grass clippings where they fall. You'll be digging them into the soil in a later step.

You can reuse the stakes and string for any number of new beds. Use the string as a guide to outline the area with a sprinkling of lime or flour.

Customized Garden Beds

▶ **Custom size.** You can use this technique to make beds of any length. Simply change the 15-foot (4.6 m) measurement to whatever length suits your needs. Just be sure you have a 3-foot (0.9 m) "leg" and a 5-foot (1.5 m) "hypotenuse."

▶ **Custom style.** Use the method to lay out a single wide bed in a lawn area or, after tilling a large garden, multiple wide beds within the entire space.

The Magic Triangle

About 4,000 years ago, the Egyptians used a simple mathematical formula to lay out the pyramids. They called it the "magic triangle," and it's still magic today. We can use it to help lay out our garden beds.

The formula is this: If one leg of a triangle is 3 units, the second leg is 4 units, and the hypotenuse is 5 units, then the angle between the legs is a right angle.

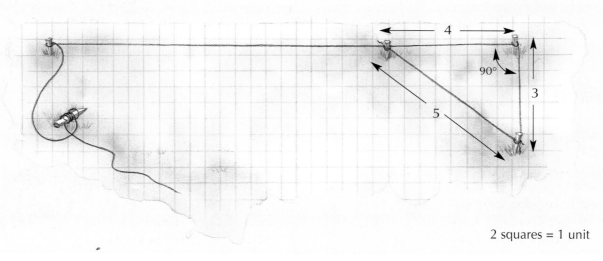

2 squares = 1 unit

Laying Out a Wide Bed

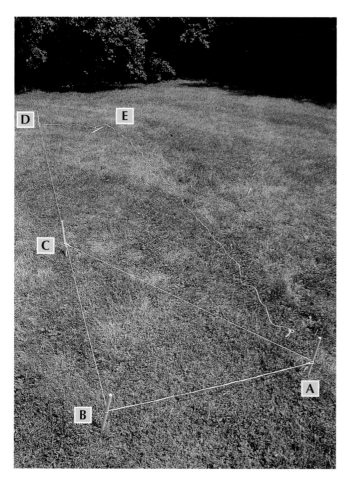

For a bed 3' x 15' (0.9 x 4.6 m):

About 50 feet (15.2 m) of garden twine

Five 1-foot (30 cm) stakes

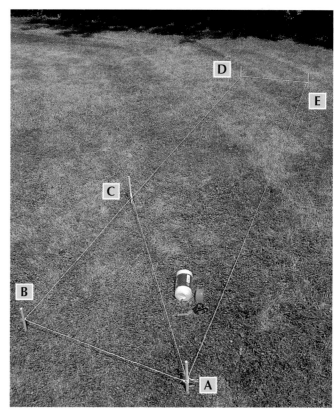

1 Attach stake A at one end of the twine; stake B, 3 feet (0.9 m) beyond that; stake C, 4 feet (1.2 m) beyond that; stake D, 11 feet (3.3 m) beyond that; and stake E, 3 feet (0.9 m) beyond that.

- Measure another 15 feet (4.6 m) of twine beyond that and cut the twine.
- Measure a 5-foot-long (1.5 m) piece of twine, and tie it to stake C.
- Following the pattern in the photo, position the stakes in the following order: first B and D, and then C so that the twine lies straight between B and D.
- Stretch the 5-foot-long (1.5 m) piece of twine from stake C to stake A, and position stake A so that the twine is taut on all sides.

2 Position stake E so that all the twine is taut. And there it is, a perfect 3' x 15' (0.9 x 4.6 m) rectangle! Leave the twine in place, or use a sprinkling of flour or lime to outline the area marked by the string and remove the stakes and string.

Stake out.
Measure out your lengths of twine and prepare your stakes before you go out in the garden.

Digging a New Wide-Bed Garden

Wherever you live, preparing a new garden involves three things: dealing with whatever is already growing there (usually grass), loosening the soil that lies beneath whatever is growing there, and improving the soil by adding organic matter. You can do these things whenever you have the motivation and time to do it, but the best time for your new garden is in late summer or fall the year before you plan to plant.

When Spring Comes . . .

If you dug your new bed in the fall, remove the mulch as soon as you can in the spring, so the soil can warm. As soon as the soil is dry enough to work, spread an inch (2.5 cm) or so of compost and work it into the soil with a garden fork. Try to accomplish this without walking in the bed.

FALL START-UP

Starting in fall means that you do your share of the work of soil improvement, but you also get a lot of volunteer help from worms and other creatures living in the soil. These little garden leupracauns will work through the colder months and digest a lot of organic matter while simultaneously aerating and loosening the soil. This extra help provides a couple of added bonuses that save you work: You can leave the sod in the bed where it will decompose, rather than having to remove it, and you can add uncomposted or partly composted organic materials, such as chopped leaves, instead of completed compost.

SPRING START-UP

If you start a new bed in spring, on the other hand, there won't be time for your volunteer helpers to decompose the sod before you plant, so you'll have to remove it instead of turning it into the bed. Save the sod and add it to your compost pile, sandwiching it between layers of other organic matter, or compost it separately by stacking it in a pile, root-side up. The sod will take about a year to break down and turn into a rich brown compost. Then bring it back to the garden and turn it into the soil.

Begin by laying out the area you plan to dig, following the steps on page 19.

Preparing New Garden Beds with a Rototiller

It's possible to use hand tools to dig a new garden, especially if you're an olympic weight lifter or your garden is small, but I like to use a big rear-tine rototiller when I'm starting a large, new garden. Tilling, however it is accomplished, is a three-step process:

1. Cut the sod free and into small pieces that will be easy for soil organisms to break down.

2. Loosen and aerate the soil.

3. Mix the sod and other organic material evenly into the loosened soil.

Using a rototiller for this process is a lot less work than digging a big garden by hand, and the tiller does a better job of chopping sod and other organic matter into small pieces and distributing them throughout the top 9 inches (22.5 cm) or so of the soil. If I manage to schedule time for it, I like to prepare the ground in the fall, because that's when there are lots of leaves to till in.

Step-by-Step to a Simple Wide Bed

1 Use a spade to edge the bed all the way around. You'll find this is much easier if you use a well-sharpened spade.

2 Cut out blocks of sod. Hold the spade at a very low angle to the ground, so that you take only a thin layer of sod.

3 Turn the blocks of sod over, making sure the grass is deeply buried, and use the spade to chop the blocks of sod into pieces

4 Work well-rotted manure, compost, leaves, and/or grass clippings into the soil, and then add at least 6 inches (15 cm) of topsoil to create a raised bed.

Fast Mulch Tip

Leaves are particularly good for the garden because tree roots reach deep into the sub-soil and absorb trace minerals, which then appear in the leaves. If you're planning to work leaves into your garden beds to enrich the soil, put them through a shredder or spread them on an area of lawn where you can mow them with a power mower to chop them up. You'll find it's easier to work them in, and they'll break down more quickly after you add them to the soil.

Deeper Beds for Super-High Yields

A simple wide-bed garden will give you a very big advantage over a traditional row-style garden, because you're providing 5 to 10 times more uncompacted soil to your plants for root growth in the same amount of space. But with a little more work, you can get even greater increases in plant vigor and yield. Look again at the drawing of plant roots (page 5) that indicates the need for wider and deeper growing spaces. As you can see, roots can grow deeper than the 9 inches (22.5 cm) or so of soil that you loosen with garden fork or tiller. You can provide for this additional growing depth by working the soil either by double-digging or broadforking. I prefer broadforking, because double-digging involves a lot more work for no more gain.

GETTING TO THE BOTTOM OF THINGS

Loosening the soil farther down usually involves getting into a different kind of soil — subsoil, as distinct from topsoil. Although subsoil contains very little organic material and therefore few of the nutrients plants need most, it often contains various other nutrients (micronutrients) that plants need in smaller amounts, which are often not present in the topsoil. In addition, by loosening subsoil you can increase its capacity to receive and store water; this can become critical to plants' health during dry times. You initiate a process whereby plant roots and worms can enter the area much more easily and continue the loosening and aerating process. They will slowly improve the subsoil structure and build capillaries to connect it with the topsoil.

DOUBLE-DIGGING

Double-digging is often seen as the defining technique of Biodynamic/French Intensive gardening, as described by John Jeavons (see the appendix). Its advantage is a very thorough loosening of the subsoil. The disadvantages are that it takes a lot of time and work; it also results in more mixing of soil layers than does broadforking. You'll need a spade and a garden fork to double-dig. Here's how to do it:

Dig a trench about the width of your spade and about a foot (30 cm) deep across the width of the bed, putting the soil you're removing in a wheelbarrow. (You'll need it at the far end of the bed.) Loosen the exposed subsoil. If compaction is not too severe, just insert the garden fork and pry downward on its handle. If the soil is really packed, break it up first with the spade and then work it with the fork. Now dig the top layer of soil from one side of the trench and put it on top of the loosened soil in the first trench. Continue to the end of the bed. Fill in the last trench with the soil from the wheelbarrow.

Using a Garden Fork

If you don't have a broadfork, you can get something of the same effect using a garden fork. Thrust the fork down into the soil as deep as you can get it, then rock it back and forth to loosen the subsoil.

Using a Broadfork

1 To avoid compacting the soil, stand on a piece of plywood while using your broadfork. Grab a handle in each hand, place the tines in the soil, and step on one side and then the other to get the tines in as far as they'll go easily.

2 Centering your weight over the bar, step on the bar with one foot and work it farther into the soil. Move the handles forward and back to work the tines into the compacted subsoil.

3 Step backward and lower the handles in a smooth and easy motion. If the fork brings up large clods, agitate it from side to side to break up the clumps. Move the broadfork 8 inches (20 cm) or so and repeat.

How Loosening Subsoil Benefits Your Plants

▶ Subsoil contains small amounts of certain nutrients (micronutrients) that aren't always available elsewhere.

▶ Subsoil can serve as a reservoir for moisture.

▶ Roots and worms can enter the area much more easily and continue the loosening and aerating process

Tools for Deep Digging

All broadforks consist of a 14- to 24-inch-long (35 to 60 cm) crossbar with 4- to 5-foot-long (1.2 to 1.5 m) handles attached to each end. Along the crossbar are five to seven 9- to 14-inch-long (22.5 to 35 cm) tines. There are also some very important differences among broadforks:

What to look for. The most useful broadforks have tines with a parabolic curve at the top. The tines are attached to the rear of the bar. This design allows the tines to work with a rolling rather than prying motion, thereby making the tool much easier to use.

What to avoid. Two features make broadforks harder to use: straight tines that are attached to the bottom of the bar and additional crossbars a few inches up the handles and/or near the top. These interfere with the best way to use the tool.

Use it respectfully. A well-made broadfork is very effective for loosening topsoil and breaking up subsoil compaction. Don't use it for removing rocks or roots, however, because even the strongest tines will bend under the weight of those tasks.

Pile It On: Another Way to Add Depth

Loosening the subsoil with a broadfork or double-digging are two ways to get a deeper bed, but you can also provide more depth for root growth by adding topsoil to the bed. If your beds are bordered by lawn or you left grass walkways, this option involves importing some soil. If, however, you are building beds in the midst of a larger area of prepared soil, the material you need, fully enriched and loosened, is already there in what will become the walkways between the beds. It would be a shame to waste this beautiful stuff growing weeds that you'll later have to grub out of the walkways, when all you have to do is rake or shovel it out of the walkway area and over the beds!

Because there is less area in walkways than in beds, and because you won't be taking all the topsoil in the walkways, bed depth will probably increase no more than 3 or 4 inches (7.5 to 10 cm), but even this is enough space for a lot of root growth. Just watch what happens when you plant carrots in a bed with this much more topsoil. The extra vigor and growth they exhibit will amaze you. Beds made this way will keep their shape without support if the sides have a gentle slope.

After the area is tilled, rake it smooth and then follow the steps on page 19 to outline each bed. Leave about 1½ feet (45 cm) for the walkways between each bed.

▼ **Better garden beds equal better gardens.** The plants below are growing in wide, deep, raised beds. With room for their roots to grow, these vegetables are amazingly vigorous and healthy.

Raising the Bed Level

1 Standing on one side of the bed, shovel 4 or 5 inches (10 to 12.5 cm) of topsoil from the walkway and put it on the bed. Work down the length of the bed, then move to the opposite side and repeat the process. Remove the guide string when the bed is shaped.

2 Rake the top of the bed as level as possible, then use the back side of the rake to smooth the length of the bed.

3 If you didn't add compost or manure when you tilled the area, spread 1 or 2 inches (2.5 to 5 cm) over the bed now and work it in as you smooth. This is also a good time to add other soil amendments, such as greensand.

4 To make your walkways carefree, cover them with three to six layers of newspaper, followed by a layer of clean, seed-free straw.

When You Want to Support Your Raised Beds

Deep-digging methods give you about 18 inches (45 cm) of cultivated soil. If you bring in more soil, you'll probably need to provide some support for it, such as boards, timbers, or cement blocks. This step involves a substantial increase in time, labor, and probably money, but the result is neat looking beds. Supported raised beds are especially appropriate if your beds are in a lawn or you have limited garden space.

A supported raised bed is surrounded by a retaining structure about 8 to 12 inches (20 to 30 cm) high, of sufficient strength to hold that amount of soil. You can use wood — anything from boards or planks to timbers or even logs — as well as stones, bricks, or cement blocks. (See the box on page 28 for the advantages and disadvantages of other materials.) The photos here show how to build a raised bed supported by boards.

Trick or Treat

There has been much controversy concerning the safety of using pressure-treated wood for raised garden beds. Treated wood commonly contains chromated copper arsenate (CCA), which inhibits fungal rot. The chromium, copper, and arsenic, all toxic to some degree, have been shown to leach from the wood into the surrounding garden soil, usually in low levels. The CCA then binds to soil particles, which limits absorption into plants. If you are concerned about the potential health effects of treated wood, don't use it. Try plastic wood, which doesn't rot, is lighter than regular wood, and doesn't leach CCA into the soil.

▶ **Pack it in.** This 4' x 12' (1.2 x 3.7 m) raised bed made of spruce boards provides a good quantity and impressive variety of crops for a small family. As shown, it offers celery, cabbages, cherry tomatoes, and two kinds of peppers (Italian frying peppers and a handsome purple variety). Pink snapdragons add a spark of color.

Creating a Raised Bed with Plank Sides

Building the Wood Frame

What You'll Need

For sides
Two 12-foot (3.7 m) pieces of
2" x 12" (5 x 30 cm) lumber

For ends
Two 4-foot (1.2 m) pieces of
2" x 12" (5 x 30 cm) lumber

For stabilizers
Two 4-foot (1.2 m) pieces of
2" x 2" (5 x 5 cm) lumber

For corner supports
Four 1-foot (30 cm) pieces of
2" x 2" (5 x 5 cm) lumber

1 lb. (454 g) of 10d nails or 1 box
of 3-inch (7.5 cm) galvanized
deck screws

1 Screw or nail one end piece to one of the side pieces, butting the side piece against the end piece. Screw or nail the second side piece in the same manner. Repeat at the other end to create a box. Use three fasteners at each corner. Use a carpenter's angle to make sure that each corner is square.

2 Measure and mark 4-foot (3.7 m) intervals on each side for the placement of the two stabilizers. The stabilizers will be at the bottom of the raised bed when you put it in place.

3 Set one stabilizer so it is flush with the edge at each side. Screw or nail in place.

4 Set one of the corner supports at the inside of a corner. Screw or nail it in place from the outside, at both the end and the side. Repeat with the remaining corners.

Creating a Raised Bed with Plank Sides (continued)

Preparing the Site

5 Place the completed wood frame on your planting site. Sprinkle lime or flour around the outer edge of the frame to mark the area to be dug. (You can also mark the area with stakes and string.) Set the frame to one side.

6 Using a sharp garden spade, cut around a section of sod about 1 foot square (30 cm²). With the spade held at a very low angle to the ground (about 10°), cut into the marked section just beneath the root zone of the grass. Remove the sod and place it on a tarp. Continue to remove all the sod in the bed area.

SOME FACTS ABOUT RAISED-BED MATERIALS

Material	Advantages	Disadvantages
Planks (1½–2", or 4–5 cm, thick)	Easy to handle	Require support at corners and every 4 feet (1.2 m) or so Will rot
Timbers (4" x 4" to 8" x 8") (10 x 10 cm to 20 x 20 cm)	Longer lasting than planks Larger ones hold back soil even if partly rotted 6" x 6" (15 x 15 cm) and larger don't need support Provide a place to sit while tending plants	Expensive Will rot eventually Smaller sizes require support at corners
Logs	Inexpensive if you already own some surplus trees and a way to move them to the garden Lasts many seasons	Cumbersome and heavy, especially the larger sizes
Cement blocks	If leveled with some care, won't require additional support Retain heat, allowing soil to warm more quickly and stay warmer	Most expensive Can be unattractive Not comfortable to sit on

7 Using a garden fork, loosen the soil about 8 inches (20 cm) deep over the entire bed. You don't need to turn over the soil; just rock the fork back and forth to break it up evenly over the entire bed.

8 Put the frame on the bed. Replace the sod *upside down*, breaking it up with a garden fork or spade as you lay it on.

9 Spread a layer about 1 inch (2.5 cm) deep of compost and/or well-composted manure into the loose sod. Work this into the surface with the garden fork.

10 Fill the frame with a mixture of good topsoil and more compost. You'll probably want to bring the soil to within 1 to 2 inches (2.5 to 5 cm) of the top of the frame.

11 Rake the area, breaking up any clumps as you go. Allow the bed to settle for a week before planting.

CHAPTER 2

Planning Your Garden, Growing Your Plan

It's late in December. The temperature is way below freezing; the days are short and seldom sunny. Today, summer seems more a dream than a memory, and the garden beds are just humps in the blanket of snow. I'm bundled to the ears, trudging through drifts to get the mail. I open the box, and there it is. The first seed catalog!

For me, that shivering moment in front of the mailbox is the beginning of the end of winter. Spring is still a long way ahead, and there will be many days yet just as cold and snowy as this one. But from here on in, I'm no longer moving farther away from last year's garden; I'm moving closer to next year's garden. We'll begin the journey tonight, in front of the fire, with this first seed catalog and a big sheet of paper titled, "Garden Plan."

Selecting Savory Seed Catalogs

Open the January issue of any popular gardening magazine and turn to the section where all the seed companies are listed. Page after page after page! How are you ever going to winnow that list down to the half dozen or so you'll actually end up doing business with? This is how I've gone about it.

STICK PRETTY CLOSE TO HOME

Most of my long-time favorite seed companies are based in the northeastern part of the country, which is also where I live and garden. That's no accident.

Although a seed company may or may not have grown its seeds in the same area the company is located, it usually carries only seeds that will grow well in that region. Most of the companies I trade with maintain trial gardens to test their seeds to ensure this.

Some vegetable varieties grow well almost anywhere, but others do well only in particular climates. I have the best chance of getting varieties that grow well in my garden if they have been tested in gardens with a similar climate.

SOME KERNELS OF WISDOM WITH YOUR KERNELS OF CORN

Just as I'll patronize a store where the salespeople know their products and can help me make informed decisions, I'll buy from seed companies whose catalogs give the facts I need to choose wisely and the cultural information I need to ensure a successful harvest. In this regard, there are some very big differences among catalogs.

In one catalog a typical bush bean description says the beans are tasty and tender and that the seeds should be planted after the last frost because they need to grow in warm soil. That's it.

▲ **Inside tips right from the horse's mouth.** My favorite seed catalogs are also among my favorite garden books.

A second catalog sells the same variety of bush bean, but with a whole lot more useful information as a bonus. The bean is described as somewhat more tender than a currently popular variety, tasty when used fresh, but not very good for canning or freezing. I also get germination temperature, pH preference, disease resistance, and a definition of warm soil as being at least 60°F (16°C). As I flip through the pages, I notice that I also get cultural information, such as a plant's ability to tolerate heat or cold, and harvest and storage hints.

The second catalog makes it much easier for me to choose among bean varieties and helps me succeed with whatever I decide to plant. My favorite seed catalogs really have a place among my favorite garden books. I refer to them often for information on planting, growing, harvesting, and pest and disease control.

THE PRICE IS RIGHT

I won't choose one seed company over another because of 5 or 10 cent price differences. But when one company charges $1.80 and another charges $.80 for the same size packet, I'm likely to patronize the latter.

Some seed houses offer very small packets of seeds for similarly small prices. That's not much help when I'm buying carrot or radish seeds because I usually plant all I get in a standard packet. But I use only two or three of the 20 or 30 seeds in a standard packet of any summer squash. If I can buy small packets, I can then afford to buy several different kinds. Similarly, I much prefer being able to get a half dozen small packets of different tomato varieties rather than a single, large pack of just one kind.

SUPPORT DIVERSITY

In a few instances these rules don't apply. I will go on trading indefinitely with some companies for other unique reasons. For example, sometimes a particular seed company is my only source of a favorite variety. In another instance a company may have very large selections of vegetables I like to experiment with, like lettuces, tomatoes, or beans. Then there are some small companies that carry specialized plants. One such company I buy from every year sells local heirloom varieties. Another caters to short-season gardeners with a wide selection of early varieties. There are also some interesting companies that specialize in preserving not just heirloom but historic varieties. I like to send at least some business to these companies every year, just so they'll be there when I need them.

▲ **These take the prize.** Once you learn the vocabulary of seed catalogs, you can select seeds with the qualities that mean the most to you. The catalog said "these beans are sure-fire blue-ribbon winners," so we put them to the test. Our blue ribbon at the county fair proved the catalog was right on the mark.

Catalogs That Are Really Useful

Seed catalogs need to give you more information than catalogs that sell many other products. A vacuum cleaner can clean a rug in California as well as in Maine. But a variety of onion that grows beautifully in warm regions may do nothing in cold climates. It won't be too hard to single out the most helpful seed catalogs if you keep these principles in mind. Look for the following:

▶ A company that's located in your region

▶ A catalog that is clearly written with lots of useful information

▶ Seed packet sizes that suit your needs and your pocketbook

▶ A catalog with a large selection of the plants you like

▶ A company that offers personal, customized service

Seed Catalogs as Garden Tools

A tool is anything that helps you accomplish a task or purpose. A good seed catalog can be a very useful garden tool to help you decide which crops and varieties to grow in the garden. But having a good tool is only half the battle; you also have to know how to use it. Study this sample catalog entry for Big Beef tomatoes, which provides explanations for what to look for and how to interpret the information you find.

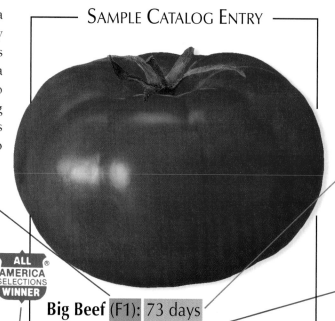

SAMPLE CATALOG ENTRY

Big Beef (F1): 73 days
(V, FF, N, T, As, L)
A beefsteak-type tomato with meaty, tasty fruit and an old-time tomato flavor. Early maturity and superior disease tolerance. Large (avg. 8-10 oz), mostly blemish-free globe-shaped red fruit. Produces well, even under adverse conditions. Indeterminate.
PKT $2.20; ¹⁄₁₆ oz. $9.90

F1 versus OP

The varieties in seed catalogs are commonly of two types: open-pollinated (OP) or F1 hybrids.

Open-pollinated varieties. These varieties are genetically stable, which means that seed collected from OP plants will produce offspring very similar to the parents. Heirloom varieties are open-pollinated.

F1 varieties. When two genetically dissimilar but related plants are crossed, the resulting offspring show increased vigor and yield. To control this phenomenon, scientists create very stable, genetically pure varieties and then cross them. The resulting seed is called F1, which means *first filial generation*. F1 hybrid seed produces vigorous, high-yielding plants. The downside of hybrid vigor is that it lasts only one generation. Seeds collected from F1 hybrids usually produce weak, inferior plants.

Cracking the Codes

Along with straightforward descriptions of each vegetable variety, you'll often find a lot of information disguised as icons or enclosed in tables. For instance, instead of mentioning cold tolerance, a catalog might use a snowflake icon. The All-America Selection (AAS) Winner notes varieties that have been recognized for superior qualities by this nonprofit gardening organization. Look for keys to this information in both the general introduction and the introductions to each section.

Weather Tolerance

This category includes things such as frost tolerance or resistance to flowering (bolting) in hot weather. Look for environmental qualities when you wish to extend your season or if your season is marginal for growing that plant. For example, lettuce is a cool-weather crop that bolts in warm weather. To extend the lettuce season, plant a heat-tolerant variety to mature during the warmer weeks of summer.

Days to Maturity

The number listed as "days to maturity" lets you know how long it takes from sowing the seed to harvesting the vegetable. On some long-season crops that are started indoors, this number is calculated from transplanting rather than sowing. It's important to determine which starting point the catalog is referring to.

Days-to-maturity numbers can be very helpful estimates when you are planning your planting and harvesting schedules. They are especially important for gardeners like me who live in an area with a short growing season. A variety that takes longer to mature than the number of frost-free days I'm likely to have is not a good choice for my garden.

You'll find variations in maturity dates from catalog to catalog, due to differences in growing season, soil fertility, and other conditions where they were tested. Remember that the date is an educated guess — sometimes a very good guess, but still a guess.

Disease Resistance

This is perhaps the least glamorous quality included in plant descriptions and is often relegated to the last sentence. Though not glamorous, disease resistance is very important. The more resistant or tolerant a variety is, the less likely disease will ruin your crop. After you've narrowed your list by using qualities such as flavor, whittle it down more by including only those varieties with good disease resistance. Each supplier provides a key to the disease-resistant qualities it touts.

Description

I've found that reading seed catalogs is a little like reading used-car ads: What is not said is sometimes more important than what is said. Up here in snow and road-salt country, if a car is free of rust, the ad will say so. If it doesn't say so, it very likely has rust. With this in mind, I look for what isn't said when I'm trying to decide on this year's varieties. If I need a bean that freezes well and the description doesn't mention this, then I assume it doesn't freeze well. When I'm choosing tomatoes, flavor is my prime concern, so I like it when flavor is the first thing mentioned, not an afterthought. What I avoid is a variety that brags about color, firmness, yield, freedom from blemishes, its ability to ship well, or its appeal as a market favorite. These are all important qualities to commercial growers, but since all I have to worry about is getting my tomato from the garden to the table, flavor is the first quality I look for.

Vegetable Size

Size is most often mentioned if the plant is substantially smaller or larger than others of its kind. For example Wee-B-Little pumpkins average 10 ounces (284 gm) each, but Atlantic Giant can weigh 500 pounds (206 kg) or more. In between is New England Pie, which weighs about 6 pounds (2.7 kg) and is noted for its superb flavor, not size. When folks choose a variety based on its size, they often aren't looking for much else. Varieties that produce big crops, such as beefsteak tomatoes, also take much longer to mature than smaller-fruited types. Supersteak tomato takes 20 days longer to mature than Early Girl. Still, some people say that big is better. If you're one of those, look for varieties that promise you big plants or fruit.

Getting Down to Decisions about What to Plant

The "what" question really has two parts: What vegetables will I grow? And what varieties of those vegetables will I grow? There are as many answers to these questions as there are gardeners. Here are some principles I follow to help me determine what my garden will look like each year.

GROW WHAT YOU'LL EAT AND AS MUCH AS YOU'LL EAT

On the surface, this sounds simple. But when I first gardened, I discovered that to think with my head and not with my stomach when I planned the garden was more difficult than I anticipated. Although we did eat some of everything we grew, we didn't eat all of everything we grew. Our experiences with beets and zucchini provide good examples of what I mean.

▲ **Lock out.** It's said that in some towns, August is the only time folks lock their car doors. Why? To keep over-blessed gardeners from dumping extra zucchini on them.

Can't beat those beets. Up until a few years ago, we always grew beets for storage in the root cellar, but we used only about a tenth of what we'd stored, the rest ending up on the compost pile in spring. We finally realized that beets were not our favorite winter food. On the other hand, we did like beets during the summer but were growing too few at that time. To solve the problem, we replaced the large planting of storage beets with small succession plantings of summer beets — varieties that are especially good when eaten young and fresh.

The ever-prolific zucchini. Another learning experience involved zucchini. We always grew three or four zucchini plants each year. You know the rest of that story. We ate zucchini. When we couldn't eat any more, the chickens ate zucchini. And when the family and the animals had had their fill, the plants were still producing zucchini. Now I grow one zucchini plant each year and that satisfies all our needs. I'm surprised by how many of these examples I can think of. Many gardeners grow certain vegetables in certain amounts just because that's the way they've always grown them, or their parents have, or neighbors have. By making sure we grow what we really like to eat — in amounts that we really will eat — we can easily increase the useful yield of the garden with little effort.

TRY SOMETHING NEW

Like many gardeners, I'm a creature of habit. Sometimes this is good, but when routine becomes a rut, it's good to give myself a boot and try something new. The garden is a great place to do this. Fortunately trying something new has never been easier. Each spring I find vegetables in the seed catalogs I've never heard of before. In fact, sometimes all the vegetables in some catalogs are new to me. A few years ago, vegetables from Europe, Japan, and

Africa were rarely available in North America. They are now, and each year brings a greater variety. I like to try at least one new vegetable each year.

Not only are many new vegetables on the market, but now you can find many unusual kinds of all sorts of common vegetables. Twenty years ago the catalogs and garden centers carried half a dozen varieties of tomato that would grow well in my garden. Today my favorite seed catalog lists 40 varieties of tomato. Another catalog lists well over 300 varieties of tomato! Even the local garden center grows two dozen varieties, including some heirlooms. With this selection it's easy to find something new to grow in the garden every year.

I don't try every new variety that comes down the pike, but I do grow at least one or two new varieties and one or two new vegetables each year. I have to remind myself not to fall in love with a new variety right away. I like to grow it in the garden and see how well it performs. If I like it, then I grow more of it the next season.

◀ Farmers Long eggplant and ▼ Treasure Chest watermelon are two new varieties to experiment with.

Picking Favorites

If a variety performs well in your garden year after year, it is not just a variety but a favorite variety. "Favorite" is not a title gardeners bestow lightly. It must be earned. The trouble is there are so many vegetables and so little time! It would take a lifetime to try all the varieties in just one good garden catalog. Fortunately there are ways of narrowing the selection of candidates before you send in each spring's order of seed.

Chatting over the neighbor's fence. Whether you're just starting out or you're looking around for something new to try, ask your neighbors. The nearest approximations of the conditions in your garden are found in your neighbors' gardens. What works for them is most likely going to work for you.

Reading the literature. Every once in a while I'll try a new vegetable or new variety because it was recommended by a garden writer, particularly if I know that conditions are similar in our respective gardens.

Combing catalogs. One of my favorite ways to pick new varieties is leafing through the new seed catalogs and reading carefully between the lines (see pages 34–35).

Exploring the local nursery. Go down to the local garden center and ask a lot of questions. They can't afford to sell plants that won't grow well for their customers.

Time to Plan Is Time Well Spent

Spring is here. The beds are ready. The birds are singing. I have all my seeds. Impatience is in the air. It's very tempting to pull on a pair of boots, grab a trowel or a hoe, and start planting. Sometimes a garden planned as a by-product of spring fever works out fine. Sometimes it doesn't. Spring is not an easy time to be patient, but patient planning can make the rest of the garden season much more rewarding and enjoyable.

I've already decided what to grow in the garden. Now I have to decide where in the garden everything should grow. Gardening is fun, and I don't want to clutter the garden planning with unnecessary restrictions, so I follow just a few simple rules.

▲ **Perfect pairs.** Dill and nasturtium both make good companions for squash and cucumber because they repel squash bugs and attract beneficial insects.

A Buddy System for Plants: Companion Planting

When I planted my garden in rows, it never occurred to me to plant more than one kind of vegetable in any row. That's just not the way it's done. But when I started planting in beds, it seemed reasonable to consider mixing different sorts of plants in a bed. I like the notion in a general way, because it's closer to the way things occur in the natural world. Nature tends to mix things up instead of planting big blocks of just one kind of plant.

Some plants have a synergistic relationship with certain other plants. One or both of them grow better, yield more, and sometimes even taste better when they grow near one another. These are often called "companion plants." In other cases, plant partnerships have negative effects: One plant inhibits another's growth. Understanding plant relationships is an important part of planning any garden, but particularly a bed-based garden.

Eliminate the Negative

Let's start with the inhibitors. In a traditional garden, the root systems of plants in adjacent rows are kept apart by a wide band of compacted soil that is largely impenetrable to roots. In beds, on the other hand, plants may be only inches apart, and roots spread and intermingle freely. In fact, there can be some degree of contact between the roots of plants as much as 5 or 6 feet (1.5 to 1.8 m) apart. Thus, both positive and negative effects among those plants will be more pronounced in beds than in single rows. It is therefore particularly important to avoid antagonistic relationships — those in which the growth of either or both plants is inhibited. Place antagonists no closer than 6 feet (1.8 m) apart in a bed, or better still, put them in separate beds.

Although you may find long (and sometimes contradictory) lists of plants that do or don't get along together, some general rules can guide your planning. You can avoid many problems by keeping a few plant families away from one another. (See the chart on pages 40–41.) For instance, members of the cabbage and onion families don't get along with members of the tomato and pea (legume) families. Yes, there are exceptions to this rule, or at least disagreements among gardeners. For instance, some consider onions and tomatoes companions; others feel chives and garlic make good companions for tomatoes. Experiment a little to see what works in your garden.

ACCENTUATE THE POSITIVE . . . CAREFULLY

When I plan my garden, I look for positive relationships between plants with clear benefits. I plant onions among members of the mustard family to keep cabbage moths at bay. And radishes go anyplace where flea beetles are a problem, because flea beetles would sooner eat radish leaves, especially young and tender ones, than they would any others.

Very little is known about why some of these relationships exist. It is clear, for instance, why carrots benefit from having onions, leeks, rosemary, wormwood, or sage nearby: Carrot flies, whose larvae attack young carrot roots, are repelled by the aromas these plants give off. But why do carrots grow with tomatoes or lettuce to mutual benefit? Why do celery, parsnips, and dill inhibit carrots? Nobody knows for certain, and most of the evidence is anecdotal. Consider all the advice, including the suggestions in this book, as a starting point, not gospel. Keep track of the results and compile your own list of garden companions.

For more information about planting to deter garden pests, see pages 151–155.

Let the Sun Shine In . . . Most of the Time

Most of the plants in the garden do best with at least 6 hours a day of full sun, some even more. To make best use of the sun, I put tall plants like corn and trellised tomatoes, beans, and peas toward the northern side of the garden. You'll notice that your garden gets the most sun at about the time of the summer solstice. In fact, at 10 A.M. in mid-June a 6-foot (1.8 m) pole placed in the middle of one bed will barely cast a shadow to the center of the next bed. But the sun angle gets progressively steeper as the summer wears on, and tall crops can sometimes produce enough shade to hurt their neighbors. It can be even more of a problem if your garden is already shady for a significant part of the day. It's best to keep tall plants on the northern side.

▲ **Move to the rear, please.** I keep trellised plants and corn on the north side of the garden so that these tall crops don't shade lower-growing vegetables.

PLANT FAMILIES

You can usually plan on placing family members near each other, because relationships of plants within families are generally either positive or neutral. An exception to this rule is the tomato family. Some tomato family plants include tomatoes, potatoes, eggplants, and peppers. Both tomatoes and potatoes grow well next to peppers and eggplants, but tomatoes and potatoes do not grow well next to each other.

Plant Family	Vegetable/Herb/Fruit	Plant Family	Vegetable/Herb/Fruit
Beet	Beet, spinach, Swiss chard	Mallow	Okra
Buckwheat	Red orach, rhubarb	Mint	Basil, marjoram, oregano, sage
Cabbage	Arugula, broccoli, broccoli-raab, Brussels sprouts, cabbage, cauli-broc, cauliflower, Chinese cabbage, cress, horse-radish, kale, kohlrabi, mizuna, mustard, pak choi, radish, rutabaga, turnip	Morning glory	Sweet potato
		Onion	Asparagus, chive, garlic, leek, onion, scallion
		Pea	Bean, pea, peanut
		Purslane	Claytonia
Carrot	Carrot, celeriac, celery, chervil, cilantro/coriander, dill, fennel, parsley, parsnip	Rose	Alpine strawberry
		Sunflower	Artichoke, endive/escarole, Jerusalem artichoke, lettuce, radicchio, sunflower, tarragon
Cucumber	Cucumber, gourd, melon, summer squash, winter squash	Tomato	Eggplant, pepper, potato (white), tomatillo, tomato
Grass	Corn		

SOME GARDEN FRIENDS AND ADVERSARIES

Plant	Garden Friend	Garden Adversary
Asparagus	Basil, nasturtium, parsley, tomato	Garlic, onion
Bean, bush	Beet, cabbage, carrot, cauliflower, celeriac, celery, chard, corn, cucumber, eggplant, leek, marigold, parsnip, pea, potato, radish, rosemary, strawberry, sunflower	Basil, fennel, kohlrabi, onion family
Bean, pole	Carrot, cauliflower, chard, corn, cucumber, eggplant, marigold, pea, potato, rosemary, strawberry	Basil, beet, cabbage, fennel, kohlrabi, onion family, radish, sunflower
Beet	Bush bean, cabbage family, corn, leek, lettuce, lima bean, onion, radish	Mustard, pole bean
Broccoli	Beet, bush bean, carrot, celery, chard, cucumber, dill, kale, lettuce, mint, nasturtium, onion family, oregano, potato, rosemary, sage, spinach, tomato	Pole, lima, and snap bean, strawberry
Brussels sprout	Beet, bush bean, carrot, celery, cucumber, lettuce, nasturtium, onion family, pea, potato, radish, spinach, tomato	Kohlrabi, pole bean, strawberry

Plant	Garden Friend	Garden Adversary
Cabbage	Beet, bush bean, carrot, celery, cucumber, dill, kale, lettuce, mint, nasturtium, onion family, potato, rosemary, sage, spinach, thyme, tomato	Pole bean, strawberry
Cantaloupe	Corn	Potato
Carrot	Bean, Brussels sprout, cabbage, chive, leaf lettuce, leek, onion, pea, pepper, red radish, rosemary, sage, tomato	Celery, dill, parsnip
Cauliflower	Beet, bush bean, carrot, celery, cucumber, dill, kale, lettuce, mint, nasturtium, onion family, potato, rosemary, sage, spinach, tomato	Pole bean, strawberry
Celery	Bush bean, cabbage family (especially cauliflower), leek, parsley, pea, tomato	Carrot, parsnip
Corn	Bush bean, beet, cabbage, cantaloupe, cucumber, morning glory, early potato, parsley, pea, pumpkin, squash	Tomato
Cucumber melon	Bush bean, cabbage family, corn, dill, eggplant, lettuce, nasturtium, pea, radish, sunflower, tomato	Potato, sage
Eggplant	Bush bean, pea, pepper, potato	None
Kale	Beet, bush bean, cabbage, celery, cucumber, lettuce, nasturtium, onion, potato, spinach, tomato	Pole bean
Kohlrabi	Beet, bush bean, celery, cucumber, lettuce, nasturtium, onion, potato, tomato	Pole bean / Bush
Leek	Beet, bush bean, carrot, celeriac, celery, onion, parsley, tomato	Bean, pea
Lettuce	Everything, but especially carrot, garlic, onion family, and radish	None
Lima bean	Beet, radish	None
Onion family	Beet, cabbage family, carrot, kohlrabi, leek, early lettuce, parsnip, pepper, strawberry, spinach, tomato, turnip	Asparagus, bean, pea, sage
Parsley	Asparagus, corn, tomato	None
Parsnip	Bush bean, garlic, onion, pea, pepper, potato, radish	Caraway, carrot, celery
Pea	Bean, carrot, celery, chicory, corn, cucumber, eggplant, parsley, early potato, radish, spinach, strawberry, sweet pepper, turnip	Gladiolus, onion family, late potato
Pepper	Carrot, eggplant, onion, parsnip, pea, tomato	Fennel, kohlrabi
Potato	Bush bean, cabbage family, corn, dead nettle, eggplant (as trap crop), horseradish, marigold, parsnip, pea	Cucumber, pumpkin, raspberry, rutabaga, squash family, sunflower, tomato, turnip
Pumpkins	Corn, eggplant, nasturtium, radish	Potato
Radish	Bean, beet, cabbage family, carrot, chervil, corn, cucumber, leaf lettuce, melon, nasturtium, parsnip, pea, spinach, squash family, sweet potato, tomato	Hyssop
Rutabagas	Nasturtium, onion family, pea	Potato
Spinach	Cabbage family, celery, legumes, lettuce, onion, pea, radish, strawberry	Potato
Squash	Celeriac, celery, corn, dill, melon, nasturtium, onion, radish	Potato
Strawberry	Bean, borage, lettuce, onion, pea, spinach	Cabbage family
Tomato	Asparagus, basil, bee balm, bush bean, cabbage family, carrot, celery, chive, cucumber, garlic, head lettuce, marigold, mint, nasturtium, onion, parsley, pepper, pot marigold	Pole bean, dill, fennel, potato
Turnip	Onion family, pea	Potato

Replace Your Garden Chores with a Garden Plan

In addition to traditional companion planting for pest control and other reported, but less understood, benefits, plants can be paired because certain of their physical characteristics can aid their neighbors. Among other benefits, plants can fight weeds, provide support for neighbors, and offer cooling shade or moisture-retaining mulch. These partnership techniques are called interplanting.

One crop that can benefit from interplanting is tomatoes. In warm climates unmulched soil can become so hot that the vitality and yield of the plant is affected. Growing Swiss chard or another low, leafy crop close to tomatoes shades the soil, reducing evaporation and moderating its temperature. This improves vigor and yield.

Here's another example: Pole beans can grow with corn and squash. This is an ancient example of interplanting practiced by Native Americans for generations, with each plant benefiting from the arrangement. The pole beans, which need something to climb to grow and yield well, use the cornstalks as "poles." The corn acts as a windbreak for the squash and the squash serves as a living mulch that shades the soil, reducing evaporation and moderating soil temperatures. In addition, some gardeners find that raccoons, who love to raid the corn patch, don't like walking over

squash vines to get to the corn. And that leaves more sweet ears for dinner!

Use the interplanting ground rules in the box below as the situations arise. For example, it's time for another sowing of Bibb lettuce, and there's room on the shady side of the peas. Peas and lettuce are not listed as companions, but the lettuce will definitely like the cool conditions, won't mind the partial shade, and might enjoy the extra nitrogen. Lettuce won't help the peas, but it won't hurt them, either. So that's where the Bibb lettuce goes this time.

▲ **Take advantage.** This cool-weather kale grows where an early crop of lettuce has already been harvested. The kale will be at its peak of flavor in fall.

Interplanting Ground Rules

▶ Plant light feeders, like carrots, with heavy feeders, like tomatoes.

▶ Match deep-rooted plants, like parsnip, with shallow-rooted plants, like onion.

▶ Plants that prefer cooler temperatures, like lettuce, can benefit from the partial shade of tall companions, like pole beans.

OPPORTUNISTIC PLANTING

In our garden, a lot of succession planting happens without a whole lot of planning. When the spinach is harvested for salad, that creates a small hole in the garden that is filled with lettuce or whatever happens to be next on the planting plan.

We've learned that some natural successions are quite reliable. For instance, where we are, in Zone 4, the garlic that was sown the previous fall is ready for harvest in late July. We replace it with lettuce, spinach, radicchio, or Chinese cabbage, all vegetables that can be sown in July and harvested before the end of the growing season. Similarly, early lettuce and spinach crops occupy the space that will be filled later by storage crops of carrots and beets. Bush beans are succeeded by sowings of kale for fall and early-winter harvest.

SUCCESS WITH SUCCESSION PLANTING

Spring is often called the "planting season," but we make a mistake if we think of spring as the only season we can plant. A garden planted in spring can have half its space harvested and lying empty by late summer. That's a lot of wasted space, but there's an easy method of filling all those empty places throughout the growing season. Succession planting is a way of increasing production by making sure that all the space in your garden is growing something all the time. It makes use of the vacant space left after you harvest a crop, by replacing it with a new, fast-maturing crop.

The dos and don'ts of succession planting are simple:

▶ **Do.** Whenever a bed becomes available, plant a crop that can easily mature in the time remaining in your growing season.

▶ **Don't.** If possible, avoid planting the same crop (or one of the same family) in the same place more than once a season.

Waste Not, Want Not: Using Green Manures

Whenever you have an unclaimed space in your garden, sow a crop "for the garden." Here are two ways to do this:

Peas. If you have some leftover pea seeds, broadcast them over one of these unused spaces in the late-summer garden. Poke the seeds in with your finger where they fall. At the least, you have a nitrogen-fixing green-manure crop to till in or to harvest for the compost pile. At best you get all the preceding *and* a bunch of tasty peas.

Green manures. Buckwheat, winter rye, and annual alfalfa are known as "green manures," because they are often grown to be turned into the soil while they are actively growing. Green manures add organic matter to the soil and increase its nutrient content. To use the crop as a green manure, let it grow for a season and then chop it into the soil with a sharp hoe. You can also cut the crop down before it sets seeds and add it the compost pile.

▲ **Buck up.** Wait until buckwheat is just beginning to flower, and then turn it into the soil as green manure.

Crop Rotation: Musical Chairs in the Garden

When I make garden plans each year, I check my records of the past few years and make sure I don't plant any crop, or even one of the same family (for plant families, see the chart on page 40), in the same place two years in a row. Any break in the cycle is good, and longer breaks are even better. Two or three years between similar crops are better than one, and it may take five or even seven years to starve out a disease like clubroot. Crop rotation is standard practice for farmers, but the technique is equally important and beneficial for home gardeners, for both soil nutrition and pest and disease control.

BEEF UP THAT SOIL: ROTATION AND NUTRITION

Each kind of plant takes from the soil a particular combination of nutrients in particular amounts. The same crop, grown in the same spot year after year, uses up some of those nutrients, and even the best soil-maintenance practices won't always restore all the nutrients to the levels that crop requires. The longer they grow in the same spot, the more the condition of the soil worsens and the greater the resulting stress on the plants. Depleted soil equals defeated plants.

HIDE-AND-SEEK: ROTATION TO AVOID DISEASE OR PESTS

Many pests winter in the soil as eggs or larvae. When they emerge in spring, they depend on finding their favorite food growing nearby. No need to cruise around for burgers when the friendly gardener always builds a fast-food place right next to your house. Fortunately, if the bugs' preferred meal isn't handed to them, they don't know where to go. The farther a hungry bug has to go in search of a proper meal, the less likely it is to find it and the less likely it is to survive. Soilborne diseases, too, can stay dormant over the winter and even for many years, but most cannot survive for long if the plants they thrive upon have left the neighborhood.

The Case of the Villainous Cucumber Beetles

The mystery of the cucumber beetles began a while back when a friend asked me what to do about a major cucumber beetle infestation of his winter squash. He had been adding compost and rotted manure to the soil for years and had enviable results with most crops, but not winter squash. I knew the villain, cucumber beetles, and I was familiar with the scene of the crime. In the course of discussion he mentioned that, while he'd moved other crops around the garden from year to year, the squash patch had been in the same place for over 20 years. The solution was to rotate the squash. Case closed.

Rotation Guidelines

The principles of plant rotation are very similar to those for interplanting and succession:

▶ Follow heavy-feeding plants with light feeders.

▶ Put deep-rooted vegetables where shallow-rooted plants previously grew.

▶ Avoid rotating plants of the same family within the same bed, because they tend to have similar nutritional needs and are often prey to the same pests and diseases.

Two Sample Rotations

On paper a rotation plan could have different plants moving from one bed to the next around the garden until they arrived back at their starting point. In a real garden with real plants it's not that easy, especially if you combine companion planting and rotation, as I do. For instance, real-life crop rotation may find onions and radishes appearing just about anywhere.

When you begin to plan a rotation scheme, one of the first things you realize is that not all the beds in a garden are really available to all the plants. If I put the corn or the trellis-grown tomatoes, peas, and beans along the southern edge of the garden, the plants in the next few beds would have to grow in the shade for a good part of the day. Some of them would find this acceptable, but most would not. It's good planning to restrict all the tall plants and those growing on trellises to the northern and northeastern sides of the garden, as much as possible. The way I manage this is to have two rotations, one for low-growing plants and one for sun blockers.

The Sun-Blocker Rotation includes corn, as well as the plants I grow on a trellis or poles (tomatoes and beans or peas). I also include squashes and squash family crops here. Although I grow the cucumbers on trellises, the other squash relatives aren't particularly tall. These squashes tend to spread, however, so I usually plant them along the northern and eastern edges of the garden, the same area where the sun blockers live. I don't have to worry about related plants following one another, since none of these plants is in the same family.

A Sun-Blocker Rotation

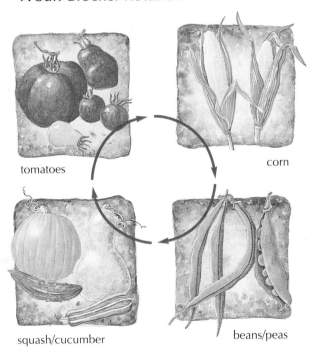

tomatoes

corn

squash/cucumber

beans/peas

▲ Trellised tomatoes, beans, peas, and cucumbers, along with corn, can grow 8 to 10 feet (2.4 to 3 m) tall. To avoid these taller plantings casting shade on other crops, I keep these in one rotation on the northeastern side of the garden.

A Low-Grower Rotation

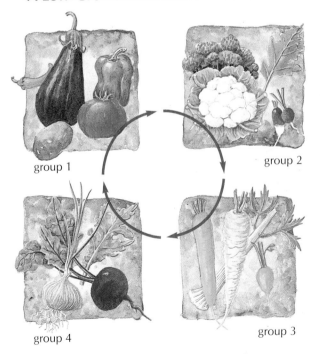

group 1

group 2

group 4

group 3

▲ This scheme groups family members to make the rotations. Group 1 consists of potato, pepper, eggplant, and/or determinate tomato. Group 2 is any member of the cabbage family. Group 3 is the carrot family, including carrots, parsnips, and celery. Group 4 covers everything else.

Giving Your Plants the Elbow Room They Need

The primary reason to garden in beds rather than in single rows is to provide plant roots with the room they need to grow, but wide, raised-bed planting also saves garden space. Many plants can be grown much closer together in beds than in rows, with the result that a bed-based garden can be much smaller than a row-based garden while still producing the same yield. (See the drawing on page 47.)

HOW TO DETERMINE PLANT SPACING

Most seed catalogs and seed packets give recommended spacing for seeds and transplants. But this spacing is based on planting in rows, since that's the method most gardeners have used in recent years. We lack data for making rules about spacing in wide beds. In addition, not all beds are equal. You can grow plants a lot closer together in a bed 5 feet (1.5 m) wide, 2 feet (0.6 m) deep, and full of compost-enriched soil than you can in a bed 2 feet (0.6 m) wide and 8 inches (20 cm) deep with a marginally fertile soil.

In part 3, as part of the cultural information for each vegetable, you'll find suggestions for spacing in beds. You may have to experiment to customize these recommendations for your own situation. The recommendations are good starting points if your beds are at least a couple of feet (60 cm) wide, broadforked or double-dug, and have at least 8 inches (20 cm) of topsoil with good nutrient balance and high organic-matter content. If you can't provide these conditions, space your plants a little farther apart. As you make your decisions, be sure to consider two important factors: how you're providing for your plants' access to sunlight and how much nutrients and moisture they'll receive.

Sunlight. Garden plants need sunlight. It is what drives the life-sustaining process of photosynthesis. Plants can grow close enough so that

▲ **Don't touch.** As these beets and broccoli plants grow, we thin them so that their leaves just touch but don't crowd each other.

their leaves barely touch, but no closer, lest they shade one another. When you plan spacing, you need to know how large an area the plant's foliage will occupy when mature.

Nutrients and moisture. Plant roots do not compete for environmental resources the same way as plant foliage. Leaves cannot share space without shading one another, but roots can intermingle in their quest for nutrients. The limiting factor is not the size of plant root systems but the number of plants compared to the amount of nutrients available. Although at a certain point plant size will be restricted by lack of nutrients, you can compensate either by decreasing the number of competing plants or by increasing the supply of nutrients.

MAKING A GARDEN PLAN

A garden plan doesn't have to be complex. In fact, it probably shouldn't be, or it won't get done in the first place. These drawings show my kitchen garden first in early summer, and then later when the fast-growing crops are replaced by succession plantings. Each plant is identified at the right by a number.

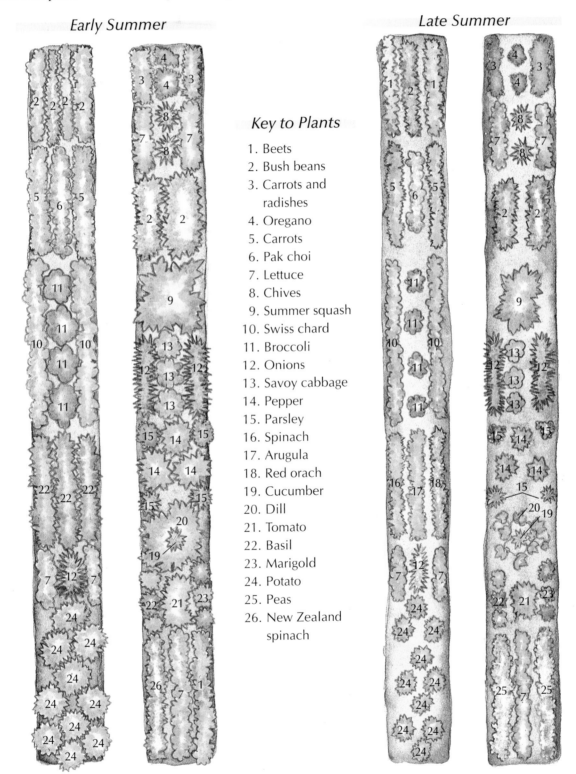

Early Summer

Late Summer

Key to Plants

1. Beets
2. Bush beans
3. Carrots and radishes
4. Oregano
5. Carrots
6. Pak choi
7. Lettuce
8. Chives
9. Summer squash
10. Swiss chard
11. Broccoli
12. Onions
13. Savoy cabbage
14. Pepper
15. Parsley
16. Spinach
17. Arugula
18. Red orach
19. Cucumber
20. Dill
21. Tomato
22. Basil
23. Marigold
24. Potato
25. Peas
26. New Zealand spinach

Plans for Small Gardens

Whether your garden is large or small, a garden plan is important to its success. The commercially made cedar-sided raised bed pictured on page 9 is only 3' x 6' (0.9 x 1.8 m), but with a plan for succession planting, it can provide a steady supply of good-tasting vegetables from spring through late fall. Not only that, but the herbs and flowers look great!

You could adapt the plans shown here to grow the vegetables you and your family like most. Instead of celery, you might like to try more herbs, such as oregano and dill. Herbs make great fillers in a small garden like this. You could even use them instead of the flowers. In summer, plant New Zealand spinach or eggplant instead of some, or all, of the peppers. Be sure to plant tomatoes, or any other tall-growing crop, on the north side of the garden so that they don't cast shade on the other plants.

You can either stake the tomatoes or use a trellis similar to the one on pages 72–73. It's especially easy to install trellises in a raised bed: Simply fasten the posts to the inner sides of the wooden bed with a metal strap. Remember to prune your tomatoes when they reach the top of their support so that they don't slouch over the other plants.

Garden Journal

Good books about gardening can be a big help. Along with general information about soil temperature, soil moisture, pH, air temperature, and day length, they often contain new ideas as well as inspiration that can add to the challenge and pleasure of gardening. But what may come to be your most helpful gardening book isn't available in any bookstore. It's the one you write yourself — your garden journal. This is the best possible garden book because it's all about *your* garden and how your garden is unique. A well-kept garden journal can be one of the best gardening tools you'll ever own.

Among the things I think worth noting in a garden journal are these:

▶ Soil and air temperature at particular times of the day, including daily maximums and minimums, and degrees of frost, if any

▶ Temperatures under row covers and beneath plastic mulches

▶ Weather, especially unusual occurrences such as heavy storms, extended droughts, or long periods of either very hot or very cool weather

▶ Watering record

▶ Planting or transplanting dates, germination dates, and harvest dates for each crop, including cover crops

▶ Starting and finishing dates for compost piles

▶ "Rogues' Gallery" — insect pests and/or diseases. What? When? How many bugs? How bad the disease? What did I do, and how well did it work?

▶ Harvest notes. How much? How plentiful?

▶ Soil maintenance and development. When and how much? Compost? Leaf mold? Rock powders? Other supplements?

Mid-May Garden

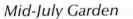

3' (0.9 m)

6' (1.8 m)

Mid-July Garden

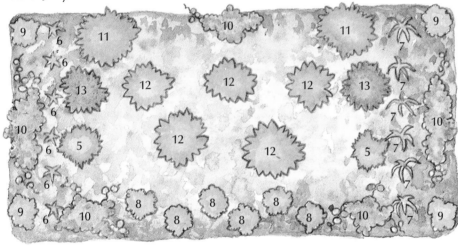

Early September Garden

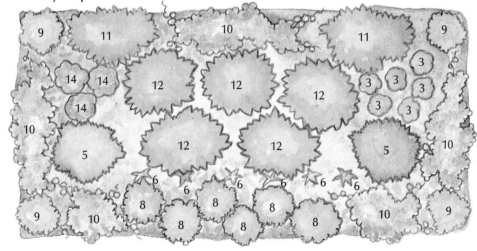

Key to Plants

1. Spinach
2. Beet
3. Lettuce
4. Radish
5. Celery
6. Garlic
7. Leek
8. Parsley
9. Marigold
10. Nasturtium
11. Tomato
12. Pepper
13. Basil
14. Kale

CHAPTER 3

Jump-Starting Your Garden

W hat will end as the harvest, starts with the seeds, and the seeds start out in one of three places: indoors, in the cold frame, or right in the garden.

Plants that need a long growing season, such as tomatoes, peppers, onions, celery, eggplant, melons, and winter squash, begin life on a sunny windowsill or in the greenhouse. These plants are joined by a few cabbage, broccoli, lettuce, and basil plants. They don't need a headstart, but I start a few indoors anyway to get an early harvest.

The rest of the cabbage and broccoli, along with cauliflower and Brussels sprouts, are nursed along in the cold frame. When they're little, these plants can have a rough time competing with weeds and surviving attacks from leaf-loving pests. Once the plants are big enough to fend for themselves, I transplant them to the garden.

The remainder of the seeds, from corn to radishes, and beets to carrots, wait in the seed packet until conditions are just right, and then I sow them right in the garden.

51

Starting Seeds Indoors

Most seeds are easy to get along with and don't demand much from us. Wherever they start life, whether in a seed flat or sown in the garden, seeds have the best chance of becoming vigorous, productive plants if you give them what they need:

▶ A loose, disease-free planting mixture, kept evenly moist
▶ A complete, low-analysis fertilizer
▶ A seed-starting container with good drainage
▶ The appropriate amount of light
▶ The right germination temperature

For advice about soil temperature, planting depth, germination times, and so on, refer to specific vegetables in part 3.

GETTING THE PLANTING MIXTURE RIGHT

From the germination period until the first few true leaves emerge, the crops you're most likely to start indoors are very susceptible to diseases. Since most of these diseases are soilborne, the best way to keep young seedlings healthy is to use a pasteurized or sterilized soilless seed-starting mixture rather than garden soil.

Soilless mixtures, which are available from garden centers and many mail-order and Internet seed companies, typically contain about 40 percent milled sphagnum peat moss, 50 percent medium-grade vermiculite, and about 10 percent horticultural-grade perlite. The finished mix is fine and light, and it holds moisture well. Many soilless mixtures also contain fertilizer, which gives the seedlings a boost that lasts for a few weeks. If your mix doesn't contain this nutrient charge, fertilize the seedlings once their first true leaves have emerged. I use fish emulsion or fish-and-seaweed liquid fertilizer at half strength once a week.

Renew, Reuse, Recycle

The seed-starting kits I use, as well as other store-bought units, work well and are fun to use, but they're not your only option. Many, many tomato plants begin productive lives every year in cutoff milk cartons or foam cups. I've yet to find anything better for starting celery than the plastic trays that tofu comes in. Remember to poke drainage holes in the bottom of whatever container you use: "If the pot doesn't drain, the plant doesn't grow."

PUTTING THINGS WHERE THEY BELONG: SEED-STARTING CONTAINERS

You'll find many kinds of seed-starting containers, including trays, trays segmented into cells, plastic pots, peat pots, clay pots, soil blocks. The good news is that you can't make a bad choice, as long as the container has drainage holes in the bottom. Some seem to work better than others, and over time I have acquired a favorite.

I like to use a compartmented foam seed-starting kit. Each seedling grows in a small Styrofoam cell, which protects against wide temperature fluctuations because it's well insulated. At the bottom of each cell is a large drainage hole that puts the growing medium in contact with a capillary mat (a feltlike cloth that absorbs water like a thin sponge). One end of the mat sits in a water-filled reservoir, so that the seedlings get a continuous supply of water from below, keeping them just-moist at all times. The whole thing is topped by a transparent plastic lid, creating a mini greenhouse, which also helps maintain proper temperature and moisture levels during germination and just after the plants emerge.

Sowing Seeds in Containers

1 Pour about 6 quarts (6 l) of soilless seed-starting mixture into a large waterproof container. Use warm water to make a mixture that is evenly moist but not soggy. Fill the seedling container with the soilless mixture.

2 Press the pegged stand gently but firmly into the planting compartments. This ensures that each compartment is filled to the bottom, so that the planting mixture contacts the capillary mat, which will wick a steady supply of moisture to it.

3 Sow two seeds in each cell and cover them lightly with the seed-starting mixture as recommended under specific vegetables in part 3.

Caring for Seedlings

Light. After the seeds have germinated, they require 12 to 16 hours of light a day. When the seedlings are up, move the setup to a sunny window. On cold nights, protect them from drafts. If you don't have a sunny spot, rig up adjustable fluorescent lights over the seedling trays. Keep the lights about 3 inches (7.5 cm) from the tops of the plants.

4 Dip the capillary mat in water to wet it thoroughly. The mat will conduct an even, steady flow of water to the cells in the seed tray. Place the mat on top of the pegged stand. Fill the plastic-lined reservoir with warm (80°F; 27°C) water.

5 Set the seed tray on the pegged stand and cover it with the plastic lid. Place the seed tray atop a refrigerator or a radiator to keep it warm. Monitor both the planting mix and the surrounding air temperatures with soil and air thermometers.

Heat. Try to keep the temperature near the recommended optimum for the plant's growth.

Water. Make sure the planting mix never dries out. If you can't arrange bottom watering, use a watering can that provides a fine stream (see page 68) to avoid damaging the tender seedlings.

Fertilizer. Once a week, give your seedlings a half-strength mixture of fish or fish-and-seaweed fertilizer when you water.

Moving Your Plants Along

Shortly after the first set of true leaves appears (see True or False? in the box below), transplant tomatoes, peppers, and eggplant into 4-inch (10 cm) pots. Onions, celery, and lettuce can stay in the flats.

When I prepare the planting mix for these transplants, I begin introducing the plants to garden soil. I use a combination of one-third soil-less seed-starting mix, one-third compost, and one-third garden soil. The stems and leaves of these plants grow quickly and their roots grow even faster. Moving the plants into this larger growing space prevents the roots from becoming cramped, which can slow down or even stop growth. The larger pots also encourage the plants to produce sturdier stems.

True or False?

Seeds are a miracle of miniaturization. Each one contains all the bits and pieces of an entire plant. Of course, the seed doesn't look like a plant when we sow it. But even when the plant first emerges from the soil, we can't usually recognize what kind it is until it grows the kind of leaves we're familiar with — its true leaves.

Seedlings generally have two types of leaves. The first to appear we call seed leaves or cotyledons. After these, the first set of true leaves develops and expands above the seed leaves. For example, with broad-leaved vegetables, such as beans or squash, the arched stem of the seedling emerges first, followed by a pair of thick seed leaves, often with the seed coat still attached, and finally the first pair of seed leaves.

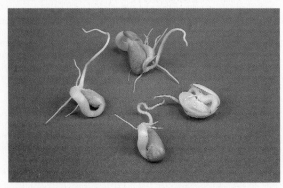

Sprouting bean seeds

There are some exceptions to this pattern:

▶ **Peas.** When peas germinate, the seed leaves stay underground, so the first leaves you see are true leaves.

▶ **Narrow-leaved vegetables.** Some crops, such as corn and onions, produce only one seed leaf instead of two, and the seed leaf is very similar to the true leaf. The best way to tell if true leaves are emerging from narrow-leaved vegetable seedlings is to count the leaves. If there are two or more leaves on a seedling, then true leaves have formed. Corn and onions have another interesting complication: The true leaf forms beneath the seed leaf, rather than above it as in broad-leaved vegetables.

Seed leaves   "True" leaves

Transplanting Seedlings into Larger Containers

Never Handle a Seedling by Its Stem

Once damaged, a stem usually doesn't recover, and the plant may die. If you bruise or break a piece of leaf, on the other hand, the plant will survive.

Follow this method for safe handling: Cradle the root ball in your hand and steady the plant by gently holding a leaf between your fingers.

1 Mix together 1 part each of planting mix, compost, and garden soil and moisten well with warm water. It should be evenly moist but not soggy.

2 Fill 4-inch (10 cm) containers with the planting mixture. Use a trowel or other tool to make a hole in the center of the soil mix.

3 Loosen the seedling from the original container and lift the rootball gently into the prepared containers. In spite of all the garden tools out there, I find that this job is best accomplished with a pair of kitchen spoons or forks. They work well and don't damage the seedlings or the roots. Press soil gently but firmly around the rootball. Water again to moisten thoroughly.

The Cold Hard Facts about Cold Frames

A cold frame is one of those tools I didn't know I needed until I got one. Now that I have one, I don't know how I got along without it.

This garden tool isn't complicated. It's just a box with no bottom and with a top that lets in light and can be opened or removed. Its purpose is to create a friendly environment outdoors where plants grow faster and healthier than in unprotected garden beds.

READY-MADE COLD FRAMES

My Juwel cold frame has held up very well for more than 10 years, and I use it all year long. At about 9 square feet (0.8 sq m), it isn't big. It's made of aluminum, which means that it's lightweight yet strong, and I can easily carry it around from one garden assignment to the next.

Both side and top panels are made of double-wall translucent polycarbonate. The sides of most cold frames are opaque, so plants receive light only through the top. But the Juwel frame's translucent sides allow more light inside the box, with the result that plants are stronger and stockier. The double-wall glazing reduces heat loss and cuts down on condensation.

Juwel cold frame

A House of Straw for Your Garden

If you have four bales of hay or straw and an old storm window, you have the makings of a basic cold frame. Although this frame can't do all the things a more refined unit can, it works very well both for starting some of your seeds and for hardening off transplants in spring. You'll use it again in fall to provide frost protection for low-growing plants, so that you can keep some of the more cold-tolerant vegetables and herbs (hardy lettuce, kale, and parsley, for instance) growing late into fall.

Arrange four straw bales around a prepared seedbed, with the straw laid vertically. Be sure to overlap the ends with the sides, to avoid exposure at the corners.

Check to be sure your storm window will rest securely over the opening. Storm windows have glass and it's easy to accidentally break the panes and end up with shards in your plants. To avoid

such a mess, remove the glass and then cover the frame with 4 or 6 mil clear plastic and staple it in place.

Please note: If you suspect that a storm window contains lead-based putty or paint, it's best not to use it around food plants. A lot of the storm windows old enough to be candidates for cold frame tops are also old enough to have lead-based paint and/or lead-based putty holding in the glass.

Starting Seeds in a Cold Frame

Avoid Fried Seedlings!

Leave the cover off your cold frame when temperature permits, so that plants don't get too hot on sunny days and so that they get moisture when it rains.

1 Seedlings will emerge faster and be healthier if you first super-charge the seedbed with some compost. Spread about an inch (2.5 cm) of compost on the soil and work it into the top 3 inches (7.5 cm) or so. This will help keep the soil loose and improve moisture retention as well as providing the nutrients the seedlings will need.

2 After seeds germinate, thin them to stand about 2 inches (5 cm) apart. Because the plants will still be fairly small when they leave the cold frame, you can grow them this close together and still leave enough room for them to develop healthy root systems.

3 Monitor the temperature in the cold frame and open or close the top to keep temperatures within the range each crop prefers. An automatic vent opener is a real help here, especially if you are often away from home. Cold frames can easily overheat on sunny days, even in cold weather. Automatic opening devices require no electricity and operate using thermal energy.

A Year in the Life of a Cold Frame

Here's how we've learned to keep our cold frame in action all year long: When the garden is full of snow in late winter, our cold frame is full of delicious spinach. After growing these greens until spring, we use the cold frame to harden off tomatoes and peppers. In early summer it does the job of a mini greenhouse, boosting the growth of heat-loving peppers. Then, as the cold returns, it becomes home to late-fall lettuce and winter spinach.

Turn Winter into Summer: Greenhouse Growing

Late in March, with snow still hiding the grass, I raise the top on the cold frame — and everything is green. Deep green spinach, medium green kale, and light greens on lettuces and claytonia. Perhaps I can find a pill like the one Alice in Wonderland took, to shrink me down so I can spend the rest of the day in among the warmth and greenery and forget the winter for a while. Or, failing that, perhaps I could find a cold frame big enough so I could fit inside. And that is what I did. Our solar greenhouse is a cold frame big enough for our whole family to fit inside among the beds full of salad greens. We spend hours there, puttering among the plants or just reading or playing cards, forgetful of winter, unmindful of the cold and barren snow. With such a greenhouse, the joys of vegetable gardening have expanded to fill the whole year.

▲ **The heart of the garden.** Our greenhouse, with all of its potential, has changed the way we garden and also given us the chance to enjoy fresh produce throughout the year.

A BIG GARDEN BED WITH A COVER

Rather than install tables in our greenhouse, we created an in-ground bed by deeply loosening the soil with a broadfork and then raising the soil from the walkway. Supported by wood sides, the U-shaped bed runs along both sides of the greenhouse and across the short end opposite the door. Down the middle, we constructed a simple walkway of 18-inch-square (45 cm) cast-concrete pavers.

Built from a kit, the greenhouse itself is an aluminum-framed shedlike design with walls and roof of double-wall resilient plastic. Anyone fairly handy with construction tools could build a suitable structure from scratch and cover it with greenhouse plastic. A good solar greenhouse handles heat well, both capturing and holding it, and letting it go.

◄ **You don't have to be Alice.** Walking into our greenhouse on a snowy winter day, we're engulfed by the colors and scents of summer.

A YEAR-ROUND GARDEN TOOL

The greenhouse has its greatest impact during winter, keeping fresh greens on our table and smiles on our faces, but it's an important part of the garden every day of the year. It's great for starting heat-loving, cold-sensitive plants (tomatoes, peppers, basil, and squashes) that will later live in the outdoor garden. We sow them both in flats and right in the in-ground beds. We also use the greenhouse in summer for these crops:

Cabbage family. Cabbages and their kin stay in the greenhouse until they're big enough to survive the rigors of outdoor life.

Eggplant and basil. We begin particularly fussy sorts like eggplants and basils that do not like even short periods of cool temperatures.

Tomatoes. We grow a few tomatoes inside the greenhouse all summer, so that we can have tomatoes even after the first fall frosts.

Spinach, claytonia, winter lettuce. Before the last tomato leaves the vine, the first seedlings of the winter garden emerge — spinach, claytonia, and all sorts of winter lettuces.

Garden transplants. As more greenhouse-grown summer vegetables finish, we transplant lettuces, kale, and chard from outdoors and get the greenhouse ready to feed our bodies and spirits through late fall and winter. These hardy salad makings will feed us until a new spring and another cycle.

But They'll Freeze!

In December, January, and February, night temperatures in our greenhouse dip well below 0°F (–17°C), and all the plants therein freeze solid. If we pick them while they're frozen, the result more closely resembles mush than salad. But if we wait until the sun has warmed the soil and thawed the leaves, we have a salad that has even more depth of taste than any the summer can produce. The secret to this success is that you not water the plants during the coldest times of the winter. If there's too much moisture in the cells, they burst, and the plant will not recover. We stop watering in mid-December and don't start again until mid-March.

▲ **Winter salads.** Our fresh-picked winter salads from the greenhouse are even tastier than those we harvest from our summer garden.

▲ **Spring start-up.** The greenhouse is the perfect place to get seeds off to the right start. We start plants both in containers and directly in the ground.

▲ **Summer home.** Even in July and August, we keep some plants going inside the greenhouse. Here, we get an extra boost of heat for long-season melons.

Just-Right Conditions for Sowing

You can sow many seeds directly in the garden, where they sprout and grow into vegetable plants. Even if the conditions are poor, some seeds usually come up. Yet for plants to be their strongest, the seeds they come from must germinate quickly and vigorously, and for that they need temperatures and moisture conditions to be just right. When the conditions in the garden match the requirements of the seed, it's time to sow. Refer to specific vegetables in part 3 for advice about the growing conditions for each crop.

SOME LIKE IT HOT, SOME LIKE IT COLD

Many plants have definite soil temperature preferences. Give them what they need and watch the germination times markedly decrease.

▶ **Spinach** takes about three weeks to germinate at 40°F (4°C) and only one week at 60°F (16°C).

▶ **Broccoli** takes about four weeks to germinate at 40°F (4°C), about three weeks at 50°F (10°C), and only one week at 70°F (21°C).

▶ **Peppers and eggplant** take about three weeks to germinate at 65°F (18°C), and they won't germinate at all below that temperature. They germinate best at 85° to 90°F (29° to 32°C).

▶ **Tomatoes,** which have as much tropical ancestry as peppers and eggplant, like it hot. They can tolerate 75°F (24°C) but germinate and grow better above 80°F (27°C).

▶ **Most lettuce** varieties, which sprout and grow best in cool temperatures, won't germinate at all when the soil temperature is above 75°F (24°C), and germination is spotty above 65°F (18°C).

▶ **Most cool-season vegetables,** such as peas and radishes, really do like it cool. These plants do best if they start life around 65°F (18°C).

KNOWING WHEN THE MOISTURE LEVEL'S RIGHT

Not only must soil temperature be right, the soil's moisture level must also be optimal for the best seed germination. Once temperature and moisture levels are reached, they must remain steady until plants are well established. Proper moisture not only aids seed germination but helps protect soil as we slice and dice it with hoes and trowels.

▲ **Putting the squeeze on a soil wet test.** Take a handful of soil and squeeze it. If you squeeze out water, or if the soil compresses and stays that way when you loosen your grip and try to crumble the soil, it's too wet (A). If it just flows off your hand like talcum powder, it's too dry (B). Soil with proper moisture should compress and hold together but then crumble when worked gently between your fingers (C).

JUST-RIGHT SOIL TEMPERATURES FOR GERMINATION

For each kind of seed, there is a "just-right" soil temperature for germination. When the soil is warmer or colder than that, fewer seeds germinate, and they take longer to do so. A long, slow germination subjects plants to severe stress right at the beginning of life. They don't grow as fast, and they aren't as able to cope with stresses like insects, fluctuations in temperature and moisture, and diseases like damping-off. Recent data suggests that stressed plants emit chemicals that attract pests to the plant. If soil temperatures are way off the mark, none of this matters — the seeds probably won't germinate at all.

For the best germination and strongest seedlings, seeds need soil that not only starts out at the right temperature, but also stays that way. One year, we planted the first batch of corn when the soil was 75°F (24°C). It stayed that way for a week, and the corn was up. At the end of that week, just before a cool snap, we planted another batch. The soil temperature suddenly dropped to 65°F (18°C), and the corn that eventually germinated took more than two weeks to come up.

Soil Thermometer

Mounted within a metal tube strong enough to withstand the rigors of being pushed into the soil repeatedly, soil thermometers make monitoring soil temperature easy. Push the thermometer 1 or 2 inches (2.5 to 5 cm) into the soil, and take a reading after the fluid stops moving, usually about a minute.

New-Fashioned Bed Warmers

To give seeds the warmth they need earlier than it occurs naturally, you can raise soil temperature by applying plastic mulch at least a week before you sow seeds or transplant. All plastic mulches are not created equal. They come in different colors, and each color differs in its ability to warm garden soil.

▶ **Clear plastic,** or builder's plastic, is inexpensive and warms soil very well. But, because it allows all wavelengths of light to reach the soil, it also encourages weeds.

▶ **Black plastic mulch.** For years, this was the plastic of choice for heating up the soil while blocking weeds. It worked well and was quite inexpensive. It's still inexpensive but now there are plastics that warm the soil even better.

▶ **IRT plastic mulch.** The initials stand for Infra-Red Transmitting. This brownish green plastic sheeting allows infrared light to pass through it to warm the soil, but blocks wavelengths of visible light that weeds need to grow. It warms the soil almost as well as clear plastic, though it costs a little more. IRT produces especially good results for melons, but also works well for eggplant, corn, peppers, squash, and pumpkins.

Laying IRT plastic mulch

Just-Right Temperatures for Growing

Once seeds have germinated, complications sometimes set in, because plants don't always *grow* best at the same soil temperatures at which they *germinate* best. And some actually prefer cooler growing temperatures than they need for germinating.

▶ **Cabbage and beans** grow best at 60° to 65°F (16° to 18°C), but cabbage germinates best at 85°F (29°C) and beans at 80°F (27°C).

▶ **Peppers** germinate best above 85°F (29°C) but grow best at 75°F (24°C).

▶ **Corn** germinates best at 80°F (27°C) but grows best below 75°F (24°C).

Most plants are pretty resilient and will sprout and survive even if you ignore these differences. They may even produce what looks like a decent crop. But they aren't as vigorous, healthy, or productive as they might be. For the biggest, best-tasting harvest as early as possible, provide your seeds and plants with the soil and air temperatures they prefer.

Warming Them Up . . .

When there is a wide gap between the ideal germination and growth temperatures of a plant, you can still give it what it needs. Here are two different ways you can accommodate a plant if the seedbed is at the right temperature for growth but too cool for optimum germination:

Indoor or cold frame environments. Start your plants indoors or in a cold frame, where proper germination temperatures can be more easily maintained. This works for many plants but is especially good for cabbage and peppers.

Plastic mulches and row covers. Warm the soil with plastic mulch before sowing, then use row covers to maintain proper temperature during germination. Let all the seedlings emerge, then remove the covers during the day. You can use a max-min thermometer (see the box on page 63) to determine whether night temperatures are dropping much below best growing temperatures.

▲ **Protected peppers.** You can monitor and control both soil and air temperatures if you grow seedlings in a cold frame.

▲ **A cozy situation.** The seedlings in this mixed planting are protected from chilly nights, as well as insect pests, by a row cover that can be removed during the day.

. . . Or Cooling Them Down

If your challenge is a seedbed that is just right but growing conditions that are too warm, try the following:

Organic mulch. After the seedlings emerge, apply a thin layer of organic mulch to lower and moderate soil temperatures. Gradually increase the depth of the mulch as the plants grow. This works particularly well for corn.

Give Jack Frost the Cold Shoulder

After they emerge from the relative protection of the soil, plants must contend with the weather. If seeds are sown too early, the seedlings can be subjected to frosty mornings that they aren't prepared to deal with. Many of our favorite vegetable plants are either damaged or severely stressed by near freezing temperatures. Many of these vegetables are the ones whose seed packets direct you to sow "after danger of frost has passed" (see box at the right).

Some plants are so sensitive to cool weather that they balk even at cool temperatures well above freezing. For some, 40°F (4°C) is too cool; for others, even 60°F (16°C) is chilly.

Your best tactic for managing these fussy plants is to monitor day and night temperatures with a max-min thermometer (see the box below) and delay sowing until temperatures are consistently within the preferred range for that crop. Sometimes patience is a gardener's best tool.

▲ **Summer coolers.** Corn actually needs cooler temperatures when it's growing than when it's germinating. Applying a good mulch helps keep the soil cool.

Understanding What "Last Frost Date" Means

In order to follow seed packet advice about sowing after danger of frost has passed, you need to know the "last frost date" for your area. These dates are based on the average temperatures reported over a period of time. Consult your local Cooperative Extensive Service for advice about frost dates in your area. As the date approaches for your area, pay attention to your extended local forecasts and sow accordingly.

Measuring Highs & Lows

A max-min thermometer records the high and low temperatures since it was last reset. Place the thermometer on the north side of the garden out of direct sunlight. For the most accurate readings, make an open box for it, so that you can mount it inside, where it will be protected by a top and slanted sides. Paint the box white so it doesn't accumulate heat and give you false readings. If you can't provide shade, hang a piece of shade cloth over the front to block much of the sun.

Providing the Cover-Up

You can give young, frost-sensitive plants some protection by covering them with floating fabric row covers or creating tents of plastic stretched over hoops. Row covers are pretty grand, and there is one for just about every purpose. Row covers can protect plants against insects as well as frost, or even create a mini greenhouse where you can grow things you otherwise have no business growing in your climate. Judicious use of row covers can make a big difference in how well you can provide for the needs of diverse garden plants. This, in turn, will make a difference in the size and quality of your harvest.

The most commonly used row covers are made of fabric. Reemay was the first of these covers, originally available in just one weight. Its success with gardeners has spawned a bunch of variations with different weights and subtly different applications. The lighter covers can rest right on top of most plants. If you use a heavier cover or your plants are delicate or pointy, it's best to install supports for the cover. Garden suppliers sell hoops for this purpose, or you can make your own with ½-inch-diameter (1.3 cm), flexible PVC pipe, available at hardware stores.

As useful as row covers are, they can present some challenges all their own. Row covers need to be anchored so they don't blow away or tear in the wind. Yet they also need to be easily removed from the bed in order to weed or harvest plants. Although many experts have given a lot of advice on how to do this, I've never found a method that really worked and was practical. So I came up with one of my own that allows the row cover to be easily set in place and removed, even for one person. Once in place, the cover reliably stays put, even in windy weather. There's another benefit: The lengths of wood used to anchor the Reemay also make the row covers easy to store in winter.

ROW COVERS COMPARED

Type	Weight in oz./sq. yd. (gm/sq. m)	Light Transmission	Frost-Protection Value	Purpose
Lightweight	0.3 (6.7)	90%	Poor	Very effective control for cool-season vegetables (such as spinach and lettuce) against root maggots, flea beetles, leaf miners, aphids, thrips, and whiteflies without increase of temperature
Medium Weight	0.5–0.6 (11–13)	85%	4°F (2.2°C)	Heats the soil, speeding up the growing season for heat lovers by 2 weeks or more
Heavy Weight	0.9 (20.2)	70%	4–6°F (2.2–3.3°C)	Primary use is for frost protection
Extra Heavy Weight	1.5 (33.6)	50%	6°F (3.3°C)	A frost blanket; remove as soon as temperatures rise above freezing

Making Row Covers Manageable

1 Sandwich the long edges of the row cover between two thin slats of wood (such as lath). Use box nails to fasten the wood together and then turn the piece over and hammer down the protruding nail ends.

2 Set the supports in place. You'll need enough supports to place them about 3 or 4 feet (90 or 120 cm) apart along the length of the bed. Follow the manufacturer's instructions for purchased supports.

3 Lay one side of the row cover along one side of the bed, and then gently unroll the fabric and set the other side in place. Fasten the ends to the soil with U-shaped wires. When you need to tend the plants simply roll up the fabric around the wood strips.

Other Protection against Cold Weather

If you have only a few, or scattered, plants, you may want to protect plants individually with "hot caps."

Be sure to remove the hot caps before plants blossom: Tests show that yields are reduced if plants are not weaned from hot caps before blossom time.

▲ **For a homemade hot cap,** cut the bottom off a plastic milk container and set this over the plant. Remove the cap on hot, sunny days.

▲ **A very effective commercial hot cap** is called Wall-O-Water, a teepee-shaped construction of plastic, water-filled cylinders. Here, it covers eggplant.

Seeds: Putting Them in Their Place

In addition to its embryonic plant, each seed contains another important component. Within the seed is a small amount of stored energy, which the germinating plant uses to push through the soil into the sunlight. If the journey through the soil is too far because the seed was planted too deep, or too difficult because the soil is crusted or compacted, the little plant runs out of gas before it ever sees the light.

The smaller the seed, the smaller the embryonic plant and its energy reserves. And, as a general rule, the smaller the seed, the closer to the surface the seed should be planted. To ensure vigorous seedlings and productive plants, follow the recommendations for planting depths for each vegetable in part 3.

When sown, most seeds should be covered with loose, compost-enriched soil to help keep the seed moist and provide the darkness they need to germinate. The seeds of some plants, such as lettuce, are not only small but need light to germinate. Sow these seeds on the surface or cover them very lightly with screened compost or vermiculite. Avoid hoeing soil over the furrow, because it's hard to gauge how much soil ends up on top of the seeds. Be sure to keep the seedbed evenly moist until the seedlings emerge.

Seed-Sowing Tips

▶ To plant large seeds, like corn or beans, make the furrow a little less than the desired depth and push the seeds in level with the soil (A). This ensures that the seeds stay where you want them (for instance, sow beans with the "eye" down) and that they'll have good contact with the soil so they can absorb moisture quickly and evenly.

▶ Plant peas in drills by laying the seeds on the soil surface in the pattern you want and then poking each one in, to the first joint of your finger (B). Push soil gently into the holes and smooth it over.

▶ To plant small seeds, like carrots, roll them between your thumb and first two fingers. This makes spacing of the seed easier.

A

Planting beans in a furrow

B

Planting peas in drills

Sowing Seeds Outdoors

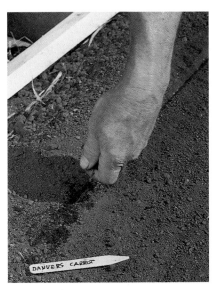

1 Use the back of a hoop rake to make the seedbed smooth and level. This makes it is easier to place all the seeds at the same depth. Remove any pebbles or large bits of organic matter.

2 To make a furrow for sowing seeds, use a long piece of 1-inch (2.5 cm) square lumber. You can easily regulate depth and make a nice, straight row. Just lay the piece of wood along the bed where you want your row and gently press it into the soil to the desired depth.

3 After sowing, fill the furrow by dribbling a handful of soil into it, crumbling any lumps as you go. Gently pat the soil to make sure it contacts the seeds, but don't pack it down.

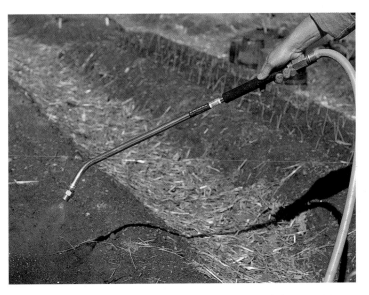

4 Label the row, so that you'll know what you planted and when.

5 Water the bed very gently, but evenly and thoroughly. Check the moisture daily and water again as necessary. The goal is to moisten the bed, not to make it soggy.

Bed Time for Young Seedlings

It's time to get the transplants you started indoors into the garden when the soil temperature meets their growing needs. Just as with sowing seeds, you can gain a bit of leeway here by using plastic mulch to warm the soil and row covers to warm the air. Transplanting on a cloudy day or in the evening will reduce transplant stress. If you must transplant on a windy day, cover plants with row covers after planting.

BEFORE YOU BEGIN

At least a week before you plan to transplant, prepare your planting bed and add any soil amendments. This will give the soil time to settle.

PLANTING DAY

Water the trays of seedlings thoroughly, and then let them stand for about an hour or until the planting mix is well drained. The mix should be moist enough to hold together, but not dripping. I like to water the plants the evening before I expect to plant. This ensures that the soil is moist and the seedlings are refreshed.

Hardening Off

At least a week before you plan to transplant your young crop outdoors in the garden, it's time to begin the process of "hardening off." This is like a little boot camp for vegetables. The plants learn to cope with direct sunlight, wind, and a wide range of temperatures. This is accomplished by exposing the plants to each one of these conditions, a little bit at first and then more and more as time goes on.

To harden off your seedlings, put them in a cold frame or shady spot in the yard for 1 hour the first day, then 2 hours the next day, and so on.

Tools for Transplanting

The only tools needed for transplanting are a trowel and watering can or hose.

TROWEL. Choose a trowel with a strong blade and shaft and a comfortable handle. You should be able to grasp it with either a "handshake" grip or what I call a "dagger" grip. When I'm transplanting, I use the dagger grip to plunge the blade straight down in the soil, make an opening by pulling back on the handle, and pop in the plant.

WATERING CAN. When you choose a watering can, look for one that's well balanced when you tip it, so that it's easy to pour.

Be sure the can has a rose. The rose attaches to the end of the nozzle and breaks the flow of water from a stream to a spray, so you don't wash away seeds or bludgeon little seedlings. The smaller the holes, the better. Haws cans, like this one, are designed so the rose directs the flow upward and the water comes down like gentle rain.

rose

Transplanting Lettuce Seedlings

1 Just before planting, rake the seedbed to smooth the surface. Remove any stones, sticks, or other debris.

2 Mark the soil where you wish to put your transplants. When planting lettuces, you can stagger them in order to take full advantage of your wide bed.

3 Remove the seedling from its container by pushing up on it from below. Take care not to disturb the root system.

4 Plunge the blade of your trowel into the soil to a depth slightly deeper than the height of the rootball. Draw the blade back to make a hole about 1½ times the size of the root ball.

5 Gently put the seedling into place. Firm the soil around the base of the plant just enough to stabilize it, but don't pack it down hard.

Caring for New Transplants

▶ Water newly planted seedlings frequently for the first few days after planting, especially in hot, sunny weather.

▶ For the first day or two after transplanting, use shade cloth or invert a plastic pot or a bushel basket over each seedling to give it protection against sun and wind.

Coming Up in the World: Vertical Gardening

The first time I heard the phrase "vertical gardening," I had visions of vegetables growing on very, very steep slopes. In reality, vertical gardening is a term used to describe growing certain plants on a support of some sort, such as a stake, trellis, or fence. Although it's common to grow pole beans or peas this way, tomatoes, cucumbers, and even vining squash and melons can be grown vertically, saving space and improving the quality of the harvest.

Space. When they are allowed to wander at will, cucumbers, squash, and indeterminate tomatoes take up a lot more garden space than they need to. When these same plants climb a fence or trellis, lots of fertile garden space is freed up, which substantially increases your garden's productivity per square foot.

Yield. Measured as the number of fruits produced, yield per plant may actually be somewhat less from a trellised plant. However, usable yield — the number of fruits that make it to the table in good condition — often increases because:

▶ **Tomatoes** on a trellis won't rot from contact with wet soil or be eaten by slugs. They're also less likely to be lost amid the foliage and overlooked until overripe.

▶ **Cucumbers** grow longer and straighter and are less likely to escape harvest. As soon as some of its fruits reach maturity, the cucumber plant calls it a job well done and stops producing, so fruits that escape harvest and reach maturity can reduce your total yield substantially.

▲ **Teepees.** Whether commercially produced or homemade, teepees are effective, traditional trellises for green beans.

▲ **A-frames.** Filled with 7-inch (17.5 cm) netting, A-frame-style trellises provide reliable support for peas.

A Simple Trellis: Vertical Gardening Made Easy

The trellis I like best is fairly easy to build, provides good support, and can be used for peas, cucumbers, and even melons (on netting) or beans and tomatoes (on twine). The instructions that follow are for a 15-foot-long (4.6 m) trellis, about 5 feet (1.5 m) high in deeply loosened soil. Make the posts shorter if your soil is not that loose or longer if you want a higher trellis.

Use rot-resistant lumber. I like white cedar, which is available locally, but anything with some rot resistance will do. You can increase the wood's life span by applying a nontoxic wood preservative. Don't use pressure-treated wood or toxic preservatives. There is no way to keep those poisons out of the garden soil and out of the food that grows there. See page 72 for a recipe for a nontoxic wood preservative.

You'll need stakes to hold the netting down or anchor the lower end of the strings that support the tomatoes and beans. For stakes, I use wood scraps about 12" x 1" x ½" (30 x 2.5 x 1.3 cm), with an angled notch cut near the top.

▲ **Versatile homemade trellises.** These sturdy structures can be fitted with twine for beans and tomatoes (above) or with netting for peas, cucumbers, or melons (right).

Installing a Garden Trellis

Homemade Wood Preservatives

Nontoxic wood preservatives are available commercially (see the appendix). Or you can homebrew a batch: Melt 1 ounce (30 g) of paraffin in a double boiler. Remove from heat. Stir the melted paraffin into 3½ quarts (3.3 l) of turpentine. Stir ½ cup (120 ml) of linseed oil into the paraffin-turpentine mixture.

1 Point one end of each of the three posts with an ax or hatchet.

2 Set the two end posts 15 feet (4.6 m) apart. Start the holes for the posts with a crowbar, and then drive them in with a sledgehammer until they don't wiggle. The posts need to be firmly set, as they'll be supporting a lot of weight. Take pains to strike the posts squarely with the sledgehammer, so you don't split the tops. Cutting a chamfer on the top of the post will also help prevent splintering.

3 Line up the spot for the middle post, and start the hole with a crowbar. Drive the post in firmly, as in step 2. After it's in place, check whether the three posts are level. If not, adjust so that you'll be able to set the top pieces on fairly level.

4 Cut a 6-inch-long (15 cm) half-lap on one end of each top piece. This joint will lie on top of the center post. In step 6, you will drill right through both pieces to fasten them together and to the post.

5 Along the centerline of what will be the upper side of the top pieces, drive roofing nails at appropriate intervals to attach netting or twine.
  • *For twine,* space nails about 15 inches (37.5 cm) apart.
  • *For 7-inch (17.5 cm) netting,* set nails 7 inches (17.5 cm) apart. In addition, drive roofing nails at appropriate intervals into the two end posts.

6 Place a crosspiece so one end rests atop an end post and the end with the half-lap rests on the center post. Position this first crosspiece so that the second crosspiece will fit atop the half-lap. Position the second crosspiece. At each post, drill through the top into the post, and then drive a common galvanized nail through the hole into the post. Make the hole through the top slightly larger than the nail, so the top pieces can be removed easily.

7 **If you're using twine,** you'll need twelve 6½-foot (2 m) lengths. Tie one end of each length of twine to one of the nails on the crosspiece and the other end around one of the stakes. Pound each stake into the ground at a slight angle, directly below the corresponding nail. Adjust the twine to fit snugly.

8 **If you're using netting,** slip the top line of the netting over the nails on the crosspiece and the side lines over the nails on the posts. To keep the bottom snugly aligned, you can also drive stakes at intervals along the length of the bed and tuck the bottom line of netting into the notches in the stakes.

CHAPTER 4

Growing a Self-Sufficient Garden

One of the nice things about gardening is that plants are so forgiving. With a few fussy exceptions, vegetable plants will burst forth, grow, and yield at least something of a harvest, even when we gardeners just barely and intermittently meet their needs.

The earliest, biggest, and best-tasting harvest, however, comes from plants whose needs are fully met, on time. Plants do best when their growth, from germination right through maturity and harvest, is steady and uninterrupted. Just as stop-and-go driving is bad for the family car, stop-and-go growing is bad for garden plants.

We can ensure steady, uninterrupted growth in the garden by giving plants the food, moisture, and temperature they need when they need it, and by protecting them from anything that hinders their growth, be it bug, disease, or weed. Much of our success in this endeavor depends on how we weed, fertilize, and water the garden.

Meeting the Needs of Your Plants

Whether it's a seedling or a ready-to-harvest crop, every plant needs the same things to thrive:

▶ Ample air, sunlight, and room to grow roots
▶ Soil and air temperatures within the plant's preferred range
▶ Enough, but not too much, water
▶ The right nutrients in the right amounts

Think of a plant as a bank with a number of vital customers that deposit money each week. As long as the customers — in this case, sunshine, water, and other essential elements — keep depositing funds, the bank gets larger and stronger. If some of the depositors disappear, the bank stops growing and must exist on its reserves, which makes it weaker.

Whenever a plant lacks one or more of these essentials for too long, it becomes stressed and growth slows or stops. When a plant moves from "growth mode" to "crisis mode," changes occur that affect both the size and the quality of its yield. Leaves become tougher and more fibrous, often developing a bitter taste, and roots and fruits lack sweetness. Some plants may bolt or try to set fruit. If stress continues, plants never catch up with others of the same age, resulting in lower yields.

As caretaker, your job is to keep out the bully weeds that rob garden plants of the precious air, light, and moisture they need, apply mulches and covers to help moderate soil and air temperature, and supply additional water and nutrients to make up for what is not naturally available. The techniques you use include weeding, mulching, protective covering, watering, fertilizing, and guarding against pests and diseases. You'll find information about pests and diseases in chapter 8; right now, let's look at some old and new ways to deal with garden weeds.

▲ **Off to the right start.** Provide plenty of water from the time your plants are very young. The amount of water needed varies from plant to plant, so check part 3 for information about what you're growing.

▲ **Payoff.** Early care leads to a healthy, plentiful harvest. If your aim is to give your plants all that they need for steady, uninterrupted growth, your reward will be a high-yield garden.

Some Weed-Fighting Strategies

Weeds are plants growing where you don't want them to grow. Whether their seeds have arrived in your garden courtesy of the wind or were brought in by animals, or if runners have crept beneath the garden fence from other areas, these unwanted plants compete with garden plants for growing space, nutrients, water, and sunlight.

Garden plants are bred and selected by horticulturists for qualities such as taste, disease resistance, color, and size. Weeds, on the other hand, are bred and selected by nature for one quality — survival. In general, weeds germinate faster and grow faster than the garden plants they compete with, and the garden plants often won't do well unless they get some help from us.

You can deal with weeds by preventing them, anticipating them, or eradicating them. Although all garden plants are affected by competition from weeds, some are much more at risk than others, and all are much more vulnerable when they're young than when they're at or near maturity.

DON'T LET THEM GET STARTED

When I prepared my garden with a rototiller, I had terrible weed problems. What I didn't know was that the rototiller was actually planting a new crop of weed seeds as it agitated the soil and brought the seeds to the surface. The tool I thought was going to help my weed problem was making it worse. Now, the guiding principle for my weed-fighting strategy is to keep weeds from germinating in the first place. In my deeply dug, raised beds, protected by mulch each fall, the soil is hardly disturbed at planting time. I've found that since I've gardened this way, very few weeds appear. One more terrific benefit of the deep, wide-bed technique!

A Whole Lot of Seeds

A cubic inch (16 cm^3) of soil can contain as many as 5,000 weed seeds, many of which can remain viable for decades.

GIVE YOUR GARDEN PLANTS A HEAD START ON THE WEEDS

When little weeds and little vegetable seedlings compete on even terms, the weeds win. You can tilt the playing field in favor of the vegetable plants by giving them a head start. Start weed-challenged plants like cabbage and its cousins indoors or in a cold frame, and transplant them to the growing bed when they are big enough to compete with the weeds.

▲ **A protective nursery.** Growing young plants in a cold frame makes it easier to protect them from weeds until they're big enough to fend for themselves in the garden.

Tools for Weeding

SWAN AND COLINEAR HOES. Swan and colinear hoes are real weed-killers! On each, a narrow blade is attached to the handle at about a 70° angle, allowing you to move the blade easily along the soil, parallel to the surface and just below it. You can sever or uproot weeds without disturbing the soil and bringing new weed seeds to the surface to germinate. For years I used a swan hoe. Its tapered shape makes it easy to use very near plants and among close plantings. Recently, I bought a stainless-steel colinear hoe, and it's my new favorite. It's just as maneuverable as a swan hoe, but the blade is even thinner and easier to draw through the soil. Being stainless steel, it won't rust, and although it is harder to sharpen, it holds an edge longer.

swan hoe

colinear hoe

CAPE COD AND FARMER'S WEEDERS. Intensive planting in wide beds saves space, but it can make weeding difficult because there isn't enough room between plants for even a slim-bladed hoe. I've found the Cape Cod and farmer's weeders very helpful, each for a different kind of "close-in" weeding.

The Cape Cod weeder has a small blade held at right angles to a short handle. You draw this blade through the soil just below the surface to sever or uproot weeds and loosen the soil.

When I go after long-rooted grasses like orchard grass or witchgrass, or deep-rooted dandelions or milkweed, I leave all the other weeding tools in the shed and take the farmer's weeder.

Cape Cod weeder

▲ **The kindest cut.** Use a farmer's weeder to pry, grub, and cut roots as much as 8 inches (20 cm) down.

◀ **Sweep away those weeds!** You grasp and use a swan or colinear hoe much the way you hold a broom when sweeping the floor. It's important to keep the angle of the blade parallel to the ground, so don't extend your arms too far ahead of you. Instead of thinking of this tool as a hoe, I have found it useful to think of it as a knife on a long handle. I draw it through the soil with a sideways slicing action and picture the blade severing weed stems.

The Sharper, the Better

When most people say that something is "dull as a hoe," they mean it is very, very dull. But *dull* is not a word to describe a properly maintained hoe. The only job a dull hoe does well is to aggravate gardeners who are trying to use it. To do its job, a weeding hoe needs to be sharp so that it can sever weeds from their roots, not grub them from the earth, roots and all. You don't need to be able to shave with your hoe, but you should be able to peel little curls from a piece of pine lumber. See the box below for how to sharpen these tools

Sharpening a Colinear Hoe

The procedure for sharpening a stainless-steel colinear hoe is the same as that for sharpening steel hoes, but because stainless steel is much harder than ordinary steel, you can't cut it with a file. Instead, I use a fine-grit diamond sharpening stone. Getting a good edge on a stainless-steel tool takes longer, but it also lasts a lot longer.

Smart Clips

Vegetable plants are most sensitive to competition when they are little, with small and poorly developed root systems. This is also when they are most likely to be damaged or even uprooted when you are hoeing or pulling weeds near them. So change weapons. Put down the hoe, pick up a pair of scissors, and clip the weeds right at the soil surface. The roots probably won't have enough strength to grow a new top, and when they shrivel and decompose, they leave air spaces behind and add a little bit of organic matter to the soil.

Sharpening Garden Hoes

1 The steel in most hoes is soft enough to be sharpened with an ordinary file. Hold the hoe firmly in a vise and file a bevel on the inside edge (the side facing toward the handle).

2 After you have a sharp edge, shift the hoe in the vise so that the other side is up and file it lightly to remove any large burrs.

Mulching for Weed Control

The effectiveness of mulches as weed suppressants depends on how well they prevent light from reaching the soil surface. A variety of mulches, both organic and inorganic, and even a "living" mulch, provide good choices for almost every garden.

ORGANIC MULCHES

This category includes any mulch comprised of dead plant material. It can be either in natural form, like straw, hay, grass clippings, pine needles, leaves, or bark, or in processed form, like cardboard or non-colored newspaper. Any of these spread in a thick enough layer to block light can suppress weeds.

PLASTIC MULCHES

Plastic mulches make effective weed fighters, although they don't have some of the side benefits of organic mulches. It's important to consider what effects the mulch may have in your garden in addition to weed control. For instance, plastic mulches, as well as black planter's paper, warm the soil. This is fine for heat-loving crops but detrimental for those that either grow slowly or decline in quality when the soil in their beds gets too hot. And some of the plastic mulches don't allow water to penetrate to the soil. Use the chart on page 81 to help guide your decisions.

LIVING MULCHES

You can place your plants so close together that nothing else can grow there. The plants can be all one crop or mixed. Good vegetables to plant densely include kale, spinach, and lettuce. It's not possible to treat all plants in this manner. For instance, beets will stunt one another if planted too close. Cabbages and other mustard family members aren't very effective shade producers. Tomatoes and peppers aren't effective shade producers until they're mature. For plants that can't provide their own living mulch, interplant with other companionable vegetables. Try these combinations:

▶ Grow lettuce among onions, carrots, corn, beets, and cabbage. Because it's a light feeder, it doesn't rob the soil of the nutrients these other crops need, and it benefits from the somewhat cooler soil provided by shade from the other plants.
▶ Fast-growing lettuce and radishes can shade the soil between tomatoes or peppers until they mature enough to do it themselves.

▶ **Mulch that you can eat.** The fast-growing lettuce planted between these rows of corn keeps weeds down when the corn is young. In turn, the growing corn shades the lettuce during the hottest part of summer.

Weed Control and Beyond: Organic Mulches

Organic mulches help control weeds, but that's not all they do in the garden. They also conserve soil moisture, moderate soil temperature, and provide food for soil-dwelling organisms; some even change soil pH. Before you choose a weed-controlling mulch consider how it may affect your garden.

Moisture conservation. Although organic mulches help conserve soil moisture, mulches like leaves, cardboard, and newspaper can make it harder for water to soak into the soil quickly, particularly during heavy rains, when runoff is common. Other materials, such as straw, hay, and grass clippings, help with water absorption by soaking up any excess that the soil cannot absorb immediately.

Soil temperature. Organic mulches, particularly those applied in thick layers, lower and moderate soil temperatures. Although sometimes desirable, it's not helpful when it retards soil warming in spring or prevents heat-loving plants from getting what they need.

Nutrient content. Because they come from plants in the first place, organic mulches provide food for soil-dwelling organisms and eventually become part of the soil, adding to its organic content.

Soil pH. Pine needle mulches lower pH and should therefore be used only where this effect is desired.

◄ **Clockwise from top left,** leaves, straw, pine needles, bark chips, grass clippings.

WEED-KILLING INORGANIC MULCHES COMPARED

Type	Effectiveness	Other Factors
Clear (or builder's) plastic	Poor weed control, unless hot enough to fry weeds	Warms soil; prevents water from penetrating soil
Black plastic	Good weed control	Cheapest; warms soil; prevents water from penetrating soil
IRT (infrared transmitting) plastic	Good weed control by blocking visible light that weeds need for growth	Costs more than black plastic; warms soil better than black plastic; prevents water from penetrating soil
SRM (selective reflective mulch) (red) plastic	Poor weed control	Warms soil; prevents water from penetrating soil
Planter's paper mulch	Good weed control	Water permeable; biodegradable
Landscaping fabric	Excellent weed control	Water and air permeable; moderates, but doesn't raise, soil temperature; 4 times more expensive than plastic; long lasting
Ewe mulch (made from wool fibers)	Excellent weed control	Water permeable; moderates, but doesn't raise, soil temperature; costly

CHRONIC WEED PROBLEMS: KEEP THEM IN THE DARK

Sometimes weeds either start out in control of a new garden or become so much of a problem that simply hoeing or pulling can't keep ahead of them. Witchgrass, orchard grass, and purslane can do this. Extreme measures are called for. Although this sometimes means you have to sacrifice a particular area of the garden for one growing season, it may be worth it in the long run. The three most effective ways to rid a garden bed of weeds are an organic mulch of newspaper and straw, black plastic mulch, and cover crops.

▲ **Extreme organic mulch.** This method works well as the first step for a new garden or garden extension: Cover the invaded area with cardboard or with at least two layers of newspaper. Cover this with a thick layer of straw. Leave it for a year. By the next spring, the weeds should be gone; the soil should also be richer and well worked by worms and other soil organisms.

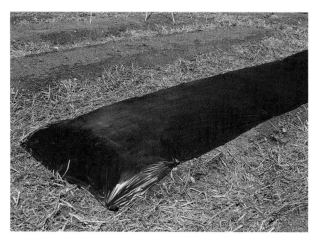

▲ **Extreme plastic mulch.** Cover the area with black or IRT plastic for the growing season. Remove the plastic in fall and mulch with leaves or straw for winter.

▲ **Cover crops.** To obliterate a really pernicious weed, plant a living mulch in the form of a cover crop that grows thick and heavy for one growing season. Buckwheat works well for this purpose. As soon as it begins to flower, I use a scythe to mow it down or till the plants into the soil as green manure. If you mow it, compost what you cut down. Make a second planting and then mow or till again. By the end of the season, those weeds should be gone. And as a bonus, there will be a lot more organic matter in your soil.

FLAME WEEDERS

My reaction when I first read about flame weeders was that they may involve a bit of overkill. Using a propane-fueled torch to go after weeds seemed a little like using a 2 x 8 to swat houseflies. I reconsidered when I remembered my chronic problem with purslane. It grows like mad, and when you dig it out, half the time it reroots itself. If you chop it up, each piece becomes a new weed. It makes the multi-headed Hydra look like a house pet. When I put a flame weeder to this test, I was convinced that this tool is well worth adding to the weed-control arsenal, particularly if you have a big, weedy garden.

When you use a flame weeder, the objective is not to burn a weed completely to the ground, but just to heat it up so the cells burst and the plant dehydrates. It's very effective for eradicating small weeds in an unplanted bed, but because it doesn't distinguish between weeds and vegetable plants, and its heat can affect plants well beyond the visible flame, it's not for weeding in beds that have already been planted.

WALKWAY WEEDING

Weeding is not my favorite part of gardening, and weeding in the packed soil of the walkways is my least favorite kind of weeding. Pulling walkway weeds is futile; they usually break off instead of coming out, and the root left behind soon grows a new top. Hoeing with a swan or colinear hoe does not work very well either, because the soil is too compacted to let the hoe pass through it, and these hoes are not good hacking tools. Fortunately, however, a stirrup, or scuffle, hoe can handle walkway weeding.

▶ **Stirrup or scuffle hoe.** This handy tool has two sharpened edges, allowing it to cut on both its push and pull strokes, shearing weeds off slightly beneath the soil surface.

▲ **Firing up.** A flame weeder is most useful for tending paths or the sides of raised beds, where it's less likely to cause erosion than if you hoe or hand-pull the weeds. If these areas are mulched, be sure to wet the mulch very thoroughly before flaming the weeds, and work with a helper who has a hose at the ready to douse any fires that might get going in the mulch.

An Ounce of Prevention Is Worth a Pound of Weeds

Even with the right tool, walkway weeding is not very high on my list of favorite ways to spend time in the garden. I'd much rather avoid the problem in the first place. So, to prevent and control the problem I mulch between and around all the garden beds with a two-layer mulch. The first layer, which consists of at least two thicknesses of newspaper or cardboard, blocks the light. The second layer of straw or mulch hay holds the first layer in place and provides something pleasant to walk on and look at. You can use water-permeable plastic mulch or landscape fabric for the first layer, but newspaper works as well and is a lot cheaper.

More Than One Way to Fertilize

I used to think that the phrases *weeding with a hoe* and *cultivating soil* meant pretty much the same thing. This isn't the case. In reality, soil cultivation involves more than just weed control. Its purpose is to introduce air into the soil, which in turn increases the activity rate of certain bacteria. This activity results in the release of soil nutrients. So, gently agitating the soil surface with a hoe or curved-tine cultivator is actually one way of fertilizing your plants. Periodic cultivation is thus a good idea whether or not the garden is in need of a weeding.

PROS AND CONS OF FERTILIZING

The notion that fruitful gardens and regular sidedressing with fertilizer go hand in hand is an axiom for many gardeners. Let me suggest a heretical notion: Once you have good soil for

▲ **Killing two birds with one technique.** Gentle cultivation with a curved-tine cultivator like this one introduces air into the soil, which in turn releases soil nutrients.

growing vegetables, you'll get better yields and higher-quality vegetables if you don't fertilize plants at all during the growing period. Here's why: Plants grow fastest and best, are most vigorous and healthy, and produce the largest and best-tasting harvest if their growth is steady and uninterrupted. Whatever gardening techniques you use should be tested against the question: Does this promote steady, uninterrupted growth?

The key to avoiding growth interruptions is to keep the plant constantly supplied with the things it needs in order to grow. Growth slows in dry soil and speeds up in moist soil. Similarly, if the soil is too wet, growth slows, then resumes when the soil is again moist. If the soil is too hot or too cold, growth slows, and then speeds up when temperatures return to the optimum range. If there aren't enough nutrients available to a plant, growth slows, and then it speeds up again when and if the nutrients become available. If you fertilize plants during the growing season, you encourage fluctuations in their growth — an acceleration when the fertilizer is applied, gradual decrease as it is used up, then another acceleration when more fertilizer is applied.

THE IDEAL: BALANCED NUTRITION

If a garden soil has plenty of organic matter in various stages of decomposition, sufficient major and minor nutrients, and a high level of biological activity, the plants living there will have all the food they need for growth, and this food will be supplied to them gradually and as they need it.

If you've been adding plenty of compost fortified with rock powders, paying attention to soil pH, and growing your plants in deep and wide beds, you won't need to (and shouldn't) add extra fertilizer, aside from a continually maintained layer of finished compost on the soil surface.

REALITY CHECK: TIME AND WORK

Unfortunately, gardens don't reach this blessed state overnight. It takes work, and it takes time. If you're starting a new garden or making the switch from traditional row-based gardens, your soil may not yet provide all the plants with all they need all season long. You'll probably have to supply some supplements. In addition, some plants require more food than others and will be more likely to need some extra help. In part 3, I make some suggestions for fertilizing the plants most likely to need it when growing conditions are short of optimum. If you're in doubt, fertilize. Little fluctuations in plant growth are a lot better than abrupt stops.

If your soil tests consistently indicate high fertility, however, and the less demanding plants are doing fine without supplements, it's okay to start the weaning process. Fertilize just part of a crop and see how things go. As you cut back on fertilizer, notice how the plants respond.

MORE THAN ONE FISH IN THE SEA: WHICH FERTILIZER?

Fish or fish-and-seaweed emulsions are well-balanced and fast-acting fertilizers for supplemental feedings, as is compost tea. They provide the major nutrients and a wide spectrum of minor elements as well. Follow the manufacturer's directions for the amount and frequency of application, depending on the crop you are fertilizing. You have several choices of how to apply, including foliar feeding and sidedressing.

Making Compost Tea

To make compost tea, mix a bushel of finished compost into about 20 gallons (76 l) of water in a plastic garbage can. Let it brew for at least four days, agitating it once a day.

Note: You can make "manure tea" using this same method. Use well-rotted manure.

Use fish emulsion or compost tea if you want a fast remedy. Foliar feed in the evening or on a cloudy day, because wet leaves, particularly if the moisture contains fertilizer, are easily damaged by sunlight. Label the spray bottle and use it just for fertilizing.

▲ **Foliar feeding.** Mix the fertilizer with water according to instructions on the package, pour the mixture into a spray bottle, and then spray it directly onto the plant's foliage.

▲ **Sidedressing.** Following package directions for how much to use, sprinkle the fertilizer well beyond the plants' leaf line.

Why Watering Is So Important

Adequate water is crucially important for vegetable plants — just as important as nourishment, because nutrients can pass from the soil to the plant only in the presence of water. Over the many years I've gardened, I suspect I've lost more yield to mistakes in watering than to anything else. Part of the problem was what I didn't know, but part was what I did know, but didn't do.

WATER, WATER EVERYWHERE

Water is important to your garden because, like humans, vegetables are mostly water. In order to continue to live and grow, plants, like humans, need to replace the water they lose each day. A tomato plant that's starved for water will produce smaller, less juicy fruits and fewer of them.

WATER AS TRANSFER AGENT

There is another, more subtle but even more important, reason why water is essential to plants. Nutrients pass from the soil to the plant through a film of water surrounding the tiny root hairs that grow from the plant's roots. If the film of water is not there, the nutrients do not get to the plant. Anytime the soil immediately around any of a plant's root hairs becomes too dry, the transfer of nutrients slows, and the plant's growth slows as well. If enough of the soil, and enough of the root hairs, are involved, the plant stops growing. It moves from growth mode to crisis mode, and a series of changes begins, each of which decreases the plant's ability to deal with other stresses and ultimately decreases its vigor, quality, and yield. Leaves toughen, blossoms appear too early, sugar content of fruits decreases, plants bolt and send up seed stalks, roots die, and leaves are shed. As if all of this isn't bad enough, plants in stress also become more attractive to pests and diseases.

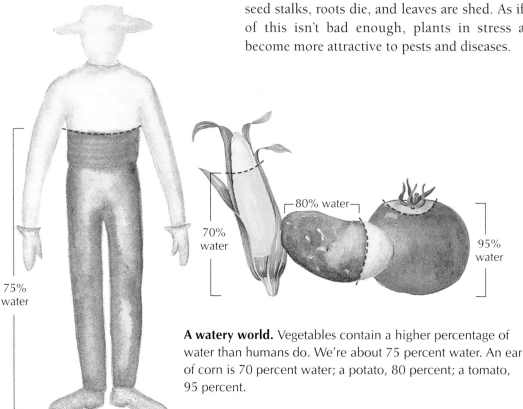

75%
water

70%
water

80% water

95%
water

A watery world. Vegetables contain a higher percentage of water than humans do. We're about 75 percent water. An ear of corn is 70 percent water; a potato, 80 percent; a tomato, 95 percent.

The extent of the damage depends on the extent and duration of the growth interruption, but some damage occurs every time a plant runs short of water. In fact, the major cause of growth interruption is water interruption. Since your primary goal is to avoid any interrupted growth, providing a steady supply of water is key.

THE WATER-FRIENDLY GARDEN

Ensuring sufficient water for plants involves a lot more than just turning on the hose or tipping the watering can, and most of what it involves happens long before you reach for either. You really start watering the garden when you prepare the soil and plant in wide, deep beds. In other words, many of the techniques that benefit your garden for other reasons also help create a garden that is less likely to have water problems at all. Here are some examples:

More loose soil. By gardening in beds rather than single rows, you increase the volume of loose soil and decrease the amount of compacted soil. And loose soil can absorb and retain much more water than can compacted soil.

More water-permeable soil. By adding lots of organic matter, particularly compost, you increase the soil's ability to hold water. Compost can hold six times its weight of water. Soil-conditioning greensand also increases the moisture-holding capacity of the soil.

More soil-dwelling organisms. The organic matter provides food for soil-dwelling organisms, which in turn improve soil structure and increase the soil's ability to accept and store moisture and move it from moister to drier areas.

More space for water storage. By loosening the subsoil and increasing the depth of the topsoil layer, you reduce compaction and provide more space for water storage.

▼ **Look for the silver lining.** Nothing pleases a gardener more than a good soaking rain after several summer days of hot, dry weather. But your garden won't receive full benefits unless the soil is receptive to the dousing.

MAKING THE MOST OF YOUR WATERING METHOD

Even with the best-prepared soil and most careful moisture conservation, most crops in most gardens will need at least some additional water from time to time in order to produce the highest yields. There's a big difference between how much water plants need to survive and what they need to produce the highest yield and best quality. Most garden plants are surprisingly forgiving of watering mistakes. They'll go on growing and produce some sort of a crop even when their water needs are just barely satisfied. But my most successful gardens have resulted when I've watered better — not just more, but where and when it will do the most good.

The usual rule of thumb is to be sure your plants receive at least an inch (2.5 cm) of water a week from rain or supplemental watering. But such amounts may be inadequate for young seedlings, and established plants may get water they don't need. Judging how to give your plants the amount of water they need, at the stage they need it, depends on a specific and measurable guiding principle — put the water where the roots are (or before germination, where the seeds are). This means that the amount of water, and the depth to which it's needed, is different for each plant and different at various times in each plant's life cycle.

MULCH IS A WATER CONSERVATIONIST'S BEST FRIEND

Evaporation happens. You can't really stop it, but you can certainly slow it down. And when you slow it down you are conserving water. One of the best ways to reduce evaporation in the garden is to cover your soil. Mulch, which you use to control weeds by keeping sunlight out, can also be used to keep water in. What mulch to use depends on the special needs of your garden.

▶ **To keep soil cool.** Apply a layer of grass clippings, straw, or rotted hay.
▶ **To keep soil warm.** Use a plastic mulch.
▶ **For additional nutrients.** If the crop you're mulching is a heavy feeder, use compost.
▶ **To create a living mulch.** For plants that tolerate close spacing, thin so that the mature plants just touch their neighbors. This living mulch greatly reduces water loss from evaporation.

Working with Plastic Mulches

Plastic mulches effectively conserve soil moisture, but they have some disadvantages compared to organic and living mulches: They cost money, need to be disposed of, and add nothing positive to the soil. In addition, they largely prevent water from soaking into the soil. In spite of those disadvantages, you may decide to use plastic mulch. If so, you can overcome the watering problem by removing the plastic when it rains or when you water or, better still, by installing a soaker hose under the plastic mulch.

Soaker hose under red plastic mulch

Judging How Much Water to Give

Too wet. When you're uncertain about whether to water, think of it this way: If you don't know where you're going, you won't know when you've arrived. You need to have a good idea of what properly moist soil is before you can judge whether your garden needs more water. Here's how to tell: Take up a handful of soil and squeeze it. If you can squeeze water out, the soil is too wet. It's still a little too wet if a clod of soil comes apart in lumps.

When Is It Time to Water?

Don't wait until your plants wilt before you water. Plants showing signs of wilt have already absorbed the last of the water available to their root hairs and have begun to withdraw water from their extremities. This means they're already stressed, already in the first stages of crisis. It's not too late to save the plant, but it is too late to prevent a growth interruption and some side effects you may not find out about until harvest.

Too dry. Open your hand. If the clump just falls apart by itself, the soil is too dry.

Just right. If it crumbles evenly into small granules, it's pretty close to just right.

Calibrate it. Use a moisture meter to get a reading that indicates this ideal condition. From then on, you can use the meter to perform spot checks on moisture conditions at various depths and different locations.

Watering Guidelines for Germinating Seeds

Seeds have to absorb moisture from the time they are sown until they germinate and emerge from the soil, so the seedbed must be evenly and constantly moist throughout this period.

WATER NEEDS FOR THE SMALLEST SEEDS

The tiny seeds — carrots, celery, and most of the cabbage family — are all planted about ¼ inch (6 mm) deep. Their seedbeds need to be constantly moist at least 1 inch (2.5 cm) down. This may require a light watering once a day or, in dry periods, twice or even three times a day. Until they have developed a minimal root system, small-seeded, shallow-rooted seedlings like these remain very sensitive to moisture deficiencies near the soil surface. For a week after emergence, continue monitoring and water as necessary so that no more than the top ¼ inch (6 mm) of the soil is dry.

PROVIDING FOR LARGE SEEDS

Although beans, peas, and other large-seeded plants are sown deeper, at 1 inch (2.5 cm) or more, their seeds are larger and therefore have to absorb a lot more water. They'll tolerate some dryness right at the soil surface but do best if their seedbed stays evenly moist during the entire germination period. Now is the worst time to skimp on water, and extra attention will pay dividends later on. Plants get off to the best start if germination happens as fast as it can. A germination process that drags on is itself a form of stress. If soil temperature is appropriate, germination problems are usually caused by insufficient soil moisture. In rainy periods, you may not need to water, but check to make sure the rain is penetrating deeply enough to reach the seeds. After the seedling emerges, keep the soil moist to at least 2 inches (5 cm) deep for the first week.

Caring for Cantankerous Carrots

Carrots are particularly fussy. If you don't keep their seedbed moist all the time, they'll just sit there and wait for rain. If they sit long enough, they won't come up at all. Still, you can ensure their germination by a simple trick.

Sow the carrot seeds as usual, water the bed, and then place a wide board over the entire area. The board protects the area from sun and drying winds and keeps the soil moist until the seeds germinate. After 7 to 10 days remove the board.

▲ **Steady does it.** If you provide your seedlings with consistently moist soil, you'll be rewarded with healthy plants and a successful harvest.

Watering Guidelines for Seedlings

As vegetable plants grow from seeds to seedlings, their water needs change. Some plants, such as onions, naturally grow all their roots fairly close to the soil surface (see photo at right). Others grow some roots close to the surface and also some farther down. And a few grow most of their roots deep into the soil, sometimes 3 feet (0.9 m), 4 feet (1.2 m), or more down. Let's look at particular plants:

▶ **Cabbage family.** Cabbages and other members of this family have both shallow and deep roots. They tolerate some dryness in the top 1 inch (2.5 cm) of soil, but they need moderate, even moisture deeper than that.

▶ **Beets and carrots.** Once they're established, beets and carrots begin developing a very wide, deep root system. They're not bothered by moisture changes in the top 1 or 2 inches (2.5 to 5 m) of soil, and they may not need extra water unless there is a long rainless period. But remember, when you do water, water deeply.

WATER NEEDS OF SANDY AND CLAY SOILS

Clay soils retain water well, but they also take it in more slowly. You will generally have to water less often but for a longer time.

Sandy soils absorb water quickly and seem to lose it just as fast. Expect to water more often and for shorter periods. Check the moisture level of the soil condition frequently.

▲ **Coddle your onions.** With their small, relatively shallow roots, onions are easily stressed if the soil is dry even 1 inch (2.5 cm) below the surface. Check every three or four days, and water to a depth of at least 3 inches (7.5 cm) whenever the top inch (2.5 cm) of soil gets even moderately dry.

Checking Your Watering Technique

▶ Work your hand right into the soil near the edge of a bed before and after watering to be sure you're getting water down at least 6 inches (15 cm).

▶ Better still, purchase a moisture meter and use it not only to determine when to water but also to check the effectiveness of the job.

Watering Guidelines for Mature Plants

Shallow-rooted plants. As they mature, shallow-rooted plants such as corn can tolerate low moisture levels in the top couple of inches (5 cm) of soil, though most of them do better when they're mulched to maintain even moisture throughout the soil. Although these plants may seem shallow rooted, many have some of their roots a foot (30 cm) or more down when they mature, so don't limit watering to just the top couple of inches. All mature plants need a good soaking when they get water.

Deep-rooted plants. Beets and other plants that naturally grow deep root systems actually benefit from a couple of inches (5 cm) of relatively dry soil near the surface. This is because too much surface moisture encourages the plant to grow extensive surface roots, which are then subject to stress if the soil does dry out later. In this case, the condition of the top few inches of the soil doesn't tell you about conditions down where the plants' roots are.

This is when the "inch a week" rule finally becomes useful. Whenever a week or so has passed without about an inch (2.5 cm) or so of rainfall, give the whole garden a good watering. Be sure to water the entire bed, not just the area right around each plant. Make sure the water permeates deeply (see page 91).

Causes of Puddling

What appears to be a problem of "too much watering" may really be something else, like inadequate drainage, compacted soil, or insufficient organic content. Chapter 6, Nurturing Vegetable-Friendly Soil, tells you how to correct each of these problems.

KNOWING WHEN TO STOP

Yes, it is possible to water too much, especially if your soil doesn't drain well in the first place. Plants need air as well as water, and they won't get enough air if too many of the spaces in the soil are filled with water. Plant growth stops when all the soil pores are filled with water for more than a few hours.

If water sits on the surface for more than 15 seconds without penetrating, stop watering. Check 12 hours later to assess whether the soil is adequately moist, but not soggy. Adjust your timing based on what you find. For instance, if the soil is too dry after 12 hours, in the future you'll need to water until the surface water stays on for perhaps 20 seconds. If it's too wet, stop when the water takes only 10 seconds to penetrate.

▶ **Bring them up right.** In a well-prepared bed, most vegetable plants are able to grow extensive and far-reaching root systems, and they'll do so unless you train them to do otherwise by providing water and food in only a small circle right around the stem.

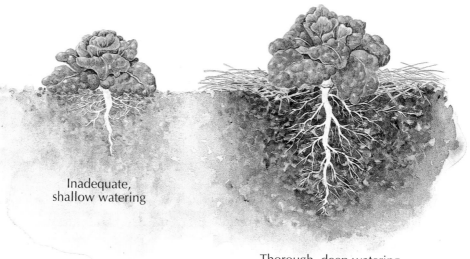

Inadequate, shallow watering

Thorough, deep watering

CHOOSING THE BEST TIME OF DAY TO WATER

The earlier in the day you water, the more of that water will be lost to evaporation during the day. If you water too late in the day, however, plants may stay damp all night and be more susceptible to diseases such as mold and rot. For these reasons, I prefer to water in the late afternoon. My second choice is early morning. Still, your own garden soil, local weather patterns, or other factors may mean that another time is ideal for you. For instance, if it's very humid, you might want to avoid watering in late afternoon and water early in the morning instead. The fact that leaves dry quickly in the morning and shade the soil may offset the natural evaporation that occurs. Wherever you garden, you might want to give an extra watering to seedbeds and young seedlings in the morning to be sure they don't get too dry during the day.

▼ **The magic wand.** Two hose attachments, a watering wand and a flaring rose, allow you to direct water right to the root zone.

COMMON-SENSE WATERING

Nature waters from above. Rain soaks the soil and also the plants. Usually, gardeners are best off if they copy nature, but watering is an exception to the rule. Tomatoes, peas, beans, melons, and squash are all more susceptible to diseases like late blight when their leaves are wet, especially in muggy or humid weather. Overhead watering is also more wasteful, because most of the water that ends up on the leaves, rather than in the soil, is lost to evaporation. These are two good reasons to use watering methods that help you get the water where you want it — onto the soil and down to the root zone of the plant.

Like most people, I am not fond of tedious jobs. When watering the onions means hauling a watering can 500 feet (150 m) back and forth from the faucet to the garden, that's a tedious job, and a job I'm likely to skip, rush through, or do poorly long after I should have. But if watering the onions means turning a spigot, picking up a hose, and waving a watering wand, the onions will get watered when they need it.

Watering Tools That Make Both You and Your Garden Happy

WATERING CANS. I'm a sucker for good tools, and usually I don't regret buying them. Nice (and usually expensive) tools work better and are more fun to use. Nonetheless, I've recently replaced the ordinary galvanized watering can I bought years ago for five dollars at a yard sale. I wish I'd done it sooner, because there are subtle but important differences between an ordinary watering can and a very good watering can.

As described on page 68, my favorite watering can has a well-designed rose and good balance. Its long spout allows me to direct-water beneath plant leaves, which moistens the soil while keeping the leaves dry. The large, well-shaped shield prevents water from splashing out when the watering can is very full. And its comfortable handle means I can hold it in one position as it empties, with no strain on my hand.

Haws
watering
can

HOSES. I thought I was saving money by not buying some extra hoses for the garden. By trying to save money, I diddled around and ended up doing too little watering, which reduced the harvest. Finally I broke down and got enough hoses to reach all over the garden. I sure wish I'd done it sooner. Save yourself frustration and do your garden a favor by getting enough hose to service the garden you're going to grow.

I've found that really cheap hoses aren't worth the little money they cost. But there's no need to go top-of-the-line either. Low-end commercial hoses, available from nursery and farm supply catalogs, are good enough and are sometimes cheaper than upper-end hoses from a garden center or hardware store. Look for a vinyl or rubber hose reinforced with polyester cords, which not only strengthen the hose but give it resistance to kinks as well. It should test to 500 psi, which means it will withstand pressure of up to 500 pounds per square inch (35 kg per cm^2). Two 50-foot (15 m) hoses cost a little more than a single 100-footer (30 m), but they're a lot easier to roll up and carry around.

While you're shopping for hoses, you'll also want to consider some helpful attachments:

shutoff
valve

SHUTOFF VALVE. This attaches to the business end of the hose so you can control the flow of water from there instead of racing back to the faucet. They're available in both brass and plastic. Plastic is less expensive, but brass lasts much longer.

WATERING WAND. This device acts like a long spout on a watering can and lets you easily direct water onto the soil and below plant foliage, so that the soil gets moist, but the leaves stay dry. It also means you can do your watering standing up.

watering wand

ASSORTED ROSES. A flaring rose attaches to the end of the hose, or to the end of the watering wand, and breaks the water flow into a wide, Y-shaped, gentle spray that's easy on the plants and the soil while covering a wide swath. You can also purchase roses in other sizes and shapes. The round roses shown here direct the spray to more specific areas.

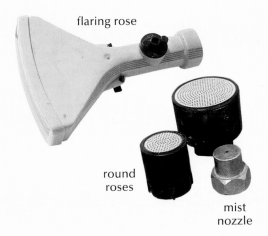

flaring rose

round roses

mist nozzle

AUTOMATIC WATER TIMER. An automatic timer allows you to regulate watering sessions to last between 5 minutes and 2 hours. It will even water while you're not home.

RAIN GAUGE. You don't need to guess how much rain fell last week if you have one of these simple, inexpensive tools. Now you'll know if your garden really got that 1 inch (2.5 cm) of rain last week.

MOISTURE METER. Insert a probe in the soil and get a moisture reading on a gauge. Guesswork over. (For photo, see page 91.)

rain gauge

▲ **Getting the right balance.** The watering can on the left is awkward to use, because its poorly balanced design allows water to spill over the top when the can is tipped. Contrast this with the well-engineered can on the right, which is a delight to use.

Irrigation Systems

Inexpensive, do-it-yourself kits make both soaker hoses and drip irrigation systems a reasonable option for home gardeners. It's quite easy to install either of these in an hour or two, depending on the size of your garden. The only tool you'll need to complete the installation is a pair of scissors. Once you have an idea of how long it takes to reach the moisture level you want with either system, you can add an automatic timer to it to make your watering chores even easier.

Drip system. These kits allow you to customize your watering system to fit the size and layout of your garden. They come equipped with connectors, caps, and vinyl tubing with tiny perforations spaced about 1 foot (30 cm) apart along the entire length. When you turn the water on, it drips slowly out of each of these holes.

You may also see a variation on this system, which includes solid mainline tubing, with narrow "spaghetti" tubing that you can space however needed. This type is especially useful when you have widely spaced plants (tomato plants, for instance); the perforated version is more appropriate for closely planted wide beds.

Soaker hose. A soaker hose is designed to carry water and leak at the same time. They are made from a rubbery material that feels like a wetsuit. Soaker hoses are flexible and can be snaked over beds so each plant gets the water it needs. They can also be buried to provide water nearer the root zone. Some gardeners find that soaker hoses are less likely to clog than drip systems.

▲ **Easy does it.** Before you begin your installation, lay out all the parts and plan the route your system will take through the garden.

▶ **Ready, set, water.** A drip setup like this one contains all the tubing, connecting Ts, and corner connectors you need to easily install an automatic watering system for your wide bed. Your hand-watering time will be reduced to a bare minimum.

Installing a Drip Watering System

1 Beginning where you can connect with the water supply, run the tubing along one side of your garden at a right angle to the length of the beds. You will install drip lines from this main line down each of the beds, using T and corner connectors as needed.

2 To install a drip line, lay out the parts needed to connect it to the main line. You'll need the T itself, as well as another length of tubing cut to the length of the bed.

3 Cut the main line where you want to make the joint. The drip line should lie along the center of the wide bed.

4 Fit the T to the drip line and to one end of the cut main line.

5 Complete the joint by fitting the other end of the cut main line to the second arm of the T.

6 Close off the ends of each of the drip lines with the cap supplied in the kit.

Keep Your Watering System Working Well

▶ **Winter care.** Be sure to take the entire system up and store it indoors over winter. Remove the caps and drain the lines before storing.

▶ **Clean up your act.** Flush the entire system with water before you install the caps. You should do this when you first install the system, as well as each time you put it in place after winter storage.

CHAPTER 5

Enjoying the Harvest & Tucking the Garden In

F ar too often, a harvest that should have been bountiful falls short of the goal right at the end. We may tend the garden just as we should all season long, and then miss the reward because we harvested too soon or too late, or made some mistake in curing or storing the crop. Timing and care at harvest can make the difference between bounty and mediocrity.

The slender filet bean that's perfect today is stringy tomorrow. Just a day changes peas from sweet and crisp to bland and mealy, and corn that's sweet picked before breakfast has a hint of starch if picked in the late afternoon.

Potatoes, gently dug, well cured, and stored at the right temperature and humidity will last into spring. So it is, too, with garlic and onions, carrots and beets, cabbages and winter squash.

The choices we make at harvest determine whether our crops enrich the table or the compost pile.

Knowing Ripe from the Wrong Time to Pick

Ripeness means one thing to the vegetable plant and quite a different thing to the gardener. For plants, ripeness is most often a measure of the maturity of the seeds. The more mature the seeds, the riper the fruit. After all, a vegetable's idea of a successful life is to make seeds that will eventually sprout and carry on the family name. The gardener's criteria are different from the vegetables'. To us gardeners, ripe is when we find the fruit most desirable, whether the seeds are mature or not. Here are some examples of what I mean:

▶ **Tomatoes.** A ripe tomato has mature seeds, so it's technically ripe from the plant's point of view. It also is at its peak of juiciness and flavor, so it's ripe from my viewpoint, too.

▶ **Beans.** When the seeds of a French filet bean are ripe and mature, the bean has more in common with a leather belt than dinner. A ripe filet bean to me is slender with tiny seeds.

▶ **Squash.** Squash plants and I agree on ripeness for winter squash, but not for summer squash, which is most flavorful when very small and tender, with immature seeds.

▶ **Peppers.** Pepper plants agree with my notion of ripeness when my taste runs to red fruits, but not when I prefer them green.

WHEN RIPE IS RIPE

We harvest portions other than the fruits of some plants, such as onions, garlic, and potatoes. These crops are ripe when the plant wilts or dies back — signs that are pretty easy to see. But the signs of ripeness are not so dramatic and obvious with other plants, like tomatoes and melons, whose fruit we harvest. The signs of ripeness in these crops are much more subtle. Instead of affecting the entire plant, signals of the perfect time to pick are often restricted to the area right

Plants that are tastiest when their seeds are ripe

▲ **Hot tomato!** When tomatoes are most juicy and flavorful, their seeds are also mature. Not only does a ripe tomato color up nicely, but it easily comes away from the vine when you gently tug it.

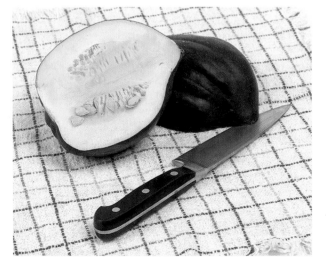

▲ **Winning winter squash.** Unlike summer squash, which is best when its seeds are small and unformed, winter squash is most tasty when its seeds are mature.

around the ripening fruit. For example, when a tomato or melon ripens on the vine, the plant is healthy, green, and vigorous, but the stem holding the ripe fruit begins to change, turning yellowish and loosening its grip on the fruit. A fully ripe tomato will slip loose from the plant if lifted gently. A ripe cantaloupe will come free from the plant with a gentle push of your thumb against the stem. One melon that gives a different readiness signal is the Chantais melon: You can tell that it's ripe when the small leaf next to the melon turns light brown.

Of course ripeness can usually be gauged by looking at the fruit. Tomatoes, and many other vegetables, noticeably change color as they ripen. Some crops, such as tomatoes, are forgiving as well and will ripen even if they are picked before they reach their peak. Others, such as strawberries, must be picked when absolutely ripe as they will not ripen further after being harvested.

▲ **Seedy and down at the heels.** The oversize, seedy zucchini on the left doesn't compare in texture or flavor with its tender sister on the right. As summer squash matures, not only do the seeds become large and tough, but the area around them becomes stringy, soft, and flavorless.

Plants that die back when they are mature

▲ **Onion family signals.** You'll know it's time to harvest garlic and onions when their tops brown and flop over.

▲ **One potato, two potatoes.** Get ready to dig your potatoes when you see the tops wilt and die back.

Two Kinds of Ripe

Sometimes ripe is simply a matter of personal taste. When is a pepper ripe? Or a green bean? Or a turnip? In each case, there's more than one right answer.

Peppers. Bell-type peppers are edible when they're green and immature, but they may be red, yellow, orange, or brown when they mature, and they're edible everywhere between their green and fully colored states. Mature peppers are sweet, while green peppers are tangy. Harvest them when they taste good to you. Picking peppers at the green stage means you'll end up with a bigger crop per plant. If you keep picking the fruits before they fully ripen, the pepper plant goes on making new ones.

Green beans that are to be eaten fresh or preserved by freezing or canning taste best fairly early in their development, long before the seeds within the pods are fully grown. Beans that grow much beyond the diameter of a pencil decline quickly in tenderness and taste; the bigger they get, the worse they taste. When they get really big ("ripe" from the bean plant's view of things), they are edible again. Now, however, it's not the pods you eat, but the seeds, which are very tasty as shell beans.

Root crops. Turnips, as well as beets and carrots, have multiple "ripenesses," depending on what you plan to do with them. Turnips and beets can be called ripe very early in life and cooked along with their greens. Turnips, beets, and carrots are all the most tender, tasty, and sweet at medium sizes, but they store better if they're bigger.

The More You Take, the More You Get

Call it the harvest paradox: The more summer squash, cucumbers, peas, or green and yellow beans you pick, the more you get to pick. A pea plant's goal in life is not to produce small, tender sweet peas to feed us, but to produce big, tough,

▲ **Pick a peck.** You can harvest and enjoy bell peppers throughout their growing stages. A young green pepper will have more of a tang than a fully mature, sweet red pepper.

Jumping the Gun

You can harvest some onions (not garlic) and potatoes early in the season and provide yourself with special treats that only gardeners can usually enjoy:

▶ Plant some onion sets or plants very close together and then eat the thinnings as scallions or little creamed onions.

▶ Reach into the soil beneath a potato plant and filch a few when the peas are ready. A dish of new potatoes and tender young peas is a fine way to eat butter.

starchy, inedible peas that will be the seeds for next year's pea plants. As soon as a pea plant succeeds in producing some seed-sized peas, its mission is accomplished, and it stops producing any more food-sized peas for you and me. The same is true of summer squash, cucumbers, and beans.

An easy way to increase your harvest is to harvest regularly, when the fruits are young and tender.

SEIZE THE MOMENT

Carrots are tasty from the time they're as big as your little finger to when they're full sized, so carrot harvest time spans most of the summer. The flavor and nutritional value of carrots changes over time. Baby carrots taste better, but big carrots are more nutritious. Some vegetables are another matter entirely. A French filet bean that was too small yesterday may be too big tomorrow, making its harvest time today, and today only. If I want the best filet beans, I pick all the ripe ones every day. Ordinary beans, peas, and summer squash offer a bit larger window of opportunity, but I still check every day and pick at least every second day.

Salad radishes start tasting good to me as soon as they're the size of little marbles, but when they're the size of big marbles, they're just a day or two from splitting open and becoming infested with root maggots. I try to harvest them all before this happens and store them in the refrigerator. The radishes keep better there than they do in the ground.

◀ **It's a pea-pickin' thing.** If you diligently keep pea and bean vines picked, they will continue to produce.

◀ **Marbles, anyone?** Pull and refrigerate radishes when they're still small. They keep longer and their flavor is better.

◀ **Sunny side up.** Young carrots are one of those gourmet treats that keep gardeners going. These early carrots are at their most tender, tasty stage, though carrots are higher in nutrients and store better when dug a bit later.

Keeping the Harvest: Storage Options

In winter, when the taste of ripe tomatoes is but a memory, I will still be eating winter squash, if I took time to store it correctly. The storage requirements of vegetables that can be saved for winter eating are given in part 3. The key to successful storage is finding or creating conditions that match these requirements.

MAKING USE OF WHAT YOU HAVE

For those vegetables that like to be kept cool and dry, you may be able to locate a spot in your house that provides just what they need without customizing a special room. Put a thermometer in various nooks and crannies around the house — in closets, under beds, in rooms either unheated or underheated during the winter — and in different areas of the basement, if it's fairly dry. Note each vegetable's requirements and then see if any of the conditions you find matches these needs.

▲ **Storage candidates.** Potatoes, onions, carrots, and beets are all reliable root cellar storables.

ROOT CELLARS

For the storage crops that want it cold and damp, you're not likely to find the right conditions unless you have an unheated basement. Even if you do, you may want to partition an area especially for food storage.

A root cellar that is perfectly adequate for most family's needs is large enough to store carrots, potatoes, beets, and other root vegetables, plus some cabbages. Sometimes the phrase *root cellar* conjures up visions of an immense underground cavern. It doesn't have to be huge, but it does need to be moist and cool: about 35 to 38°F (2 to 3°C) is ideal. If you store potatoes, it must also be dark.

To build a root cellar in a heated basement, the area you choose has to be isolated and insulated. If you need to keep your root cellar very humid, use cement blocks with foam insulation on the outside. If you'd prefer to use wood with fiberglass insulation, you can simply add the moisture to the storage containers of the crops that most need it (carrots and beets, for instance).

To maintain cool temperatures, make sure there's a window (blacked out, so that the space inside stays dark) or a vent to the outside to admit cold air as needed and provide air exchange.

Sand or Sawdust?

Most garden books that deal with winter storage suggest bedding carrots and other roots in either damp sand or damp sawdust. I've had much better luck with sand. When I used sawdust, the roots began to shrivel after two months or so, because they gave up too much moisture to the sawdust, which in turn gave up too much to the air. Sand seems to stay moist all winter. I have problems with sand only if I make it too wet in the first place. The sand should be quite damp, but not wet.

A Built-In Basement Root Cellar

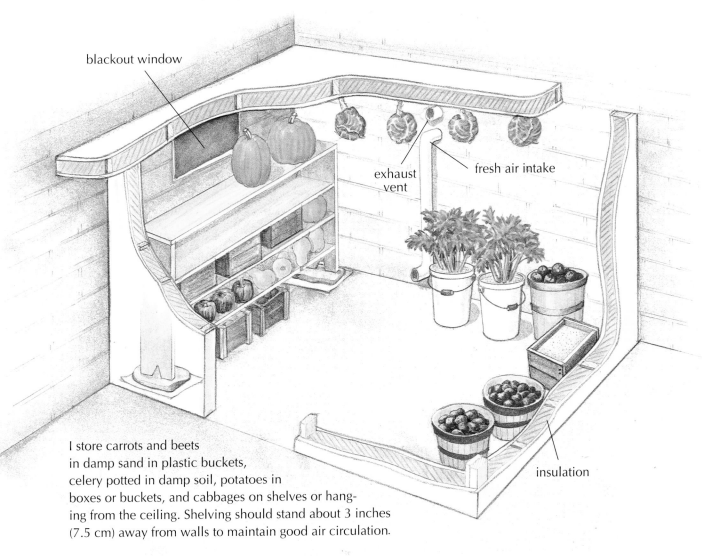

blackout window

exhaust vent

fresh air intake

insulation

I store carrots and beets in damp sand in plastic buckets, celery potted in damp soil, potatoes in boxes or buckets, and cabbages on shelves or hanging from the ceiling. Shelving should stand about 3 inches (7.5 cm) away from walls to maintain good air circulation.

Storing the Harvest

When you store your vegetables for winter use, remember that some crops prefer to be kept dry, whereas others like it moist. Garlic does best when you keep it cool but dry. Winter squash and dried beans need warm, dry spots. Store the following vegetables in a cool, moist place:

Beets, in damp sand
Brussels sprouts, on
  stems, in damp sand
Cabbage, wrapped in
  newspaper

Carrots, in damp sand
Celeriac, in damp sand
Celery, planted in a
  bucket of damp soil

Jerusalem artichoke,
  in damp sand
Onions, in baskets or
  braided

Potatoes, in baskets
Rutabaga, in damp
  sand
Turnips, in damp sand

The Year-Round Garden

When I first started gardening, the growing season was pretty clearly defined. I followed the same traditions that gardeners had been using for generations. Gardening started in early spring when we planted the peas and a few leaf crops like lettuce. Then we paused to wait the coming and going of the last frost, about Memorial Day in Vermont, when the rest of the plants went in. In fall, the first killing frost marked the end of the garden and we all switched our attention to other things.

Now, however, things are very different. Row covers, cold frames, and garden greenhouses mean that we can keep something growing in the garden all year long. And it isn't just new hardware that helps create the year-round garden.

Plant breeders have developed a number of frost-tolerant vegetable varieties that we can grow even in some of the unprotected parts of the garden long after the first "killing frost."

The first hard frost has been changed from an ending to a turning point. Although much of the garden does stop, some continues to go on. With the cold weather it's time for a change of focus, of keeping some things growing while also looking ahead to next year. What you do in the garden after the Big Frost is in one sense the ending and cleanup of the old garden, but in another it's the beginning of a new garden. What you do now in fall and early winter can have an important effect on what will happen in your garden next spring and summer.

▲ **Even Santa Claus can grow iceberg lettuce all year round.** Hoe, hoe, hoe! Once upon a time, it was easy to tell the growing season from the rest of the year. The last frost allowed it to begin, and the first frost ended it. Now, with row covers, greenhouses, and cold frames just about anyone can grow nutritious vegetables in any season of the year.

Recycling the End-of-the-Garden Wastes

With less day-to-day work in the garden, you often have more time for some important long-range improvements to your garden soil. In part 2 you'll find some specific information on how to make compost and how to test and amend your soil. Here are some tips for things that are best to do right now.

RECOGNIZING THE HALF-FULL GLASS

A lot in life depends on how you view things. Are you more likely to see the half-full or the half-empty glass in certain situations? Looking at the garden right after the first really hard frost, some people see a mess to clean up. Others seeing the same scene find one final, glorious harvest, not for the table, but for the compost pile. Fall is the perfect time to start making the compost you'll need next spring and summer.

Much of what goes into compost piles in spring and summer is ready to compost without being chopped, ground, or otherwise reduced in size. This includes tender young weeds, grass clippings, high grass and weeds mowed from around the garden or beside the driveway, and the harvest from cover crops grown especially for compost.

▲ **The kindest cut.** Tough stalks and overgrown vegetables will decompose more quickly if you chop them up before adding them to the compost pile.

On the other hand, much of what remains in the garden in fall breaks down slowly and poorly unless it is chopped, shredded, or beaten to render it more edible by bacteria. For instance, broccoli, Brussels sprouts, and cauliflower plants — along with tomato vines, cornstalks, and melon and squash vines — all decompose faster if chopped into smaller pieces, exposing more surface area to the ravenous bacteria.

You need to take these additional steps in fall not only because the composting material itself is likely to be tougher, but also because time is not on your side as the seasons slip toward winter. Cold temperatures of late fall and winter slow down bacterial activity. And once it gets really cold, the kinds of bacteria that prefer higher temperatures simply call it quits until spring.

FALL IS THE BEST TIME TO TEST AND AMEND YOUR SOIL

Like many gardeners, I sometimes test my soil in spring, because that's when I think of it. But fall is a better time, really a much better time, for this important activity:

▶ **Lead time.** If you discover problems, you have plenty of lead time to apply long-term solutions rather than quick fixes that don't last. For instance, rock powders, which are used to modify soil acidity and maintain nutrient levels, are more effective if given months to work rather than weeks. Giving them a whole winter to settle in is better than adding them in spring.

▶ **Ideal temperatures.** In early autumn, soil temperatures are optimum for biological activity — neither too cold, as in early spring, nor too hot. Because biological activity affects the availability of soil nutrients, tests for these nutrients are most accurate when soil life is most active.

Planning Ahead Can Improve Next Year's Garden

If everything has gone about as you had hoped, planning next year's garden involves no more than putting the plant rotations through one cycle. (For details about crop rotation, see pages 44–45. If you're thinking about adding or dropping a vegetable or variety, now is a good time to make the decision so you can make proper preparations for the newcomers.

Many gardeners start the planning for the next year's garden in winter, when the seed catalogs start arriving in the mail, or even later, when the seeds themselves arrive. But there are some very good reasons to do a lot of the planning in fall, right after the garden has been put to bed and the last frosted remnants of last summer's plants have been consigned to the compost pile:

▶ **For carrots.** If you decide in fall where next year's carrot patches will be, you can increase the chances for a terrific, good-tasting harvest by adding some autumn leaves or, even better, leaf mold to these beds. Just spread the leaves over the bed and chop them into the soil with a hoe. Soil creatures, such as earthworms, will spend the winter working on the leaves, breaking them down and liberating their nutrients for use by the carrots next summer.

▶ **For cabbage family crops.** If clubroot has attacked any of the cabbage family crops, add lime or wood ashes in the beds where they will be next year to raise the pH to a neutral (7.0) or even slightly alkaline level.

▶ **For acid-loving plants.** If pH levels are too high in any bed where acid-preferring plants will grow, work in some peat moss or sawdust. The months ahead give plenty of time for these to have some effects before you plant next year's garden.

▶ **For asparagus.** For a such a skinny little vegetable, asparagus is hungry all the time. To supply this plant with the nutrients it needs, apply an inch (2.5 cm) of compost to this bed in fall and cover it with straw mulch to protect the asparagus roots from cold.

▲ **Fallen treasure.** Leaves are one of the best "free" materials for improving your garden. I chop in a layer several inches thick, water it down to get the biological activity going, and then top it off with a thick layer of straw, which I water down as well.

Fall Forking

I prefer to do my broadforking in fall, rather than spring. The worms then have the fall, winter, and the beginning of spring to repair the inevitable damage that the digging causes to their network of tunnels.

Coverlets for the Garden Beds

While homes filled with people are well cared for, no one takes care of an empty house. Abandoned houses fall apart soon after people move out. The same is all too often true of gardens. Many folks abandon their gardens in winter and soon find out that bare soil is a lot like an abandoned house. It doesn't do well unless something — even weeds — is growing there. You can easily keep the garden alive and active in winter by sowing cover crops or applying organic mulches in fall.

WINTERING OVER WITH WINTER RYE

Sow a cover crop of winter rye in fall, and the garden will be a garden all winter long — and a whole lot better off. Winter rye sends out extensive roots that make the soil more friable. When the roots die and decompose, they leave behind countless spaces for air and water, along with lots of organic matter. Although winter rye doesn't add nitrogen to the soil, it does capture nitrogen already in the soil and prevent it from being leached away.

Mature winter rye can reach 4 feet (1.2 m) in height, but in the home garden it's best to harvest it earlier, while the stems are still young, tender, and easy to break down. Here are three ways to use it:

- At 8 to 16 inches (20 to 40 cm) high, work it into the soil by chopping with a hoe or tilling.
- Wait until flowering and mow it down for the compost pile.
- At flowering, mow and leave on the ground; mulch over it with straw.

WINTER MULCHING

Spreading a thick layer of organic mulch over the beds is the single best thing you can do for your whole garden as winter approaches. A good mulch insulates the soil, which either keeps it from freezing, or keeps it from freezing as deeply

or quickly as it otherwise would. This has some very beneficial effects:

- Soil that has gone through a deep freeze and thaw is more compacted in spring than it was in fall. Mulch mitigates the freeze cycles and helps maintain soil friability over winter.
- Mulch applied after the first hard freeze, but before daytime temperatures stay below freezing, allows soil organisms (worms in particular) to go on working the soil for much longer than they otherwise could. And when freezing temperatures do invade the soil, the mulch slows the freezing process, allowing worms time to migrate deeper into the earth instead of being caught by a sudden cold spell and freezing to death.

Straws in the Wind

I've found that leaf-mulched beds show even more worm activity in spring than do straw-mulched areas. I like to put down a layer of leaves for the worms and then top it off with some straw for extra insulation.

▲ **Deep sleep.** One of winter's true satisfactions is to consider the energetic promise of our wide beds, slumbering under a deep covering of snow.

PART 2

The Healthy Garden
Above and Below Ground

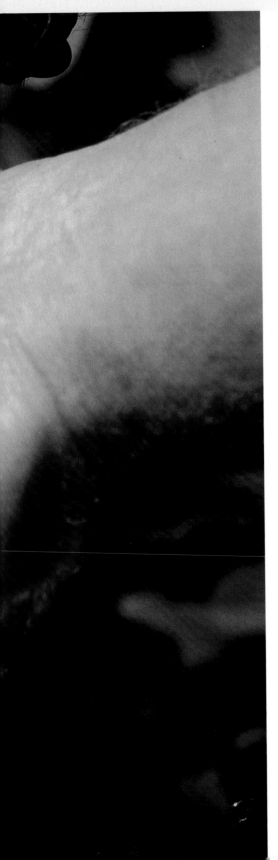

CHAPTER 6

Nurturing Vegetable-Friendly Soil

Although it is often disparaged as just dirt, garden soil is in fact the keystone in the arch that reaches from the seed's promise to the harvest's fulfillment. No matter what else we do right, the garden will not reach its highest potential if the soil within it is less than the best it can be. Yet many gardeners view soil as something that can't be changed. In their search for a better garden, they try new vegetables, and different fertilizers and watering methods, but never think of improving the soil.

Great garden soil is a balance of the right ingredients nurtured by worms and other essential organisms. The result is a vibrant, vigorous garden.

If you improve your garden soil, regardless of what type your garden presently has, you will improve your garden. You may not feel as if you are building something great as you dig compost or freshly cut buckwheat into the soil, but you are. You are placing the keystone to a garden that will be the best you ever had.

A Recipe for Garden Success

To grow as well as they can, plants need many different nutrients. Nine of these — carbon, hydrogen, oxygen, nitrogen, phosphorus, potassium, calcium, magnesium, and sulfur — are required in relatively large amounts. These nine are called the macronutrients. Among the others are iron, boron, manganese, copper, zinc, and molybdenum. These, called micronutrients, are needed in smaller amounts — sometimes very small.

To a vegetable plant, all the nutrients are important, but some are more likely to be in short supply, and these require more of the gardener's attention. For instance, carbon, hydrogen, and oxygen are free for the taking from air and water. Nitrogen, phosphorus, and potassium, on the other hand, are lacking to some degree in most soils. Even if they are present in sufficient amounts at the beginning of the gardening year, these elements may be used up and require replenishing each year or after each growing cycle, and usually require supplementing, sometimes after each growing cycle. Calcium, magnesium, and sulfur are usually present in adequate amounts, but not always.

To properly evaluate your soil's nutrient content, you will need to test your soil (see how to do this on page 116). But the plants growing in it can also offer you clues to what it contains. The chart on the next page gives you some tools to read the signs. Notice that signs of excess are included along with signs of deficiency: "Moderation in all things" is as good a rule for plants as it is for people. Too much of some plant nutrients can be as bad as too little.

▲ **It's great being green.** Healthy corn needs healthy soil with plenty of nitrogen to produce heavy crops and green leaves.

▲ **A pale shadow.** Plants growing in poor soil are off color and spindly.

SOME CLUES TO WHAT NUTRIENTS YOUR PLANTS NEED

	Element/Symbol	Signs of Deficiency	Signs of Excess	Sources
ELEMENTS FROM WATER & AIR	Carbon/C	None known	None known	Air (carbon dioxide)
	Hydrogen/H	Wilting	Drowning	Water
	Oxygen/O	White areas in veins; high nitrates	None known	Air and water
PRIMARY ELEMENTS	Nitrogen/N	Light green to yellow leaves; growth stunted	Dark green leaves; excessive growth; maturity slowed; bud or fruit loss	Blood meal, fish emulsion, manure
	Phosphorus/P	Red or purple leaves; cell division slowed	Other essential elements sometimes tied up	Bonemeal, rock phosphate, superphosphate
	Potassium/K	Vigor reduced; susceptible to disease; thin skin; small fruits	Coarse, poor-colored fruit; intake of magnesium and calcium reduced	Greensand, muriate or sulfate of potash, seaweed, wood ashes
SECONDARY ELEMENTS	Calcium/Ca	Growing point of plants damaged	Intake of potassium and magnesium reduced	Gypsum, limestone, oyster shells, slag
	Magnesium/Mg	Yield down; old leaves white or yellow	Intake of calcium and potassium slowed	Dolomite, magnesium sulfate (Epsom salts)
	Sulfur/S	Light green to yellow leaves; growth stunted	Combined with too-low pH, sulfur "burn"	Sulfur, superphosphate
MICRONUTRIENTS	Boron/B	Small leaves; heart rot (corkiness); multiple buds	Yellowish red leaves	Borax
	Copper/Cu	Multiple buds; gum pockets	Intake of iron prevented; roots stunted	Copper sulfate, neutral copper
	Iron/Fe	Yellow leaves; veins remain green	None known	Chelated iron, iron sulfate (copperas)
	Manganese/Mn	Leaves mottled with yellow and white; growth stunted	Small dead areas with yellow borders on leaves	Manganese sulfate (tecmangam)
	Molybdenum/Mo	Varied symptoms	Poisonous to livestock	Sodium molybdate
	Zinc/Zn	Small, thin, and yellow leaves; yield low	None known	Zinc sulfate

Let a Test Tube Be Your Crystal Ball

The ultimate test of any soil is the condition of the plants growing in it. Vigorous, healthy plants and a bountiful, tasty harvest mean the soil is just fine. Most garden soil isn't great, though, and would benefit from an addition of the right amendments in the right amounts. But before you can improve the soil, you have to know what it needs and what it doesn't need. Some gardeners claim they can test soil by tasting it; I haven't tried that. Most of what I need to know I learn from scientific soil tests, which give me reliable information about solving soil deficiencies before they affect my garden plants.

You can test your soil yourself or have it done at a laboratory, either through your state's Cooperative Extension Service or a private lab. To help you choose which method is best for you, here are some advantages and disadvantages of each.

DO-IT-YOURSELF SOIL TESTS

Easy-to-use and inexpensive, do-it-yourself kits contain individual tests for pH as well as for nitrogen, phosphorus, and potassium. A nice thing about do-it-yourself soil tests is that you get your results right away. And because the kits are adaptable, you can test individual beds and fine-tune the soil for the vegetables you plan to grow there. Home test kits can be purchased at nurseries and garden centers as well as from mail-order suppliers.

LAB-STYLE SOIL TESTS

If home test kits haven't solved your garden soil problems or you need information that home kits can't supply, laboratory soil tests may be

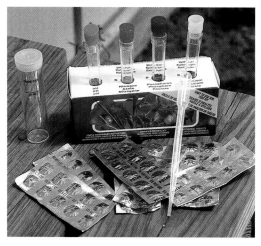

▲ **Home-style chemistry.** Do-it-yourself kits are fun to use and provide a surprising amount of helpful information.

what you need. Compared to home tests, lab tests provide more information, more accurately, including pH, nitrogen, phosphorus, and potassium levels, as well as values for secondary elements and micronutrients. Most labs also test for the amount of organic matter, and some test for the amount and kind of biological activity going on in the soil.

That's a lot of very valuable information, but these benefits come at a cost, partly in money, partly in time. Soil tests by a state Extension Service are generally less expensive than those by private labs, depending on the range of the report. In either case you don't get instant results — particularly not in spring, when labs are often swamped with requests from other gardeners and farmers wanting their soil tested.

THE BEST OF BOTH WORLDS

I use both kinds of tests. I test my soil with a kit at least once a year to monitor soil pH and major nutrient levels, and I test particular beds to match or adjust their characteristics to the needs of the plants I want to grow there.

When I'm starting a new garden or making a significant addition to an old one, I have a lab test done to make sure the soil doesn't have any major problems. Ideally, I like to do this in fall, when labs are less busy. In addition, every three or four years I have a complete laboratory test done on the entire garden to make sure my soil care is on track.

An accurate soil test often depends on how carefully the soil sample has been gathered. Here's how to do it.

How to Make a Soil Sample for Testing

1 After scraping away any surface litter or mulch, use a trowel to dig a circular hole about 5 inches (12.5 cm) in diameter and as deep as the topsoil layer — 8 to 18 or more inches (20 to 45-plus cm), depending on how deeply the garden is dug.

2 Slice a strip of soil about ½ inch (13 mm) thick from the side of the hole and lay the sample on a sheet of newspaper. Take samples from at least 10 different places in your garden. Mix the samples well, breaking up any clumps and removing any stones or other litter.

3 Follow any further particular instructions for preparing the sample for home testing or shipment to the lab. For example, you may be asked to dry the sample to a particular degree before beginning tests or shipping.

Soil-Sampling Savvy

Soil test kits measure chemical reactions, which is one reason why they are so reliable. Just as with any other scientific research, however, the accuracy of the test depends on the quality of the soil sample you collect and prepare. This is true whether you do your own soil tests or have them done by a lab.

► Follow the test lab or test kit manufacturer's instructions carefully.

► Take samples before working the soil.

► Home tests involve mixing water with soil samples. It's best to use distilled water; it is pH neutral and does not contain any dissolved minerals that might affect test results.

► Use a clean trowel and wear clean latex gloves so you won't contaminate the samples.

► You'll get more accurate results, particularly for nitrogen tests, if the soil is warm and neither very dry nor very wet.

► Don't take samples from areas you know to be atypical, such as the spot where you piled the manure or compost before you spread it on other parts of the garden, or a depression where runoff collects.

► Don't take samples within two weeks of adding fertilizers.

► Be sure to keep records of your results, including the date, weather conditions, and location of soil samples, along with the readings.

Using Home Soil Test Kits

The two most popular types of home soil tests are chemical and electronic. Both are easy to use, but that's about all the two have in common. In general, chemical kits are more affordable than electronic tests and offer good accuracy for the money. Home electronic testers are usually more expensive than chemical kits, but in my experience the additional cost is not reflected in increased accuracy. Both chemical kits and electronic testers can be purchased from local and mail-order garden supply companies.

Chemical kits supply different chemicals to measure soil pH along with phosphorus, nitrogen, and potassium levels. After mixing a small soil sample with distilled water, you add a chemical from the kit that changes the color of the solution. Then you compare the color of the solution with a color chart.

Using an Electronic Soil Tester

With an electronic tester, you need only a trowel, water (distilled water, if possible), and the special cleaning pad supplied with the tester. To get a reading, you simply plunge the probes into wet soil and throw a switch. Move the switch one direction to get the pH value and the opposite way to measure fertility.

This device can be reused almost indefinitely, and it's somewhat faster to use than a chemical kit. On the other hand, while it can give you a fairly accurate reading of soil pH, its fertility reading is vague, so you won't know what specific nutrients your soil lacks.

Testing Your Soil pH with a Chemical Kit

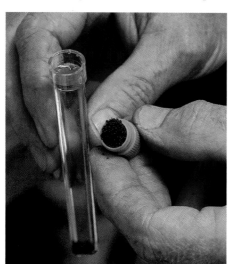

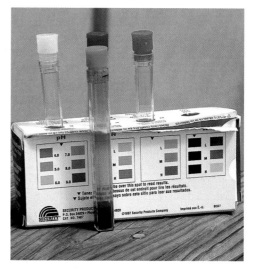

1 Following the package instructions, combine the soil sample and water with the chemical pH indicator supplied in the kit. Most kits supply test tubes for this purpose.

2 With the color chart placed so that a light source is behind it, hold the test tube about ½ inch (13 mm) away from the chart and compare the color reaction against the samples on the chart.

Soil pH: The Latch on Your Garden Gate

After you've tested your soil, you're left with a bunch of numbers that represent everything from pH to nutrients. What do they mean, and why do they matter? Let's start with pH, which I believe is the most important factor. My own early garden experience tells why.

Many years ago my wife, Sylvia, and I started a new garden in the Berkshire hills of western Massachusetts. It was the worst garden we have ever had. Most of the seeds didn't germinate at all, and many of those that did gave up quickly. The tomato plants grew to be 9 inches (22.5 cm) high and bore no fruit at all. The corn never got more than a foot (30 cm) tall.

All this trouble in soil that looked beautiful! It had wonderful tilth, a deep, dark brown color, plenty of organic matter. Soil tests showed no significant nutrient deficiencies. But what the tests did show was a pH of 4.5. With soil that acidic, none of the rest mattered. To be of any use to plants, nutrients in the soil must be available to them, which means they must dissolve in water. Most nutrients will not dissolve when the soil is either too acidic or too alkaline. And 4.5 is way too acidic.

The following year we added ground lime to the soil to bring the pH up to about 6.5. This single change allowed the nutrients to become available to the plants, and we had one of our best gardens ever. I have paid attention to pH levels ever since.

Understanding pH

Soil pH is a measure of how acidic or alkaline the soil is. The pH scale runs from 1 to 14, with 7 signifying neutral. Values below 7.0 indicate acidity, and numbers over 7.0 indicate alkalinity.

▲ **A matter of pH.** Each year Nathan tests and adjusts the soil pH before growing another crop of his specialty, Roy's Calais Flint heirloom corn.

Matching Soil pH to Your Plants' Needs

Most garden soils have a pH of between 4.0 and 8.0. Most of the vegetables we grow in the garden do best with a soil pH of between 6.0 and 7.0, but there are some exceptions. Carrots, eggplant, sweet corn, and potatoes grow well at 5.5, while cabbage and cauliflower can tolerate a pH of 7.5.

Gardening in beds makes it possible to have each vegetable growing in soil that is at or close to its optimum pH. After testing I assign each vegetable to the bed that is closest to its ideal pH conditions. Or I may adjust the pH up or down by adding an appropriate conditioner in fall.

IDEAL pH RANGES FOR PLANTS

Plant	pH Range	Plant	pH Range	Plant	pH Range
Alpine strawberry	5.0–7.5	Corn	5.5–7.5	Parsley	5.0–7.0
Artichoke	6.5–7.5	Cucumber	5.5–7.0	Parsnip	5.5–7.5
Arugula	6.5–7.5	Dill	5.5–6.7	Peanut	5.0–6.5
Asparagus	6.0–8.0	Eggplant	5.5–6.5	Pea	6.0–7.5
Basil	5.5–6.5	Endive/Escarole	5.8–7.0	Pepper	5.5–7.0
Bean, lima	6.0–7.0	Fennel	6.0–6.7	Potato	4.5–6.0
Bean, pole	6.0–7.5	Garden cress	6.0–7.0	Potato, sweet	5.5–6.0
Beet	6.0–7.5	Garlic	5.5–7.5	Radicchio	6.0–6.7
Broccoli	6.0–7.0	Gourd	6.5–7.5	Radish	6.0–7.0
Broccoli-raab	6.5–7.5	Horseradish	6.0–7.0	Red orach	6.5–7.0
Brussels sprout	6.0–7.5	Jerusalem artichoke	6.0–7.0	Rhubarb	5.5–7.0
Cabbage	6.0–7.5	Kale	6.0–7.5	Rutabaga	5.5–7.0
Cantaloupe	6.0–7.5	Kohlrabi	6.0–7.5	Sage	6.0–6.7
Carrot	5.5–7.0	Leek	6.0–8.0	Salsify	6.0–7.5
Cauli-broc	5.5–7.5	Lettuce	6.0–7.0	Sorrel	5.5–6.0
Cauliflower	5.5–7.5	Mache	6.5–7.0	Spinach	6.0–7.5
Celeriac	6.0–7.0	Marjoram	6.0–8.0	Squash, summer	6.0–7.5
Celery	6.0–7.0	Melon	5.5–6.5	Squash, winter	5.5–7.0
Chervil	6.0–6.7	Mizuna	6.5–7.0	Sunflower	6.0–7.5
Chinese cabbage	6.0–7.5	Mustard	6.0–7.5	Swiss chard	6.0–7.5
Chive	6.0–7.0	Okra	6.0–7.5	Tarragon	6.0–7.5
Cilantro/Coriander	6.0–6.7	Onion	6.0–7.0	Tomatillo	6.7–7.3
Claytonia	6.5–7.0	Oregano	6.0–7.0	Tomato	5.5–7.5
Collard	6.5–7.5	Pak choi	6.5–7.0	Turnip	5.5–7.0

SELECTED PLANT pH PREFERENCES AT A GLANCE

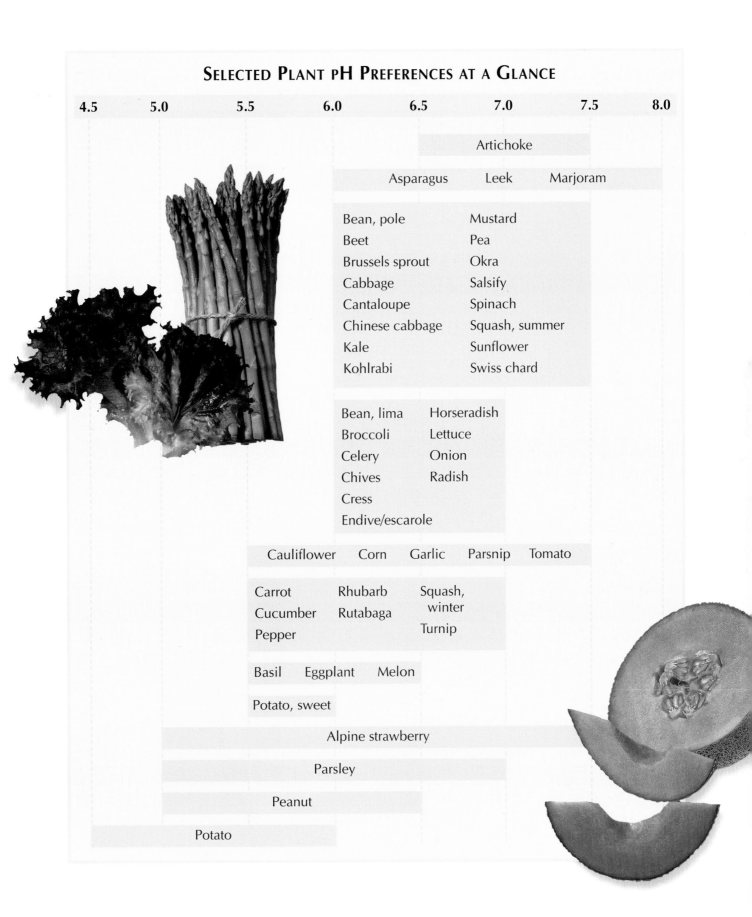

4.5	5.0	5.5	6.0	6.5	7.0	7.5	8.0

Artichoke

Asparagus   Leek   Marjoram

Bean, pole	Mustard
Beet	Pea
Brussels sprout	Okra
Cabbage	Salsify
Cantaloupe	Spinach
Chinese cabbage	Squash, summer
Kale	Sunflower
Kohlrabi	Swiss chard

Bean, lima	Horseradish
Broccoli	Lettuce
Celery	Onion
Chives	Radish
Cress	
Endive/escarole	

Cauliflower   Corn   Garlic   Parsnip   Tomato

Carrot	Rhubarb	Squash,
Cucumber	Rutabaga	winter
Pepper		Turnip

Basil   Eggplant   Melon

Potato, sweet

Alpine strawberry

Parsley

Peanut

Potato

Putting pH Test Results into Action

As the result of a pH test, you'll have a number that indicates how acid or alkaline your soil is. If that number is within 0.5 of the number preferred by the plants you want to grow, you don't have to do anything. If it's more than 0.5 outside your plants' range, though, you'll have to add something to the soil to move its pH into the range preferred by the plants you're hoping to raise.

HOW TO SWEETEN ACIDIC SOILS

The most common way to raise soil pH is to add lime to the soil. Calcitic and dolomitic limestone, as well as wood ashes, all contain lime. Calcitic limestone is primarily calcium, dolomitic limestone is a combination of calcium and magnesium, and wood ash is composed of about one-third calcium with significant amounts of potassium and magnesium. Which amendment you choose depends on whether nutrient soil tests show that your soil is deficient in potassium or magnesium.

As you can see by the chart on the next page, it takes quite a bit more lime-containing additive to raise your pH if you have clay soil or soil with a lot of organic matter.

HOW TO IMPROVE TOO-ALKALINE SOILS

The best long-term solution for improving alkaline soils is to add acidic organic matter such as peat moss, pine needles, leaf mold (particularly oak leaves), or aged sawdust or shavings. This not only reduces pH but also helps improve soil content and structure.

A quicker fix, but one that does not last as long, is to add agricultural sulfur. Like lime, it is best applied in fall, but

you can apply it in spring if you do so early. Spread it and fork it in just the way you would add lime.

TIMING YOUR CORRECTIONS

To correct acidity. Fall is the best time to add lime to your soil to reduce its acidity, but if you find the problem in spring, deal with it in spring. Do so as early as you can, though — and at least three weeks before planting, because it takes a while for the pH to begin to change.

To correct alkalinity. Because organic materials take a while to act, and they tie up nitrogen while decomposing, it's best to add them in fall.

◀ **A quartet of pH adjusters.** Clockwise from top left, peat moss, pine needles, wood shavings, and leaf mold will make your soil more acidic.

Applying Lime to Make Soil Less Acid

◀ Be sure to wear a dust mask for this process. Spread the lime or ashes evenly with a scoop or trowel. (*Note:* It takes about 30 percent more wood ash than ground limestone to raise the pH one unit.) Work lime into the top 6 inches (15 cm) of soil with a garden fork.

How Lime Raises Soil pH

Doing a pH test is like taking a census, but instead of counting people it counts two types of hydrogen molecules — a positively charged one (acid) and a negatively charged one (base). As long as the positively charged molecules outnumber the negatively charged molecules, the soil is acidic. The greater the difference, the more acidic the soil. When you add lime to the soil, you're adding lots of the negatively charged molecules, which makes the pH go up.

HOW TO CHANGE YOUR SOIL'S PH

Improving Acidic Soils

To raise pH by 1 unit, apply lime at the following rates for every 100 square feet (9.3 m²):

Soil Texture	Calcitic Limestone	Dolomitic Limestone	Wood Ashes
Sandy	2½ lbs. (1.1 kg)	2–3 lbs. (0.9–1.4 kg)	3–4 lbs. (1.4–1.8 kg)
Loam	6½ lbs. (3.0 kg)	6 lbs. (2.7 kg)	8 lbs. (3.6 kg)
Clay	9 lbs. (4.1 kg)	7–8 lbs. (3.2–3.6 kg)	9–10½ lbs. (4.1–4.8 kg)

Improving Alkaline Soils

To lower pH by 1 unit, apply sulfur at the following rates for every 100 square feet (9.3 m²):

Soil Texture	Powdered Sulfur	Aluminum Sulfate	Iron Sulfate
Sandy	1 lb. (0.5 kg)	2½ lbs. (1.1 kg)	3 lbs. (1.4 kg)
Loam	1½ lbs. (0.7 kg)	3 lbs. (1.4 kg)	5–5½ lbs. (2.3–2.5 kg)
Clay	2 lbs. (0.9 kg)	5–6 lbs. (2.3–2.7 kg)	7½ lbs. (3.4kg)

Nitrogen, Essential for Vigorous Leaves

Nitrogen is among the nutrients that plants need for healthy leaf growth. It is therefore particularly important for plants such as lettuce, spinach, and cabbage, whose leaves are the parts we want. If your plants' leaves are light green or yellow and their growth is stunted, you can suspect that your soil needs more nitrogen.

WHEN YOUR SOIL NEEDS A NITROGEN BOOST

The best way to achieve and maintain a steady and sufficient supply of nitrogen in your soil is to add compost. If you find that your soil needs a nitrogen boost during the growing season, however, one or more of the following strategies should make a difference.

Green manure. Plants that are grown to maturity and then plowed back into the soil to enrich it are called green manures. Some plants that are particularly high in nitrogen, such as alfalfa, make excellent green manures. Known as nitrogen fixers, these plants take nitrogen from the air in the soil and change it into a form that plants can use. In order to benefit from the nitrogen these plants contain, you must incorporate the entire plant — roots, fruits, leaves, and all — back into the soil. Wait at least two weeks before planting a new crop in the treated bed. This gives the green manure a chance to decompose and release the nitrogen into the soil.

Blood meal and fish emulsion. It may sound like a horror story, but turning plants into vegetable vampires can cure many nitrogen-deficiency problems. Blood meal contains about 12 percent readily available nitrogen. For even faster results, give your plants a foliar feeding of fish emulsion. These remedies work only for a short time and should be followed with more long-lasting treatments. Follow the application advice on the package carefully, especially when using blood meal, since it's very rich in nitrogen. You don't want to overdose.

Waiting in the Wings

A nitrogen deficiency can sometimes occur even when there's plenty of nitrogen in the soil. This problem occurs when nitrogen is temporarily locked up or when soil conditions discourage microbacterial activity.

Locked-up nitrogen. When fresh organic matter begins to break down in the soil, nitrogen can be temporarily "locked up" and made unavailable to plants. Normally the microorganisms in the soil break down organic matter slowly, making nitrogen available to plants as they work. Fresh organic matter, however, breaks down very quickly — so quickly that the microorganisms remove available nitrogen from the soil, locking it away from plant roots. For example, nitrogen can become locked up when raw compost is spread. It's also temporarily unavailable for one or two weeks after a green manure has been turned into the soil. Once the breakdown of the organic matter is complete, the nitrogen is again available to the plants.

Weak microbiological activity. Nitrogen is less available when the soil is cold, dry, or wet — all conditions that decrease biological activity in soil. If you test your soil under these conditions, you may get a low nitrogen reading, when in fact a change in weather may show that nitrogen is nearly ideal.

Planting a Green-Manure Crop

Having Too Much of a Good Thing?

If you have ever grown an absolutely beautiful, big, leafy, dark green tomato plant that bore almost no fruit, you know that it's possible to have too much, as well as too little, nitrogen. All plants — even the leafy greens — can pig out on nitrogen if there is too much of it around, often in the form of too much manure. You should suspect that you've got an over-abundance of nitrogen if leafy greens are bitter tasting or fruiting plants have luxuriant leaves but no blossoms or fruit.

1 Prepare the seedbed as you would for any crop, applying slow-release nutrients such as greensand and rock phosphate. Rake it smooth and remove stones and other debris.

2 Broadcast seeds generously over the area, rake the seeded area thoroughly, and then cover it with straw.

3 When the crop begins to form flower heads, use a common hoe to chop it up and turn it into the bed.

Slow-Growing Gardens May Lack Phosphorus

A healthy tomato plant should have rich, medium green leaves. But have you ever seen a tomato plant with purple-green leaves or leaf stems with a reddish purple cast? This strange coloration is an easy-to-detect sign of phosphorus deficiency. Unfortunately, the effects of insufficient phosphorus extend far beyond discolored foliage to touch every part of the plant. Tomatoes with phosphorus deficiency have slower growth and poor production of flowers and fruits, both symptoms of too little phosphorus. In many areas phosphorus is the plant nutrient most likely to be deficient or to become deficient in soils. This is so common that it's wise to add phosphorus, in the form of rock phosphate, whenever you start a new garden. Use about 10 pounds (4.5 kg) per 100 square feet (9.3 m²). To guard against future deficiencies, add rock phosphate to compost piles.

This Product Really Rocks

Don't be misled when you read on a package of rock phosphate that its phosphorus content is only 4 percent. That 4 percent represents the immediately available phosphorus. The product is actually about 30 percent phosphorus, with more than 25 percent of it in a slow-release form that will become available over time.

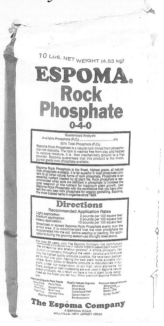

▲ **Topnotch tomatoes.** Healthy, delicious-tasting tomatoes result only when they're grown in great soil.

▲ **Phosphorus poor.** If your tomato plants show a poor purplish color like the plant on the right, you can suspect that your soil lacks phosphorus. A good dose of rock phosphate should correct the problem.

Plant Weaklings May Lack Potassium

Some plant nutrients are real showboats. If a plant has pale green leaves and you toss it some nitrogen — wham, the plant greens up in no time. Give phosphorus to your tomato plant with purplish leaves and in a few days it is lush and green again. But potassium is different. You can have a garden full of plants deficient in potassium and you may not notice it. The plants may appear a bit small or thinner than usual, but not enough to get your attention. They don't look sick, but they are.

WHAT POTASSIUM DOES FOR PLANTS

Potassium is important to plants in many ways. It helps regulate critical plant processes, including photosynthesis, moisture content of plant cells, and the stomata, which control carbon dioxide exchange. It even helps move vital nutrients from place to place within the plant. Potassium also aids in the formation of proteins, which directly affects the nutritional value of vegetables. Plants grown in soils deficient in potassium often contain less protein than those grown in potassium-rich soils. Finally, potassium is critical to good soil health. For example, the microorganism responsible for fixing nitrogen in legumes needs a potassium-rich soil to function at its optimum.

POTASSIUM-POOR SOIL: THE SIGNALS AND THE FIX

Despite the subtleties of potassium deficiency, there are some symptoms to look for that may alert you to a lack of potassium in your garden. A plant with potassium deficiency often appears weak and spindly, attracts more pests and disease than usual, and bears small, thin-skinned fruits that often lack good flavor. This is most likely to occur in sandy soils, where the potassium is easily leached by irrigation and rain. Potassium deficiency can be corrected by adding greensand, granite dust, and wood ashes.

Greensand — Nutrient Additive and Soil Conditioner in One!

In addition to supplying potassium, greensand is also a very good soil conditioner: It loosens clay soils, binds sandy soils, increases water retention, and stimulates biological activity.

Greensand. Yes, it is really green and has the texture of sand. It is also the best source of potassium for the garden. Greensand is mined in places that used to be the bottom of ancient oceans. It contains not only potassium (1 percent immediately available, and 6 percent available over time) but also iron, magnesium, calcium, phosphorus, and more than 30 trace elements. Apply greensand directly to new gardens (about 10 pounds per 100 square feet, or 4.5 kg per 9.3 m^2) and whenever a soil test indicates a deficiency. Add it to your compost pile to ensure against future deficiencies and improve soil condition.

Wood ashes contain about 5 percent potassium in a relatively quick-release form. Because wood ashes also raise soil pH, apply these to your garden only after you test for pH, and do not use them if your soil is already alkaline. Wood ashes can burn sensitive plants, so it's best to add them to the soil when the garden is bare of growing plants, such as late fall, winter, or early spring.

Granite dust is a rock powder that helps restore a potassium balance to the soil in two ways; it provides a supply of water soluble potassium that the plant can use immediately, as well as amounts of mineral potassium that become available to the plant over time and form a reservoir of soil potassium to inhibit future deficiencies. Granite dust is about 6 percent potassium; 3 percent is immediately available and 3 percent is available over time. It does not affect pH.

Soil Structure: A Delicate Matter

Plants do best in soil that stays loose and thoroughly aerated throughout the growing season. This is because plant roots do not just grow to a certain size and then stop, thereafter simply sucking up nutrients. Given the space, roots continue to grow and grow and grow. Located at the head of the growing root tip, fine root hairs absorb most of the nutrients that nurture the plant. These root hairs generally slough off after only a few days, but new ones appear as the root tip lengthens. This process is most effective when the soil contains root-friendly spaces — spaces large enough to gently direct growing roots around and between soil particles while also channeling the air and water that carry nutrients to the roots.

Instead of being simply fluffed up, a soil full of long-lasting air spaces has structure. Within a well-structured soil, particles of clay, silt, sand, and organic matter are actually bound together by a waterproof "glue," which is the by-product of the feeding activities of millions of soil organisms. The result is soil crumbs or, more accurately, aggregates. Because they are waterproof, soil crumbs remain intact through cycles of wetting and drying, and the soil retains the important air spaces that channel the air and moisture that carry nutrients to the plants. The spaces also make it easier for roots to spread freely and deeply into the soil in search of those nutrients.

ROTOTILLING: FRIEND OR FOE?

If you're starting with a compacted, heavy clay soil containing little organic matter, rototilling will improve conditions a lot. A tiller is a very efficient way to loosen and aerate severely compacted soil and to chop and mix a large dose of organic matter into it. But if you are starting with soil that has decent structure and adequate amounts of organic matter, rototilling can easily destroy the worm-welcoming environment that already exists. This is because the pulverizing action of the tiller breaks up soil aggregates, disrupts capillaries, and demolishes worm-tunnel networks.

For more than twenty years I rototilled the garden three times a year, twice in fall and once in spring. I did all this tilling because I believed it was the best way to maintain and improve soil, as well as to create the best conditions for growing plants. I was wrong. It was a painful lesson to

◀ **A hairy system.** Delicate plant root systems, like those of this sweet potato, need a soil that provides a friendly environment — one that contains water and air and plenty of room for the root system, to develop and take in nutrients. If a soil is to provide for these needs, it must be "full of holes," and it should stay that way throughout the growing season.

learn: Instead of improving the garden, the rototiller gave me more weeds and poorer soil. Here are the three problems tilling creates:

1. **The problem of compaction.** Rototilling does loosen and aerate the soil, but it doesn't stay that way. In contrast, the air spaces that form naturally in soil are a result of microorganisms working in the soil. The air spaces formed by rototilling are a result of the tines breaking up that structure. Consequently, although tilled soil is fluffy, its air spaces are fragile. In addition, the tiller destroys soil aggregates, which in turn decreases the water stability of the soil. As the soil settles over the growing season, the air spaces disappear until, long before the growing season is over, most are gone, and the soil is hard and compressed. Tilling creates a catch-22 for the gardener: The more you till, the more you need to till.

2. **The problem of the tiller pan.** The downward-beating action of the tiller tines compacts the soil at the maximum depth the tiller can reach. This is called tiller pan, a special case of subsoil hardpan. This compacted subsoil layer makes it harder for plant roots, worms, and water to enter.

3. **The problem of inversion.** Tilling also brings about wholesale inversion of the soil and the creatures living there. Bacteria that were perfectly suited to certain temperature and moisture levels are suddenly disrupted and put where different temperatures and drier or wetter conditions prevail. Worms, if they aren't killed, are driven away.

Is Double-Digging Double Trouble?

Lest I leave any sacred cows alive, I should point out that a lot of what is true of rototilling is also true of double-digging. Although double-digging doesn't do as much damage to soil aggregates, worm tunnels can't survive the practice. Also, much of the double-dug soil is inverted, displacing soil organisms from the temperature and moisture levels they prefer. Double-dig when it is needed, such as when you're creating a new garden. The rest of the time, though, let the worms do the work.

healthy, well-structured soil

tiller pan

Tiller troubles. Although rototilling has its place, gardeners should know that it can cause soil to compact, create tiller pan, and destroy beneficial worms and other soil organisms. Note that the untilled soil ahead of the tiller is loose and deeply aerated. Once the blades churn through the bed, they disturb the channels naturally formed by the microorganisms and compact soil into tiller pan under the tiller tines.

Help Wanted: Structural Workers

Gardeners can do a lot to improve their soils. If the soil is too acidic or not acidic enough, you can add limestone or peat moss to change this. You can add greensand or phosphate rock or other nutrient sources if the soil is deficient in nutrients. But if the soil doesn't have good structure, it's not something you can fix. You have to hire the work out.

WORMING YOUR WAY TO BETTER SOIL

Some of the most important organisms to work your soil into shape are worms. As they munch their way through the soil, worms ingest clay, silt, and sand particles as well as bits of organic matter. These nutrient-rich ingredients are eventually expelled as water-stable granules called castings. The castings make the soil more granular, which helps create soil capillaries and other spaces that improve soil structure while allowing air and moisture to flow freely.

In addition to these castings, worms also make tunnels that permeate the topsoil, allowing easy and quick access for water and air. These tunnels even penetrate into the subsoil (though to a lesser extent), facilitating deeper root growth and providing additional water-storage space. Soil that has been well worked by worms can take in water four times faster than soil that hasn't. This reduces runoff and prevents water loss through evaporation from puddles that form when soil cannot absorb rainfall quickly enough.

YOU CAN COUNT ON WORMS

Scientists use complicated tests to determine whether soil is healthy. All you really have to do, though, is go out to your garden and count your worms. While worms are by no means the only important inhabitants of the soil, they are the most obvious. If there are many worms in the soil, it's because the soil contains plenty to eat and is a friendly place to live and raise little worms. Worm-friendly soil has lots of organic matter, is well aerated and drained, and has a pH of about 6.0 to 7.0. Because the rest of the soil population has similar needs, the worm population is a mirror of soil life in general. And the soil life is a reflection of the health of the soil.

▲ **That's the way the cookie crumbles.** Well-structured soil is crumbly, much like the leftovers from a chocolate cake. Soil scientists call these particles of soil *aggregates*, but I like the term *crumbs*, because it describes the texture so accurately.

How Worms Affect Soil Structure

Castings. Worms are among the soil-dwelling creatures that form soil particles into aggregates.

Channelings. Worms perforate the soil with a network of tunnels that create spaces where plant roots can grow.

WHEN TO TAKE THE CENSUS

A worm census is most accurate in spring or fall, when soil temperatures are comfortably warm. In summer, when soil temperatures rise above 60°F (16°C) — the comfort zone for garden worms — they move to deeper, cooler levels or die.

LET'S DO THE NUMBERS

Fewer than 10 worms in a 12" x 12" x 7" (30 x 30 x 17.5 cm) soil sample is bad news. The lower the number, the more serious the problem. You'll need more than a quick-and-dirty test to figure out exactly what the problem is, but the soil is probably woefully lacking in organic matter, and organic matter is the breakfast buffet to a worm. Worms do two things very, very well. They eat and make more worms. Add organic matter to the soil and you supply them with food, and with food nearby, they'll happily make lots more worms.

If you find more than 10 worms, rejoice! Word has gotten around the worm world that your garden is a nice place to live. The more, the merrier; you can't have too many worms. A high score means that the soil is well stocked with organic matter and that the worms and other creatures eating this organic matter are significantly improving soil structure and fertility.

Thousands of Worker Worms

A census of 60 worms means that there are about 24,000 worms at work in a 20' x 20' (6 x 6 m) garden, producing miles of irrigation lines and many pounds of rich castings.

Taking a Worm Census

1 With a spade, outline and remove a block of soil about a foot (30 cm) square and 7 inches (17.5 cm) deep.

2 Spread the soil on a board and, as you break up the clumps of soil, gently extract and count the worms. Little ones score the same as big ones.

HOSPITALITY 101:
MAKING WORMS FEEL WELCOME

Worms have a very simple mission in life: eat and make more worms. The more worms eat, the more worms they make, and the better off your garden will be. Where there is little for worms to eat, there will be few worms. Where there is a lot for worms to eat, there will be lots of worms — as long as the soil temperature, moisture, and pH are acceptable. Also, worms like a peaceful neighborhood. Run the rototiller through the garden too much and the worms will bid your garden goodbye. The best way to ensure conditions conducive to happy worms is to mix plenty of compost into your soil, protect it with organic mulch, and keep the rototiller in the tool shed.

SERVE UP SOME
COMPOST AND MULCH

The best food for worms is, providentially, also the best food for garden plants — compost. This is nice to know because it supplies the answer to the question of when to apply compost. This answer is: All the time.

Worms are most content and most productive in loose soil, what agronomists call friable soil, that is moist but not soggy, about 60°F (16°C), with a pH of 6.0 to 7.0, and replete with organic matter. Worms slow down or die when it gets too hot or too cold, especially when that change happens quickly. Organic mulch helps keep soil moist, protects the soil from rapid changes in temperature, and, like compost, provides additional, high quality food for worms.

An automatic moisturizing system. As anyone who has picked up worms knows, they are moist creatures. To survive, they need soil that stays about as moist as they feel when you hold them in your hand. Mulch is an excellent way to retain soil moisture.

A built-in cafeteria. Mulch is food. Worms will eat just about any organic matter suitable for use as a mulch.

▲ **A cozy blanket.** A covering of mulch can be particularly important as winter approaches. The mulch ensures that freezing temperatures penetrate the soil gradually, allowing worms enough time to move to deeper levels. In unprotected areas, the soil can freeze rapidly, and worms trapped near the surface freeze to death.

Should I Add Worms to My Garden?

If worms are so important, and there aren't enough in the garden, why not just buy some and solve the problem that way? This sounds like a solution, but many times it isn't.

If there are few worms in your garden, it's probably not because there are few worms in your neighborhood. There are likely plenty living beneath the lawn or in the woods nearby. They aren't in the garden because it doesn't provide them with what they need — moisture, proper temperature, and food. If you import worms, they will leave, for the same reasons that they didn't move in of their own accord.

▲ **Environmental protection for the worm population.** For topnotch soil, be generous with your compost and then turn your soil-improvement work over to the worms and other soil dwellers. Soil organisms can have a profound and cumulative effect on garden soil, but only if our tillage practices allow them to do their work uninterrupted and unmolested.

CHAPTER 7

Rot & Recycle: Making & Using Compost

Whenever somebody tells me that I need just one answer for all my questions, I get suspicious. The snake oil that cures all ills doesn't really cure anything; the multi-purpose tool does none of its many tasks very well; and the one-size-fits-all garment doesn't really fit anybody.

But then there's compost. Compost sounds too good to be true, but it actually is as good as it sounds.

Compost nourishes both the garden plants and the creatures that live in healthy soil. It makes it easier for soil to receive and retain air and water, while stabilizing soil pH at the level most plants prefer. Compost even helps protect plants against some diseases and pests. It has been called "gardener's gold," and that's no exaggeration. The path to the garden of your dreams leads right through the middle of a compost pile.

135

What Compost Is

Compost is partially decomposed organic matter, mostly plants and the manures of plant-eating animals. Because it consists primarily of plants in the first place, compost often contains the elements plants need for growth in roughly the proportion they're needed. Gradual decomposition of compost by soil organisms releases these nutrients slowly, at a rate plants can use.

Compost helps the garden in many ways. It:

▶ **Provides nutrition.** It is a source of all the basic nutrients required for vigorous plant growth.
▶ **Improves soil structure.** Because it separates soil particles, it improves soil tilth by creating aeration.
▶ **Increases the ability of soil to retain water.** Because it is naturally absorbent, compost improves water retention.
▶ **Contributes to the health of plants.** It helps prevent some plant diseases.

▶ **Moderates soil pH.** Most compost has a pH level at which most plants thrive, and it helps keep the soil pH in that range by increasing the buffer capacity of the soil.
▶ **Encourages soil microorganisms.** Most important, it is a food source for legions of soil-dwelling organisms whose activities are essential for plant health and continual soil improvement. Before it becomes food for plants, compost is food for countless soil-dwelling organisms whose activities greatly improve soil structure, increase aeration and water retention, and make it easier for roots to grow. (See also pages 130–131 in chapter 6, Nurturing Vegetable-Friendly Soil.)

▼ **A truckload of gold.** We use so much compost that we supplement the amount we can create from home and garden waste with a truckload of purchased compost from a local supplier.

Good Humus

Humus, the end product of fully decomposed compost, contains humic acid, which makes the essential minerals that are already present in the soil more available to plants. It also stimulates seed germination and plant growth, reduces the need for fertilizers, and encourages better yields.

When You Can't Make Your Own Compost

Not very long ago, the only way to get compost was to make it. Now, with organic vegetables featured in supermarkets and organic gardening gaining popularity, compost has become big business and is commercially produced out of everything from autumn leaves to residue from breweries. The resulting product is uniform, high-grade compost that can be purchased in bags at nurseries and garden and home centers.

If you are just starting to garden, or just starting to make compost, buy some of the commercial stuff to get your garden off to a good start. Don't skimp and don't shortcut. Compost is crucial to a healthy, productive garden, and any money spent now will come back to you in many ways, many times over, especially when it comes time to harvest.

If you have a large garden, or if your soil test indicates the need for a hefty initial dose of organic matter, consider buying compost by the cubic yard (meter) rather than by the bag. I am fortunate to live only 25 miles from a commercial composting operation. I can buy about 1,200 pounds (545 kg) for what 200 pounds (91 kg) would cost in bags. Even if you have to pay someone else for hauling, you will likely come out way ahead.

COMPOST CREDENTIALS

Not all of what passes for compost belongs in the garden. Buy the compost you use to grow vegetables as carefully as you would buy vegetables. Although the label may not mean as much applied to compost as it does applied to lettuce, I'd sooner buy "organic" compost. I always read the ingredients list to make sure it contains things I want to put in my garden.

Buying compost, no matter how good it is, is just a temporary solution. The best way to get the compost you need is to make it yourself. Making your own is certainly cheaper than purchased compost. Most of the ingredients are things you presently throw away. Even more important, if you make your own compost, you know what's going into it. You grow your own food so you'll be sure it is safe and nutritious, and "growing your own" compost ensures that it, too, will be safe and nutritious.

▶ **Give your garden a head start.** Some people use leftover beer to catch slugs, but breweries make use of their leftovers by producing a very high quality, inexpensive compost.

Composted Sludge: Hazardous or Not?

Composted sewage sludge is the by-product of municipal sewage treatment plants. Because municipal sewage usually includes chemical waste from factories and cleaning plants, the resulting sludge may be contaminated with heavy metals, which are not good for plants or people. I don't like taking chances with my food or family, so I don't use or recommend compost made from sewage sludge.

Compost: Nature's Recycling Method

When you make compost, you're doing what nature does all the time, only a little faster. Compost-making is nothing more than the fine-tuning and acceleration of a process that goes on all around us as bacteria and other soil-dwelling organisms break down organic matter and produce food for new plants. Composting is nature's method of recycling.

For many people, composting is a way to turn otherwise bothersome waste products from their kitchens, yards, and gardens into a valuable resource. But most gardeners soon find that the ordinary stream of household and yard waste isn't enough to produce the amount of compost they need. Although I recycle any organic matter I can from my home and garden, I wouldn't have enough compost if I depended on only that. My garden requires a lot of compost, so I've had to come up with ways to compost more material and design a composting system with my needs in mind.

What to Compost

Just about anything organic can be made into compost, but some things are better for composting than others. You'll end up with more balanced compost, and have it sooner, if you're a little choosy about what goes into it. If you're really particular, you may want to be sure your compost ingredients are organically grown.

Alfalfa meal and hay

Algae (pond weeds)
Apple pomace (from cider pressing)
Ashes (wood, not coal)
Bean shells and stalks
Broccoli stalks (but not roots)
Buckwheat hulls or straw
Cabbage stalks and leaves (but not roots)
Citrus rinds
Clover
Cocoa hulls
Coffee grounds
Corncobs (chopped)
Cottonseed hulls
Cowpeas
Cucumber vines

Eelgrass
Eggshells (crushed)
Farm animal manures
Flowers
Fruit peels
Granite dust
Grape pomace (from wine making)
Grass clippings (in thin layers)
Greensand
Hay
Hedge clippings
Hops (from beer brewing)
Kelp
Leaf mold and leaves
Lettuce and other greens

Melon vines, leaves, and rinds
Oat straw
Olive residue
Peanut hulls
Pea pods and vines
Peat moss
Phosphate rock
Potash rock
Potato skins and vines (unless diseased)
Rhubarb leaves
Rice hulls
Shells (ground clam, crab, lobster, mussel, oyster, well buried in the pile)
Sod
Soybean straw

Sphagnum moss
Sugarcane residue
Tea leaves
Vegetable peels, stalks, and foliage
Vetch
Weeds
Wheat straw

Getting the Right Balance

Everything that grows is made up of many different elements. Two of the most important are carbon and nitrogen. Composting occurs fastest and most completely when you use about 30 parts of carbon to 1 part of nitrogen, by weight. Since people don't usually remember which materials supply which of these elements, I like to think in terms of 30 parts "brown" (for the carbon) and 1 part "green" (for the nitrogen).

COMPOST BROWNS: SOURCES OF CARBON

Generally speaking, the browns are the dried-out stems, stalks, and leaves of plants.

Straw. Of the browns that I use, I like straw best. Straw is composed of hollow stalks, which ensures good action in the compost pile. Any sort of straw is good, including oats, barley, wheat, and rye.

Hay. This may contain weed seeds, only some of which may be killed by the heat of composting. I use it anyway if I run short of straw. If you use cow or horse manures, you'll probably end up with some hay, too.

Cornstalks and pea and bean vines. When allowed to wither and dry out, cornstalks, as well as pea and bean vines, are useful browns.

Autumn leaves, even if they are shredded, tend to mat together and prevent enough air from entering the pile. (A whole other bunch of bacteria start working in airless or low-air conditions. You'll know that this has happened if things start to stink.) It is okay to mix some leaves into the straw, but don't make them the main ingredient in your brown layers. Leaves are a valuable addition to garden soil, but rather than composting them, it's better to incorporate them directly into the soil (see page 108).

Wood shavings and sawdust decompose much more slowly and have a lower pH than the rest of the pile. I don't usually add these, but because they're used as bedding materials for farm animals, they often end up in the pile if I use animal manures.

Pine needles also break down slowly and are very acidic. I use these materials as mulches for acid-loving plants like blueberries, but not in the compost pile.

Do Activators Help?

To get the composting process going, you need a "starter" population of the microorganisms that will actually do the work. Under most conditions, the best ingredients, called *activators*, are garden soil and compost.

▲ **A balancing act.** Try to keep a balance of 30 to 1 between the carbon-rich ("browns") and nitrogen-rich ("greens") materials you add to your compost pile.

COMPOST GREENS: SOURCES OF NITROGEN

Important "greens" include just about any fresh or slightly wilted plant matter. Grass clippings and kitchen scraps are obvious examples, but all nonpoisonous weeds (before they go to seed) are also good additions to the pile. Seaweed, especially kelp, is a very good green because it is likely to contain trace minerals. Plant residues from the garden can go into the compost pile as long as they are not diseased and have not gone to seed.

Creating More Greens

If you want to make a lot of compost, it may be difficult to come up with enough greens. One solution is to grow some. If there is extra space in your garden, plant a crop of buckwheat, annual alfalfa, cowpeas, or field peas. These plants are often referred to as green manures. Instead of tilling in these plants, as you normally do with green manures (see page 43), mow or pull them and add them to the compost pile. Or plant perennial alfalfa in an otherwise unused garden space; you may get as many as three harvests a year from a good stand.

▲ A green manure crop of buckwheat

If you can find a nearby source, pond weeds, apple or grape pomace, and bird feathers can go in the pile as nitrogen-rich greens. (Some nitrogen-rich compost materials, such as these weeds, pomace, and feathers, as well as manures and alfalfa hay, aren't actually green but still belong in the "green" category.)

WHAT NOT TO COMPOST

Diseased plants. Don't compost any part of a diseased plant. Some plant parts, like the roots of any cabbage family member, are likely enough to harbor soilborne diseases that they shouldn't be composted at all. Some plant diseases can survive in even the hottest hot piles, and many more will survive if the pile doesn't get hot enough and stay hot long enough. Play it safe and keep diseases out of the compost. If you burn the diseased plants, the ashes are safe for the garden.

Weeds gone to seed. Most weeds are okay, but if they've gone to seed, don't add them to a cold pile. Avoid pieces or whole roots of weeds, like witchgrass, that propagate themselves from roots.

Ashes. Coal ashes can be toxic to plants, so don't use them. Wood ashes are a source of considerable disagreement. They raise pH, and I may not want to change the pH of either the compost or the particular bed to which it will be added. Instead of using wood ashes in the compost pile, I add them directly to the garden if I need to adjust the pH of the soil.

Some manure. Don't use manures of cats and dogs in the compost pile. Manures of animals other than herbivores may contain diseases or parasites that are harmful to people.

Some lawn clippings. Some people use herbicides on their lawns. If you use grass clippings from these lawns in your compost, you'll end up applying herbicide to your garden. If you collect grass clippings from your neighbors or from a lawn-care service, make sure the clippings have no herbicides.

Getting Your Compost Pile Started

Composting methods, and the compost piles that result, can be identified as either "hot" or "cold." As is often the case with such neat divisions, the reality is a bit more complex. All composting gives off some heat, the by-product of bacteria digesting organic material. The heat generated by bacteria that prefer temperatures at about 55°F (13°C) gradually raises the temperature to a level where different bacteria are more comfortable, between 70° and 90°F (21° and 32°C) — which is about the limit for a cold pile. These bacteria, in turn, may raise the temperature still further, beyond their own comfort range, and create conditions for yet another bunch of bacteria whose feeding activities may raise temperatures as high as 160°F (71°C). This kind of pile is a hot pile. You get a cold or hot pile depending upon how you build and maintain it.

QUICK AND SURE: HOT COMPOSTING

A hot compost pile is the best way to produce large amounts of compost fairly rapidly. It has the further advantage of killing many of the pathogenic organisms and weed seeds that may be present in the composted materials. A hot pile works best if it is made up all at one time and then allowed to compost completely without further additions of material. Because of this, it's best to build hot piles when it is easiest to come by the materials, particularly the greens. I have a lot of green matter in late spring, when I mow around the garden and along the driveway. There are a lot of greens at harvest, but not necessarily enough for a pile; I therefore plan a green-manure harvest at the same time.

SLOW BUT STEADY: COLD COMPOSTING

Cold compost piles take longer and do not destroy pathogens or weed seeds, but they can be built over a period of time. They are ideal for recycling small, steady streams of organic matter. Bacteria that prefer either cool or moderate temperatures do all the work in cold piles, which usually don't heat up beyond 90°F (32°C).

Once the cold pile is constructed, you can take some time off and let nature do the rest of the work. Monitor the moisture level, and add water if necessary. After a few months, turn the pile, bringing material from the middle out to the edges. Rewater if necessary and fluff the material well. It will take a year or more to get finished compost, but you can use it sooner as a topdressing or mulch, or you can mix it into the soil in fall.

Where to Put Compost Piles

Compost bins. Any place fairly near the garden with good drainage can be the site for a compost pile or piles. Before you put any composting material in place, loosen the soil where you intend to build your compost pile so worms can get in. If possible, make more than one compost setup. Put a cold pile near the kitchen to handle the small but constant stream of kitchen and garden wastes. In addition, build a hot-pile setup wherever convenient for you.

In-garden compost piles. If there's enough room, you can put your compost pile right in the garden. Make the compost pile a part of the crop rotation and put it in a different spot each year. Any compost left behind still enriches the garden, and any nutrients that leach out of the compost settle in the soil. Additionally, worms can help a lot with the later stages of compost development, and, if things are going as they ought in your garden, you should have plenty of worms in the beds.

Composting Hardware: Bins and Tools

Compost bins aren't necessary, but they are desirable. An unrestrained pile can be messy, and it can get a lot messier if animals get into it. A good bin also makes the process easier and more fun.

Size. Hot compost requires a bin at least 3' x 3' x 3' (0.9 x 0.9 x 0.9 m). A smaller pile won't heat up enough. A pile larger than 4 feet (1.2 m) on a side will need additional ventilation in the center. Bins for cold piles can be smaller but should be large enough to handle the volume of kitchen waste you anticipate.

Shape. Most bins are square or rectangular, though some are round. They can be made of wood, wire, wood and wire, plastic, cement blocks, straw bales, or metal. I like a bin to be enclosed on all sides to give the pile support all the way around. I also like easy access to one side when turning the pile or removing finished compost, and I prefer not to have to take the whole bin apart to get this access.

Here are three very different, but acceptable, composting bins. Choose the one that meets your needs and fits your budget.

A COLD COMPOSTOR FOR A SMALL KITCHEN GARDEN

You'll find quite a variety of polyethylene composters at garden centers and from mail-order suppliers. One example is the Biostack, a bin made of polyethylene, with a fitted top that keeps out both rain and animals. Its size, 28" x 28" x 34" high (70 x 70 x 85 cm), is marginal for hot composting, but this is a perfect bin to put in or near the kitchen to receive garden trimmings and kitchen waste for a cold pile. (Keep some straw and leaves in a container nearby so that you can add browns from time to time to keep the carbon-nitrogen ratio in balance.) It is handy to have two of these bins: One can be filling while the other is composting. The tiers are separable, so turning the pile is easy.

WOODEN COMPOST BIN

We use bins that are made of white cedar, a naturally rot-resistant wood. The wood isn't treated with any chemicals and it lasts for years. While white cedar is one of the best woods to use for compost bins, other good choices are redwood, tamarack, even oak.

Our bins are a good size for hot compost making and well-enough braced so they needn't be fixed to the ground. Portability is a nice feature, if

▲ **The path to success.** Our compost bins are conveniently located, along with our greenhouse, right in the middle of the garden. Here, they're not only easy to fill and access, but they remind us that they really are the key to our success.

you'd like to place your compost bin in the garden and move it from spot to spot over the years. The angled slots on the front hold the wooden slats and allow the lower slats to be removed while the upper ones remain in place. This feature makes loading, repiling, and unloading easy.

A trio of these wooden bins makes a nice compost factory. Compost can be turned from one bin into the next. Then a new pile goes in the first bin.

STRAW BALE HOT BIN

I like this bin because it is both functional and inexpensive. It isn't the prettiest thing, but it does make good compost, which is what matters most. The straw bales will hold together longer if the baling is plastic or wire; if not, tie new twine around them once a year. After a few years, the bales will decompose, and you can add them to the compost pile and create a new bin. Arrange the bales in much the same way as for the straw bale cold frame pictured on page 56. As your compost grows, simply pile on additional straw bales.

Compost Ventilating System

To ventilate a large compost pile, insert a 4-foot-long (1.2 m) piece of perforated plastic drainage pipe as soon as the pile is deep enough to support it. Continue to build the pile up around the pipe.

Tools for Compost-Making

Although compost-making is a natural and simple process, a few tools can make the operation go more smoothly.

SHREDDER. This expensive tool is optional. Materials like cornstalks and tomato plants will be easier to handle and compost a lot faster if chopped. Instead of an expensive shredder, you can use a machete and a chopping block for this task; it just takes more time and energy.

LAWNMOWER. You can shred leaves and other composting materials by running over them with a lawnmower a few times, then raking up the clippings and tossing them on the pile. The smaller the material is, the faster it will compost, provided it doesn't pack down and exclude air. To avoid this, if you're using finely chopped material, make your green layer thin.

WATERING CAN OR HOSE. Add water as you build the pile. The whole pile needs to be moist but not soggy.

SIX-TINE MANURE FORK. The tines of this fork are slim and pointed, more like the tines of a pitchfork than those of a garden fork. They enter the pile easily. This is the best tool for making, turning, and aerating the pile.

COMPOST THERMOMETER with a 20-inch (50 cm) probe. Taking the temperature of your hot compost pile tells you whether it's behaving correctly, when to turn the pile, and when the compost is finishing.

compost thermometer

six-tine manure fork

If You Build It, You'll Get Compost

Hot and cold piles are built the same way, but the recipe for a hot pile is a little more exact. Also, a cold pile is created gradually, as materials become available, whereas a hot pile is built all at once. A cold pile that isn't quite perfect just takes longer to break down, but an improperly made hot pile may not heat up at all, or it may not stay hot long enough to produce the best compost.

Ideally, all the ingredients in a compost pile should be mixed together. In practice, layering works fine, provided the layers aren't too thick. "Too thick" depends on what makes up the layer, so here are some guidelines that apply to both hot and cold piles.

GARDEN LASAGNA

Start with a layer of straw about 3 inches (7.5 cm) deep. Add 1 to 6 inches (2.5 to 15 cm) of green material. The looser the material, the thicker the layer you can add without risking compaction and loss of air. For instance, you can safely add pea or bean vines in a thick layer (6 inches [15 cm]). Mowings from green-manure crops, weeds, and hay (either green or dry) can be piled about 3 inches (7.5 cm) deep. Grass clippings and kitchen scraps will mat together and exclude air if they're piled more than an inch or so deep. There's a bit more art here than there is science. Just keep this rule in mind: Leave room for air to circulate throughout the pile.

On top of each green layer, sprinkle about ½ inch (13 mm) of soil (no more). If you're using manure, this is where it should go. This time, use no more than an inch (2.5 cm) and mix it with soil. The bio-activator for the pile, soil contains the organisms that will break down the organic material into more soil. Unless the soil is seriously deficient in organic matter, and therefore in biological activity, ½ inch (13 mm) should be enough. If you're in doubt, add some compost as a starter.

Add another straw layer and keep building, "lasagna-fashion," until the pile is about 4 feet (1.2 m) high. The pile will settle, and it needs to be at least 3 feet (0.9 m) high after settling to heat up properly.

How Much Compost Should I Make?

In cool climates you'll want to spread compost at least an inch (2.5 cm) deep on every bed, with some available for sidedressing during the season.

If you live in a warm region, you'll need even more compost. The warmer your climate, the more quickly soil organisms will digest compost, because there's more biological activity as soil temperatures rise, and the activity goes on for more of the year. In the warmest regions, you may need 2 or even 3 inches (5 to 7.5 cm) of compost a year for each bed.

4 Easy Steps to Hot Composting

1 Make succeeding layers of straw, green material, and soil lasagna-fashion as described on page 144 until the pile is about 4 feet (1.2 m) high. As you spread on the layers, fluff them to allow spaces for air to circulate through the pile.

2 Compost needs moisture just as it needs air. Your goal should be to get a mixture that feels something like a squeezed-out sponge, damp to the touch but definitely not soggy. Add water to the brown layer, which is the driest, as you build the pile.

3 When you've finished making the pile, cover it. This reduces evaporation from the top of the pile and also prevents accidental overwatering from rain. You can cover it with a nylon-reinforced tarp, as shown, or use black plastic, which absorbs sunlight and adds warmth to the pile. White plastic reflects sunlight and can keep the compost pile too cool.

4 You'll get better results with a hot compost pile if you check it and tend it regularly. Using a compost thermometer, preferably one with a long probe, take the temperature of the pile daily. If everything is going as it should, the pile should reach 140° to 160°F (60° to 71°C) within a few days. Whenever the temperature starts a steady drop, turn the pile. With each turning, moisten the pile if necessary, fluff it for aeration, and move the material from the outside into the center.

Don't Leave Out the Leaves

Leaves, particularly oak leaves, are very good for garden soil. They contain micronutrients drawn from the depths of the earth. Unfortunately, in a compost pile they mat together and promote the growth of anaerobic bacteria, the smelly ones we don't want (see The Good Guys vs. the Bad Guys below).

A better way to add leaves into the garden is to work them directly into the soil. You can do this by first putting them through a shredder or running over them a few times with a power mower and then using a three-tine cultivator to mix them into the soil. You can also till them in, but I prefer the gentler method (see page 108).

LEAF MOLD

Another way to get the benefits from leaves is to make leaf mold. The end product of leaves decomposed in a moist environment primarily by fungi, leaf mold is the rich-looking, crumbly material that lies beneath the layer of recognizable leaves on the floor of a deciduous forest. It is very good for plants, particularly carrots and members of the cabbage family.

Making leaf mold is very easy. Wait for the leaves to fall from the trees and then simply make a leaf pile. If the leaves aren't wet, water them down. Then, just like the cold compost pile, let them sit. It takes a bit longer to make leaf mold than compost — about two or three years — but it's worth the wait. Just turn the pile once a year to give the fungi that are doing all the work a breath of fresh air.

As is the case with compost piles, a bin keeps things neater. A circular bin 3 to 5 feet (0.9 to 1.5 m) in diameter made of heavy-gauge wire fencing works well. You can also make a serviceable bin from a length of snow fence. Just form it into a circle and secure with wire. A few large rocks or concrete blocks placed around the base of the bin will help to keep it from bulging.

The Good Guys vs. the Bad Guys

Aerobic bacteria need oxygen; anaerobic bacteria don't. Both kinds of bacteria act upon and break down organic compounds, but the former are a lot more helpful if what you want is a plentiful supply of compost. Aerobic bacteria work much faster, and they do a more thorough job. The end products of their work are basic plant nutrients in a form readily available to plants. Anaerobic bacteria are slow, and they leave the job only partly done. Their end products leave many nutrients still locked in compounds and unavailable to plants, or even toxic to them. Finally, as if to let us know that they really aren't being much help to us, anaerobic bacteria create a monstrous stink.

▲ **Fall roundup.** Use fencing to make a movable bin for leaves. In two or three years you will have leaf mold, one of the best soil amendments, especially for carrots and cabbage family members.

COMPOST TROUBLES SOLVED

Symptom	Possible Cause	Solution
Unpleasant odor	Lacks air, because of compaction	Aerate.
	Lacks air, because of overwatering	Add browns, which will absorb moisture, and aerate.
	With ammonia smell, too much nitrogen	Add browns and aerate.
	Lacks nitrogen	Add greens like grass clippings, fresh manure, or blood meal.
	Too wet	Add straw or other brown and turn pile.
Pile doesn't heat up	Lacks moisture	Poke holes in pile so you can water well inside.
	Needs turning	Use manure fork to bring materials from the outside to the center of the pile.
	May be finished	If it's dark, crumbly, and earthy smelling, you have finished compost.
Hot pile cools off	Needs turning	Use manure fork to bring materials from the outside to the center of the pile.
Pile is damp and warm only in the center	Pile is too small	Gather more materials and rebuild a larger pile.
	Not enough nitrogen	Add nitrogen source, such as manure or fresh grass clippings.
Animals get into pile	Meats and/or dairy products attract them	Avoid adding meats and dairy products. Throw a loose covering, such as a piece of chicken wire or fencing, over the pile.
Some material doesn't break down	Lacks nitrogen and/or moisture	Add water. Cover pile and water whenever it feels dry. Add nitrogen source, such as manure or fresh grass clippings.
	Needs mixing	Turn pile, breaking up any whole or matted material and mixing it in.
	Pieces too large or woody	In the future, chop coarse material before adding it to pile. For now, sift compost to remove large pieces.

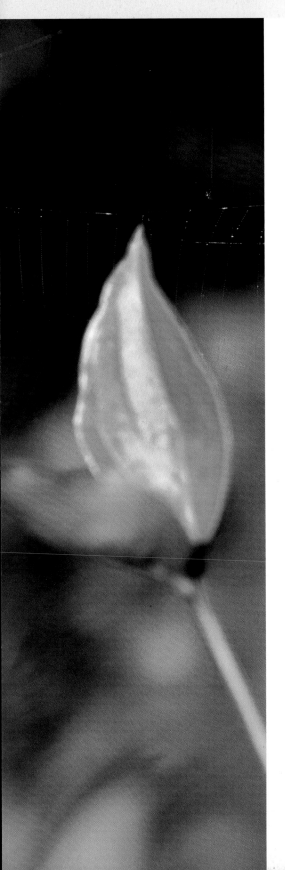

CHAPTER 8

Banishing Bugs, Slugs & Things That Go Chomp in the Night

When I was growing up, we had a large, family vegetable garden, which my mother tended and which she also used to introduce each of her children to the plants and animals that lived there. I remember one warm spring day when she led me to a section of the garden between the wire fence and a tomato plant where we discovered a broad silken web delicately outlined in dew. In the center of the web was a large black-and-yellow garden spider busily darning a captured carrot fly into a silken cocoon. I was not a natural fan of spiders, but that day Mom spent the time to teach me how valuable spiders are — especially garden spiders. That lesson was my first step in a long journey of learning about the world of nature and natural pest control. In this chapter are the tools that will help you distinguish the good guys from the bad in your garden and craft a healthy environment where pests and diseases are no longer a problem.

Natural Pest Control That Really Works

The methods of controlling pests and diseases in the garden are changing. It used to be that you had the choice of dusting your vegetables with toxic chemicals, either synthetic or botanical, or going "natural" and eating vegetables with worms in them. Now, thankfully, there's a third choice that is much better than the first two. I call it ecological pest and disease control.

The easiest way to understand pests, as well as diseases, is to view them as predators out on the hunt. Instead of a pride of lions circling a herd of wildebeest on the Serengeti, however, you've got hungry aphids devouring tomatoes in the garden. Just as lions select the weakest wildebeest, aphids are drawn to the weakest plants. They'll even bypass healthy, vigorous plants to attack the stressed ones. Stresses include extreme fluctuations in soil or air temperature, too little or too much water, interruptions in the supply of any nutrient, compacted soil, and improper soil pH. Anything you can do to improve growing conditions for a plant makes the plant less likely to be attacked by pests and disease. Good pest and disease management means understanding that pests and diseases are not problems in themselves, but symptoms of problems.

LIKE SHOOTING YOURSELF IN THE FOOT

Traditional pest control using pesticides as primary problem-solvers tends to poke holes in your garden's ecosystem by completely removing vast numbers of organisms and upsetting a critical natural balance those organisms create. It's all too true that nature abhors a vacuum, and it often fills those holes with greater numbers of pests and diseases than ever.

A balanced ecological approach to pest and disease control not only works better than traditional methods, but it's also less work. Balanced pest and disease control uses the natural relationships between plants, insects, and other organisms to minimize populations of pests and diseases and keeps more intrusive interventions to a minimum.

THE THREE U'S

Three easy guidelines to natural pest and disease control make it possible to grow healthier plants, get more bountiful harvests with less effort, and have fewer pests and diseases in the garden:

▶ Make the habitat unacceptable.
▶ Make the habitat unavailable.
▶ Make the habitat unsurvivable.

You can follow each of these guidelines separately or in combination to control many pests and diseases with little or no chemical controls. In the next pages, you'll find out how.

▲ **Ladybug, ladybug, we want you at home.** A few aphids in a garden don't usually cause a problem, and they supply food for beneficial insects like lacewings and ladybugs. If you use pesticides to kill the aphids, you may also kill the beneficials. When the aphids return (and they will), no beneficial insects will be there to help control them.

Make the Habitat Unacceptable

An unacceptable garden habitat is one that pests and diseases just don't like. Making your garden habitat unacceptable is usually quite easy and can be as simple as lowering the pH in the soil to reduce scab on potatoes.

FERTILIZE WISELY

When you fertilize your plants, you may not realize that fertilizer does more than provide nutrition to the plants. Fertilizing can also make your pest problems better, or it can actually make them worse. For example, plants grown in soils rich in nitrogen are more attractive to pests like aphids, mites, and whiteflies. On the other hand, plants grown in soils rich in phosphorus and potassium have fewer populations of pests like wireworms.

You can reduce the negative effects of fertilizers by using kelp or seaweed extracts, which contain the three primary elements of nitrogen, phosphorus, and potassium, as well as trace minerals. Monitor plants for any signs of nutrient deficiency (see page 115), and correct problems quickly with fast-acting liquid fertilizer or foliar sprays.

GET THE pH RIGHT

By keeping the pH of the soil at the optimum value for the plants you grow, many pest and disease problems can be greatly reduced or eliminated. The proper soil pH allows the plant access to the nutrients it needs, which keeps it from being stressed and in turn reduces pest problems. Diseases like clubroot or scab can also be managed by monitoring and adjusting soil pH.

USE COMPANION PLANTING

One of the easiest and most effective ways to make the habitat unacceptable to pests is to use companion planting specifically for pest control. We know that particular pests prefer to feed on particular plants or groups of plants. In addition, those pests very often have dislikes as well, plants they cannot stand to be around or that just confuse them. In companion planting for pest and disease control, we interplant these plants. Here are some specific examples:

▶ Onions, garlic, and other members of the onion family are universally despised by pesky bugs, probably because the onion group is stinky. Almost all other garden plants will be less bothered by insects if they live among onions.
▶ Garlic offends Japanese beetles, vegetable weevils, and spider mites.
▶ Celery deters the white moth that begets the green caterpillar that eats cabbage, broccoli, and other cabbage family crops.
▶ Beans and potatoes live nearby to mutual benefit, not interplanted, but in adjacent beds. The beans repel Colorado potato beetles; the potatoes reciprocate by driving away Mexican bean beetles.

▲ **Buddy up.** Celery offends the moth phase of the cabbage worm, but if you plant celery and cabbage in the same bed, be sure to give them extra compost, because they're both heavy feeders with shallow root systems.

HERB AND FLOWER DETERRENTS

If you're going to make life miserable for pests and diseases, you might as well enjoy it — so say it with flowers and herbs. Many plants give off volatile chemicals that are attractive to the pests that feed on them. If you plant stronger-scented plants among your vegetable crops, you may be able to disguise or hide the crops' attractive scent so that the pests are confused and never find dinner. For example, onions, chives, and garlic can block ants, aphids, and flea beetles. Marigolds are useful against aphids, Colorado potato beetles, and whiteflies. And rosemary deters carrot flies and cabbage moths. At the same time that these aromatic herbs and flowers confuse insect pests, many of them also attract beneficial insects.

Here are some other combinations to try:

▶ Hyssop, wormwood, thyme, and sage all repel the cabbage moth.
▶ Rue and white-flowered geraniums are offensive to Japanese beetles.
▶ Sage repels both carrot flies and cabbage moths.
▶ Tomato hornworms don't like borage or basil.

▶ French marigolds, planted among tomatoes or in ground recently home to tomatoes, destroy nematodes. Marigolds also repel whiteflies, tomato hornworms, bean beetles, cucumber beetles, and asparagus beetles.
▶ Neither squash bugs nor whiteflies can abide nasturtium.

nasturtium

marigolds

Don't Let the Cure Be Worse Than the Disease

Mint discourages cabbage moths and ants, and horseradish repels bean beetles. That's the good news. Mint and horseradish are hardy perennials that, left uncontrolled, will quickly spread all over your garden and become pests in themselves. That's the bad news. But there's more good news. You can still use mint and horseradish in the garden by planting them in large clay pots set in the appropriate beds of vegetable plants.

▲ **Make a mint.** Tuck pots of mint in the cabbage patch to deter cabbage moths.

thyme

sage

borage

Make the Habitat Unavailable

Remember the story of the fox and the grapes? The fox wanted to eat the grapes, but they grew just high enough to be out of reach. After much effort, the fox gave up, claiming the grapes were sour anyway. There are many morals to this story, but the one applicable to your garden is that pests won't steal your vegetables if they can't reach them. Making the habitat unavailable makes pests and diseases leave your garden empty-handed.

TRICKS OF TIMING

cabbage worm damage

In search of the earliest harvest in the neighborhood, many people sow seeds as soon as they can in spring. Unfortunately, early crops often end up with a lot of pest problems. Choosing the right time to sow or transplant is an easy way to avoid some of the worst pests in the garden. For example, if you wait until the peonies flower to plant cabbage family crops, you'll have very little damage from cabbage worms.

You can also use timing to buy your plants some time to toughen their defenses. Keep small transplants in the cold frame or cover seedlings with a light row cover to keep flea beetles from eating the leaves. Once the plants are bigger, the flea beetles won't damage them as much.

WEEDING WORKS

Keep after the weeds, especially when plants are young and very sensitive to competition. Weeds include those volunteers that sprout from seeds shed by last year's vegetables. It's tempting to let the plants grow, just to see what they turn into. More often than not they turn into the same thing —

trouble. Like weeds, volunteer plants can attract pests that specialize in munching on your garden, as well as serve as reservoirs for pests and diseases.

SOW CONFUSION WITH INTERPLANTING

Bad bugs and diseases just love the way most gardens are laid out. All the carrots go here, all the tomatoes there, and all the onions together somewhere else. The technical term for this is *monoculture*. Such a garden is giving your garden's pests one-stop shopping — a mini-mall for munching bugs that start at one end and eat an entire row.

Breaking up the pattern makes it harder on the pests and easier on the garden and the gardener. An onion disease harbored by some of the onions grown from sets will not infect the onions grown from seedlings if the seedlings are in a separate bed some distance away. The greater the distance any bug has to cross from one snack to the next, the greater the chance that the bug itself will become snack for some other predator.

Tips for a Healthy Garden

▶ **Keep at least a ½-inch (1.25 cm) layer of compost on growing beds all the time.** Compost not only ensures a steady flow of balanced nutrients to the plants, but also has been shown to inhibit many plant diseases. (See pages 135–140.)

▶ **Make sure plants have enough water.** By the time it begins to look droopy, a plant is already stressed, and a stressed plant is an open invitation to pests and diseases. (See pages 86–97.)

▶ **Use mulches and row covers to maintain soil and air temperatures** within the plant's preferred range. (See pages 62–65.)

CAMOUFLAGE OUTFITS

You can take confusion to a higher level by actually scattering different crops in the same bed. Planting in this fashion intermingles the odors of the plants, so pests have a more difficult time finding lunch, while increasing cover used by insect predators. Diverse planting often increases the number of beneficial insects while decreasing the number of pests.

SUCCESSION HARVESTING

Succession planting was developed to extend the harvest time of a crop by planting small amounts over a period of weeks, allowing each sowing to mature at a different time. But you can also use succession planting to control pests. When you harvest a succession planting, try to harvest the entire mature planting in a few days, rather than gathering a little here and there. Some pests and diseases seek out overripe fruit. Reduce spoilage of crops by harvesting them on time, when the vegetables are mature.

ROTATING YOUR GARDEN

Rotating plants from one part of the garden to another after each crop cycle keeps you one step ahead of the pests and diseases. It works best for pests that don't move around much, such as those that live primarily in the soil, as well as those that don't survive very long without a suitable place to dine.

Avoid planting any crop in the same place two years in a row. To pests, this is a little like their favorite restaurant moving but not leaving a forwarding address. All of your plants will benefit by having a fresh supply of the nutrients they require, and insect pests will be discouraged from depending on the availability of the plants they prefer. Here's how it works:

When I was growing up, I played hide-and-seek with the neighborhood kids. The rules were

▲ **All mixed up.** Planting a number of different vegetables in the same bed diffuses the plants' attractive odors, making it harder for pests to find their favorite food. As a bonus, interplanted beds are also more resistant to drought than conventionally planted gardens.

easy — hide well enough so the seeker couldn't find you. The kids that were really good at the game learned one important thing early on: Don't hide in the same place two times in a row. The same idea holds true when avoiding pests and diseases in the garden.

If your eggplant is attacked by fusarium rot, that is not only a problem for the current growing season. It affects future ones as well, because the fusarium fungus can survive in the soil for more than one year. If you plant eggplant in the same spot in the garden the next season, it doesn't take a rocket scientist to guess the outcome. The solution is to play hide-and-seek with your vegetables. If you don't want your eggplant attacked by a pest, move it to a spot where the pest won't find it.

The Subtleties of Spacing

Closer spacing grows better vegetables. Plants, especially broccoli, cauliflower, and other cabbage family members, that are planted with lots of space between them can actually attract pests. Standing out by themselves apparently makes them easier to find and recognize. Space plants slightly closer than recommended on the seed packet to reduce pest problems.

Co-Hosts: Pairings to Avoid

Some insect pests have a taste for several different plants, so it's important to know those and avoid planting them near one another so that you aren't providing a buffet just as appetizing and easy to access as a monoculture. Here are a few to guard against:

▶ **Corn and tomatoes.** If found in an ear of corn, it's called a corn earworm; if found in a tomato, it's called a tomato fruitworm. It's the same beast. Keep some distance between the corn patch and the tomatoes.

▶ **Potatoes, tomatoes, peppers, and eggplant.** Although it is called Colorado potato beetle, this pest will feed on any plant related to potatoes, such as tomatoes, peppers, or eggplant. It actually prefers eggplant to potatoes.

▶ **Cucumbers, squash, melons, and pumpkin.** Pickleworms, which bore into fruits and stems, probably prefer cucumbers but will not turn down a nice melon, squash, or pumpkin either.

Cover Ups

Row covers, which come in various weights, have several good uses in the garden. The heavier ones are often used in cool weather because they provide significant frost protection in addition to thwarting bugs (see pages 64–65). During summer, use the lightweight versions, so the plants don't heat up too much. The new ultra-lightweight covers let in the most light (90 percent), with very little heat increase, and still keep the pests out.

For pest control, apply row covers right after planting, either supporting them with hoops or laying them loosely right over the soil. The lighter-weight covers will not impede plant growth and will be lifted by the plants as they grow. You can seal the row cover by covering the edges in soil or securing them to the ground with row cover staples (long metal pins that look like half of a giant paperclip). I like to reinforce the long edges with wooden slats, which make it much easier not only to put the row covers in place but also to roll them back to tend or harvest the plants.

Row covers are especially effective against the pests that bother greens, such as spinach, as well as cabbages, broccoli, squash, radishes, and even potatoes.

If you are protecting a crop that needs pollination from insects, such as squash, be sure to remove the covers when blossoms appear.

An Ounce of Prevention: Row Covers

Once a pest is living on or in a vegetable plant, there may be a dozen more or less acceptable ways to prevent or minimize harm to the plant. The problem is a whole lot simpler if you can keep the pest from getting to the plant in the first place, and one of the best deterrents is a row cover. These lightweight polypropylene blankets lie atop a row or bed and protect the plants beneath. They let in most of the light, air, and rain but block wind and insects.

Make the Habitat Unsurvivable

Making the habitat unsurvivable used to mean poisoning everything in sight. It took several generations before we learned how much damage that course of action caused, not just on farmland, but to everything from soil organisms to birds to water supplies to ourselves. But ecological gardeners can make the habitat unsurvivable without using the arsenal of synthetic and botanical poisons that have caused such damage. We have at our hands an amazingly wide array of methods that will dispatch the pests that damage the garden, without damaging the garden or the world around it.

HANDPICKED SPECIALTIES

Check the undersides of leaves where beetles often lay eggs. You'll easily spot the bright orange egg clusters of the Colorado potato beetle and the shiny golden brown eggs of squash bugs. Pick these off the leaves before they ever have a chance to develop. Unless there are an awful lot of them, you can control the adult Colorado potato beetles by regular handpicking, too. If you have young children in the

squash bug eggs

family (or the neighborhood), try offering a beetle bounty. Our daughter, Lindsey, at four, learned to count so she could keep track of her beetle earnings. A couple of years later she picked 450 beetles at a neighbor's garden at ½ cent each to earn the purchase price of three ducklings.

CALL IN THE TROOPS

A number of living organisms like your garden pests as much as you dislike them, earning them the name biological controls. With a little bit of

▲ **A soapy death.** Handpick caterpillars by knocking them gently from the plant into a can of water with a bit of dish detergent added. The detergent reduces the surface tension of the water, so that the caterpillars readily sink beneath the suds.

▲ **Just rewards.** Our daughter, Lindsey, earned the money to buy these ducks by handpicking Colorado potato beetles from a neighbor's garden.

knowledge, you can enlist them as your helpers to control a number of garden pests, from caterpillars to Colorado potato beetles. The smallest of them are forms of bacteria, so small as to be microscopic. Products containing these organisms are easy to use and more specific than old-fashioned pesticides. Here are some of the most common.

Bacillus thuringiensis (Bt). Sold under many brand names, *Bt* is a bacterium that, when ingested by various caterpillars, including cabbage worms, hornworms, corn borers, and the like, paralyzes the gut, giving the insect a fatal case of indigestion. Specialized strains of *Bt* are effective for specific pests, including Colorado potato beetles.

Milky spore. Milky spore disease is a biological control of Japanese beetles caused by the bacteria *Bacillus popillae* and *Bacillus lentimorbus*. Apply it over grassy areas, such as lawns, where adult beetles lay eggs and larval grubs feed on the roots of grasses. The grubs will ingest the bacteria and die within two or three weeks. The white spores that fill the grub's body will then reenter the soil waiting for more grubs to come along. It can take two or three years for milky spore to become established in a treated area.

Milky spore has been used for over 50 years, and in some regions, signs are that Japanese beetles are developing resistance to the bacteria. A good plan to control Japanese beetle uses beneficial nematodes (see next entry) in combination with milky spore. When using either beneficial nematodes or milky spore, avoid applying chemical pesticides to the same areas.

Beneficial nematodes. The nematodes we usually hear about are the bad guys that mess with vegetable roots. But not all nematodes are garden enemies. The ones sold for insect control feed on soft-bodied, soil-dwelling pests such as wireworms and root maggots. They are not interested in earthworms or plant roots. These are so tiny that you apply them to the garden by suspending them in water and using a spray attachment on your hose.

Nothing's Perfect

Bt is a safe, reliable tool for controlling pests in the garden, but it isn't perfect. In addition to controlling pests, it can also be harmful to the larvae of certain butterflies, including swallowtails and monarchs.

▶ **Swallowtail caterpillars,** also called parsleyworms, can often be found nibbling on parsley, dill, celery, cilantro, parsnip, and carrots. Parsleyworms are pale green, accented with

Swallowtail caterpillars

stripes of black and yellow. Before spraying *Bt* in the garden, handpick the parsleyworms and relocate them to a place away from the garden, such as a patch of wild carrot, also known as Queen Anne's Lace.

▶ **Monarch caterpillars** prefer to hang around milkweed, which is their favorite food, and don't usually wander into the garden. When applying *Bt,* take care not to spray plants adjacent to the garden.

Monarch butterfly

ATTRACT THEM AND THEY WILL COME

A great way to control pests in the garden is to attract creatures that prey on pests. This is known as calling in the good bugs to get rid of the bad bugs, another kind of biological control. It's amazing how many different kinds of good bugs are out there. And they have such healthy appetites, too.

You can buy these biological controls if you choose, or many times you can make the garden attractive to them — and they will come. Some garden plants attract beneficial insects. For example, morning glory vines attract ladybugs and hoverflies, while goldenrod beckons ladybugs, assassin bugs, and parasitic wasps. Many gardeners plant a windrow near the garden to serve as habitat for beneficial animals. This windrow can be as simple as planting some grasses, perennial alfalfa, goldenrod, or hairy vetch in front of a row of fruit-bearing shrubs. If your property is small, locate your perennial garden near the vegetable garden so it can serve the same purpose. Intersperse a few fruiting shrubs, such as swamp holly or cranberry bush, as well. The flowers and grasses can harbor many beneficial insects, while the shrubs are home to birds that think garden pests are great hors d'oeuvres. Finally, don't forget the flowers and herbs. The flowers attract pollinating insects, and the aromatic herbs, such as dill and thyme, attract beneficial insects that prey on pests. Here are some of the most effective and common "good bugs."

Beneficial Insects to Attract to Your Garden

Assassin bug. These ½-inch-long (13 mm) insects look like a miniature robot monster from some science fiction movie. What they lack in beauty, however, they more than make up for in appetite for pests. Assassin bugs eat many different types of pests, and a few are always nice to have around.

Green lacewing. This is a real Jekyll-and-Hyde sort of bug. In its adult phase, the green lacewing eats only pollen and nectar, as befits its delicate appearance. But in larval form, this is the famous "aphid lion," a creature that devours soft-bodied insects such as aphids, scale, thrips, mealybugs, spider mites, whiteflies, the nymphs of leafhoppers, and the eggs of many caterpillars. Green lacewings can be purchased as eggs, larvae, or adults. You can also attract them with special bug foods.

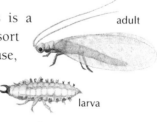

adult

larva

Hoverfly. If you watch hoverflies long enough, you just might start liking flies. Hoverflies, also called syrphid flies, have black and yellow stripes. These master flyers are able to zip around, hover, and even fly backwards. Adults feed on nectar and deposit eggs on leaves of plants. The eggs hatch into ugly little maggotlike larvae that feed on aphids and other small, succulent bugs.

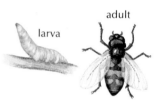

larva

adult

Ladybug. Also known as lady beetles, ladybugs are colorful, small, and cute. How can you not like a bug that looks like a little Volkswagen? But aphids don't think ladybugs are cute. Neither do asparagus beetles, Colorado potato beetle larvae, chinch bugs, bean thrips, mites, nor numerous other soft-bodied insects. Each adult ladybug can consume about 5,000 aphids in its lifetime.

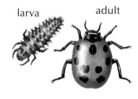

larva

adult

Even the black-and-orange alligator-shaped larvae eat 50 or 60 aphids a day.

You can buy ladybugs in lots of ¼ pint (118 ml) (about 2,300 adults) to 1 gallon (3.8 L) (72,000, give or take a few), but, unless you have a very, very large garden and an overwhelming aphid problem, that may not be the best way to go. If you bring in too many predators at once, they'll wipe out all the prey, and then they'll leave because there's nothing left to eat. When the next hatch of pests appears, there's nobody to eat them.

A better plan is to attract ladybugs by providing their favorite plants, like goldenrod, yarrow, and morning glory vine. In addition, supply the ladybugs a place to hide when they're not eating. These methods may help you establish an ecological balance in which there are always some prey insects available and always some predator insects to keep the pest population from getting large enough to inflict crop damage.

Ladybug Larvae

Everything the adult ladybug is by way of cute, the larva is not. It is aptly described as dark, flightless, and alligatorlike with orange spots. If you don't know that this apparition is really your friend, you will be sure that it is one of the bad guys and be tempted to dispatch it forthwith. Don't!

ladybug larva

Minute pirate bug. As the name suggests, these are very small, as are their prey — mites, aphids, thrips, and tiny caterpillars. They work in the garden but are particularly effective in a greenhouse because they like the high temperatures and humidity.

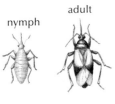

nymph   adult

Praying mantid. Possibly best known of the beneficial insects, praying mantids are also the most over-rated. Given their size, they don't eat much, and when they're eating, they'd just as soon munch good insects as bad ones. To a mantid, if it moves, it's food. Honeybees are just as tasty as bean beetles. The one exception is that they seem to find ladybugs bitter (though I don't know who interviewed the mantid to find this out).

Spined soldier bug. This bug likes to harpoon its prey, which includes hornworms, potato and bean beetles, and cabbage worms. It then injects a paralyzing venom and sucks the victim's body fluids. With that as a modus operandi, it is somehow appropriate that this creature is a member of the stinkbug family.

Trichogramma wasp. This is the best known of a group of parasitic wasps. The adult wasps feed on nectar, but they lay their eggs within the eggs of garden pests like corn earworms, cutworms, cabbage worms, and various borers. The newborn wasp starts life by feasting on the embryo of the host.

NATURAL PESTICIDES THAT ARE KIND TO NATURE

We can't get away from the fact that the pesticides we apply to our crops are poisons, whether they come from a chemistry lab or, like pyrethrum, from a daisy. In fact, many natural pesticides, including pyrethrum, rotenone, and sabadilla, are just as nasty as their synthetic brethren. But several botanical pesticides do work well, with few drawbacks: garlic spray, hot pepper wax, insecticidal soap, and neem. When applying these or any pesticides to your garden, be sure to read and follow label directions carefully.

Garlic spray. Garlic repels a wide range of pests, including aphids, spider mites, and whiteflies. Simply spray on plants before pests appear and the garlic spray does the rest. You'll notice a garlicky odor when you first spray it, but once dry, the smell disappears. Garlic spray does not affect the flavor of vegetables, and it's environmentally safe and biodegradable.

Hot pepper wax. A blend of food-grade paraffin wax, herbs, and capsaicin (the active ingredient in hot peppers), hot pepper wax is derived from cayenne peppers. Many garden pests, including aphids and whiteflies, don't like spicy things and avoid plants sprayed with hot pepper wax. In addition to repelling pests, hot pepper wax also helps protect plants from dry or windy weather. The plants don't absorb the spray, so it doesn't alter the flavor of the vegetables. Simply wash the vegetables under warm running water to remove any remaining wax before preparing. Capsaicin can irritate your skin and eyes.

Insecticidal soap. If you'd like your pest problems just to dry up and blow away, use insecticidal soap. As its name implies, insecticidal soap is a biodegradable soap used to control pests. Its most common active ingredient, potassium salts of fatty acids, is derived from plants. When sprayed on a pest, the soap damages cell membranes, making them more permeable. Vital cellular fluids then leak from the cells and the pest dies of desiccation.

The Facts on Insecticidal Soaps

▶ Not harmful to most beneficials

▶ Low impact on mammals, birds, aquatic organisms, and other wildlife

▶ Damaging to predatory mites and some insects, such as hoverflies, in their larval stage

Insecticidal soap is most effective on soft-bodied pests, such as aphids, and must stay in contact with the pest for as long as possible to work well. It's less effective when mixed in water containing high amounts of minerals such as iron or calcium. Apply it in the early morning or late afternoon when it takes the longest to dry.

▲ **It leaves them be.** Neem won't harm or discourage beneficial organisms such as butterflies, spiders, bees, earthworms, or ladybugs.

Neem is derived from the seeds of the neem tree, which is found in southern Africa, India, Australia, and southeast Asia. The active ingredient, azadirachtin, blocks the progression of the insect pest's life cycle. Although it sometimes takes days to kill the pest, neem has another trick up its sleeve: Azadirachtin also acts as an appetite suppressant. One or two nibbles on a treated plant and the pest stops feeding.

Applied as a spray, neem is a refreshingly safe pesticide that has little to no effect on beneficials, such as butterflies, spiders, bees, earthworms, and ladybugs. In addition, the evidence we now have shows it has little impact on birds, aquatic organisms (including fish and mammals), or other wildlife. You may also find neem oil insecticidal soap, which combines the two products.

A Toad by Any Other Name Is Still a Prince

Is it toads or frogs that, when kissed, change into handsome princes? It doesn't really matter. Toads are welcome in my garden just as they are. They probably eat more bugs as a toad than they would as a prince anyway.

Toads are a help in any kind of garden, but they're especially helpful if you're bothered by slugs and cutworms. Toads seem to love these garden pests, and toads are most active at night, when slugs and cutworms come out. Toads also eat gypsy moth larvae, sowbugs, armyworms, and various beetles, up to 15,000 noxious garden pests a year. And all they ask for this work is room and board.

Any garden offers food aplenty for toads, but they won't take full advantage of the "board" unless they can also find a "room" in or very near the garden. Toads need a cool, moist, ventilated, and fairly dark place to hide away from sun, predators, and disturbances like lawn mowers. If you provide that hiding place, you'll have toads. They are creatures of habit and will return to the same place each night and even year after year.

A toad house can be as simple as a board or a flat rock propped at an angle over some loose soil in a little-traveled spot in the garden. A clay flower pot, upside-down and propped with a stone to allow access, or with a gap broken out of the rim, will also make a fine toad house.

▲ **Board and room provided.** We found a quiet corner of the garden to tuck away this little toad house, consisting of a flat rock propped over a couple of rock "walls."

It's for the Birds . . . and Bats

Above the earth and garden plants is the open sky. And if you're fortunate, that sky will be a flyway for birds. In early spring, when most other migratory birds are still enjoying southern vacations, the phoebes are already at work snatching insects from the air or soil surface itself. A few weeks after the phoebes' return, the tree swallows come back, followed by the barn swallows, and if we're lucky, bluebirds. At night, there are bats. All of these creatures live around the garden throughout the summer, eating insects that eat the garden, as well as those that eat me as I tend the garden, spoiling half the fun of being there.

The phoebe likes a place to perch while surveying the garden, and nests in a nearby open shed, as does the barn swallow. Tree swallows and bluebirds like birdhouses. If you live where purple martins are found, attract them with a communal house. Hummingbirds, which eat insects as well as nectar, like to perch in tree or shrub branches along the edge of the garden. The birds don't require large trees and shrubs, but they prefer their resting places to be densely branched.

▲ **House for rent.** Birds can be some of the most useful tenants of your garden. It pays to do all you can to entice them to stay around.

PEST CONTROLS AT A GLANCE

Pest	Control
Aphid	Yellow sticky traps, green lacewings, ladybugs, garlic spray, hot pepper wax, insecticidal soap, neem, neem oil soap, water spray
Armyworm	*Bacillus thuringiensis* var. *berliner (Btb)*, beneficial nematodes, spined soldier bugs
Asparagus beetle	Green lacewings, ladybugs, praying mantids, neem
Bean beetle	Handpicking, beneficial nematodes, green lacewings, ladybugs, praying mantids, spined soldier bugs, neem
Broccoli worms (cabbage worm)	*Bacillus thuringiensis* var. *berliner (Btb)*, green lacewings, ladybugs, praying mantids, spined soldier bugs, trichogramma wasps, garlic spray, neem oil soap
Cabbage looper	Yellow sticky traps, *Bacillus thuringiensis* var. *berliner (Btb)*, green lacewings, ladybugs, praying mantids, spined soldier bugs, trichogramma wasps, beneficial nematodes, neem oil soap
Cabbage root maggot	Beneficial nematodes
Colorado potato maggot	Handpicking, *Bacillus thuringiensis* var. *san diego (Btsd)*, beneficial nematodes, green lacewings, ladybugs, praying mantids, spined soldier bugs, neem
Corn earworn	Beneficial nematodes, green lacewings, ladybugs, praying mantids, trichogramma wasps, garlic spray, neem
Cucumber beetle	Beneficial nematodes, green lacewings, ladybugs, praying mantids, neem oil soap
Diamondback	*Bacillus thuringiensis* var. *kurstaki (Btk)*, *Bacillus thuringiensis* var. *berliner (Btb)*, trichogramma wasps, garlic spray
Earworm	*Bacillus thuringiensis* var. *berliner (Btb)*
European corn	Beneficial nematodes, *Bacillus thuringiensis* var. *kurstaki (Btk)*, green lacewings, ladybugs, praying mantids, trichogramma wasps
Flea beetle	Beneficial nematodes, neem oil soap
Fruitworm	*Bacillus thuringiensis* var. *berliner (Btb)*
Hornworm	Handpicking, *Bacillus thuringiensis* var. *berliner (Btb)*, spined soldier bugs, neem oil soap
Japanese beetle	Handpicking, diatomaceous earth, beneficial nematodes, milky spore *(Bacillus popillae)*, neem, neem oil soap
Leafhopper	Insecticidal soap, neem, neem oil soap
Leaf miner	Yellow sticky traps, beneficial nematodes, green lacewings, ladybugs, praying mantids, neem
Mite	Green lacewings, ladybugs, minute pirate bugs, neem, neem oil soap, water spray
Mosquito	*Bacillus thuringiensis* var. *israeliensis (Bti)*
Root maggot	Beneficial nematodes, insecticidal soap, water spray
Slugs/snail	Copper tape or foil barrier, diatomaceous earth, slug and snail traps, sawdust, wood ashes
Squash bug	Praying mantids, garlic spray
Squash vine borer	Beneficial nematodes, garlic spray
Striped blister beetle	Diatomaceous earth, beneficial nematodes
Thrip	Blue sticky traps, yellow sticky traps, diatomaceous earth, green lacewings, ladybugs, minute pirate bugs, praying mantids, garlic spray, insecticidal soap, neem
Tomato fruitworm	Beneficial nematodes, green lacewings, ladybugs, trichogramma wasps
Tomato pinworm	Beneficial nematodes, green lacewings, ladybugs, trichogramma wasps
Whitefly	Yellow sticky traps, green lacewings, ladybugs, praying mantids, garlic spray, insecticidal soap, neem, neem oil soap

DISEASE CONTROLS AT A GLANCE

Disease	Control
Anthracnose	Plant resistant varieties; rotate crops annually; spray foliage with compost tea; avoid getting foliage wet when watering.
Aster yellows	Cover plants with row covers; remove infected plants and nearby weeds; plant resistant varieties.
Bacterial blight	Apply neem oil; plant resistant varieties; remove severely infected plants; add organic matter to soil.
Bacterial wilt	Cover plants with row covers; rotate crops annually; remove infected plants.
Black leg	Rotate crops annually.
Blossom-end rot	Keep soil at proper pH for crop; mulch around plants; avoid high-nitrogen fertilizers; add organic matter to soil.
Catfacing and cracking	Mulch around plantings.
Clubroot	Keep soil pH above 7.0; solarize soil; rotate crops annually; add organic matter to soil.
Curly top	Cover plants with floating row covers; remove infected plants.
Damping-off	Sow seeds in sterilized media containing sphagnum peat moss; avoid overwatering; water with compost tea.
Downy mildew	Apply neem oil; rotate all crops annually; eliminate weeds; spray foliage with compost tea.
Early blight	Apply neem oil; plant potato-leaved tomatoes and other resistant varieties; spray foliage with compost tea; use row covers to exclude flea beetles.
Fusarium wilt	Solarize soil; rotate crops annually; plant resistant varieties; add organic matter to soil.
Gray mold (Botrytis)	Apply neem oil; space plants farther apart; spray plants with compost tea.
Late blight	Apply neem oil or plant certified seed; spray foliage with compost tea.
Leaf blight	Apply neem oil.
Leaf spot	Apply neem oil; spray foliage with compost tea.
Powdery mildew	Apply neem oil; spray with chamomile tea or baking soda.
Root-knot nematode	Plant French marigolds; add chitin to soil; add organic matter to soil; solarize soil; plant resistant varieties.
Root rot	Remove infected plants; avoid overwatering; rotate crops annually; solarize soil; add organic matter to soil; water plants with compost tea.
Rust	Apply neem oil; spray foliage with compost tea.
Southern blight	Add organic matter to soil; drench plants with compost tea.
Sunscald	Avoid leaf drop from moisture stress or leaf diseases.
Tobacco mosaic virus	Plant resistant varieties; remove infected plants.
Verticillium wilt	Rotate plants annually; plant resistant varieties; add organic matter to soil.

Some Common Insect Pests

APHIDS

Plants affected: Just about everything

Description: Aphids come in a wide variety of sizes and colors, but they all are shaped pretty much the same, like little pears. During the warmer months, aphids reproduce asexually, with females giving birth to live young. This makes a lot of aphids very quickly. Aphids prefer to feed on soft growth and cluster on buds, young leaves, and stems. The insects suck sap from the plants, causing the leaves to become deformed and growth to be stunted. As the population increases on a plant, winged aphids appear and then fly off to infest other plants.

Control: Use yellow sticky traps; spray with neem, insecticidal soap, or neem oil soap; and encourage lacewings and ladybugs. Apply garlic spray or hot pepper wax spray. You can also use a water spray to control aphids, but it has to be just the right type of water spray and it's time consuming. Attach a mist nozzle to a hose and adjust the flow of water so that it knocks the aphids off the plant without damaging leaves and flowers. It does take time to do this correctly. I can't help but think this method takes too much time.

ARMYWORMS

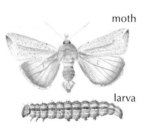

moth

larva

Plants affected: Bean, beet, cabbage, corn, cucumber, lettuce, pea, peanut, pepper, spinach, and tomato

Description: Armyworms are 1- to 2-inch-long (2.5 to 5 cm) caterpillars that range from greenish blue to brownish, usually with prominent stripes down their sides. They feed at night or on cloudy days, chewing ragged holes in leaves and fruit. Armyworms are a persistent problem in warm climates, where they can cause damage most of the year. In cool regions, infestations most often occur in fall.

Control: Beneficial nematodes and spined soldier bugs are good long-term solutions. For more immediate control, spray with *Btb* (*Bacillus thuringiensis* var. *berliner*) or handpick.

ASPARAGUS BEETLES

Plants affected: Asparagus

Description: Asparagus beetles are small, about the size of a ladybug, and come in many colors, from blue and black to brown and russet. They begin feeding on asparagus as soon as the spears begin to emerge in the spring. They lay dark-colored eggs on the spears, from which blackish larvae emerge. Both larvae and adults feed on the spears and, later in the season, the ferny leaves.

Control: Handpick both larvae and adults. Predators include ladybugs, lacewings, praying mantids, and spined soldier bugs. You can get fast control by spraying plants with the botanical insecticide neem.

CABBAGE WORMS AND CABBAGE LOOPERS

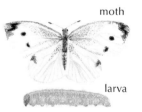

moth

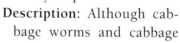

larva

Plants affected: Cabbage family crops

Description: Although cabbage worms and cabbage loopers are different pests, they usually occur together in the garden. Cabbage worms are medium green, 1-inch-long (2.5 cm) caterpillars, marked with subtle yellowish stripes along their sides and covered with short fuzzy hairs. The adults are antique white butterflies with two or three black dots on each upper wing.

Cabbage loopers acquired their name because they arch, or loop, their backs as they move along. These green caterpillars have faint whitish stripes along their sides. The adults are grayish night-flying moths with a silver chevron on each wing.

Both cabbage worms and cabbage loopers are serious pests to cabbage family crops. Leaves develop ragged-shaped holes, and cabbage and broccoli heads become a hideaway.

Control: Handpick both pests. Natural predators include lacewings, ladybugs, praying mantids, spined soldier bugs, and trichogramma wasps. Yellow sticky traps are effective, especially for loopers. For immediate control apply *Btb* (*Bacillus thuringiensis* var. *berliner*) or neem oil soap.

COLORADO POTATO BEETLES

Plants affected: Eggplant, pepper, potato, and tomato

Description: These fingernail-sized beetles have dome-shaped shells brightly decorated with black and yellow stripes. The adults lay clusters of orange eggs on the undersides of the leaves. The eggs then hatch, revealing larvae that look like dull reddish orange blobs with black legs and head.

Control: Spray with neem or *Btsd* (*Bacillus thuringiensis* var. *san diego*). Beneficial nematodes, praying mantids, lacewings, spined soldier bugs, and ladybugs are all helpful.

Handpicking is also effective for eggs, larvae, and adults. Dusting seed potatoes with sulfur reduces damage, as does mulching around susceptible plants.

CORN EARWORMS

moth

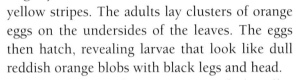

larva

Plants affected: Bean, corn, pea, pepper, potato, squash, and tomato

Description: Earworms, also called fruitworms, are about 1-inch-long (2.5 cm) caterpillars that can range in color from green to brown to yellowish tan, with dark stripes down their sides. The pale tan adult moths lay single, cream-colored eggs on leaves or corn silk in spring. On corn, the earworm consumes the silk before eating its way into the developing ear. After a month, it drops to the soil to pupate. On other crops, earworms feed on stems, leaves, and fruits.

Control: Spray with *Btb* (*Bacillus thuringiensis* var. *berliner*) in spring, when young are hatching. Introduce beneficial insects, including spined soldier bugs, lacewings, and trichogramma wasps.

CUCUMBER BEETLES

Plants affected: Cucumber, melon, potato, squash, and other plants

Description: Cucumber beetles come spotted and striped. Each is about ¼ inch (6 mm) long with shiny yellow wingcovers decorated with either 11 black spots or 3 black stripes. Larvae are thin whitish grubs with brown or black heads.

Control: Adult beetles emerge in spring and lay eggs on soil near plants. After hatching, the larvae enter the ground to feed on roots. Apply beneficial nematodes in spring to attack larvae in the soil. Adults can be controlled by spraying plants with neem oil soap as needed. Introduce green lacewings, praying mantids, and ladybugs, all of which feed on cucumber beetles.

EUROPEAN CORN BORERS

moth

larva

Plants affected: Bean, corn, and tomato family crops

Description: European corn borers are about the same size as corn earworms, but they are lighter colored, usually tan to antique white, with brown spots on each body segment. Another way to tell the two apart is by counting how many worms are in each ear of corn. There is usually only one corn earworm in each ear, while as many as three to five European corn borers can occupy a single ear. European corn borers are most numerous in cool climates during warm summers.

Control: Spray *Btk* (*Bacillus thuringiensis* var. *kurstaki*) a week or so after you notice the white eggs clinging to corn leaves. Natural predators include lacewings, ladybugs, praying mantids, and trichogramma wasps.

FLEA BEETLES

Plants affected: Just about everything, but especially tomato, cabbage, and beet family plants

Description: Flea beetles are the pinhead-sized dark brown to black beetles that jump away, just like fleas, when threatened. Though small, these little pests can quickly pepper leaves full of tiny holes so affected foliage looks more like a screen door than a leaf. They also spread plant diseases as they bounce around the garden.

Control: Spray plants with neem oil soap. Apply beneficial nematodes for long-term control.

LEAF MINERS

Plants affected: Beet, lettuce and other leafy greens, spinach, and Swiss chard

moth

larva

Description: Leaf miner is a term that refers to the larvae of a collection of moths, beetles, and flies. The leaf miner that affects vegetables is a small grayish yellow fly. The flies lay tiny white eggs from which small green maggots emerge. The maggots chew tunnels in the leaves for a few weeks, and then they drop down to the ground to pupate. In about three weeks, the adult fly emerges to begin the cycle all over again.

Control: Grow crops beneath floating row covers. Remove infested leaves as they appear. Natural predators include lacewings, ladybugs, and praying mantids. For long-term control, treat the area with beneficial nematodes. You can also use yellow sticky traps to catch adult flies. For fast control, spray plants with neem.

MEXICAN BEAN BEETLES

Plants affected: Bean

Description: Mexican bean beetles look similar to ladybugs in size and shape. They have a coppery-tan back sprinkled with black dots; the young adults have no spots. Mexican bean beetles have huge appetites and feed on bean leaves and fruit, leaving skeletonized foliage and nibbled pods. Eggs are yellowish and appear on the undersides of bean leaves. Larvae, which also feed on bean plants, are light colored with a spiny appearance.

Control: Handpick or apply beneficial nematodes. Natural predators include lacewings, ladybugs, praying mantids, and spined soldier bugs. For fast control, spray plants with neem.

MITES

Plants affected: Just about everything

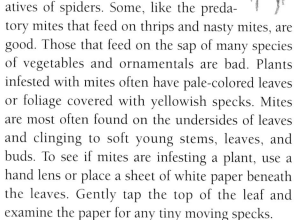

Description: Mites are very, very small relatives of spiders. Some, like the predatory mites that feed on thrips and nasty mites, are good. Those that feed on the sap of many species of vegetables and ornamentals are bad. Plants infested with mites often have pale-colored leaves or foliage covered with yellowish specks. Mites are most often found on the undersides of leaves and clinging to soft young stems, leaves, and buds. To see if mites are infesting a plant, use a hand lens or place a sheet of white paper beneath the leaves. Gently tap the top of the leaf and examine the paper for any tiny moving specks.

Control: Natural predators include lacewings, ladybugs, minute pirate bugs, and predatory mites. Deliver a water spray using a mist nozzle head placed an inch or two (2.5 to 5 cm) from the plant. For quick control, try applying the botanical insecticide neem or neem oil soap.

SLUGS AND SNAILS

Plants affected: Just about everything

slug

snail

Description: If you're going to be a pest, you might as well be slimy — it fits the job description. Slugs and snails are slimy. They feed on the soft tissues of a number of vegetables and flowers, leaving raspy, rough-edged holes and slime trails to mark their passing. Like vampires, they usually work at night or on cloudy days.

Control: If you can't sleep at night, grab the flashlight and go slug and snail hunting. After dark, they are easy to handpick and drop in a can of soapy water. Other methods include setting boards, stones, or overturned pots as traps in the garden. Check them in the morning, pick off any slimy visitors, and drop them in a can of soapy water. Apply an unbroken line of wood ashes, diatomaceous earth, or sawdust around susceptible plants. Tack copper foil to the sides of supported raised beds or stick copper strips vertically in the soil. The copper gives the slug or snail an electrical shock, which discourages further travel.

SQUASH BUGS

Plants affected: Cucumber, gourd, melon, pumpkin, and squash

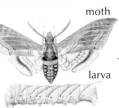

Description: Squash bugs are from ½ to 1 inch long (1.25 to 2.5 cm), black to gray, with a back as flat as an aircraft carrier. They pierce the outside skin of plants and suck out the juices, leaving infested plants dotted with yellow or brown spots. In severe cases the plants are pale green to yellowish and stunted, with few fruit.

Control: Plant resistant varieties when possible. Many winter squash, including butternuts and Hubbards, are resistant, while other squash, such as Pattypan, are more susceptible. Sprays of insecticidal soap help. Apply garlic spray regularly, starting early in the season. Rotate plants annually.

SQUASH VINE BORERS

Plants affected: Cucumber, melon, pumpkin, and squash

moth

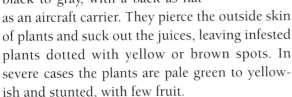

larva

Description: Squash vine borers are the plump, 1-inch-long (2.5 cm) larvae of a winged moth with two black and two transparent wings. The adults lay eggs on plants in early summer. On hatching, the larvae tunnel into the stem, where they feed. Squash vine borers weaken the plants and can damage them so much that the vines wilt and die.

Control: Apply beneficial nematodes for long-term control. To repel moths from plants, regularly treat leaves and vines with garlic spray. Grow young plants under floating row covers to exclude moths from plants. Grow resistant varieties.

TOMATO HORNWORMS

moth

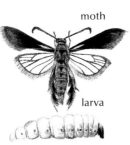

larva

Plants affected: Tomato

Description: As much as 4 inches (10 cm) long and as thick as your pinky finger, hornworms are pale to medium green with chalky white streaks across the body. Small eyelike spots decorate their sides; their backsides sport a red or black spiky tail. They can devour most of a tomato plant in a day or two. Adults are large (4 to 5 inches [10 to 12.5 cm]), brownish gray moths with orange spots on the abdomen. Eggs are tiny greenish yellow balls on the undersides of tomato leaves.

Control: Spray small ones with Btb (Bacillius thuringiensis var. berliner) or neem oil soap. When they're larger, handpick and drop them into a can of soapy water. If you find a hornworm wearing clusters of small white eggs on its back, it's best to leave it be. The eggs belong to a small braconid wasp that parasitizes and destroys the worm.

WHITEFLIES

Plants affected: Cucumber, potato, and tomato

Description: Whiteflies are small — a little larger than a pinhead — with tiny snow white wings. Walking through a severely infested garden is like strolling through a snow globe with specks of white swirling around. Whiteflies suck the sap from plants and usually gather on the undersides of leaves or near soft, succulent growth.

Control: Natural predators include lacewings, ladybugs, and praying mantids. Use yellow sticky traps near target plants to capture adults. Spray with neem, insecticidal soap, or neem oil soap for immediate control. Use garlic spray to repel whiteflies from plants.

Common Diseases and Some Balanced Solutions

ANTHRACNOSE

Plants affected: Many, including bean, cucumber, eggplant, lettuce, melon, pea, pepper, potato, radish, rhubarb, spinach, tomato, and turnip

Description: "Out, damned spot! out, I say!" is a quote from Shakespeare's *Macbeth,* but it could easily have been uttered by any gardener with vegetables infected with anthracnose. This disease produces small spots on leaves, stems, and fruit. The spots typically grow in size and subsequently cause the plant to die back.

Control: Spray plants with compost tea. Rotate crops annually and use resistant varieties.

BACTERIAL BLIGHT

Plants affected: Bean, cabbage family plants, and pea

Description: In cabbage family plants, early infection results in stunting, with one side of the plant often larger than the other. Mature plants often lose older leaves. On pea and bean plants, dark or light green spots appear on leaves. As the disease progresses, the spots dry out, becoming bronze or brown. The disease, which is most common in humid areas, can also infect flowers, pods, and stems.

Control: Use resistant varieties when possible. Remove and destroy severely infected plants. Spray plants with minor infections with neem oil.

BACTERIAL WILTS

Plants affected: A broad range, including carrot, cucumber, eggplant, some melons, peanut, pepper, potato, pumpkin, rhubarb, squash, sweet potato, tomato

Description: Bacterial diseases are often characterized as slimy and smelly, which is an apt description for bacterial wilts. Infected plants often have a brown, soft lesion on the stem, which enlarges until the plant is girdled. The plant then rapidly wilts, sometimes briefly recovering during the night. The stems develop brown streaks before dissolving into a brown jelly.

Control: One type of bacterial wilt lives in the gut of cucumber beetles, while another overwinters in the soil where it can survive for over five years. Cover plants with row covers to protect from cucumber beetles. Rotate crops on a four- or five-year cycle. Destroy infected plants as soon as you notice them.

BLOSSOM-END ROT

Plants affected: Pepper, squash, tomato, and watermelon

Description: Blossom-end rot is not caused by an organism but by environmental conditions, including soils deficient in calcium and long periods of wet weather followed by dry. It begins with the appearance of a dark, watery spot at the blossom end of the fruit. The spot slowly enlarges, sometimes engulfing most of the fruit. Small fruits may quickly drop from the plant, while larger fruits often persist. Secondary rots are common.

Control: Test soil before growing season begins. If your soil needs calcium and the pH is also low, add limestone. If pH is not excessively acidic, add gypsum. Mulch plantings to maintain even moisture. Avoid excessive fertilizing.

CLUBROOT

Plants affected: Broccoli, Brussels sprout, cabbage, cauliflower, Chinese cabbage, kale, kohlrabi, mustard, radish, rutabaga, and turnip

Description: Clubroot is a disease that infects vegetables of the cabbage family. The disease is caused by a funguslike organism that destroys the plant's root system, producing swollen, lumpy roots and wilted, yellowish leaves. If you allow the roots and plants to rot, disease spores are released into the soil where they can be spread to other locations by dirty shoes and tools or even manure from animals grazing on infected plants.

Control: Remove infected plants as soon as you notice them. Enrich the soil with compost instead of manure, plant resistant varieties when available, and raise soil pH to at least 7.2.

CRACKING

Plants affected: Celery, rhubarb, and tomato

Description: In tomato, the fruit splits longitudinally, while in celery and rhubarb, the leaf stem splits. Cracking in tomato is caused by a quick change in soil moisture, usually from dry to wet. In celery and rhubarb, cracking is caused by a deficiency of the trace element boron.

Control: Mulch tomatoes to help regulate soil moisture levels; water during dry periods. Harvest ripe fruit promptly. Test soil before growing season begins and add amendments as needed.

CURLY TOP

Plants affected: A wide range, including bean, beet, cabbage family crops, carrot, celery, cucumber, eggplant, melon, pumpkin, spinach, squash, Swiss chard, and tomato

Description: Curly top is a viral disease. It's most prevalent west of the Rocky Mountains, but it can appear anywhere. Symptoms include an upward curling of leaves accompanied by a thick, leathery appearance. Beans buck this trend by having their leaves bend downward. This disease affects so many plants that often more than one crop in the garden is infected. It is spread by leafhoppers.

Control: Cover plants with row covers. Remove infected plants promptly. Keep weeds in and around garden under control.

DAMPING-OFF

Plants affected: Everything

Description: Damping-off is a disease that most often infects seedlings. It's caused by many different fungi. There are two forms of the disease: pre-emergent, where the seedling rots before it emerges from the soil, and post-emergent, where the stem and roots rot after they emerge from the soil. Manage both forms the same way.

Control: Discard seedlings with damping-off and disinfect the containers. To prevent the disease, sow seeds in clean, sterilized containers and sterilized or pasteurized seed-starting mixture. Water with compost tea, but avoid overwatering. If germinating seeds are in a covered container, remove the cover as soon as plants emerge. If you sow outdoors, avoid spacing seeds too close together. If possible, avoid sowing when the weather is expected to be warm and humid.

DOWNY MILDEW

Plants affected: A wide range of plants, including those of the sunflower, cabbage, pea, onion, beet, and carrot families

Description: Downy mildew is a fungal disease that thrives during times of cool, humid nights with heavy dew, and warm days. Symptoms first appear as spots on leaves, followed by a fluffy, often violet, mold over the spot; the mold grows on both sides of the leaf. Other fungi then invade the plant, causing extensive rot.

Control: Spray foliage with neem oil or compost tea before symptoms appear. Plant resistant or tolerant varieties where available. For example, red onions seem more resistant than other onions. Remove weeds, as they may harbor the disease, and rotate plants annually.

EARLY AND LATE BLIGHT

Plants affected: A variety of plants

Description: Although these diseases affect similar plants, they're caused by very different fungi. Early blight most often appears before the first fruits have ripened. It produces brown, circular spots on leaves, each spot marked with concentric rings. Plants are most often infected during periods of warm, humid weather.

Late blight, which can attack seedlings or mature plants, sounds like a tardy sibling of early blight, but it isn't. It's called late blight because it most often appears during spells of warm, wet weather — conditions that most often occur late in the growing season. Late blight is the disease that caused the great potato famine in Ireland in 1845. The scientific name of the fungus that causes the disease translates as "plant destroyer." The disease first appears as dark spots on the leaves, which often have a strong, offensive odor. Eventually the plants rot and collapse.

Control: *To control early blight,* spray plants with neem oil or compost tea. Avoid damaging plants when cultivating, remove weeds regularly, plant resistant varieties, and use row covers to exclude flea beetles that can spread the disease.

To control late blight, spray plants with neem oil or compost tea at the first sign of the disease. To prevent the disease, rotate crops annually and plant certified seed.

FUSARIUM AND VERTICILLIUM WILTS

Plants affected: Many crops, including bean, cucumber, dill, melon, pumpkin, squash, sweet potato, and tomato

Description: In many plants, the leaves turn yellow and then brown as the disease advances up the stem. Stems can turn brown and split.

Control: Remove and destroy infected plants. Before the growing season begins, solarize soil and add additional organic matter. Rotate plants annually and plant resistant varieties.

GRAY MOLD (BOTRYTIS)

Plants affected: Just about everything

Description: Gray mold is one of those diseases that seems to pop up here and there throughout the growing season. It can infect seedlings as well as mature plants, and it even attacks fruit and flowers. The most common symptom is the appearance of an airy gray mold above a brown, water-soaked, rotten area on stems, leaves, flowers, or fruit. Gray mold can be lethal to seedlings but is largely just a nuisance on larger plants.

Control: The best way to control gray mold is sanitation. Keep seed-starting supplies clean, provide plants with good air circulation through proper spacing, and remove dead leaves and flowers from the garden promptly. Spray plants with neem oil or compost tea.

POWDERY MILDEW

powdery mildew

Plants affected: A broad range of plants, including those of the squash and pea families

Description: Powdery mildew is a very common disease that coats leaves, buds, and flowers with a powdery white coating. Powdery mildew weakens plants, deforming young leaves and flowers and reducing yields. The disease is most often a problem late in the growing season and during periods of hot, humid weather.

Control: Keep susceptible ornamental plants, such as phlox and bee balm, away from vegetable plantings. Spray plants with neem oil or baking soda spray. Chamomile tea spray also works well but should not be sprayed on plants in direct sunlight.

ROOT-KNOT NEMATODES

Plants affected: A broad range of vegetable, ornamental, and other plants

Description: Root-knot nematodes are tiny worms that parasitize the roots of plants. They draw food from the plant, damage or destroy the roots, open wounds where disease organisms can enter, and ultimately kill the plant. Other types of parasitic nematodes attack potato tubers (potato rot nematodes); onion bulbs (stem and bulb nematodes); and celery, bean, corn, and pepper (awl nematodes). Vegetables infested with root-knot nematodes are often stunted and sickly, with roots covered with small galls that cannot be broken off. In contrast, you can easily break the beneficial nodules on legumes from the roots. Root-knot nematodes were once considered a problem only in warm climates, but it's now recognized that they can become a problem just about anywhere.

Control: An attractive and effective way of managing nematodes is to grow marigolds (*Tagetes* spp.) in infested soil. You can attain subtle effects by growing marigolds near susceptible plants, but for the best control, grow marigolds as a cover crop and turn them into the soil as soon as the plants begin to flower. This treatment is usually effective for about one year.

Other solutions include soil additives, such as chitin, a natural substance found in the shells of some shellfish, to encourage nematode predators, and organic matter, as well as solarizing infested soil and planting resistant varieties.

▲ **A beautiful control.** To discourage nematodes, dig Lemon Gem marigolds into your soil.

ROOT ROT

Plants affected: Just about everything

Description: Many organisms cause root rots, but the majority have similar symptoms and controls. Root rot typically results in a wilting of the plant along with a yellowing of lower leaves. The wilting can be very gradual or rapid, and it occurs in moist or wet soil. The roots are brown to black, often soft and easily broken, and sometimes smell foul. Root rots most often occur during wet, cool weather.

Control: Remove infected plants as soon as you notice them. Water plants with compost tea before symptoms appear. Before the growing season begins, solarize the soil and add more organic matter. Rotate crops annually and avoid overwatering plants.

RUST

Plants affected: Many plants, including asparagus, bean, beet, carrot, chard, corn, onion, pea, peanut, spinach, and sunflower

Description: You'll most often see rusts late in the season during periods of wet weather. The fungi infect foliage, producing red, yellow, or orange dots, usually on the underside of the leaf. On onion and asparagus, the tips of the foliage become brownish red. Rust infection can range from being a nuisance that blemishes leaves to a virulent disease that destroys crops.

Control: You can control rust to some extent by spraying plants with neem oil or compost tea before symptoms appear. Plant resistant cultivars, but be forewarned that some previously resistant varieties, such as Martha Washington asparagus, are not resistant to newly emerged strains of rust.

SOUTHERN BLIGHT

Plants affected: Just about everything

Description: Southern blight begins as a web of white to pinkish fungal growth that appears at the base of the stem at the soil line. As the stem is attacked, the leaves turn yellow and drop.

Control: Remove infected plants and surrounding 6 inches (15 cm) of soil. Add compost or other organic matter before the growing season begins. Water plants regularly with compost tea before symptoms appear.

TOBACCO MOSAIC VIRUS

Plants affected: Pepper and tomato family crops

Description: Infected plants have yellow to pale green leaves, often smaller than normal, mottled, and deformed. Plants are often stunted, and yields are reduced or negligible.

Control: Tobacco mosaic is transmitted by contact — by touching an infected plant and then handling a healthy one. Remove infected plants as symptoms appear, disinfecting hands and tools before again working near plants. Plant resistant varieties when available.

Repellents: The Smell of Success

There is a story about a gentleman sitting on a bench in Central Park, tossing confetti. "Why," he is asked, "are you throwing confetti?" "To repel tigers," he replies. "But there are no tigers in Central Park," he is told. A knowing smile crosses the man's face. "I know. Works pretty well, doesn't it?"

Repellents are relied on by some and laughed off by others. Yet there is ample evidence that some repellents can dissuade many pests, from deer to voles, from feasting on the garden.

SCARECROWS

Scarecrows have been used to repel pests as long as there have been gardens. A scarecrow is likely to be more effective if it doesn't just hang around. Some have active parts that move or make noise that really does confound the nuisances. You can make a minimalist scarecrow by hanging aluminum pie plates or strips of shiny foil from fencing and branches. Or, you can purchase big balloons decorated with huge eyes that float in the wind. You'll even find that some mail-order sources carry a high-tech scarecrow with a built-in brain, in the form of a heat-and-motion sensor. If motion is detected, it shoots a spray of water at the intruder. You'll want to remember to turn this one off before you go in the garden, or you'll be the target!

ELECTRONIC REPELLENTS

Some electronic devices rely on soundwaves to keep pests away from an area. Small models have different frequency settings to repel insects, mice,

squirrels, and even spiders. Larger units are used to repel dogs, cats, skunks, raccoons, and other animals.

NATURAL REPELLENTS

Repellents protect something tasty (the garden) with something that is offensive but harmless (the repellent). The marketplace is a grab bag of repellents. Some smell bad. In fact, some smell so bad they repel you as well as the pests from the garden.

Garlic and hot pepper products. Some repellents use garlic and hot peppers to repel both insects and larger animals. One commercial spray smells like a combination of rotten eggs, hot peppers, and garlic. But it's not for use on edibles, so spray it around the garden edge, not on plants.

Plastic clips. These devices contain a very concentrated garlic oil. The clips may be either pushed into the soil near the target plants or hung around the edge of the garden.

Hair. Ask at your barber shop or beauty parlor for the clippings they sweep up each day, and spread the hair around the edge of the garden or near susceptible plants.

Blood meal. Sprinkle blood meal right on plants, not just near them, and be sure to renew it after each rain.

Soap. Tie bars of deodorant soap to stakes and place them around the garden among the target plants.

HOME RECIPES FOR WHAT AILS THE GARDEN

Just as wisdom handed down from grandparents is sometimes better than that delivered by strangers, so homemade remedies can sometimes be better than store-bought concoctions. Although many recipes for curing plant diseases or killing bugs aren't worth the time of day, those that follow are among the most trusted.

Homemade Pest- and Disease-Control Remedies

COMPOST OR MANURE TEA

Compost and manure teas are useful fertilizers, and they can also help prevent many plant diseases.

  1½ gallons (5.68 L) fresh compost or
        aged manure
  4½ gallons (17 L) warm water

Put the compost or manure into a sack and tie the open end closed. Pour the water into a 5-gallon (20 L) bucket and immerse the sack in it. Cover the bucket and allow the solution to steep for three to seven days. Pour the solution into a watering can or plant mister and apply to plants.

CHAMOMILE TEA

Chamomile is a useful preventative, as well as treatment, for powdery mildew. Avoid spraying chamomile tea in direct sunlight, as it can damage the leaves of some plants.

  4–6 tablespoons (40–50 g) dried chamomile flowers
  2–3 cups (472–700 ml) boiling water

Place chamomile flowers in a heat-resistant container. Pour boiling water over herbs. Steep until cool. Place in a hand sprayer. Use within two or three days.

ORANGE DELIGHT

Here's a remedy that smells wonderful and at the same time helps control many types of insects.

  2 lemons
  1 orange
  1 quart (1 L) boiling water

Grate the citrus rind and place it in a heatproof container. Pour the boiling water over the rinds. Cover and steep until cool. Strain into a hand-held sprayer and apply.

BAKING SODA SPRAY

Using baking soda in spray form helps prevent or manage plant diseases, including black spot and powdery mildew.

  1½ tablespoons (22.5 g) baking soda
  1 tablespoon (15 ml) vegetable oil
  1½ gallons (5.68 L), plus 1 cup (236 ml)
        warm water

Combine the baking soda and oil in 1 cup (236 ml) of warm water. Stir until the baking soda is dissolved. Add the baking soda mixture to the 1½ gallons (5.68 L) of warm water and stir until blended. Pour into sprayer; use immediately.

BUG SPRAY

Many pests, from insects to squirrels, are quickly repelled by the taste and odor of hot pepper. This homemade spray helps you use their distaste to your advantage. Caution: The active ingredient in hot pepper, capsaicin, can produce skin and eye irritation. Use care when preparing or applying this remedy.

  7 cloves of garlic
  1 tablespoon (15 g) powdered
        cayenne pepper
  3 cups (700 ml) hot water

Crush the garlic and place it in a heat-proof container. Add the cayenne. Pour the hot, but not boiling, water over the garlic and cayenne. Stir to combine completely. Allow the mixture to steep for two to three days. Strain and pour into a hand-held sprayer.

Big-Time Pests: Guess Who's Coming to Dinner?

Deer are beautiful animals, but gardens and deer just don't go together. It takes a whole lot of flea beetles to do much damage to a cabbage plant, and a dozen or more Colorado potato beetles are needed to lay serious siege to a potato plant. But in just one night a single deer can munch the tops off all your storage carrots. And deer aren't the only furry bandits to worry about. Raccoons can destroy your corn patch; rabbits or woodchucks have a liking for anything green and tender; and dogs, cats, wild turkeys, and skunks can just make a mess of things. Your garden shouldn't also be a petting zoo, and fortunately, a wide array of solutions can humanely help you keep wildlife on the outside of your garden, looking in.

THE BEST OFFENSE IS A FENCE

A 3-foot-tall (90 cm) nylon mesh or chicken-wire fence will keep most animals, such as rabbits and woodchucks, out of the garden. Remember to set the posts no farther than 8 feet (2.4 m) apart and bury the base of the fencing at least 1 foot (30 cm) deep. These measures help keep the fencing taut and prevent animals from burrowing under it.

Raccoons are smarter than ground squirrels, woodchucks, and rabbits. In fact, in my experience, they're smarter than just about any other garden pest. A raccoon will climb over a mesh or chicken-wire fence in the blink of an eye. Sometimes a line of electric fencing strung atop the fenceposts will deter the less ambitious ones. Yet to have a good chance at preventing raccoon damage, a more elaborate system is needed. I've had good luck using a two-wire electric fence, with the bottom wire about 4 inches (10 cm) from the soil and another about 12 inches (30 cm) high.

Deer are as athletic as raccoons are intelligent. A white-tailed deer can easily leap over a 6-foot-tall (1.8 m) fence. This means that protecting a

▲ **Radical raccoon repeller.** Raccoons are determined, and they can do a lot of damage in a short period of time. I've managed to keep them away from our corn with two strands of electric fence, 4 inches (10 cm) and 12 inches (30 cm) high.

Keep the Salad Bar a Secret

It's best to erect fences before animal damage occurs. If they develop a taste for your garden, woodchucks and rabbits have much greater motivation to get inside to the salad bar.

garden from deer requires a bigger fence. Deer fences are usually 8 feet (2.4 m) tall, with some reaching 10 feet (3 m). The fencing and posts can be the same as the 3-foot (90 cm) garden fence mentioned earlier, just more of it.

If tall fences just aren't practical, another alternative is to educate your deer. The lesson begins by installing a 3-foot-tall (90 cm) fence around the garden. Next, string a strand of electric fencing

▲ **A deer-proof garden.** You'll need very tall fencing to keep out high-leaping deer. This deer fence at Shepherd's Garden Seeds, in Litchfield, Connecticut, is 8 feet (2.4 m) tall.

Be Careful What You Catch

Humane trapping is a much kinder way to handle problem animals than many traditional alternatives, but it can have a downside too. Although I've caught corn-stealing raccoons this way, I've also caught a cat and a skunk in traps meant for raccoons. The cat was quite unhappy and loudly conveyed what I'm pretty sure were cat profanities when I let it go. But a cat is a cat and profanities were the extent of its arsenal. The skunk was a different story. The first two times I tried to let it go, the attempts failed. Each time I set the door open and made my own escape, the skunk panicked, tripped the trigger, and recaptured itself. Finally, I propped the door open with a flowerpot, and the skunk crept from the trap and disappeared into the woods. At the time, I thought the skunk's cramped quarters in the trap protected me from its own version of chemical repellent. I have since learned that such is not necessarily the case, making this form of pest control potentially quite memorable. I was just lucky.

atop the posts. With the power shut off, dab some peanut butter (creamy is better than chunky) on the electric strand. Then, turn the power back on. That's it. When deer come to investigate the peanut butter, they get a harmless but memorable shock, bound away, and the garden goes unscathed.

WHEN ASKING NICELY DOESN'T WORK

Some animals, through sheer persistence, cross the boundary between being a nuisance and being intolerable. They spend more time in the garden than you do, when they're in the garden they're making a mess, and nothing seems to discourage them. These are the animals that are the best candidates for humane trapping. You can purchase humane traps (traps that capture but

cause no injury to the animal) in many sizes, ranging from mouse-size to dog-size. They are easy-to-use and maintain and can be purchased from many garden centers, mail-order catalogs, and department stores. In some areas, you may be able to rent them. Simply bait the trap with a tasty treat not found in the garden, such as peanut butter, set the doors, and wait.

Pesky animals are not created equal. Each species seems to have a different degree of susceptibilty to being captured in a humane trap. Raccoons and woodchucks are among the animals that will sometimes allow themselves to be caught in humane traps. Of course, once you've succeeded in capturing the animal, you must transport it somewhere else and release it. Ask your County Extension Service for advice about where to release the wildlife you catch.

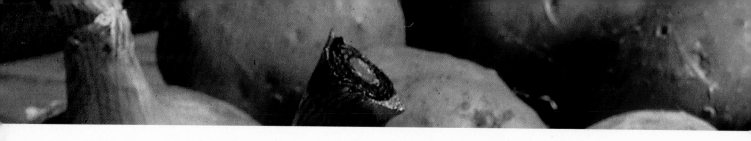

PART 3

Vegetables & Herbs, A–Z
Great Taste and More Variety

Getting to Know What You Grow

At the fair my family attended each fall was a silhouette artist. Sit still for a minute and he would make a black paper outline that, at first glance, looked just like you. That is, it did until you saw the next one he did of someone else, when you realized that every silhouette he made looked pretty much the same. When I want to know about a plant, I want real, useful information, not a cutout silhouette.

The vegetable profiles that follow will help you know each plant well — as you might if you'd grown them many times. No empty silhouettes, but detailed, descriptive portraits. Each profile takes you from seed to harvest and includes information on seed sowing, transplanting, growing, harvesting, storage, and much more. As you read, you learn about each plant's needs, as well as how it affects and is affected by others. In the end the knowledge you gain teaches you about each vegetable and how it interacts with others and its environment, helping you become as much a part of the garden as the plants you grow.

Artichokes

This gourmet-quality perennial is grown in warm climates as either a perennial or biennial but in cold climates as an annual. If that seems confusing to you, think of how it must be for the artichoke. Native to the Mediterranean, artichokes are becoming increasingly popular in American gardens from Zone 11 north through Zone 4. In North America, the ideal climate for artichokes is along coastal areas of central California, where the plants yield all year long. In other regions they need some special care — but they're worth it.

▲ **This bud's for dinner!** Whoever discovered the tender treat at the heart of this prickly vegetable? Growing artichokes successfully is almost as satisfying as eating them.

THE SITE

Where winter temperatures never go below about 14°F (–10°C; USDA Zones 8–11), artichokes can be grown as perennials, the way nature intended. During their first year, the plants make leaves, but no buds (the edible portion of the plant). The second year, they produce buds in late summer and fall. In areas with warm, dry climates, such as the southwestern United States, buds may form all year long but are of best quality in spring. In warm regions, artichoke plants can produce buds for three to five years. In colder

Sow & Grow

ARTICHOKES
(Cynara scolymus)
Sunflower family *(Compositae)*

SOWING
Seed depth: ¼" (6 mm)
Germination soil temperature: 70–80°F (21–27°C)
Days to germination: 10–14
Sow indoors: Late winter to early spring — 10 weeks before last frost
Sow outdoors: Not recommended

GROWING
pH range: 6.5–8.0
Growing soil temperature: 60–75°F (16–24°C)
Spacing in beds: 24" (60 cm)
Watering: Heavy
Light: 8 hours or more per day
Nutrient requirements: N=high; P=high; K=high
Rotation considerations: Avoid following Jerusalem artichoke or sunflower.
Good companions: Sunflower, tarragon
Bad companions: None
Seed longevity: 5 years
Seeds per ounce: 10,000 (333 seeds per g)

regions (USDA Zones 7 to 4), you'll have to fool Mother Nature to get your artichokes in one growing season.

SOWING

Sow seeds indoors in a seed-starting mix in flats or pots and set in a 70 to 80°F (21 to 27°C) spot; the seedlings should appear in about 12 days. Transplant into 4-inch (10 cm) pots as soon as the first set of true leaves begins to expand, reducing temperatures to 60 to 70°F (16 to 21°C) during the day and 50 to 60°F (10 to 16°C) at night. In warm regions, the plants are ready for the garden when they are about six weeks old. Set them in the soil and cover with a row cover for a week or two. If you live in a cool region, follow the strategy in the box You Can Fool Mother Nature.

You Can Fool Mother Nature

In cool regions, it's time to start the trickery when artichoke plants are about six weeks old. The objective is to convince the artichoke that it is two years old and ready to make buds, rather than a seedling ready to make only leaves. This is done by growing the plant at cool temperatures for a prescribed length of time. This cold treatment makes the seedling behave like a two-year-old plant ready to flower.

Temperatures during the cold treatment should remain below 50°F (10°C) but above 35°F (2°C) for at least 250 continuous hours (about 10½ days). Since it is difficult to prevent times when temperatures rise above 50°F (10°C), give the plants the cold treatment for an even longer period: from four to six weeks. Put the plants in a cold frame about six weeks before the last frost. Keep the frame open during the day for cooling and closed at night for frost protection.

When all danger of frost is past and the soil temperature is above 60°F (16°C), set plants about 2 feet (60 cm) apart in the bed.

GROWING

Fertilizing. Deep-rooted, heavy feeders, artichokes grow best in soil enriched with lots of compost. Feed once a month with compost tea or an organic fertilizer such as fish emulsion.

Watering. Water evenly throughout the growing season.

HARVESTING AND STORING

A mature artichoke bud, ready for the dinner table, is firm, tight, and a nice even green color. If it begins to open, the tenderness quickly deteriorates. The first bud to mature is the top, or terminal, bud, followed over the next few days by the lateral, or secondary, buds. The terminal bud is often a bit larger than most of the lateral ones, but they all taste great.

Using a sharp knife, cut the buds at the base. Harvest during cool, moist weather for best flavor. The buds can be refrigerated for up to two weeks.

WINTER CARE

In warm regions (USDA Zone 8 and warmer): After harvest in late fall, cut the plants at or just beneath ground level and cover with an organic mulch.

In cool areas (USDA Zones 6 and 7): Cut the plants to about 12 inches (30 cm) from the ground and mound a light organic mulch, such as oat straw, over the stumps. Cover everything with an inverted bushel basket. Mulch some more and, if practical, drape with a rainproof cover. Good mulching can bring plants through some winters even in regions as cold as Zone 5.

BEST VARIETIES

Green Globe has been *the* variety to grow for years, and remains so, but it now has competition.
Imperial Star produces up to three times more buds per plant than Green Globe.

Asparagus

Like the king who wanted only a little bit of butter on his bread, asparagus is not fussy. Just give it a good place to grow, offer the nourishment and water it needs, and keep the weeds away. Given this level of attention, an asparagus bed will provide you and your family with food fit for a king for many years to come.

THE SITE

Asparagus is a perennial. Since typical asparagus beds can remain productive for 15 to 20 years, you'll want to choose the site carefully. Too often asparagus beds are located for the gardener's convenience instead of for the plants' needs.

If you're starting a new bed, site it in the northern portion of the garden, so that the tall ferns won't shade other plants. Keep it away from the edge of the garden, too, so grass and weeds are less likely to creep in and get established.

▲ **Tender loving care** results in an abundant harvest of sweet spring treats. For the best flavor, you've got to grow your own, because asparagus quickly loses its flavor after it's been cut.

Sow & Grow

ASPARAGUS
(Asparagus officinalis)
Onion family *(Liliaceae)*

SOWING/PLANTING

Seed depth: ¼–½" (6–13 mm)
Germination soil temperature: 77°F (25°C)
Days to germination: 10–12
Sow indoors: 8 weeks before last frost
Plant outdoors: In spring, 3 weeks before last frost

GROWING

pH range: 6.5–7.5
Growing soil temperature: 60–70°F (16–24°C)
Spacing in beds: 18" (45 cm)
Watering: Heavy
Light: 8 hours or more per day for best yield; will tolerate 4–8 hours
Nutrient requirements: N=high; P=moderate; K=moderate
Rotation considerations: Avoid following onion family plants.
Good companions: Basil, calendula, parsley, tomato
Bad companions: Onion, chive, garlic, leek
Seed longevity: 3 years
Seeds per ounce: 1,400 (47 seeds per g)

Traditionally, asparagus crowns were planted in trenches 8 to 12 inches (20 to 30 cm) deep. That was when open-pollinated varieties such as Martha Washington and Mary Washington were the most popular. Times have changed — and for the better. Research at Rutgers University has produced the Jersey Series of all-male asparagus. These varieties are planted just 5 to 6 inches (12.5 to 15 cm) deep and yield up to four times as many spears as the older types.

PLANTING

It's best to prepare soil in fall for planting the next spring. In a pinch, you can prepare a new bed in spring if the pH of the soil is already within the recommended range. Cultivate soil about 16 inches (40 cm) deep. Work an inch (2.5 cm) of compost into the top 3 inches (7.5 cm) of the bed.

In most regions, you should plant asparagus crowns in early spring at about the time daffodils bloom. In very warm areas, such as the southwestern United States, fall or winter planting is preferred.

Getting the Acidity Right

Be sure to test your soil before you start planting. Asparagus does best in a slightly acid to slightly alkaline soil (6.5–7.5), a higher pH than you generally want in the rest of the garden. Dig any amendments deeply into the soil.

Planting Asparagus Crowns

1 Dig a hole about 12 inches (30 cm) deep for open-pollinated varieties such as Martha Washington, and 6 inches (15 cm) deep for Jersey hybrids such as Jersey Knight and Jersey King. Add about 1 inch (2.5 cm) of compost to the bottom of the hole. Place plants 18 inches (45 cm) apart. Don't crowd them; asparagus likes plenty of room.

2 Place the one-year-old crowns in the bottom of the hole, and spread the roots out evenly. Cover the crowns with 2 inches (5 cm) of soil. As the ferns grow during the summer, gradually fill the hole with soil, adding no more than 2 to 3 inches (5 to 7.5 cm) at a time, until the hole is filled.

GROWING

Fertilizing. As far as vegetables go, asparagus has a pretty big appetite, with good reason. Because they are perennials, the plants need to produce enough energy to feed us, produce new ferns, and survive the winter. It may be possible to overfeed asparagus, but it isn't easy. To ensure a steady source of nutrients for the plants and keep soil organisms busy loosening and aerating the soil, make regular applications of compost or rotted manure throughout the growing season.

Weed control. If asparagus has to share nutrients with weeds, its vigor is affected and its yield and longevity is ultimately reduced. Around midsummer, apply a straw or hay mulch to help with weed control as well as to moderate the soil temperature and help with moisture conservation. Create a buffer zone between the bed and garden edge by using an opaque mulch, such as layers of newspaper or cardboard covered with straw, to discourage invading grasses.

For asparagus, any competitor is a weed. This includes the asparagus seedlings that sprout from those red berries produced by open-pollinated varieties. Hoe them out, being careful not to damage the roots of the parent plants. Or you can avoid the pretty red berries entirely by growing all-male varieties such as Jersey Giant.

"Weeds" also include any potential companion plants. Tomatoes, for instance, are often mentioned as companions for asparagus, but tomatoes take a lot of nutrients from the soil.

HARVESTING

You can harvest fresh asparagus from the garden the second spring after planting (the third if you're starting from seeds). The first harvest should be light, no more than two or three spears per plant over a period of about two weeks. Each following spring, harvest spears that are more than ⅜ inch (1 cm) in diameter and 6 to 8 inches (15 to 20 cm) tall. Let the skinny spears grow into ferns. Stop harvesting when most of the emerging spears are small and the tips become loose and open; this will happen at about the time you start harvesting peas. A typical harvest lasts from four to eight weeks.

▲ **Weed no more.** A thick straw mulch around asparagus plants holds down weeds and helps keep soil moist and cool.

▲ **Nip them in the bud.** Loose tips, like the one on the left, mean stringy asparagus. Choose stalks like the one on the right with its nice, tight buds. Check your asparagus every day during the harvest season, so you don't miss the perfect picks.

There are two schools of thought on how to harvest: Cut the spear at or just below the soil with a knife; or, my preference, bend the spear until it breaks, which leaves a bit of it still above the soil.

STORING

You've got to be kidding. You don't store asparagus, you eat asparagus . . . immediately after cooking, or sooner, if you count the half-dozen spears munched right in the garden.

If you must store asparagus, either immerse the newly harvested spears in a tub of cold water or stand the bunch in a shallow container filled with 1 to 2 inches (2.5 to 5 cm) of cold water for a few minutes. Drain and refrigerate in plastic storage bags. It stays fresh for about a week. Storage temperature is important for asparagus; for best results, it must be just above 32°F (0°C).

PREPARING FOR WINTER

The thick growth of asparagus ferns, or brush, that covers the bed in late summer and early fall turns brown and brittle at the end of the growing season. In early to midfall, cut back this brush and add it to the compost pile. Test the soil and add amendments to restore soil fertility and maintain a pH of about 7.0. Next, spread compost or rotted manure at least an inch (2.5 cm) thick over the bed. Finish with a mulch of straw about 6 inches (15 cm) deep. This both protects the asparagus crowns from winter damage and allows soil organisms to continue improving the soil both in fall and spring.

BEST VARIETIES

Open-pollinated types: Martha Washington and Mary Washington are both old-fashioned cultivars that reliably produce large crops.

Rutgers hybrids: Jersey Giant, Jersey Knight, and Jersey King are all-male varieties that produce huge crops of thick, tender spears.

▲ **Bend or cut?** I prefer the bend-and-break method of harvesting asparagus because only the tenderest, most flavorful portion of the spear remains in my hand. If you cut the stalk with a knife, on the other hand, you get any tough parts as well.

Eat Now, Pay Later

Unlike other garden vegetables, which reward us only after we work all summer long to tend and nurture them, asparagus gives us the reward first. From the plant's perspective, however, the important part is still to come: It must grow lush and hardy ferns to make lots of food to store in the roots for the following spring. But we've already had what we want from the plant, and all too often we neglect it during what, for it, is a critically important time. Be fair to your asparagus: Keep it well weeded, fertilized, and watered throughout the growing season.

Bush Beans

Bush beans include such favorites as green, wax, Italian flat pod, French filet, and purple types. Add to this shell beans, lima beans, and fava beans. That's a lot of beans to choose from! What makes choosing easier is knowing that wherever you live, there are bush beans that will grow easily in your garden, taste delicious, and be good for you, too.

THE SITE

Bush beans, unlike pole beans, are determinate, which means they grow to a certain size, blossom, fruit, and stop growing. Because the best part of a bush bean harvest lasts only a few weeks, you'll enjoy more, and better-tasting, beans if you make small plantings every 10 days.

▲ **Flower buddy.** Insect pests of various sorts are less likely to bother bush beans if you grow marigolds nearby.

Sow & Grow

BUSH BEANS
(Phaseolus vulgaris, P. limensis, Vicia faba)
Pea family *(Leguminosae)*

SOWING

Seed depth: 1" (2.5 cm)
Germination soil temperature: 75–85°F (24–29°C)
Days to germination: 7–10
Sow indoors: Not recommended
Sow outdoors: When soil temperature reaches 60°F (16°C)

GROWING

pH range: 6.5–7.5
Growing soil temperature: 60–65°F (16–18°C)
Spacing in beds: *Bush,* 4" (10 cm) between plants, in rows across the bed 8" (20 cm) apart
  Pole, in hills 15" (37.5 cm) apart, 4 plants per hill

Watering: Low at planting, medium at flowering, heavy through harvest
Light: Full sun
Nutrient requirements: N=low; P=moderate; K=moderate
Rotation considerations: Because they get along with just about all vegetables except members of the onion family, bush beans can go almost anywhere and be followed by just about anything.
Good companions: Beet, cabbage, carrot, cauliflower, celeriac, celery, chard, corn, cucumber, eggplant, leek, marigold, parsnip, pea, potato, radish, rosemary, strawberry, sunflower
Bad companions: Basil, fennel, kohlrabi, onion family
Seed longevity: 3 years
Seeds per ounce: 100 (3 seeds per g)

SOWING

Starting beans too early is not doing them a favor. Cold soil slows down germination, makes the seedlings more susceptible to disease, and can damage the plants so much they never produce a good harvest. Be sure the seedbed is moist but not wet and then rake it smooth.

GROWING

Watering. Beans need just the right amount of water as they develop. Too little or too much slows or stops growth and makes the plants more susceptible to diseases and pests. Water plants lightly, but evenly and regularly, from germination to flowering. Increase the amount of water from flowering to the formation of the first pods. Increase watering again from beginning to end of harvest. Avoid overhead watering, which wets the leaves and can promote diseases such as bean rust. In arid regions, be sure to water well once blossoms appear to help ensure a heavy crop.

Fertilizing. Beans, along with peas, alfalfa, and some other plants, belong to a group called legumes. Legumes are special because they get much of their nitrogen through a partnership with *Rhizobia* bacteria, instead of relying on supplies in the soil. But it takes a little time after germination

▲ **Bean there, done that.** Instead of sowing one big crop of beans, make several small plantings about 10 days apart. You'll have a continuous harvest of tender, fresh beans over most of the garden season.

for the bacteria to become established on the roots of each plant, so for a few weeks beans need to get their nitrogen from the soil like other plants.

Fertilize young bean plants with an organic fertilizer, such as fish emulsion, every two weeks for the first six weeks, then once every three to four weeks.

Give Your Beans a Bacterial Boost

Beans and other legumes supply much of their own nitrogen needs through their relationship with certain bacteria that live in their roots. They do a better job at this and produce heavier crops if the seeds are inoculated with *Rhizobia* bacteria before sowing.

Simply put the black powder containing the bacteria (available in most seed catalogs) in a bag with the seeds. Shake the bag until the seeds are coated, and sow.

Vive la Différence!

Snap beans. These are the familiar green beans, which are eaten, pod and seeds, when they're young and tender.

Shell beans. When the seeds of some beans begin to swell, but are not completely mature and ready for drying, they make delicious eating shelled, fresh from the pod.

Dried beans. Among the best of storage crops and filled with nutritional benefits, dried beans are a valuable staple for cold-weather soups, stews, and casseroles.

HARVESTING SNAP BEANS

The easiest time to mess up a bean crop is right at the end. Until harvesttime, all bush beans look and act pretty much the same. It is when it's time to pick the pods that the differences between snap, shell, and dried beans become most apparent and important.

For snap beans to taste their best, they must be picked at the proper time. Beans that stay on the plant too long are much less tender and flavorful. And if you leave them unpicked even longer, the plant will stop producing new beans.

The better indicator of when to harvest snap beans is the diameter of a pod, rather than its length. Length can vary by variety, while pod diameter is related to the maturity of the developing seeds.

Green and wax beans. Pick these when the pods are ¼ to ⅜ inch (6 to 10 mm) in diameter, about the thickness of a pencil.

French, or filet, beans. Considered by many to be the tastiest bush bean, French beans should be harvested when they're very slender, about ⅛ inch (3 mm) in diameter. Beans allowed to grow larger quickly get tough and stringy. At times of peak harvest, this can mean picking filet beans about every other day.

BEST SNAP BEAN VARIETIES

Nickel. A French-filet type with small, very tasty, tender pods on strong, upright plants, Nickel is more tolerant of unfavorable unconditions than most.

Vernandon. A long, straight French-filet–type bean, Vernandon has pods that are both tender and crisp.

Slenderette. Sweet and delicious snap beans with no stringiness or toughness, Slenderettes are heavy bearers and resistant to many diseases.

Provider. This bean has been a favorite variety for decades, in part because the pods are sweet and meaty. But these disease-resistant plants also grow well even in cool weather and poor soil.

Goldkist. With tender, clean, yellow pods, this wax bean sports disease resistance.

HARVESTING DRY BEANS

Harvest dry beans when the pods are completely mature and dry. Good air circulation is important so that the pods don't rot before they dry, so allow sufficient space between rows. If you have a run of rainy weather after the leaves have died and the pods have begun to dry, pull the plants and hang them by the roots in an open shed.

BEST DRY BEAN VARIETIES

Etna, Midnight Black Turtle, Jacob's Cattle, Speckled Yellow Eye, Maine Yellow Eye, Vermont Cranberry, Soldier, Black Coco, Andrew Kent

◄ **Slim and fit for picking.** The two beans on the left are too large and will be tough. The two in the middle are at their peak, but those on the right are too young and will therefore lack flavor.

HARVESTING SHELL BEANS

Bush shell beans are grown the same as snap bush beans but harvested later, when the pods are swollen with plump, tender seeds. Some varieties, such as Tongue of Fire, can be eaten younger, as snap beans, and others, including Flambeau, can be used as dry beans. In cool regions, shell beans are a good substitute for lima beans, which grow best in hot weather, something northern gardeners have in short supply.

BEST SHELL BEAN VARIETIES

Flambeau, Flageolet Chevrier Vert, Borlotto, Etna

Pennies in the Sand

Collecting colorful beans from the remains of the dry pods (threshing) can be as much fun as finding pennies buried in a sandbox. We usually thresh by hand, shelling each pod and admiring the pretty colors of the beans. It's fun to do this on an early-winter evening with a fire in the fireplace. After you thresh the beans, make sure they are thoroughly dry and then store them in airtight jars. You can try either of these threshing methods:

▶ Take a handful of dried plants and gently bang them on the inside of a clean, dry trash can.

▶ Stuff the dried plants in a clean feed bag or old pillowcase and tread on it lightly. Picking the beans from the litter is a little like searching for pennies in the sand.

Winning at Shell Games: Growing Favas and Limas

Fava beans, also called broad or horse beans, are distant relatives of snap beans. Their pods look like fuzzy limas. These meaty beans have long been a staple of European cuisine, from the Middle East to Italy to northern Europe. In cool regions of North America, fava beans are used as a substitute for lima beans.

Sow fava beans as soon as the soil can be worked. Sow 1 to 2 inches (2.5 to 5 cm) deep and 6 inches (15 cm) apart. Pinching back the top of the plant when the first pods begin to form usually gives more uniform, higher-quality beans. Harvest for shell beans when the pods are plump, usually when they're about 6 inches (15 cm) long.

Caution: Some people are allergic to raw fava beans, so be sure to cook them before consuming.

Lima beans love long stretches of warm weather, a quality that makes them of questionable value for northern gardeners. In warm regions, however, lima beans prosper, yielding delectable, tasty beans that resemble the store-bought kind in name only.

Lima beans need even warmer soil (65°F; 18°C) than other beans for germination, are sensitive to even light frosts, and need warm and dry weather throughout a long growing season. Sow lima beans 1 inch (2.5 cm) deep (slightly deeper in sandy soils) and 3 to 4 inches (7.5 to 10 cm) apart. As with other beans, harvest often to increase yield.

Bush limas for cool areas: Jackson Wonder, Eastland Baby, and Packers

Bush limas for warm regions: Dixie Butterpea, Fordhook 242, and Burpee's Improved Bush Lima

Pole Beans

Flavor is always a debatable point, but most people who grow both bush and pole beans think pole beans are the sweeter, more tender, and better tasting of the two. There is no debate regarding yield. Pole beans produce more pods per plant than bush beans, plus they're much easier to pick.

SOWING AND GROWING

Most of the growing information that applies to bush beans also works for pole beans, with a few exceptions. Because pole beans are vining plants (called indeterminate), they need support to produce the best crops. You can construct a trellis like that described on pages 72–73 or create or purchase obelisk or teepee-style supports like those shown in the photos on these pages.

▲ **Beans by the pyramid-full.** Pole beans continue to grow, flower, and produce pods over a season of six to eight weeks, much longer than bush beans.

Sow & Grow

POLE BEANS
(Phaseolus vulgaris)
Pea family *(Leguminosae)*

SOWING

Seed depth: 1" (2.5 cm), 6–8 seeds per hill
Germination soil temperature: 75–85°F (24–29°C)
Days to germination: 7–10
Sow indoors: Not recommended
Sow outdoors: When soil temperature reaches 60°F (16°C)

GROWING

pH range: 6.5–7.5
Growing soil temperature: 60–65°F (16–18°C)

Spacing in beds: *In hills* (for poles), 16" (37.5 cm) apart, 4 plants per hill; *in rows* (for trellises), 3" (7.5 cm) apart
Watering: Low at sowing, medium at flowering, heavy through harvest
Light: Full sun for best yield; tolerates light shade
Nutrient requirements: N=Low; P=moderate; K=moderate
Rotation considerations: Precede corn; avoid following peas and bush beans.
Good companions: Carrot, cauliflower, chard, corn, cucumber, eggplant, marigold, pea, potato, rosemary, strawberry
Bad companions: Basil, beet, cabbage, fennel, kohlrabi, onion family, radish, sunflower
Seed longevity: 3 years
Seeds per ounce: 100 (3 seeds per g)

The vines will climb twine, poles, or netting. For twine or poles, plant seeds in groups of four to six with 16 inches (40 cm) between the groups. For netting, plant seeds 3 inches (8 cm) apart, with a row on each side of the netting; stagger the rows. Anchor the netting or twine to the ground with stakes or loops of heavy wire.

HARVESTING

Pole beans tend to stay tender on the vine longer than bush beans, but regular picking is still required to extend the harvest to its limit. When you have all the beans you need, let the remaining pods mature and use them as shell beans.

▲ **From small beginnings.** Sow a handful of four to six seeds spaced around each pole.

STORING

Pole beans freeze very well, keeping a firmer texture than bush beans.

BEST VARIETIES

Blue Lake. If you could call a bean variety tried-and-true, Blue Lake would be the one. Tender and stringless, these beans stay tasty even when big.

Emerite. For incredible flavor, it is hard to beat Emerite, a French filet bean with a deliciously sweet, nutty flavor.

Other great-flavored beans include the wax bean **Gold Marie** and the very vigorous **Fortex**.

▶ **Jack never had it this good.** This rustic obelisk makes a sturdy and attractive support for beanstalks as well as for other climbing plants.

Beets

Grown for their greens as well as their roots, beets come in many colors and shapes. While it is technically true that those reddish purple things in cans tucked in the back of your cupboard are beets, they aren't the best way to get to know this delicious vegetable. Beets baked in the oven like potatoes, or fresh baby beets and carrots sautéed in butter, are a better introduction to this flavorful, often overlooked vegetable.

THE SITE

Beets prefer a light soil with a pH of between 6.5 and 7.5. Research at Cornell University has shown that the roots of beets can grow as much as 3 feet (0.9 m) into the soil, a fact that emphasizes the benefits of gardening in deeply dug, wide, raised beds.

▲ **Can't beat this.** Keep your beets cool by growing them beneath mulches, and try to harvest them when they're no more than 2½ inches (6.3 cm) in diameter. To avoid "bleeding," remove the greens by twisting rather than cutting.

Sow & Grow

BEETS
(Beta vulgaris) Crassa Group
Beet family *(Chenopodiaceae)*

SOWING
Seed depth: ½" (13 mm)
Germination soil temperature: 75–85°F (24–29°C)
Days to germination: 5
Sow indoors: 5 weeks before last frost
Sow outdoors: 3–4 weeks before last frost

GROWING
pH range: 6.5–7.5
Growing soil temperature: 65–75°F (18–24°C)

Spacing in beds: *For greens,* 2" (5 cm); *for summer use,* 3" (7.5 cm); *for storage,* 4" (10 cm)
Watering: Moderate and even
Light: Full sun for best yield; tolerates light shade
Nutrient requirements: N=low; P=moderate; K=moderate
Rotation considerations: Avoid following spinach or Swiss chard.
Good companions: Bush bean, cabbage family, corn, leek, lettuce, lima bean, onion, radish
Bad companions: Mustard, pole bean
Seed longevity: 4 years
Seeds per ounce: 2,000 (67 seeds per g)

SOWING

Each beet "seed" is actually a dried fruit containing a cluster of two to six seeds. Sow these seeds 2 to 4 inches (5 to 10 cm) apart a month or so before the last frost. Repeat sowings every two weeks until the last frost. If you sow beets in midsummer for winter storage, the soil is likely to be warmer than beets prefer. To improve germination, sow seeds at dusk or on a cool, cloudy day. Water well and add a thin dressing of compost to help moderate soil temperatures.

After seedlings emerge, thin each cluster with floral shears or scissors. Save the most robust plant in each cluster and cut the rest at soil level. To avoid disturbing the remaining plants, don't pull out the unwanted seedlings.

GROWING

Plants that reach harvestable size during hot weather may have poor root color and flavor. Beets grow best in cool conditions and profit from cooling mulches and companion-cropping with plants that shade the soil.

Watering. Even moisture, which allows steady, uninterrupted growth, is important if beets are to reach peak quality. Don't let the soil dry out.

Fertilizing. Too much nitrogen can result in luxuriant tops but poor root development. For best root growth, fertilize every three to four weeks with a low-nitrogen, organic fertilizer, high in phosphorus and potassium.

HARVESTING

Beets taste best when harvested at about 1½ to 2½ inches (3.8 to 6.3 cm) in diameter. As the roots grow larger, they lose flavor and develop an unappetizing texture. To harvest, pull or dig the roots and remove the tops. Some people cut the greens from the roots, but this can cause bleeding, which reduces the moisture content in the root. To minimize such bleeding, grasp the root in one

◀ **Sweet beets go deep.** Pulled from a deeply dug, sandy soil, this young beet boasts a tap root of 1 foot (30 cm). Its fine root hairs probed even farther into the soil all around.

hand, the greens in the other, and twist off the tops. Place in plastic vegetable bags and refrigerate or store in damp sand in the root cellar.

BEST VARIETIES

Miniature beets. Kleine Bol (Little Ball), Gladiator, Spinel, Pablo

Specialty beets. Chioggia, Forono, Cyndor, Golden Beet

Main-crop beets. Red Ace, Scarlet Supreme, Detroit Dark Red

An Exception to Every Rule

Although in general beets grow best in cool weather, an extended cold snap (two or more weeks below 50°F; 10°C) that occurs after beet plants have formed a tidy rosette of leaves can force them to bolt, which ruins the quality of the roots. If a long cool period is expected, place a floating row cover over plants to keep daytime temperatures above 50°F (10°C).

Broccoli

You either love it or you don't. But lately, even people who don't love broccoli have found a good reason to like it. Recent research has shown that broccoli contains large amounts of sulforaphane, a compound that can prevent some types of cancer. And the good aspects of broccoli don't stop there. It also contains antioxidants that help protect the body from some other diseases.

THE SITE

Broccoli is a heavy user of nitrogen, so choose a spot where autumn leaves were added the previous fall. Don't start broccoli too early. Large or rootbound transplants may produce a tiny broccoli head, or "button." Discard these plants; they will not produce well. Long exposure to cold weather can also produce buttoning.

▲ **Hale and hearty.** Broccoli is delicious and versatile, with health benefits as well.

SOWING

Sow broccoli seeds about four to six weeks before the last spring frost. Seeds will germinate in about six days at 75°F (24°C). Once plants show true leaves, fertilize with an organic fertilizer such

Sow & Grow

BROCCOLI
(*Brassica oleracea*) Italica Group, (*B. rapa*)
  Ruvo Group
Cabbage family (*Cruciferae*)

SOWING
Seed depth: ¼" (6 mm)
Germination soil temperature: 80°F (27°C)
Days to germination: 4–7
Sow indoors: 6–8 weeks before last frost
Sow outdoors: Early summer for fall crop

GROWING
pH range: 6.5–7.5
Growing soil temperature: 60–65°F (16–18°C)

Spacing in beds: 16" (40 cm), staggered pattern, 3 rows to a wide (36"; 0.9 m) bed
Watering: Moderate and even
Light: Full sun for best yield; tolerates partial shade
Nutrient requirements: N=moderate to high; P=high; K=high
Rotation considerations: Avoid following with cabbage family plants.
Good companions: Bush bean, beet, carrot, celery, chard, cucumber, dill, lettuce, mint, nasturtium, onion family, oregano, potato, rosemary, sage, spinach, tomato
Bad companions: Pole and snap beans, strawberry
Seed longevity: 3 years
Seeds per ounce: 8,000 (283 seeds per g)

as fish emulsion at half strength. For a second, or fall, crop, you can direct-seed in late spring in cool regions and summer in warm areas.

GROWING

Broccoli transplants well, but be careful not to disturb the roots. Transplant when seedlings are about 3 inches (7.5 cm) tall, and set plants 1 inch (2.5 cm) deeper than they grew in the pots. Plant in a staggered pattern 16 inches (40 cm) apart, with 12 inches (30 cm) between rows. Three rows can fit in a 36-inch-wide (0.9 m) bed. The plants grow best when the soil pH is between 6.5 and 7.5.

Fertilizing. Fertilize every three to four weeks with an organic fertilizer such as fish emulsion. Broccoli, like all cabbage family relatives, needs significant amounts of boron, which tends to be deficient in very acid and alkaline soils and in soils with a low percentage of organic matter.

Broccoli-Raab

Broccoli-raab and broccoli are related, but you wouldn't confuse the two if you saw them side by side. While broccoli looks like, well, broccoli, broccoli-raab has thin, leafy shoots topped by small, loose clusters of buds. To grow broccoli-raab, sow indoors as for broccoli, or sow directly in the garden a week or two after peas are sown. Grow as broccoli until the shoots begin to sprout from the crown of the plant. When the shoots are about 12 inches (30 cm) tall, harvest the buds and the few leaves just below the bud. The flavor of broccoli-raab is sharper than broccoli and is excellent when mixed with other vegetables. It can be tamed a bit by boiling in one change of water.

HARVESTING

Harvest when the head is dark green and fully formed; the buds should also be tight. Any hint of yellow color in the buds is a sign the head is over-ripe. Harvest by cutting the head free of the stalk with a knife. More, smaller heads will soon form as side shoots. Harvest these every few days to keep more forming. Some varieties, such as Early Packman, Saga, Mariner Hybrid, and Premium Crop, produce abundant side shoots.

▲ **Cut-and-come-again broccoli.** After the main head has been harvested (A), broccoli continues to produce side shoots (B) for several more weeks.

BEST VARIETIES

Broccoli varieties can be divided into a few handy groups: those that do best planted early in the season, those that will produce during summer, and those planted in summer for harvest in fall or early winter.

Spring or early broccoli varieties. Early Dividend, Early Emerald, and Early Packman

Summer varieties. Genji, Mariner, Saga, and Small Miracle

Fall or winter varieties. Arcadia, Marathon, Pirate, and Saga

Brussels Sprouts

If you grow Brussels sprouts, you'll be eating from the garden after most of the harvest is only a memory. Brussels sprouts are one of the hardiest vegetables in the garden. Not only do they survive fall frosts and light snowfalls, but the cold actually makes them taste better. This is one of the few vegetables that give cool-region gardeners an edge over their warm-region counterparts.

THE SITE

Brussels sprouts are tall plants reaching from 2 to 3 feet (0.6 to 0.9 m), with thick stems and heavy bud production. Their root system, however, is close to the soil surface and, though dense, not very far reaching. These qualities mean Brussels sprouts require a rich, fertile soil and even moisture to grow their best.

▲ **Topping off.** About a month before you expect a hard freeze, top the plant by pinching out the growing tip. This directs all the plant's energy into maturing the remaining sprouts.

Sow & Grow

BRUSSELS SPROUTS
(Brassica oleracea) Gemmifera Group
Cabbage family *(Cruciferae)*

SOWING

Seed depth: ¼" (6 mm)
Germination soil temperature: 75–80°F (24–27°C)
Days to germination: 5–8
Sow indoors: 4–6 weeks before last frost
Sow outdoors: Early summer for fall crop (warm regions)

GROWING

pH range: 6.0–6.8
Growing soil temperature: 60–65°F (16–18°C)

Spacing in beds: 16–18" (40–45 cm), depending on type; staggered pattern, 3 rows to a wide bed (36"; 0.9 m)
Watering: Moderate and even
Light: Full sun for best yield; tolerates light shade
Nutrient requirements: N=moderate; P=high; K=high
Rotation considerations: Avoid following cabbage family plants.
Good companions: Bush bean, beet, carrot, celery, cucumber, lettuce, nasturtium, onion family, pea, potato, radish, spinach, tomato
Bad companions: Kohlrabi, pole bean, strawberry
Seed longevity: 4 years
Seeds per ounce: 8,500 (283 seeds per g)

Prepare the bed in fall by working in plenty of compost or well-rotted manure and autumn leaves. In spring, test the soil for nutrients and to be sure the pH is between 6.0 and 6.8. Brussels sprouts, like all cabbage family members, need significant amounts of boron. This micronutrient tends to be deficient in very acid soils, as well as in slightly alkaline soils and those with a low percentage of organic matter. If preparing the bed in spring, fork the soil well, add a layer of compost, and turn the soil again, lightly.

SOWING

Even the shortest-season Brussels sprouts take a long time to grow (about 100 days), so start the plants indoors or in a cold frame about a month before the last frost date. Seeds will germinate in about a week at 75 to 80°F (24 to 27°C). Transplant when seedlings are from four to six weeks old. If your growing season is about four months long, Brussels sprouts can be direct-sown.

In warm regions, such as the U.S. Gulf Coast, direct-sow from mid-October to Christmas for harvest in spring. Sprouts grown in warm regions are often more open and less flavorful than those grown in cool areas.

GROWING

Brussels sprouts grow best in cool, evenly moist soil. Apply an organic mulch, such as straw, to moderate soil temperature during the warm months. Maintain a layer of compost on the bed under the mulch to supply nutrients and encourage the activity of worms. In areas exposed to persistent winds, plants may need staking. Insert stakes when transplants are planted to avoid damaging the roots of established plants.

Fertilizing. Fertilize every three to four weeks from transplanting to late summer with an organic fertilizer such as fish emulsion. If your soil is rich, supplemental fertilizing may not be needed.

▲ **Losing your marbles?** Get an early start on your Brussels sprouts harvest by picking the first, marble-sized buds that form at the bottom of the plant. You'll be able to continue to harvest this vegetable long after the rest of the garden has been put away.

HARVESTING

Although the buds improve in flavor after a frost or two, harvest whenever some buds are firm, between "aggies" and "shooter" marbles in size (½ to 1 inch; 13 to 25 mm). Break off the leaf stem below the bud and either snap off or cut the bud.

If there are still sprouts left when night temperatures are near 25°F (–4°C), cut the whole plant, strip the leaves, and hang it in the root cellar; the sprouts will be good for another three weeks.

BEST VARIETIES

Dwarf types, such as Jade Cross E and Oliver, produce harvests in less than 100 days. These varieties are excellent for cool regions where the growing season is short, as well as for very warm areas where the duration of cool weather is only a few months.

Tall varieties, such as Trafalgar and Valiant, usually take from 100 to 130 days to mature and are popular in Europe and more temperate areas of North America.

CABBAGE • CABBAGE • CABBAGE • C

Cabbage

Tradition holds that babies come from the cabbage patch. I know of no one who has actually found this to be true, but it is easy to understand how the belief got started. Cabbage isn't hard to grow, but it does need the right sort of attention to turn out right. Do this and, just as kids add joy to life, the cabbage patch will be one of the nicest, most rewarding parts of your garden.

THE SITE

Cabbage prefers a rich, fertile soil with a pH of 6.0 to 7.5, with the optimum about 6.5. It does best in full sun, especially in cool regions and other areas with short growing seasons. In warmer climates, cabbage tolerates light midday shade.

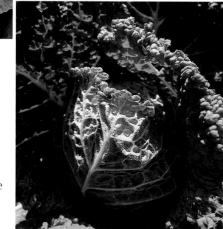

▲ **C is for Cabbage.** Cabbage is easy to grow and delicious to eat either fresh or cooked. An excellent source of vitamin C, it's useful in dishes from many ethnic traditions. Here, we have a solid head (top) and a Savoy (bottom).

Sow & Grow

CABBAGE
(Brassica oleracea) Capitata Group
Cabbage family *(Cruciferae)*

SOWING

Seed depth: ¼" (6 mm)
Germination soil temperature: 75–85°F (24–29°C)
Days to germination: 5
Sow indoors: 4–6 weeks before last frost
Sow outdoors: 10–12 weeks before first frost for fall crop

GROWING

pH range: 6.0–7.5 (7.2–7.5 to inhibit club root)
Growing soil temperature: 60–65°F (16–18°C)

Spacing in beds: *Early varieties,* 12" (30 cm); *late varieties,* 18" (45 cm)
Watering: Heavy from planting to head formation, then moderate
Light: Full sun for best yield; tolerates light shade
Nutrient requirements: N=high; P=high; K=high
Rotation considerations: Avoid following cabbage family plants.
Good companions: Bush bean, beet, carrot, celery, cucumber, dill, lettuce, mint, nasturtium, onion family, potato, rosemary, sage, spinach, thyme
Bad companions: Pole bean, strawberry, tomato
Seed longevity: 4 years
Seeds per ounce: 7,500 (250 seeds per g)

198 VEGETABLES & HERBS, A–Z

SOWING

Sow cabbage seeds for early crops in flats in early to midspring; sow late varieties in midspring. Once seedlings emerge, lower temperatures to about 60°F (16°C). When the plants have a few true leaves, transplant directly from the starting flat to a 3-inch (7.5 cm) pot. Transplant early-maturing varieties in early to midspring, spacing plants 12 inches (30 cm) apart; transplant fall varieties in early summer, spaced 18 inches (45 cm) apart. Be careful not to disturb of the rootball.

You can also direct-sow both early- and late-season cabbage, eliminating the possiblity of damaging the roots during transplanting. If you use this option, make sure that weeds don't crowd the seedlings, and use floating row covers to discourage flea beetles.

GROWING

Fertilizing. All cabbages are heavy feeders and need ample, even supplies of most nutrients, including nitrogen, potassium, phosphorus, and boron. Follow a nitrogen-fixing green-manure crop such as alfalfa. Best added to the soil in fall or late winter, wood ashes are a good source of potassium and also help raise soil pH.

Mulching. Cabbage has a shallow, dense root system, with many feeder roots very close to the surface. The roots are easily damaged by everything from cultivation to fluctuations in soil moisture to high soil temperatures. A simple way to ensure a stress-free cabbage patch is to mulch. Mulches, including straw or salt hay and "living mulch" (the shade provided by other crops, such as lettuce), reduce weeding as well as moderate soil temperature and moisture fluctuations.

No More Splits

Cabbages have a tendency to split and bolt. In general, any stress that disrupts growth after head formation can cause a head to split. These stresses include fluctuations in soil moisture and heads that have grown too large. There are a couple of ways to slow growth and thus prevent splitting:

▶ Wait until just after the heads firm up, and then twist the plants to break some roots (A).

▶ Plunge the blade of a spade into the soil on one side of the plant (B).

▶ Space the plants more closely together. For early varieties, space plants 8 to 12 inches (20 to 30 cm) apart; space late types 12 to 16 inches (30 to 40 cm) apart. Heads will be smaller, but they will also have better flavor be less likely to split.

▶ Plant a variety that is more resistant to splitting than others. Some good choices include Primax, Columbia, Dynamo, and Super Red 80.

Weeding. Early competition from weeds slows growth, particularly of direct-seeded plants, but cabbage roots are easily damaged by cultivation, so use your hoe carefully or weed by hand. In fact, if a weed is big enough or close enough to the cabbage plant to cause damage when pulled, clip the weed with scissors. Avoid hoeing or working in the cabbage patch early in the morning, when leaves are full of moisture and brittle. Once heads begin to form, put the hoe away and do any weeding by hand.

HARVESTING AND STORING

Early cabbage. Early varieties do not store well and should be harvested for use anytime after the head reaches the size of a softball. The heads can grow larger, but they are most tender and tasty at this early stage, and the plant will often produce another head or heads, with the total harvest adding up to more than a single mature head would yield.

Late cabbage. Rather than cutting late crops grown for storage, pull them from the ground, roots and all. Remove the large leaves and all but a few wrapper leaves. Take care not to bruise the heads, as this will shorten their storage life. Late-season cabbage can tolerate some frosty nights before harvest. You have several different options for storing late cabbage:

▶ Cut off the roots and any loose or damaged leaves and place on shelves in the root cellar.

▶ Prepare as above and wrap in newspaper; store as above.

▶ Hang by the roots in the root cellar.

▶ Leave the roots on and lean the plants against the root cellar wall, covering the roots with damp sand. If you use this method, you'll receive a little bonus when you get around to using the cabbage. After you have cut the head from the root, plant the root in a pot filled with damp sand and put it in a sunny window. You'll soon be harvesting small cabbage leaves for salads, right in the middle of winter.

In general, green cabbage doesn't store as well as red varieties. Scanbo is a nice exception to this rule. Until we discovered Scanbo, our green cabbages never kept as well as the reds. Now it's a toss-up. I can't report on the storage quality of savoy cabbages: We love the taste so much in late-fall salads that the savoys are always gone before we can compare storage times.

BEST VARIETIES

Early-Season Green. *Dynamo* is disease and split resistant and is an All-America winner. *Tender-sweet* is disease and split resistant, with a sweet flavor to boot.

Late-Season Green. *Storage No. 4* and *Scanbo* are disease resistant and store well.

Red. *Rona* is insect and disease tolerant, stores well, and has a mild flavor. *Super Red 80* is split resistant, with an excellent flavor.

Savoy. *Savoy King* has nice flavor, is split resistant, and is an All-America winner. *Wirosa* is a high-quality long-season cabbage that stores well.

Two Heads Are Better than One

To extend your early-cabbage harvest, try making one plant produce more than one head. When a cabbage head is ready to harvest, carefully cut it from the stalk just below the head, leaving a stump. Cut a cross pattern into the stalk, making the slice about ¼ inch (6 mm) deep. In a little while, up to four small heads will begin to appear. Harvest when the heads are about the size of baseballs.

Carrots

If you are just now making the transition to deeply worked, raised garden beds, use the first of your beds for carrots. The differences in size, shape, flavor, and yield per square foot between row-crop and wide, raised, deep bed-crop carrots are — putting it mildly — dramatic. Like the carrot on the stick that keeps the horse walking forward, the beautiful carrots you pull from your first raised bed will encourage you to grow all your vegetables this way.

THE SITE

Prepare and enrich the bed in fall by forking in a layer of fallen leaves. If you're preparing the bed in spring, mix in a generous amount of compost a few weeks before seeding. Rake and smooth the bed carefully.

▲ **A 24-karat vegetable.** When carrots are stored, they often lose their moisture and sweetness. What better reason to grow your own? Once you've experienced the pleasure of pulling those slender beauties from the earth, you're sure to be hooked on homegrown carrots.

Sow & Grow

CARROTS
(Daucus carota var. *sativus)*
Carrot family *(Umbelliferae)*

SOWING
Seed depth: ¼–½" (6–13 mm)
Germination soil temperature: 75°F (24°C)
Days to germination: 6
Sow indoors: Not recommended
Sow outdoors: Early spring to midsummer

GROWING
pH range: 5.5–6.5, but best above 6.0
Growing soil temperature: 60–70°F (16–21°C)

Spacing in beds: 2" (5 cm) apart in rows 6–8" (15–20 cm) apart, 3 rows to a 30" (0.75 m) bed, 4 rows to a 36" (0.9 m) bed
Watering: Moderate
Light: Full sun for best yield; tolerates light shade
Nutrient requirements: N=high; P=low; K=low
Rotation considerations: Avoid rotating with celery, dill, fennel, parsley, parsnip.
Good companions: Bean, Brussels sprout, cabbage, chive, leaf lettuce, leek, onion, pea, pepper, red radish, rosemary, sage, tomato
Bad companions: Celery, dill, parsnip
Seed longevity: 3 years
Seeds per ounce: 22,000 (733 seeds per g)

SOWING

Carrots can germinate in a week with a soil temperature at about 75°F (24°C). The colder the soil temperature, the longer the germination period. If it gets much below 45°F (7°C), germination may not happen at all. Plan to sow carrots about the time you sow pole beans or tomatoes.

Carrot seeds are tiny and devilishly hard to space evenly. Over the years gardeners have come up with a number of solutions to this problem. I've tried many of them but wasn't really happy with results. The easiest way to sow carrots is to broadcast them over the bed. This method takes only seconds to accomplish but the eventual thinning of seedlings can take hours. I've tried mixing the seeds with dry coffee grounds or vermiculite before sowing. That was an improvement, but I still found the spacing somewhat irregular. Pelleted seeds are easy to handle and space but add another layer of material the germinating seeds must push through before reaching daylight. Seed tapes look like a convenient idea but are too expensive for my liking. After experimenting with many ways to sow carrot seed, I've resorted to patiently sowing them one or two at a time as shown in the photo below.

One for Now, One for Later

Plant a quick-maturing variety for summer eating as soon as you like, but postpone the winter storage crop until the soil warms up, about the time you plant tomatoes.

GROWING

No matter how carefully I space the seeds, carrots always seem to need some thinning. Carrots can grow very close together and still produce excellent crops, but if they grow too close together they'll be stunted, excessively slender, or deformed.

Carrots prefer their roots to be cool and their tops to be warm. When the soil temperature rises above 70°F (21°C) carrots will be small and bland tasting. To give carrots the growing conditions they like, add a layer of organic mulch, like grass clippings, around the plants to moderate the soil temperature when the warmer days of late spring and summer arrive. Repeat as needed throughout the growing season. In addition to using mulch, grow a leafy companion crop, such as Swiss chard, which will help shade and cool the soil.

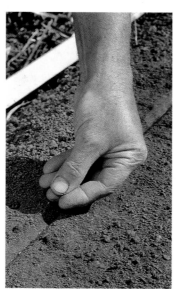

◄ **Practice makes perfect.** With a little practice, you can sow the seeds ½ inch (13 mm) apart by rolling them, a half dozen or so at a time, between your thumb and first finger, so that one (or sometimes two) emerges at a time.

◄ **Easy does it.** Thinning carrots, like sowing them, is best accomplished on days when patience can rule your actions. Thin with floral shears to no less than 2 inches (5 cm) between plants.

HARVESTING AND STORING

In loose soil, carrots can be gathered by pulling them from the ground by their tops. If the tops break off when you pull the plants, preloosen the soil carefully with a garden fork or broadfork. Clip the foliage about an inch (2.5 cm) from the root. Cull any damaged or misshapen roots; they won't store well and should be refrigerated for immediate use. Layer storage carrots in damp sand or sawdust in a bin, box, or plastic pail in the root cellar.

BEST VARIETIES

Nantes. A longtime favorite of home gardeners, these sweet, crisp, full-flavored carrots are easily recognized by their cylindrical, sausage shape and blunt tip. Some excellent Nantes varieties include Bolero, Napoli, Sweetness II, Nelson, Mokum, and Scarlet Nantes.

Imperator. This is the long, tapering supermarket carrot. Easy to harvest and ship (which means little to gardeners), Imperators have less overall flavor and crispness than many other types. Some of the best varieties in this group, including Nevis and Artist, are actually hybrids with Nantes types.

Baby or Mini. These tasty, small carrots with a range of shapes are best used fresh. This type is a bit of a catch-all category, since, if it's little, it can go here. Some popular varieties include Thumbelina, Minicore, Amsdor, and Parmex.

Chantenay. All-purpose carrots with a broad shoulder, stocky build, and blunt tip, Chantenays keep their shape better in stony or heavy soils than other carrots. Some varieties include Chantenay Red-Cored, Chantenay Royal, and Chantenay Imperial.

Danvers. These good all-around carrots are similar in shape to Chantenay, but longer. Their flavor is good, but lacks the sweetness of Nantes. Some good varieties include Danvers Red-Cored and Danvers Half-Long.

▲ **Long life.** Carrots store best if you cut off the greens, leaving about 1 inch (2.5 cm) of stem.

▲ **Hidden treasure.** Carrots grown in deeply dug beds will be larger, more shapely, and more flavorful than you can imagine.

Give Your Carrots Some Friends

Because of their small size, carrot seeds produce tiny seedlings that do not have the strength to push through crusted soil. Help them out by:

▶ **Interplanting them with radishes.** The radishes will emerge first and break up crusted surface soil.

▶ **Keeping the soil moist throughout the germination period.** This keeps the soil from crusting.

Cauliflower

Cauliflower has long had a reputation for being a vegetable prima donna. It is the easiest of the cabbage family vegetables to stress, and when it stresses, it acts like a two year old and bolts. Cauliflower can be set back by cool temperatures in spring, hot weather in summer, or dry conditions at any time. And to top everything off, of the cabbage family, it's the most sensitive to frost. Altogether, cauliflower could be called the black sheep of the cabbage family, but we still love it.

▲ **Flower power.** Harvested at its prime, cauliflower has a sweet, nutty flavor, delicious raw or lightly steamed.

THE SITE

Cauliflower requires a pH of at least 6.5, but it grows best and is most likely to be free of root diseases in a nearly neutral or slightly sweet soil (6.8–7.2).

SOWING

Start plants indoors where you can provide a germination temperature of 70°F (21°C) or more and early growth temperatures of at least 60°F (16°C). Start in flats a month before the last frost date so the seedlings will be no more than four to

Sow & Grow

CAULIFLOWER
(Brassica oleracea) Botrytis group
Cabbage family *(Cruciferae)*

SOWING
Seed depth: ¼–½" (6–13 mm)
Germination Soil temperature: 80°F (27°C)
Days to germination: 6
Sow indoors: 4–6 weeks before last frost
Sow outdoors: From last frost to late spring

GROWING
pH range: 6.5–7.5
Growing Soil temperature: 60–70°F (16–21°C)

Spacing in beds: 15" (37.5 cm) staggered pattern, 3 rows to a bed
Watering: Moderate and even
Light: Best yields in full sun; tolerates light shade
Nutrient requirements: N=high; P=high; K=high
Rotation considerations: Precede with nitrogen-fixing cover crop; avoid following cabbage family crops.
Good companions: Bush bean, beet, carrot, celery, cucumber, dill, lettuce, mint, nasturtium, onion family, pea, potato, rosemary, sage, spinach
Bad companions: Pole bean, strawberry
Seed longevity: 4 years
Seeds per ounce: 8,500 (300 per gram)

Don't Jump the Gun with Seeding Cauliflower

Time your sowing so that plants are no older than five weeks when it's safe to put them in the garden. Transplants older than this are too easily stressed by transplant shock. Older plants may also "check," which means they become root-bound and stop growing. These plants often produce only "buttons," little heads that never grow to be big heads.

five weeks old when they go into the garden. Move the seedlings from flats to 2-inch (5 cm) growing cells as soon as they can be handled. Moderate but even moisture is critical at this time.

You can direct-sow seeds in midspring for early crops or in early summer for fall crops.

GROWING

Transplant four-week-old seedlings to the garden in spring about the time of the last frost after hardening outdoors for at least a week. Transplant carefully, being sure not to damage roots.

Watering and fertilizing. Keep plants evenly watered throughout the entire growing period. Cauliflower is a heavy feeder and likes frequent waterings with compost tea or dilute solutions of fish emulsion or kelp fertilizers.

Blanching. Blanching, a technique used for white varieties, limits the amount of light that contacts the developing head. The result is cauliflower with a nice, white color, improved flavor, and none of the unappealing ricey texture that sometimes develops during hot weather. Even self-blanching varieties have the best flavor and color if blanched. It's time to blanch when the head is about 2 or 3 inches (5–7.5 cm) wide. Fold some of the leaves over the head and secure them together at the top with rubber bands or twine.

HARVESTING AND STORING

After tying leaves for blanching, check heads daily for maturity. In warm weather, harvest heads about four days after tying; in cool weather, harvest in about ten days. Don't wait longer than these recommended times to harvest, as the head may rot.

Cauliflower is ready for harvest when the head is tight and fairly regular, and the curd has not begun to separate, a condition called riciness. Purple types have a more irregular head and should be harvested when the curd looks like a tight bunch of broccoli.

You can store cauliflower in the root cellar or the refrigerator for about a month, but it tastes much better if used soon after harvest.

BEST VARIETIES

Cauliflower is sensitive to cold and hot weather. To minimize these eccentricities, horticulturists have developed varieties that are both cold and heat tolerant and are more likely to give beginner as well as expert gardeners the uniform, delicious crops they desire.

Early Dawn, Andes, Snow Crown, and **Fremont** are all varieties with both cold and heat tolerance.

A Rainbow of Cauliflower

Once upon a time, bedroom sheets, tennis court attire, and cauliflower were always white. No more. Today we have designer sheets, neon tennis clothes, *and* colorful cauliflower. You'll find the heads now come in orange, purple, and green.

Orange types, such as Orange Bouquet, get their color from increased carotene content, making these varieties high in vitamin A.

Purple types, such as Violet Queen, have heads that both look and taste a little like cauliflower and a little like broccoli.

Green cauliflower, such as Alverda, is another cauliflower-broccoli variety with distinctive cone-shaped heads and a rich flavor.

Celery

Thoreau once said that if someone doesn't keep pace with his companions, perhaps he hears a different drummer. After growing celery for some years, I think celery walks to the beat of a very different drummer. It has the reputation of being fussy, but it isn't really. It's just different. And once you take account of the differences, it's not difficult to grow and still a pleasure to eat.

SOWING

Start celery indoors at least eight weeks before the last frost date. Sow seeds on a potting mixture rich with organic matter and lightly cover with washed sand or potting mix. It's important to remember that celery seeds need light to germinate, so don't cover seeds very deeply. Moisten, cover with clear plastic, and place in a warm area with indirect light. For best germination, keep temperatures between 65 and 75°F (18 and 24°C).

▲ **Celebrating celery.** It's easy to overlook this familiar vegetable, but as long as you give it fertile conditions, it will reward you with a crisp, sweet harvest for many months.

Germination may be erratic, but seedlings should begin to appear in about one week.

When the plants are up, remove the plastic cover and move the container into a warm, sunny place. Be sure to keep the soil moist. If the plants are not already in pots or growing cells, transplant when there are two true leaves.

Sow & Grow

CELERY
(Apium graveolens var. *dulce)*
Carrot family *(Umbelliferae)*

SOWING
Seed depth: Just cover
Germination soil temperature: 70°F (21°C)
Days to germination: 7
Sow indoors: 10 weeks before last frost
Sow outdoors: Not recommended

GROWING
pH range: 6.0–7.0
Growing soil temperature: 60–70°F (16–21°C)
Spacing in beds: 8" (20 cm), 3 rows to a bed
Watering: Heavy and even
Light: Best yields in full sun, tolerates light shade
Nutrient requirements: N=high; P=high; K=high
Rotation considerations: Avoid following lettuce or cabbage.
Good companions: Almost everything
Bad companions: Carrot, parsley, parsnip
Seed longevity: 3 years
Seeds per ounce: 76,000 (2,683 seeds per g)

GROWING

Plant outdoors only after day temperatures stay consistently above 55°F (13°C) and night temperatures above 40°F (4°C). Pre-warm the soil with plastic mulch for a week before planting, and cover plants with floating row covers for about a month after planting.

Fertilizing. The key to growing good celery is organic matter. Celery has a small root system and grows best in soil rich in organic matter. Before planting, add plenty of compost or rotted manure to the bed. Add some compost to the planting hole when transplanting, and sidedress with fish emulsion during the growing season.

Weeding and watering. Because the roots are very near the surface, keep the patch weeded, but do not cultivate deeply. Check soil moisture regularly and water as needed, but don't let the bed get soggy.

HARVESTING AND STORING

Begin harvesting stalks from the outside of the plants whenever they are big enough to suit you. You can harvest whole plants by cutting them at the soil line. Gather plants when you want to; even small ones taste good. Celery can survive light frost if covered.

For best flavor and longest storage, water plants the day before harvest. Celery will keep in the refrigerator for a couple of weeks or longer in the root cellar.

BEST VARIETIES

Utah 52-70 is disease tolerant and produces reliable crops of sturdy, flavorful stalks. Blanching improves flavor.

Ventura is an early, disease-tolerant variety with an upright habit, strong stalks, and a tender, sweet heart.

Celeriac: A Celery Relative

Celeriac (*Apium graveolens* var. *rapaceum*) is a close relative of celery, though not as fussy, and grown for its roots rather than its stalks. Grow it following the same procedures as you do for celery. Harvest after the first few light frosts in fall.

To harvest, loosen the soil around each plant with a garden fork and lift the plant free. Cut the tops an inch or two (2.5–5 cm) above the root and store in the root cellar.

During the winter, plant a celeriac root in a large clay pot in damp sand. Place it in a sunny window at room temperature and keep the sand moist. In a little while you'll have small celerylike stalks and greens for fresh winter salad.

Spring Celery Bonus

Before the first hard frost in fall, I dig a half-dozen plants, replant them in sap buckets or large plastic buckets (in either case, be sure to provide drainage holes). I place them in the root cellar and water them whenever they begin to droop. We enjoy crisp, tasty celery all winter long and into the spring.

Chinese Cabbage

This Asian cousin of domestic cabbages combines a mild cabbage flavor with the look and texture of romaine lettuce. Open-head types have a loose, lettucy look, while closed-head, or Napa, types have outer leaves that wrap over the top of the slightly tighter head. Whatever shape your Chinese cabbage takes, all types taste good, with a mild, slightly pungent, spicy flavor.

SOWING

In warm regions, sow two seeds each in 4-inch (10 cm) pots in late winter; in cooler areas, sow seeds in midspring. After seedlings emerge, thin with floral shears to one plant per pot. I like to thin after the first true leaves appear to be sure the seedling I choose is the stronger of the two.

▲ **This beauty's more than skin deep.** As frivolous as this vegetable may appear, it's both easy to grow and versatile in the kitchen.

Summer crops. Set plants in the garden about four weeks after true leaves appear and night temperatures are consistently above 50°F (10°C). Don't be impatient and move this plant into the

Sow & Grow

CHINESE CABBAGE
(Brassica rapa) Pekinensis Group
Cabbage family *(Cruciferae)*

SOWING
Seed depth: ¼–½" (6–13 mm)
Germination soil temperature: 75–80°F (24–27°C)
Days to germination: 7
Sow indoors: 4–6 weeks before last frost
Sow outdoors: 10–12 weeks before first frost for fall crop

GROWING
pH range: 6.0–7.0
Growing soil temperature: 60–70°F (16–21°C)
Spacing in beds: 12–18" (30–45 cm), depending on type
Watering: Moderate and even
Light: Full sun
Nutrient requirements: N=high; P=high; K=high
Rotation considerations: Avoid rotating with cabbage family crops.
Good companions: Beet, lettuce, onion, radish, spinach
Bad companions: tomatoes
Seed longevity: 3 years
Seeds per ounce: 7,000 (233 seeds per g)

garden too early, as a week or more of nights when the temperature drops below 50°F (10°C) can trigger the plant to bolt a few weeks later. Chinese cabbage is sensitive to transplanting, so set plants in the garden very carefully so roots are not damaged.

Fall crops. Direct-seed about two months before the first frost. Open-head, lettucelike types are good for fall harvests. Plant as a successor crop to peas or early beans, which leave behind an extra shot of nitrogen in the soil.

GROWING

Like many plants in the cabbage family, Chinese cabbage has a delicate and fairly shallow root system that grows quite close to the surface. To grow the best Chinese cabbage, follow these guidelines:

General care. Water evenly from transplant to harvest, cultivate lightly and carefully, mulch during warm weather, and keep weeds under control, especially when the plants are young.

Fertilizing. Chinese cabbage can grow large and has a big appetite for soil nutrients, particularly nitrogen. Mix in plenty of compost at planting and fertilize every two weeks with fish emulsion.

BEST VARIETIES

For spring crops, it is very important to use a bolt-resistant variety such as **Blues, Kasumi,** or **Orient Express.**

Throw-Aways

Remove Chinese cabbage roots from the garden and discard them; don't compost. Chinese cabbage is subject to the same root diseases as the rest of the cabbage family.

HARVESTING

As with cabbage, Chinese cabbage can be harvested as soon as the plants are large enough to use. Cut the entire plant at the base and remove the outer, or wrapper, leaves. Freshly harvested heads of spring and fall crops will keep for about a week in the refrigerator.

Chinese cabbage keeps for several weeks in the root cellar, providing tender, tasty greens long after the garden has been put to bed for the year.

To store, wrap the cabbage in newspaper and place it on a shelf in the root cellar or other cool spot. Fall crops tend to store better than spring crops.

Pak Choi

After you taste this delightful Chinese vegetable, you'll know that pak choi spells stir-fry. Pak choi, a relative of Chinese cabbage, has a tidy rosette of upright gray-green leaves. The large, succulent leaf stems vary in color from snow white to creamy green. Try these varieties:

Joi Choi. About 12 to 18 inches (30 to 45 cm) tall with icy white leaf stems, Joi Choi tolerates cool weather and is slow to bolt.

Chinese Pak Choi. About 15 inches (37.5 cm) tall, this variety is very easy to grow and has excellent flavor. Its leaf stems are pale green and hold wide, thick, shiny leaves.

Mei Qing Choi. This dwarf, or baby, pak choi has pastel green leaves and pale greenish white leaf bases. It tolerates heat and cold well, is slow to bolt, and has an enchanting flavor.

Sweet Corn

A satisfying ear of sweet corn shouldn't taste like sugar — it should taste like sweet corn. It seems that every year the seed catalogs feature a new variety of sweet corn supposedly sweeter than last year's sweetest. I'm not a fan of supersweet corn. The main virtue of these varieties is commercial: Their sugar is slow to convert to starch after harvest, so they can mimic fresh sweet corn even after a long trip to the supermarket.

If there's not enough sweet in your homegrown sweet corn, the problem is more likely in how you're growing it rather than what you're growing. Provide your sweet corn with good growing conditions and you will be rewarded with corn that is both sweet and full flavored.

▲ **Summer rewards.** Sweet corn likes it sunny and hot with ample soil moisture and consistent fertilization. Given these things, corn will reward you with the vegetable that sings summer.

Sow & Grow

SWEET CORN
(Zea mays)
Grass family *(Poaceae)*

SOWING
Seed depth: 1" (2.5 cm)
Germination soil temperature: 80°F (27°C)
Days to germination: 4
Sow indoors: Not recommended
Sow outdoors: 1 week after last frost

GROWING
pH range: 6.0–7.0
Growing soil temperature: 65–75°F (18–24°C)

Spacing in beds: 8" (20 cm)
Watering: Moderate early; heavy from flowering to harvest
Light: Full sun
Nutrient requirements: N=high; P=high; K=high
Rotation considerations: Precede with a nitrogen-fixing crop.
Good companions: Bush bean, beet, cabbage, cantaloupe, cucumber, parsley, pea, early potato, pumpkin, squash
Bad companions: Tomato
Seed longevity: 1–2 years
Seeds per ounce: 150 (5 seeds per g)

THE SITE

Begin preparing the corn bed in fall. Apply at least an inch (2.5 cm) of compost or rotted manure and work it into the soil with a garden fork. To encourage worm activity, mulch the bed before a hard freeze.

SOWING

In spring, remove the mulch to let the soil begin heating, and apply some finished compost. Cover the corn beds with black or IRT plastic at least a week before sowing and monitor soil temperature with a soil thermometer.

Sow the seeds 1 inch (2.5 cm) deep and 8 inches (20 cm) apart, down the center of a 30-inch (75 cm) bed. To ensure good pollination, plant each variety in blocks of four short rows rather than a single long row. Sow new blocks every two weeks for successive harvests throughout the season.

After sowing, keep the soil moist and install a fabric floating row cover supported by hoops to maintain soil temperature and protect seedlings against frost. Remove the cover when night temperatures are consistently above 60°F (16°C).

GROWING

Corn is a heavy feeder — a really heavy feeder — particularly of nitrogen. Yet for a plant of its large size, corn does not have a very deep or extensive root system: A good blast of wind can flatten a corn plant. This means that corn needs deeply tilled, fertile soil with readily available nutrients. This allows the plant to produce roots that compensate in density for what they lack in range.

Like other plants with relatively shallow roots, corn is sensitive to fluctuations in soil moisture, which stress the plants. Regular and shallow (about 1½ inches; 3.8 cm) cultivation controls weeds while making nutrients available. Water regularly and fertilize every two weeks with a complete organic fertilizer, such as fish emulsion.

▲ **A moisture lifeline.** Drip irrigation laid between the rows of corn gets the right amount of moisture right to the roots.

▲ **Sunken treasure.** In dry areas, plant corn in groups of four, slightly below the level of the bed. The "bowl" that is created will collect every drop of precious water from rain or irrigation.

Keep Those Sweets Apart

If you grow any of the supersweet varieties, they must be isolated from normal sugary or sugar-enhanced types to prevent cross-pollination. You can do this either by keeping the plantings at least 25 feet (7.5 m) apart or by sowing the seeds of one at least 10 days after you sow the seeds of the other, so that they flower at different times.

HARVESTING

It's easy to know when to pick a tomato, but knowing when to harvest corn is a little trickier. The secret is to examine the silk at the top of the ear. A ripe ear of corn has a small amount of pliant, greenish silk near the top of the husk, with dry, brownish silk at the ends.

The time of day to pick is another concern, and it's one about which you'll hear different advice. Very soon after picking, the sugar in corn begins turning to starch. Some people like to pick their dinner corn a few minutes before it gets dropped into the cooking pot. These folks believe the faster an ear of corn moves from the garden to your plate, the sweeter it will taste. It makes sense. Yet corn actually has its highest sugar content in the early morning, not just before the evening meal. The old-timers I've known pick their corn early in the morning, before it's warmed by the sun, and refrigerate it in the husk until supper. I've tried both ways and come to the conclusion that the old-timers are right.

▲ **You break it, you buy it.** When it's nearly butter-and-corn-on-the-cob time, it's very tempting to open the husks when the ears are still on the stalk. But because the husk protects the corn, you should open it only when the pot is boiling and you're ready to cook. Instead of peeking, feel the husk to see if it seems full and rounded and look for greenish, pliant silk turned drier and brown at the very ends.

Fending Off Corn Thieves

Wildlife often pose more problems for corn growers than either insect pests or disease, and raccoons and birds cause the most difficulties. (For more ideas on pest control, see chapter 8.)

Raccoons. I have kept the raccoons out (so far!) with a two-strand electric fence, the lower strand at 5 inches (12.5 cm), the upper at about 12 inches (30 cm). Install the fence at least a week before the corn is ripe. The raccoons seem to consider corn ready to harvest about two days before I do.

Birds. Crows and other grain-eating birds can do a lot of damage to the corn patch. A favorite deterrent, the scarecrow, gets its name for good reason. If you use a scarecrow, dress it in light, flowing clothes that will move in the wind and decorate it with strips of aluminum foil. Another popular scare tactic is a big, brightly colored

balloon or beachball painted with large eye spots. Whichever you choose, be sure to change its location every few days, so the birds don't get used to it being in only one place.

Two strands of electric fence wire along a corn row is a good deterrent for raccoons.

BEST VARIETIES OF SWEET CORN

There are many excellent varieties of sweet corn. The trick to selecting the best ones is to bypass the supersweet hype and focus on flavor, ears per stalk, number of rows per ear and, one more time — flavor. Here are some best bets.

Double Gem is an early bicolor variety that combines great taste with high yield.

Sugar Snow is a variety from Colorado that yields large ears filled with sweet, snow-white kernels.

Seneca Arrowhead is a disease-tolerant early variety with excellent flavor.

Sundance is a vigorous variety, resistant to cold soil and birds, that yields very flavorful ears.

FIELD CORN

Field corn is a term that lumps dent, flint, and flour corn into one category. The names are unimaginative but accurate:

▶ **Dent corn** has a dent in each kernel when dry.
▶ **Flint corn** has rock-hard kernels.
▶ **Flour corn** makes the best-quality corn flour.

To harvest field corn, allow the husks to dry completely. Unlike most other corns, you can harvest field corn after a few frosts. Husk the ears and bring them to a cool, dry, well-ventilated space to finish drying. Store kernels on the cob or shuck them and store in covered glass containers.

POPCORN

Popcorn, as well as field corn and ornamental corn, has a higher starch content than sweet corn, but the growing requirements for all of these are the same as for sweet corn. The difference is in the harvesting.

Popcorn has been a part of the American diet for millennia. Native Americans have grown it for thousands of years, and the Pilgrims feasted on it hundreds of years before it became a movie theater staple. Yet many people's experience with popcorn is still limited to the snack aisle of the supermarket.

Popcorn comes in many varieties, from red and blue to white and yellow. Popcorn takes longer to mature than sweet corn, so choose a variety that has enough time to develop in a typical growing season in your area.

BEST VARIETIES OF POPCORN

Tom Thumb. A New England heirloom that is early, Tom Thumb has short stalks and bears yellow kernels.

Robust. This is gourmet-quality tender popcorn with golden yellow kernels.

Ruby Red. Burgundy red kernels are as decorative as they are tasty.

Shaman's Blue. Bluish red kernels are decorative.

Top Pop. Tall stalks have plentiful yellow kernels.

Popcorn that Really Pops

Successful popcorn growing means growing popcorn that pops. For a kernel to pop, it must have just the right amount of moisture inside it, and this is influenced by curing.

Harvest the ears before a hard frost, when the husks have dried and the kernels are plump, well colored, and shiny. Remove the husks and spread the ears out in a cool, well-ventilated space.

After they're cured for about a month, test-pop some kernels. If they pop nicely, remove the kernels from the cobs and store in dark glass containers. If they pop weakly, they still contain too much moisture. Continue curing, but test-pop every few days, because you don't want them to get *too* dry.

Cucumber

Cucumbers like to climb on things. They can't help themselves; it's in their nature. Breeders have tried to mute this by developing bush cucumbers, but even the caged bird sings. And inside every cucumber, whether bush type or vine, remains the desire to climb, and with good reason, as you'll soon find out if you grow them on a trellis. Trellis-grown cucumbers are straighter, more uniform in shape, and less likely to rot or be eaten by slugs or other pests. They are also less likely to become overripe because they've been overlooked. You don't have to grow cucumbers on a trellis, but you'll get more and better-quality fruits if you do, and you'll also use less garden space.

◀ **It's easy being green.** Cucumbers mature rapidly, and if you keep the vines picked, you'll be able to harvest them over a long season.

THE SITE

Although they're not as big as squash or pumpkins, cucumbers use a lot of soil nutrients just the same. You'll get higher yield and better-tasting fruits if you apply an inch (2.5 cm) of compost to the bed before planting and work it into the top few inches of soil.

Sow & Grow

CUCUMBER
(Cucumis sativus)
Cucumber family *(Cucurbitaceae)*

SOWING
Seed depth: ½–1" (13–25 mm)
Germination soil temperature: 80–95°F (27–35°C)
Days to germination: 3–4
Sow indoors: 3 weeks before last frost
Sow outdoors: After last frost

GROWING
pH range: 6.0–7.0
Growing soil temperature: 70–80°F (21–27°C)

Spacing in beds: *Trellised,* 18" (45 cm); *on ground,* 36" (90 cm)
Watering: Moderate until flowering; heavy from flowering to harvest
Light: Full sun
Nutrient requirements: N=moderate; P=high; K=high
Rotation considerations: Avoid rotating with other cucumber family members.
Good companions: Bush bean, broccoli, cabbage family, corn, dill, eggplant, lettuce, nasturtium, pea, radish, sunflower, tomato
Bad companions: Aromatic herbs, potato
Seed longevity: 5 years
Seeds per ounce: 1,000 (35 seeds per g)

SOWING

In cool regions, start the plants indoors rather than direct sowing. Cucumbers do not like to be transplanted, however, so handle them carefully when you put them into the ground. Sow three seeds to a 4-inch (10 cm) pot, three to four weeks before your transplant date. Keep the soil moist and temperatures above 70°F (21°C) during the day and 60°F (16°C) at night. When the first set of true leaves appears, thin to one plant per pot by cutting the extras with scissors. Transplant after danger of frost is past and the soil has warmed to about 70°F (21°C). Set out the plants on a cloudy day or in the evening, being very careful not to disturb the roots.

You can direct-seed cucumbers if the soil is at least 70°F (21°C) and promises to stay at least this warm during the germination period. Use row covers to keep the soil warm.

GROWING

This is a genuine warm-season crop, very sensitive to frost at both ends of the growing season and demanding warmth from germination to harvest. But cucumbers also mature quickly, so they don't need a lot of care.

Fertilize with a complete organic fertilizer, such as fish emulsion, every two weeks. Once flowers appear it is very important to maintain even soil moisture, or misshapen, poor-tasting fruits will result.

With guidance, cucumber vines climb pea netting on the same trellis used for other vertical garden crops (see pages 72–73). You can also construct an A-frame trellis like that at the right, and cover it with netting or chicken wire to support the cukes.

HARVESTING AND STORING

You can harvest cucumbers whenever they are large enough to use, and most gardeners find smaller fruits more flavorful than big ones. Check

Bitter Medicine

If cucumber beetles afflict your crops, grow bitter-free varieties. Cucumber plants produce a bitter compound in their skins that actually attracts cucumber beetles. Bitterless varieties, such as Aria, Jazzer, Holland, and Lemon, are less attractive to the insects. Not only that, they produce delicious fruits as well.

▲ **Growing up.** You'll get cleaner, straighter cucumbers if you support them on a trellis, like this A-frame support.

◀ **Bigger isn't better.** The two fruits on the right are much tastier, crisper, and less seedy than the overmature one on the left.

the vines daily, as the fruits grow quickly. Be sure to harvest when the cucumber is still dark green all over. A yellowing at the blossom end indicates an overripe fruit that is past its prime.

Although you can store cucumbers in the refrigerator for a week or more, they're best eaten fresh.

Eggplant

For northern gardeners, eggplant is a fussy, fussy plant. We like it once it's on the dinner plate, but in the garden it can drive you batty. Most of the gardeners in my neck of the woods have given up trying to grow it — though some just go on trying through sheer cussedness. If you garden in warm climates, you no doubt know what makes this plant happy. Eggplant's most pressing need is for warmth, and the weather must remain warm throughout the plant's growth cycle. If you live in a climate with hot summers, the plant is more forgiving than in regions with short, cool growing seasons. In cooler regions, you'll have to resort to some tricks in order to have success.

▲ **Putting your eggs in one basket.** Eggplants come in a surprising variety of sizes, shapes, and colors, from tiny-fruited kinds the size of a hen's egg, to large pear-shaped kinds, to skinny cucumberlike varieties. All eggplants have a similar flavor, though some are milder than others.

Sow & Grow

EGGPLANT
(Solanum melongena)
Tomato family *(Solanaceae)*

SOWING
Seed depth: ¼" (6 mm)
Germination soil temperature: 85°F (29°C)
Days to germination: 7
Sow indoors: 4–6 weeks before last frost
Sow outdoors: Not recommended

GROWING
pH range: 5.5–7.0
Growing soil temperature: 80–90°F (27–32°C)
Spacing in beds: 18" (45 cm) staggered pattern
Watering: Heavy
Light: Full sun
Nutrient requirements: N=moderate; P=high; K=high
Rotation considerations: Follow beans or peas.
Good companions: Bush bean, pea, pepper, potato
Bad companions: Fennel
Seed longevity: 4 years
Seeds per ounce: 7,000 (247 seeds per g)

SOWING

Start eggplant indoors eight weeks before your transplanting date. You'll want to time transplanting for when you can count on the following conditions: soil temperature of at least 70°F (21°C); daytime air temperature consistently above 70°F; night air temperature not below 60°F (16°C).

Eggplant is very sensitive to transplant shock, so instead of sowing seed in flats, start the plants in 4-inch (10 cm) pots right away, two or three seeds to a pot. Germinate with bottom heat and try to maintain a soil temperature of at least 80°F (27°C) until the seedlings emerge and 70°F (21°C) thereafter. Thin to one plant per pot by cutting the extras with scissors. Brush the plants gently with your hand twice a day to promote stocky growth and hefty stems. Grow under lights if you have them. As the plants grow indoors, prepare their outdoor planting bed by warming it with plastic mulch.

Harden the seedlings for a week before transplanting by decreasing the air temperature to 60°F (16°C) and cutting back on water. Outdoors, cut slits in the plastic mulch and transplant carefully to avoid root damage.

GROWING

Once the plants are in the garden, use floating row covers along with the mulch (see chapter 4), both to provide steady heat and to protect the plants from insect damage. Aside from its need for heat, the other challenge in producing a good crop of eggplant is bugs. Insects love eggplant. If there is only one Colorado potato beetle in your garden, it won't be on a potato plant, it will be on an eggplant. And so will flea beetles, aphids, tomato hornworms, and many others. The good news is that unlike many plants, eggplant can be grown beneath row covers from transplant to harvest.

About a month before the first frost, snip off any remaining blossoms to encourage the existing fruits to ripen.

HARVESTING AND STORING

Harvest plants anytime after they've reached half their mature size. Not only are early-harvested plants more tender, but you'll get a bigger total yield because keeping the plants picked stimulates further production. Cut the fruits from the plants with shears, leaving some stem attached. Eat soon; eggplant doesn't store well.

BEST VARIETIES

Diva. A traditional purple eggplant, Diva has thin skin and a mild flavor.

Asian Bride. Long, skinny, and pale white, like other Asian types, this variety has a subtle flavor and an unusually creamy texture.

Kermit. Small green and white fruits the size of a hen's egg are typical of Kermit's eggplant.

Machiaw. This eggplant looks like a blushing cucumber, with long, thin fruit brushed with rosy purple skin. It tastes good and yields very well.

Neon. Bright neon purple skin covers the tender, tasty flesh of Neon. Its yields are good and strikingly attractive to boot.

Rosa Bianca. Another attractive variety, Rosa Bianca has skin in shades of rose, lavender, and white that change throughout the season. Its flesh is sweet and mild.

Little Fingers. With lots of stout little purple fruits that resemble fingers, this eggplant tastes wonderful. Harvest when fruit is small for best flavor.

There's a Lot at Stake

Although many varieties of eggplant grow into bushy plants about 2 to 3 feet (60–90 cm) tall and need no staking, some, including many of the thin-fruited Asian types, do best if grown on a trellis or stake and pruned like indeterminate tomatoes (see page 293).

Garlic

I've heard it said that if you enter a restaurant and can smell garlic cooking, it's a sure sign the food's going to be great. For some cooks, all sauces, soups, and stews begin with the full, rich flavor of garlic. Fortunately, growing your own garlic is pretty easy to do.

PLANTING

Garlic likes deep, fertile soil that is well drained but has plenty of organic matter. Keep the pH where most other vegetables prefer it — at about 6.5.

Plant garlic cloves in the fall about a month or two before the soil freezes. In cool climates this can be as early as midautumn; in warm regions, early winter. For your first planting, purchase cloves from a local garden center or mail-order catalog. (In future years, you can use some of your harvest for the next year's crop.) Use only the larger cloves, which will produce larger bulbs, and eat the smaller ones.

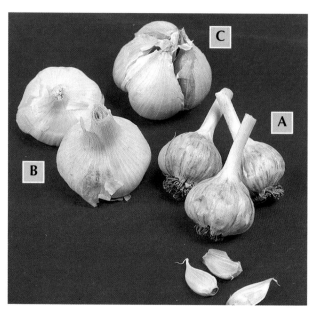

▲ **A garlic trio.** You can choose among three kinds of garlic for your garden: (A) *Stiff-neck garlic* has a single ring of cloves enclosing a stiff, central stem. (B) *Soft-neck garlic* is the kind generally sold in supermarkets; it's somewhat less hardy than stiff-neck and often does not store as well, though this largely depends on the variety grown. (C) *Elephant garlic* produces a few very large cloves with a pleasing, mild flavor. In reality a type of leek, elephant garlic is less hardy than true garlic.

Sow & Grow

GARLIC
(Allium sativum)
Onion family *(Liliaceae)*

SOWING/PLANTING

Clove depth: 2" (5 cm), with pointed end up
Germination soil temperature: 55°F (13°C)
Days to germination: Not applicable
Sow indoors: Not recommended
Plant outdoors: Late summer to fall

GROWING

pH range: 6.0–7.0
Growing soil temperature: 55–75°F (13–24°C)
Spacing in beds: 6 inches (15 cm)
Watering: Low
Light: Best yields in full sun; tolerates light shade
Nutrient requirements: N=moderate; P=moderate; K=moderate
Rotation considerations: Should not follow any onion family crop.
Good companions: Beet, lettuce
Bad companions: Bean, pea
Seed longevity: Not applicable
Seeds per ounce: Not applicable

After planting but before the ground freezes, mulch with a thick layer of straw or leaves to protect the bulbs and encourage worm activity, which helps keep the soil friable.

GROWING

In spring, when the daffodil leaves are a few inches out of the ground, remove the mulch and spread some compost on the bed. Don't water unless the ground gets very dry. The bright green leaves may already be showing, and if they aren't, they will pop out shortly. Once the plants are up, use shallow cultivation to keep the weeds under control.

▲ **Hot-weather friends.** Keep the garlic company with interplantings of lettuce or beets to help cool the soil during the heat of summer.

▲ **Nip the buds.** When flower buds appear, cut them back with scissors to promote larger bulbs.

HARVESTING AND STORING

It's time to harvest garlic in late summer when the bottom two or three leaves have turned yellow or the tops fall over. Loosen the soil with a garden fork and pull the bulbs. (A broadfork is very effective for this job.)

The key to long storage is curing. Spread the plants on a screen for good air circulation and cure in full sun. In warm climates, screen the bulbs with light shade to prevent sunscald. Cover or move to an open shed or porch if it rains. Curing, which can take as long as two weeks, is complete when the skins are dry and the necks are tight. Remove the tops and store the bulbs in a cool, dry place. Stored bulbs remain fresh for between five and eight months.

▲ **This will cure them!** Spread harvested garlic bulbs on a screen and leave them in an airy, shady place until the skins are dry and the necks tight. Trim roots and stems.

Changing a Good Thing

Garlic is a wonderfully adaptable plant that actually changes to fit the growing conditions of your garden. To customize garlic to your garden, start by purchasing and planting a variety recommended for your area. After harvesting and curing, select the largest cloves for replanting. Do this every season and the garlic will slowly adapt to the climate of your garden.

Gourds

Many garden crops don't last long after they leave the garden. And why should they? We don't grow vegetables for their looks, but because they provide nutritious and healthy food. We grow them, we harvest them, we eat them.

Birdhouse gourds don't fit this formula, however. We grow and harvest them, and then we cure them, carve them, and hang them in a tree near the garden. When spring comes, we hope a pair of birds will choose to nest in the home we've provided. When they do, we plan daily stakeouts until the babies fly off. No, we don't eat birdhouse gourds, but they do provide food for the soul.

▲ **Gorgeous gourds.** Here's a real conversation-starter crop! Gourds not only make a dramatic display in your garden, easily growing as much as 30 feet (9.5 m) in a season, but they develop into interesting shapes that can be crafted into a variety of practical and decorative objects.

Sow & Grow

GOURDS
(Lagenaria siceraria)
Cucumber family *(Cucurbitaceae)*

SOWING
Seed depth: 1" (2.5 cm)
Germination soil temperature: 80–90°F (27–32°C)
Days to germination: 4–6 days
Sow indoors: 3 weeks before last frost
Sow outdoors: After last frost (warm climates)

GROWING
pH range: 6.5–7.5
Growing soil temperature: 70–80°F (21–27°C)

Spacing in beds: 2' (60 cm) between hills
Watering: Moderate early; moderate to heavy after fruits form
Light: Full sun
Nutrient requirements: N=high; P=high; K=high
Rotation considerations: Avoid following summer and winter squash, cucumbers, and melon.
Good companions: Celeriac, celery, corn, melon, onion, radish
Bad companions: Potato
Seed longevity: 4 years
Seeds per ounce: 300 (11 seeds per g)

SOWING

Gourds prefer rich, fertile soil with plenty of organic matter. Prepare the planting bed in fall or spring by turning in aged manure or compost. Sow three seeds per 4-inch (10 cm) pot about four weeks before the last frost, or direct-sow (in warm climates only) after the danger of frost is past and the soil is well warmed. Thin with scissors to one plant per pot about one week before setting out. Transplant carefully, spacing plants 2 feet (60 cm) apart.

GROWING

Birdhouse gourds are best grown on a strong support such as a sturdy fence or trellis. A dried gourd doesn't weigh much, but a gourd on the vine is very heavy. You can also allow gourds to sprawl along the ground, but if you do so, mulch them with a bed of clean straw to minimize any discoloration.

Set floating row covers over seedlings or transplants to protect them from pests such as squash bugs and cucumber beetles. In addition to providing pest protection, row covers also add warmth to encourage fast growth. After flowers appear, remove the row covers so insects can pollinate the blossoms.

Water plants heavily from sowing to about a month before frost, then reduce moisture by about one-third. This helps prepare the fruits for drying.

▲ **An invitation to pollinators.** If you use row covers to protect young gourd seedlings, be sure to remove them when the vines blossom, so that bees and other pollinators can move among the flowers.

HARVESTING AND DRYING

Harvest a gourd when it turns pale. Gently snip the stem, being careful to leave enough stem to use as a hanger. Handle carefully, as bruised fruits often rot instead of drying. Wash the gourds gently in a 9:1 solution of water and household bleach, which also helps prevent rot. Hang in a warm, dry location until the seeds rattle when you shake the fruit. This usually takes about three to four weeks.

Making a Gourd Birdhouse

When the gourd is completely dry, use a wire brush and sandpaper to clean the outside. Use an expansion bit to cut a 2-inch-diameter (5 cm) entrance hole in the center of the gourd. Use a serrated knife to break up the pith and seeds inside the gourd, and remove all of this material. To protect the gourd from fungal molds and rots, treat it with copper sulfate. *(Caution: copper sulfate is toxic; handle with care.)* Wearing rubber gloves, dissolve 1½ pounds (680 g) copper sulfate in 7½ gallons (28.4 L) of water. Soak the gourd in the copper sulfate solution for 15 minutes, and then allow the gourd to dry.

If you wish, add a metal or plastic semi-circular canopy, 2½ inches (6.25 cm) wide and 6 inches (15 cm) long, above the entrance hole. Attach with silicone caulking.

Paint the outside with one coat of white oil-based primer and three coats of white enamel paint. This reflects heat and keeps the inside of the gourd cool.

To hang the gourd, drill two ¼-inch-diameter (6 mm) holes at the stem end and insert a 1-foot (30 cm) piece of rigid wire (such as coat hanger wire) through the holes. Fasten as shown in the drawing. Drill five ⅜-inch (1 cm) holes in the gourd's bottom for drainage. Hang from a tree branch or from wire suspended between two sturdy posts.

Greens

Sometimes you just don't notice things. For instance, I'd seen and eaten garden greens all my life. They mingled with other vegetables in salads or sat shoulder to shoulder with lettuce in the produce section of markets. They certainly were around, but didn't catch my attention. Then one spring I started growing them in my garden, and that's when I began to appreciate their individuality: the meaty tang of claytonia (miner's lettuce), the pleasant sharpness of arugula, the mild spiciness of mizuna, and on and on. When I blended these with lettuce and various other greens, I had to completely redefine my idea of salad. It was like eating spaghetti all your life and suddenly being shown the pasta aisle in the supermarket. What a nice surprise!

But variety and flavor weren't the only surprise greens had in store for me. The greatest and most welcome came one bitterly cold winter morning after an evening snowfall. Some weeks before, I'd planted a selection of greens in our small, unheated greenhouse in the garden. This little patch had supplied a regular harvest throughout the fall, but I didn't expect the plants to last through really cold conditions. It was well below freezing that morning, yet when I stepped into the greenhouse, the greens still lived up to their name — they were green. Later that day, I snipped enough of them for a nice salad, then trudged back to the house through the snow.

Perhaps it's not absolutely correct to call that experience my first impression of greens, but it is certainly the one I remember most. And I relate it now so you can see how valuable these delicious plants are to any garden, anywhere. They are easy to grow, nutritious, flavorful, and surprisingly hardy. They can transform vegetable gardening from a seasonal pastime to a year-round pleasure for just about anyone.

▲ **Gardening's Superbowl.** A selection of greens can provide bowls of delicious salads for months, from early spring to early winter.

Mesclun: A Salad in a Packet

Mesclun isn't one particular vegetable — it's a whole salad. More and more seed catalogs offer mesclun mixes, which include seeds for a variety of lettuces and European salad greens that grow well together and also taste good together. All the included varieties are easy to grow. Many catalogs offer two, three, or more different mixes. Add some mystery to your garden by trying out several kinds.

Before sowing, shake the seed packet well to mix up the seeds. Either space seeds about ½ inch (12 mm) apart in rows or broadcast them in a thin band. Cover seeds with about ⅛ (3 mm) inch of fine soil. Moisten the soil and be sure to keep it moist until the seeds have germinated.

Harvest in "cut-and-come-again" fashion at about three weeks by cutting the plants with scissors ½ inch (12 mm) above the soil. Most of the plants will regrow.

Arugula

*One of many salad greens long popular
in Europe and recently introduced in North
America, arugula adds a delightful nip to salads.
Preferring cool weather, arugula is frost hardy
enough that it will bear right through winter in a
cold frame or unheated greenhouse. The plant is
small, with a compact root system, so it is easy
to grow in containers or in a flat on a sunny
windowsill.*

◀ **Très gourmet.** Tangy is the best way to describe this easy-to-grow specialty.

SOWING AND GROWING

Prepare the seedbed by working some finished compost into the top 3 inches (8 cm) of soil. Plant seeds outdoors in spring as soon as the soil can be worked. Make additional plantings every three weeks as long as the cool weather lasts. For winter harvest, sow seeds in midfall.

HARVESTING

You'll be able to harvest leaves when they're about 2 to 3 inches (5 to 7.5 cm) long, two or three weeks after the plants germinate. Cut individual leaves or whole plants. The leaves are best when young, but they retain good flavor until the plant starts to bolt. The flowers are also edible, so let some plants blossom, gather the flowers, and toss them in among the greens of your salad.

BEST VARIETIES

Astro. Compared to most varieties, Astro is ready to harvest a few days earlier and has a milder flavor.

Rocket. Another early variety, Rocket bears tender leaves with a spicy, peppery flavor.

Italian Wild Rustic. This Old World variety has tender leaves, a spicy flavor, and excellent yields.

Sow & Grow

ARUGULA *(Eruca vesicaria)*
Cabbage family *(Cruciferae)*

SOWING

Seed depth: ¼" (6 mm)
Germination soil temperature: 40–55°F (4–13°C)
Days to germination: 5–7
Sow indoors: Late fall through early spring
Sow outdoors: As soon as soil can be worked

GROWING

pH range: 6.0–7.0
Growing soil temperature: 50–65°F (10–18°C)
Spacing in beds: *In rows,* 1" (2.5 cm); *in beds,* 6" (15 cm); thin progressively to 6" (15 cm)
Watering: Moderate and even; light in cold frame
Light: Full sun to partial shade
Nutrient requirements: N=low; P=low; K=low
Rotation considerations: Avoid following plants of the cabbage family.
Good companions: Bush bean, beet, carrot, celery, cucumber, dill, lettuce, mint, nasturtium, onion family, potato, rosemary, spinach, thyme
Bad companions: Pole bean, strawberry
Seed longevity: 5 years
Seeds per ounce: 15,000 (530 seeds per g)

Claytonia

Claytonia, also called miner's lettuce, isn't the best-known salad green, but it is certainly one of the best tasting and easiest to grow. Native to western North America, claytonia has gone largely unnoticed by gardeners for years. This is a pity, because it's another in that wonderful group of cool-weather, freeze-hardy greens that supply salads all winter from a cold frame or unheated greenhouse.

SOWING AND GROWING

Claytonia is related to the dainty spring wildflower called spring beauty, which is fitting, because claytonia is as decorative as it is tasty. Claytonia is easy to raise and able to grow vigorously even during the colder months. Like other cool-weather greens, it languishes in the heat of summer. Before planting, work at least an inch (2.5 cm) of compost into the seedbed.

In cool climates, sow seeds in the garden every three weeks from early spring to midspring, and then begin to sow again in late summer to midfall. For winter greens, put the midfall sowing in a cold frame or unheated greenhouse.

In warmer climates, sow in the garden in late fall and successively every three weeks until early winter for winter and early-spring crops.

HARVESTING

Begin harvesting as soon as leaves are of edible size. If you cut the leaves and stems as needed, the plant will continue to grow and produce. If you fall behind on harvesting, claytonia will produce little white flowers near the tops of the plants. In some vegetables this is a sign to discard the plant. Not with claytonia. The blossoms are edible and make a nice addition to salads.

◀ **Cool-weather beauty.** Easy to grow, frost hardy, and uniquely attractive and tasty to boot, claytonia is a good green to get acquainted with.

Sow & Grow

CLAYTONIA *(Montia perfoliata)*
Purslane family *(Portulacaceae)*

SOWING
Seed depth: ¼" (6 mm)
Germination soil temperature: 50–55°F (10–13°C)
Days to germination: 7–10
Sow indoors: Late fall to late winter for indoor growing
Sow outdoors: 4 weeks before last frost

GROWING
pH range: 6.5–7.0
Growing soil temperature: 50–65°F (10–18°C)
Spacing in beds: *In rows,* 1" (2.5 cm); *in beds,* 8" (20 cm); thin to 4–6" (10–15 cm)
Watering: Moderate and even; light when grown in a cold frame over winter
Light: Full sun to partial shade
Nutrient requirements: N=low; P=low; K=low
Rotation considerations: Avoid following with radicchio, endive, escarole, or artichoke.
Good companions: Other salad greens
Bad companions: None
Seed longevity: 5 years
Seeds per ounce: 45,000 (1,590 seeds per g)

Endive and Escarole

Endive and escarole are different forms of the same plant. Endive has curly or crinkly-edged leaves and a sharp, somewhat bitter taste. Escarole is hardier with flat, somewhat thicker leaves and a less bitter flavor.

SOWING AND GROWING

For spring planting, sow endive and escarole as soon as the soil can be worked. Make successive plantings every three to four weeks until the weather warms. For the winter garden, sow about two months before the first frost in fall. Plants grown in fall and subjected to a few light frosts have a richer, less bitter flavor than spring-grown plants.

Water plants evenly and regularly to keep leaves green and growing. If the ground freezes in winter, withhold water unless the top of the soil dries out, then water very lightly. Plants grown in soil with lots of organic matter, such as compost, usually need no supplemental fertilizing. In poorer soils, apply a solution of fish emulsion or seaweed once a month.

HARVESTING AND STORING

Harvesting can begin as soon as the outer leaves are of usable size. Gather the leaves as needed, or cut the whole plant at soil level. The leaves are best fresh.

BEST VARIETIES

Coral. An early-maturing escarole that produces a thick head of broad leaves, Coral is slow to bolt and well-flavored.

Sinco. A very tasty escarole, Sinco has crisp, full-flavored leaves.

Taglio. This variety matures early and is nicely flavored. It is tolerant of many conditions, from hot to cold and wet to dry.

▲ **Besting the bitters.** Endive and escarole both become bitter in warm weather. Grow them in spring or fall, and harvest them young in hot weather.

Sow & Grow

ENDIVE AND ESCAROLE *(Cichorium endivia)* Sunflower family *(Compositae)*

SOWING

Seed depth: ¼" (6 mm)
Germination soil temperature: 60–65°F (16–18°C)
Days to germination: 5–7
Sow indoors: 8 weeks before last frost
Sow outdoors: Stagger every 2 weeks from spring to early summer and from late summer to fall

GROWING

pH range: 5.5–7.0
Growing soil temperature: 45–65°F (7–18°C)
Spacing in beds: 12" (30 cm) is usually recommended, but endive will self-blanch (and be more tender) if spaced at 8–10" (20–25 cm)
Watering: Moderate; light to none when grown in cold frame over winter
Light: Full sun to partial shade
Nutrient requirements: N=moderate; P=moderate; K=moderate
Rotation considerations: Avoid following radicchio.
Good companions: Nonheading salad greens
Bad companions: Radicchio
Seed longevity: 4–6 years
Seeds per ounce: 17,000 (600 seeds per g)

Garden Cress

The most popular forms of garden cress are broadleaf cress and curly cress. Broadleaf cress has flat, wavy-edged leaves, while curly cress has leaves resembling parsley. Both are almost embarrassingly easy to grow, with some varieties going from sowing to salad bowl in less than one month. Their peppery flavor adds a pleasant zing to salads.

▲ **Greens for your windowsill.** Cress grown in containers provides a taste of spring all winter long.

SOWING AND GROWING

If the meek are destined to inherit the Earth, then cress will inherit the garden. This stuff will grow just about anywhere. You can grow cress indoors in a flat or flowerpot for sprouts anytime of year. Just fill a flat with moist seed-starter mix, sprinkle the seeds over the soil, and lightly cover with a little vermiculite or seed-starting mix. The seedlings will emerge in as little as two days and can be harvested anytime after the first true leaves begin to appear.

To grow outdoors, broadcast seeds in bands about 3 inches (7.5 cm) wide down the bed. Space bands about 4 inches (10 cm) apart. Sow every two weeks from early spring until the weather warms. Resume sowing when cool weather arrives in late summer or fall. Sow every two weeks until mid- to late fall. In warmer areas, sowing can continue through most of the winter months.

HARVESTING

When plants are 2 to 3 inches (5 to 7.5 cm) tall, harvest by cutting them at the soil line with sharp scissors. Under ideal conditions cress can be harvested in 2 to 3 weeks from sowing. If plants get too large, or if the weather warms, the leaves will develop an unappetizing bitterness. Remember that with cress, harvesting young pleases the tongue.

Sow & Grow

GARDEN CRESS *(Lepidum sativum)*
Cabbage family *(Cruciferae)*

SOWING

Seed depth: Cover lightly
Germination soil temperature: 55–75°F (13–24°C)
Days to germination: 2–6
Sow indoors: Anytime
Sow outdoors: Every 2 weeks from early to midspring, then every 2 weeks from late summer to midfall

GROWING

pH range: 6.0–6.7
Growing soil temperature: 50–75°F (10–24°C)
Spacing in beds: 1–2" (2.5–5 cm)
Watering: Moderate
Light: Full sun, but will tolerate partial shade
Nutrient requirements: N=low; P=low; K=low
Rotation considerations: Do not precede or follow with cabbage family crops.
Good companions: Bush bean, beet, carrot, celery, chamomile, cucumber, dill, lettuce, mint, nasturtium, onion family, potato, rosemary, sage, spinach, thyme
Bad companions: Pole bean, strawberry
Seed longevity: 5 years
Seeds per ounce: 10,000 (353 seeds per g)

Mustard

Mention the word mustard *and people usually think of the yellow stuff on hot dogs. It's true that mustard seed is the major ingredient in the condiment that bears its name, but this versatile plant has more than one way to please the palate. Mustard greens can add a new dimension to salads with their meaty, decidedly spicy leaves.*

◀ **Cutting the mustard.** Like other greens, mustard is tastiest when grown in cool weather.

SOWING AND GROWING

Prepare the soil as you would for cabbage, a near relative, adding compost or other form of organic matter and working it in well. Mustard is tolerant of some cold and can be sown a few weeks before the last frost. You can start plants indoors if you'd like, but direct-sown crops seem to establish themselves faster and grow more vigorously. The plants grow quickly, with most types ready to harvest about a month from sowing. For best flavor be sure to provide the plants with an even supply of moisture and adequate nutrients, especially potassium. Fish emulsion or seaweed fertilizers work well.

HARVESTING AND STORING

Begin gathering individual leaves after the plant has formed a rosette of leaves, usually when the plants are about 3 to 4 inches (7.5 to 10 cm) tall. You can cut entire plants anytime after they reach about 4 to 6 inches (10 to 15 cm) tall. If cut an inch (2.5 cm) or so above the soil line, the plants will regrow, but the resulting leaves are of poorer quality, often having a bitter taste. If some plants bolt and go to seed, you can gather the brown pods and save the seed. Mix the seed with other sprouting seeds, such as radish, cauliflower, onion, broccoli, and garden cress, for a healthy, flavorful blend of winter sprouts.

Sow & Grow

MUSTARD *(Brassica juncea)*
Cabbage family *(Cruciferae)*

SOWING

Seed depth: ¼" (6mm)

Germination soil temperature: 65–70°F (18–21°C)

Days to germination: 4–6

Sow indoors: 2 weeks before last frost

Sow outdoors: Every 3 weeks from spring to summer for early crop and from late summer to early fall for fall crop

GROWING

pH range: 5.5–7.0

Growing soil temperature: 50–70°F (10–21°C)

Spacing in beds: 6–15" (15–37.5 cm)

Watering: Moderate

Light: Full sun to partial shade

Nutrient requirements: N=high; P=moderate; K=moderate

Rotation considerations: Do not follow or precede cabbage family crops.

Good companions: Bush bean, beet, carrot, celery, chamomile, cucumber, dill, hyssop, lettuce, mint, nasturtium, onion family, potato, rosemary, sage, spinach, thyme

Bad companions: Pole bean, strawberry

Seed longevity: 4 years

Seeds per ounce: 14,000 (494 seeds per g)

Radicchio

Radicchio is a type of chicory that adds a distinctive zippy flavor to salads. It has been popular in Italy for many years, but older varieties were fussy and demanding, not qualities gardeners seek out. New varieties are easy to grow, and the lettucelike heads, boldly marked with deep red and snowy white, make both the garden bed and the salad plate look vibrant.

SOWING AND GROWING

You can grow radicchio as a spring crop, but it often matures after the days have grown warm, which makes the leaves somewhat bitter. As a fall and winter crop, however, radicchio is tough to beat. It tolerates cold and frost very well, and, if you grow it in a cold frame, you can harvest it all winter long in all but the coldest climates.

For fall and winter crops, begin sowing in midsummer, with succession sowings every 10 to 14 days for a month. For spring crops, direct-sow in the garden as soon as the soil can be worked.

HARVESTING AND STORING

Unlike the old varieties of radicchio, the new varieties don't need to be cut back before the heads form. We harvest radicchio as soon as the heads are firm. Radicchio remains fresh in the refrigerator for a few days and holds in the garden equally long if the weather is cool.

BEST VARIETIES

Giulio. An excellent variety for spring crops, Giulio produces bright red heads about 90 days from sowing. It is vigorous, slow to bolt, and delicious.

Augusto. One of the most cold-tolerant varieties available, Augusto is excellent for fall and winter crops.

▲ **The price is right.** Colorful, tart, and slightly bitter, radicchio is often costly at the market. Grow your own, and you don't have to worry about the price.

Sow & Grow

RADICCHIO *(Cichorium intybus)*
Sunflower family *(Compositae)*

SOWING

Seed depth: ¼" (6 mm)
Germination soil temperature: 60–65°F (16–18°C)
Days to germination: 5–7
Sow indoors: 8 weeks before last frost
Sow outdoors: 2 weeks before last frost and 2 months before first fall frost

GROWING

pH range: 5.5–6.8
Growing soil temperature: 45–65°F (7–18°C)
Spacing in beds: 8–10" (20–25 cm)
Watering: Moderate; light to none over winter
Light: Full sun to partial shade
Nutrient requirements: N=moderate; P=moderate; K=moderate
Rotation considerations: Do not follow escarole or endive.
Good companions: Lettuce
Bad companions: Endive, escarole
Seed longevity: 5 years
Seeds per ounce: 15,000 (530 seeds per g)

Red Orach

Orach tastes a bit like spinach. Yet, while it's easy to see the similarities, it is its differences from spinach that make orach such a special addition to the garden. There are three types — green, red, and gold — with the plant of each color having a flavor and texture all its own. Grown together in a bed or tossed in a salad, the beauty of orach's burgundy, gold, and emerald leaves is surpassed only by its flavor.

SOWING AND GROWING

Orach is a cool-weather green that is easy to grow in most fertile soils that contain some organic matter. Sow seeds every two weeks beginning in early spring and continuing until the weather warms. Orach tolerates warm weather but tastes best when temperatures are cool.

HARVESTING AND STORING

Begin harvesting leaves for fresh salads when they are 1 to 1½ inches (2.5 to 4 cm) long; if you'd like to steam the leaves, harvest them when they're 3 to 4 inches (7.5 to 10 cm) long. You can gather the leaves individually until the plants begin to flower, or cut the entire plant at the soil line when it's about 6 inches (15 cm) tall.

BEST VARIETIES

Green orach, such as *Green Spires*, produces attractive green foliage with a balanced, slightly sweet flavor.

Red orach, including *Rubra* and *Purple Savoyed*, produces dark, wine-red leaves with a rich spinachlike taste.

Gold orach, such as *Aureus*, bears yellowish gold leaves with a softer flavor than either red or green orach.

◀ **Seeing red.** Colorful in the garden and in the bowl, red orach is an excellent addition to your salad garden.

Sow & Grow

RED ORACH *(Atriplex hortensis)*
Buckwheat family *(Chenopodiaceae)*

SOWING
Seed depth: ½" (13 mm)
Germination soil temperature: 50–65°F (10–18°C)
Days to germination: 7–14
Sow indoors: 3 weeks before last frost
Sow outdoors: After soil reaches germination temperature

GROWING
pH range: 6.5–7.5
Growing soil temperature: 50–75°F (10–24°C)
Spacing in beds: 2" (5 cm); thin to 6" (15 cm)
Watering: Moderate
Light: Full sun to partial shade
Nutrient requirements: N=moderate; P=moderate; K=moderate
Rotation considerations: Do not follow or precede with beet, spinach, or Swiss chard.
Good companions: Cabbage family, celery, legumes, lettuce, onion, pea, radish, strawberry
Bad companions: Potato
Seed longevity: 5 years
Seeds per ounce: 9,000 (318 per gm)

Herbs

A vegetable garden I visited one summer stays in my memory because of what wasn't there. It was a warm, pleasant day, brushed by a soft breeze, and all around me were beds of vegetables. The tomatoes were just beginning to ripen, and the spreading leaves of cabbage plants were open to the sky. It was a beautiful garden, yet as I walked around the plantings, it felt as if something was missing, something whose absence made the entire scene incomplete. It was all the more a mystery to me, because this garden really looked terrific.

Later, in another garden, I realized what had been wrong. The second garden also had vigorous, healthy vegetables, but as I wandered about the plantings I saw other things as well. Butterflies passed by, bobbing on the breeze and settling on a cluster of chives or visiting dill blossoms. Honeybees and black-and-yellow bumblebees buzzed and danced among basil flowers. As I brushed by other plants, the air became filled with warm spicy smells. This garden was not only healthy, it seemed alive. What was missing from the first garden now became glaringly obvious — herbs.

Herbs have been a part of gardens for thousands of years, yet somewhere along the way, herbs and vegetables became separated from each other. Herbs were rounded up to grow in herb gardens, while vegetables were hustled off to vegetable gardens. And what a shame, because herbs like dill, sage, and basil, for instance, make perfect additions to the vegetable garden. Here's why.

Many times things that go well together in recipes also grow well together. So it is with many herbs and vegetables. For example, basil and tomatoes are natural companions; they go together like peas and carrots. In the kitchen, basil adds a rich flavor to tomato-based pasta sauce, and it's spectacular with sliced tomatoes. In

▲ **A treat for the senses.** Aromatic and flowering herbs add beauty and fragrance to the vegetable garden, while attracting butterflies, bees, and other beneficial insects.

the garden, basil helps repel hornworms, a major pest of tomatoes, and mosquitoes, a major pest of gardeners. In addition, basil flowers attract bees and other pollinators, which can increase yields of tomatoes and many other crops.

Herbs add enjoyment to vegetable gardening and add zest and aroma to the dishes you create from the vegetables you grow.

Basil

Basil makes the perfect partner for tomatoes, not only in the garden, where its strong scent may confuse predatory insect pests, but also chopped and sprinkled on thick slices of juicy tomatoes, still warm from the sun. Basil has become such a staple for us that we think of it more as a vegetable than as an herb.

SOWING AND GROWING

A true heat lover, basil is very sensitive even to light frosts and can be permanently set back by temperatures below 50°F (10°C). Because it matures quickly, you can direct-seed it in almost any region. It also transplants well, however, so you can get an earlier harvest if you start plants indoors two or three weeks before the last frost date.

Like many herbs, basil has a naturally low germination rate (about 60 percent). To compensate for this, sow the small seeds 2 to 3 inches (5 to 7.5 cm) apart and cover them with about ⅛ inch (3 mm) of soil. Thin to 4 to 8 inches (10 to 20 cm); the plants provide their own living mulch when mature.

Basil needs warmth and full sunlight but is otherwise undemanding. A light feeder, it's unlikely to need supplemental feedings, provided the soil is reasonably fertile. It doesn't need a lot of water, but its roots are shallow, so don't let the soil dry out.

HARVESTING AND STORING

Harvest the flower buds before they open and the leaves anytime they are large enough to use. Harvest the whole plant before frost, preferably in the morning.

You can store fresh basil in a glass of water at room temperature. You can also freeze basil, either as pesto or whirled in a blender with enough water to make a thick sauce. It's a terrific almost-fresh seasoning for winter soups and stews.

◀ **Pinch me!** To induce a full, bushy basil plant and increase yield, pinch or snip out the growing tips. The pinchings are also your first harvest. Bon appétit!

Sow & Grow

BASIL *(Ocimum basilicum)*
Mint family *(Labiatae)*

SOWING

Seed depth: Just cover
Germination soil temperature: 75–85°F (24–29°C)
Days to germination: 5–10
Sow indoors: 4–6 weeks before last frost
Sow outdoors: In warm regions, spring to late summer

GROWING

pH range: 5.5–7.5
Growing soil temperature: 75–85°F (24–29°C)
Spacing in beds: 4–8" (10–20 cm)
Watering: Light and even
Light: Full sun
Nutrient requirements: N=low; P=low; K=low
Rotation considerations: Avoid rotating with marjoram or oregano.
Good companions: Pepper, tomato
Bad companions: Beans, cabbage, cucumber
Seed longevity: 5 years
Seeds per ounce: 17,000 (600 seeds per g)

Chives

Perennial in Zones 3 through 9, chives are very easy to grow, at home in a pot on the windowsill as much as in the garden. So what's the catch? Well, sometimes chives can get a little invasive, tossing their seeds about the garden. It's a minor fault, easily remedied by snipping the flowers before they set seed.

PLANTING AND GROWING

Grown from seed, chives take about a year before they're large enough to harvest, so most folks purchase live plants. Plant in spring where plants can grow for at least three seasons undisturbed. After three years, divide the clump and replant or give away the extras.

Set plants in soil amended with compost or rotted manure; no other fertilizing is needed. Chives makes an attractive edging in the flower garden.

HARVESTING AND STORING

In cool climates, chives die back to the ground in winter, but in warm areas they can remain evergreen throughout the year. You can harvest leaves whenever they're large enough. Use scissors to snip individual leaves or give the entire clump a haircut. The flowers have a more pungent, oniony flavor than the leaves and should be gathered just as they open.

Use chives fresh in salads or blend snipped chives with sour cream, butter, or cottage cheese for dips and spreads.

BEST VARIETIES

Fine Chives. The long, very slender leaves on this variety are more attractive than many chive plants.

Purly. This variety has stout, strong leaves that grow quite straight and tall.

▲ **Spring fling.** Chives are one of the earliest plants to appear in spring, and their freshly snipped stems and flowers are a treat in first-of-the-year salads.

Sow & Grow

CHIVES *(Allium schoenoprasum)*
Onion family *(Liliaceae)*

SOWING

Seed depth: Surface or just cover

Germination soil temperature: 60–85°F (16–29°C)

Days to germination: 7–14

Sow indoors: Spring to transplant to garden; anytime for windowsill growing

Sow outdoors: Spring or fall

GROWING

pH range: 6.0–7.0

Growing soil temperature: 55–70°F (13–21°C)

Spacing in beds: 6–8" (15–20 cm)

Watering: Moderate

Light: Full sun to partial shade

Nutrient requirements: N=moderate; P= moderate; K=moderate

Rotation considerations: Do not follow or precede other onion family crops.

Good companions: Carrot, tomato

Bad companions: Beans, peas

Seed longevity: 1–2 years

Seeds per ounce: 20,000 (706 seeds per g)

Cilantro

If any plant has a split personality, it's this one. When the herb is just happily growing in the garden, it's often called Chinese parsley. When the leaves are harvested for salsas and salads, they're called cilantro. And the seeds that are gathered for mildly spicy casseroles and baked goods are called coriander. Once you get past all the confusion, though, this delicious herb is pretty easy to grow and adds zip to your recipes and aroma to your kitchen.

SOWING AND GROWING

Before sowing, amend the soil with some compost or rotted manure. Both transplanting and dry soil can cause the plants to bolt, so direct-sow the seeds and mulch plantings to keep soil evenly moist. Avoid fertilizing. For a continuous supply of cilantro, make successive sowings every three weeks from spring to late summer.

HARVESTING AND STORING

Cilantro. Harvest the entire plant when it's about 8 inches (20 cm) tall. When gathering cilantro, remember to harvest only what you need. Cilantro should be used fresh, as it quickly loses much of its potent flavor when dried or stored for more than a few days in the refrigerator.

Coriander. Allow the plant to go to seed. The seedheads will turn yellowish, then yellowish brown when ripe. Snip the seedheads, bunch them together, and store them upside down in a brown paper bag. Close the bag and place in a warm, dry place. Over the next week or so, as the heads continue to ripen, the seeds will drop to the bottom of the bag where they can be gathered. Clean the seeds of any sticks or other foreign material and store in a glass jar.

◄ **What's in a name?** Whether you call it "cilantro" and use the fresh leaves, or "coriander" and save the spicy seeds, you'll find dozens of ways to enjoy this fast-growing plant.

Sow & Grow

CILANTRO *(Coriandrum sativum)*
Carrot family *(Umbelliferae)*

SOWING

Seed depth: ¼–½" (6–13 mm)
Germination soil temperature: 55–65°F (13–18°C)
Days to germination: 7–10
Sow indoors: Not recommended; does not transplant well
Sow outdoors: *In cool areas,* after last frost and every 3 weeks until fall; *in warm areas,* fall

GROWING

pH range: 6.0–7.0
Growing soil temperature: 50–75°F (10–24°C)
Spacing in beds: 6–8" (15–20 cm)
Watering: Moderate
Light: *For seeds,* full sun; *for leaves,* light shade
Nutrient requirements: N=low; P=low; K=low
Rotation considerations: Avoid rotating with other carrot family plants.
Good companions: Tomato
Bad companions: Fennel
Seed longevity: 5 years
Seeds per ounce: 4,000 (141 seeds per g)

Dill

If dill's sole talent were flavoring pickles, that would be reason enough to include it in the garden. But of course pickles are just its opening act. Fresh dill leaves are essential to many seafood recipes, they're a great match for potatoes and onions, and they spruce up green beans and many other vegetables. And as if that weren't enough, dill attracts many types of beneficial insects to the garden.

◀ **Another good garden buddy.** Dill attracts many beneficial insects, including predatory wasps and flies. Interplant it freely in your garden to help keep insect pests under control.

SOWING AND GROWING

Dill is an independent plant that grows best if you leave it alone. If you fuss with dill, in fact, it won't grow well. As soon as you can work the soil in spring, sprinkle dill seeds on the soil surface, and then pat them into the soil and water. Once the plants are 3 inches (7.5 cm) tall, add a layer of mulch to keep weeds down and conserve moisture. In many areas, dill readily self-sows.

HARVESTING AND STORING

Begin to gather the fresh leaves as soon as the plants are large enough. You can gather the flower umbels for pickles when most of the flowers are open. Harvest seeds when they turn from yellowish to brownish tan. Gather the seedheads and turn them upside down in a brown paper bag. Collect the seeds as they fall to the bottom of the bag.

BEST VARIETIES

Dukat. Slow to bolt, Dukat produces abundant, aromatic dark green leaves noted for rich flavor.

Hercules. This dill produces very large quantites of ferny foliage.

Fernleaf. A dwarf form growing just 18 inches (45 cm) tall, Fernleaf is perfect for small spaces and container gardens.

Sow & Grow

DILL *(Anethum graveolens)*
Carrot family *(Umbelliferae)*

SOWING

Seed depth: Surface or just cover

Germination soil temperature: 60–70°F (16–21°C)

Days to germination: 7–21

Sow indoors: 4–6 weeks before planting out, but transplants poorly

Sow outdoors: *In cool regions,* every 3–4 weeks from early spring to midsummer; *in warm regions,* late summer through fall

GROWING

pH range: 5.5–6.5

Growing soil temperature: 60–80°F (16–27°C)

Spacing in beds: 6–8" (15–20 cm)

Watering: Heavy

Light: Full sun

Nutrient requirements: N=high; P=high; K=high

Rotation considerations: Follow beet.

Good companions: Cabbage family plants

Bad companions: Carrot

Seed longevity: 5 years

Seeds per ounce: 15,000 (530 seeds per g)

Fennel

Have you ever met someone with whom you got along just fine, but no one else did? Well, that's a good description of fennel. Gardeners love the stuff. Where fennel causes dissension is in the garden. Most vegetable plants just don't grow well near it. The solution is a lot like dealing with squabbling children: separation. It's a nice way to have your fennel and eat it, too.

SOWING AND GROWING

Florence fennel forms a spreading bulb at the base of the plant, celerylike leafstalks, and ferny sprays of aromatic leaves. Start Florence fennel indoors about a month before last frost. Fennel is best grown in a separate bed, so it doesn't perturb nearby vegetables. In summer, the larvae of swallowtail butterflies, called parsleyworms, often feed on the leaves. You can pick them and move them to appropriate plants, such as Queen Anne's lace, or leave them be. The plants usually require no fertilizing but need even, light watering for best growth, especially during dry times. Mulch around the base of the plant to blanch the bulb and make it more tender.

HARVESTING

Harvest Florence fennel when the bulb is about 4 inches (10 cm) across and firm to the touch. Collect the entire plant. The leaves can be used like sweet fennel. Plan on using the stalks and bulb within a day or so of harvest for best flavor.

BEST VARIETIES

Zefa Fino has thick leafstalks and softball-sized bulbs.
Rudy produces very large, flavorful bulbs.

◀ **Like having dessert for dinner.** Florence fennel has a sweet taste that makes any meal a real treat.

Sow & Grow

FENNEL *(Foeniculum vulgare)*
Carrot family *(Umbelliferae)*

SOWING

Seed depth: ¼" (6 mm)
Germination soil temperature: 65–75°F (18–24°C)
Days to germination: 7–14
Sow indoors: 4 weeks before last frost

GROWING

pH range: 6.0–7.0
Growing soil temperature: 65–80°F (18°–27°C)
Spacing in beds: 12" (30 cm)
Watering: Moderate
Light: Full sun
Nutrient requirements: N=moderate; P=low; K=low
Rotation considerations: Avoid rotating with carrots, parsnips, and other members of the carrot family.
Good companions: Fennel gets along well with mints and members of the mint family, such as sage, but that's about it.
Bad companions: Just about everything
Seed longevity: 3 to 4 years
Seeds per ounce: 7,000 (250 per g)

Marjoram

Marjoram's small green leaves, rising from a tangle of stems, have a unique fragrance, a blend of sweet and pleasantly pungent aromas that accents a wide array of dishes. Though not as easy to grow as its cousin oregano, it's not all that picky if its few needs are met.

SOWING AND GROWING

Marjoram prefers a slightly acid to slightly alkaline soil with some compost or rotted manure added. It grows well in the company of cabbage family crops, such as broccoli and Brussels sprouts. Marjoram is a tender plant that does not like cold weather and has no tolerance for frost. In cool areas, sow seeds indoors a few weeks before the last frost; in warm climates, sow directly in the garden after the last frost. Keep the soil evenly watered and mulch around the plants with a thin layer of straw.

HARVESTING AND STORING

Begin harvesting leaves when the plants are about 4 to 6 inches (10 to 15 cm) tall. Gather individual leaves for immediate use or snip entire stems for drying and storage. You can use the leaves fresh to season vegetable and pasta dishes. The volatile oils of marjoram dissipate quickly on cooking, so the leaves should be added to prepared dishes a few minutes before serving to preserve the herb's flavor. You can also dry marjoram and store it in jars for later use.

BEST VARIETIES

Most seed companies don't sell named varieties of marjoram but instead offer the species. Here is one very nice exception:

Erfo produces an abundant crop of fragrant leaves on vigorous, upright plants

◀ **Pot up some marjoram.** Enjoy marjoram fresh all year long, no matter where you live. Before the first frost of fall, dig up a plant and transplant it to a pot. Set the pot on a sunny windowsill away from drafts. You'll have aromatic leaves all winter.

Sow & Grow

MARJORAM *(Origanum majorana)*
Mint family *(Labiatae)*

SOWING

Seed depth: Just cover
Germination soil temperature: 60°F (16°C)
Days to germination: 10–14
Sow indoors: 4 weeks before setting out
Sow outdoors: After last frost

GROWING

pH range: 6.5–7.5
Growing soil temperature: 55–80°F (13–27°C)
Spacing in beds: 6–8" (15–20 cm)
Watering: Moderate
Light: Full sun
Nutrient requirements: N=low; P=low; K=low
Rotation considerations: Avoid rotating with oregano and basil.
Good companions: Everything
Bad companions: Nothing
Seed longevity: 1 year
Seeds per ounce: 120,000 (4,236 seeds per g)

Oregano

Oregano is sometimes called wild marjoram, with emphasis on the wild. Though related to marjoram, oregano has a bolder flavor as well as a hardier constitution — it survives as a perennial in Zone 5 gardens. And just taste how much zest it adds to your pasta and pizza sauces!

SOWING AND GROWING

You can grow oregano from seed, but many gardeners like to purchase plants so that they can sample the taste before the crop gets established in the garden. There's quite a bit of difference in flavor from variety to variety. If you start from seed, sow it indoors about two months before the last frost. As seedlings grow, select the most fragrant to transplant to the garden and put the remainder in the compost bin. Space plants about a foot (30 cm) apart in slightly acid to slightly alkaline soil. For the best-flavored foliage, avoid fertilizing, do not overwater, and harvest before the plants flower.

HARVESTING AND STORING

You can harvest the leaves as soon as they are large enough to use. Pick individual leaves or snip entire sprigs. An alternative method is to shear the plants about 2 inches (5 cm) from the ground just before flowering and again about a month before the first frost. Use the leaves fresh or dry them and store in a jar for later use.

Not All Oreganos Are Created Equal

Some oreganos are so mild they are of little use for seasoning. For the best, spiciest oregano, be sure to grow Greek (also called Italian) oregano. This plant bears white flowers and very aromatic leaves.

◀ **Early summer haircut.** Shear the plants about 2 inches (5 cm) from the ground just before they flower in early summer. You'll have another harvest at the end of the season.

Sow & Grow

OREGANO (*Origanum vulgare* subsp. *hirtum*)
Mint family (*Labiatae*)

SOWING
Seed depth: Just cover
Germination soil temperature: 60°F (16°C)
Days to germination: 7–14
Sow indoors: 8 weeks before last frost
Sow outdoors: 2 weeks before last frost

GROWING
pH range: 6.0–7.5
Growing soil temperature: 55–80°F (13–27°C)
Spacing in beds: 6–8" (15–20 cm)
Watering: Low
Light: Full sun to partial shade
Nutrient requirements: N=low; P=low; K=low
Rotation considerations: Avoid rotating with marjoram and basil.
Good companions: Everything
Bad companions: Nothing
Seed longevity: 1 year
Seeds per ounce: 250,000 (8,825 seeds per g)

Parsley

Mention parsley and many people conjure up images of a sprig of green tossed on the dinner plate for garnish only. It deserves better. For starters, parsley is full of vitamin C, carotene, iron, and chlorophyll. A single planting produces all summer and is often the last plant still producing in the garden, even after a few light snows. You can pot it up and bring it inside to sit in a sunny window for fresh seasonings all winter. Parsley perks up any salad and adds its unique piquancy to everything from potato soup to meatballs and poultry stuffing. In short, parsley is not a one-trick pony, and once you experience its many attributes you will probably grow it in your vegetable garden every year.

▲ **Patience's reward.** Parsley may take a long time to germinate, but it repays you for the wait with beauty, nutrients, and flavor.

Hurry Up, Please, It's Time

You can either live with parsley's slow germination habit, or you can use one or more of the ruses gardeners have come up with to speed the process:

▶ Soak or refrigerate the seeds for a day before sowing them.

▶ Freeze the seeds, or soak them and then freeze them.

▶ Pour boiling water over the soil after you've planted the seeds.

Sow & Grow

PARSLEY
(Petroselinum crispum)
Carrot family *(Umbelliferae)*

SOWING
Seed depth: ¼" (6 mm)
Germination soil temperature: 65–85°F (18–29°C)
Days to germination: 21
Sow indoors: Late winter to early spring
Sow outdoors: Early spring before last frost

GROWING
pH range: 6.0–7.0
Growing soil temperature: 60–65°F (16–18°C)
Spacing in beds: 6" (15 cm)
Watering: Light
Light: Full sun to light shade
Nutrient requirements: N=moderate; P=moderate; K=moderate
Rotation considerations: Avoid rotating with carrots, celery, and parsnip.
Good companions: Asparagus, corn, pepper, tomato
Bad companions: None
Seed longevity: 1–3 years
Seeds per ounce: 18,000 (635 seeds per g)

SOWING AND GROWING

Parsley is not at all fussy, but it does have one eccentricity — it takes three to four weeks to germinate. When other seedbeds are filled with seedlings, the parsley bed will be empty. Just remember, it's nothing you did. That's just the way it is with parsley.

Sow parsley in fertile, slightly acid to slightly alkaline soil, and it will grow well. Parsley can stand a little shade, and it's a good companion to both tomatoes and asparagus, so it can be planted among either.

Parsley doesn't need a lot of water but does have shallow roots, so don't allow the soil surface to dry out.

HARVESTING

Harvest as needed, beginning with the larger, outer leaves. To maintain production and quality, harvest the leaf stem along with the leaf blades. If you need a lot of parsley all at once, cut the whole plant a little above the soil level. It will grow new foliage.

For fresh parsley all winter, transplant one or two plants into 10-inch (25 cm) pots in late fall and grow them in a sunny window. You can also start some seeds in a pot in late summer and grow the plants outside until the first fall frost. Then bring them indoors.

BEST VARIETIES

Two types of parsley are available through most garden centers, via mail order, and from Internet sources:

Curly-leaved parsley has deeply curled leaves and a very attractive appearance. Its flavor is not as esteemed as that of flat-leaved, but still quite enjoyable. Varieties include *Forest Green*, with long, strong, nicely flavored leaves that stay green even in hot weather; and *Frisca*, which produces very curly leaves that are equally attractive and delicious.

Flat-leaved parsley, also called Italian parsley, has flat, celerylike leaves. Varieties include *Gigante D'Italia*, which bears large, dark green leaves; the strong but pleasant-tasting foliage can be eaten fresh or added to recipes. *Single-Leaf Italian* bears leaves with a rich flavor, excellent for seasoning cooked dishes.

▲ **Flat-out stronger.** Many cooks prefer Italian, or flat-leafed, parsley over curly, for its heartier taste.

Parsleyroot

All parsleys have roots, but only one type of parsley can be called parsleyroot. Although its leaves taste very good, parsleyroot (also called Hamburg parsley) is valued more for its large swollen root. It's about the size of a carrot and the color of a parsnip, with a distinctive taste all its own.

Grow parsleyroot the same way you grow other parsley. To harvest, dig the roots, remove the tops, and store them in damp sand or sawdust, just like carrots. You can also leave them in the garden with a covering of mulch and dig them in spring like parsnips.

Grate parsleyroot raw into salads or slaw or serve it fried, baked, or boiled. For a winter treat, plant the root in a pot indoors and harvest the fresh sprouts all winter long.

Sage

Sage has a lingering, slightly spicy aroma that's as warm and inviting as a country kitchen when Sunday dinner is cooking. Generations ago, it was used to restore the body. Today, its fragrant bouquet instills a sense of calm and well-being, while adding beauty and fragrance to the garden. It is as pleasant a companion as a gardener could want.

PLANTING

Sage is a perennial that is hardy in Zones 4 to 8. Instead of starting plants from seed, you may want to buy year-old plants from a nursery or garden center. This way, you'll get a rich harvest the same season, instead of the two growing seasons required if you start plants from seed.

GROWING

Sage prefers cool to warm temperatures and should be lightly shaded in hot weather and south of Zone 8. Water plants during dry periods and avoid overwatering other times. Sage doesn't like wet feet, especially during the winter months.

HARVESTING

The leaves can be gathered anytime during the growing season. They seem to be most flavorful just as the flowers begin to open. Purple-leaved varieties tend to be more aromatic than green-leaved types. Use the leaves fresh in recipes or add them sparingly to salads. You can store dried leaves in airtight, dark-colored jars for about a year.

BEST VARIETIES

Purpurea is a beautiful dusky purple, with very aromatic leaves on an attractive spreading plant.

Tricolor has white, green, and purple leaves, making this variety particularly ornamental.

◀ **Looking good.** Sage adds grace and style to the garden while repelling harmful pests.

Sow & Grow

SAGE *(Salvia officinalis)*
Mint family *(Labiatae)*

SOWING

Seed depth: Surface or lightly cover
Germination soil temperature: 65–70°F (18–21°C)
Days to germination: 7–21
Sow indoors: 6–8 weeks before last frost
Sow outdoors: Not recommended

GROWING

pH range: 5.5–7.0
Growing soil temperature: 55–80°F (13–27°C)
Spacing in beds: 12–18" (30–45 cm)
Watering: Light
Light: Full sun to part shade
Nutrient requirements: N=low; P=low; K=low
Rotation considerations: Plants should be replaced every 4 to 5 years. Avoid rotating with basil, cucumber, marjoram, and oregano.
Good companions: Broccoli, Brussels sprout, cabbage, carrot, cauliflower, kale, and kohlrabi
Bad companions: Cucumber
Seed longevity: 2 years
Seeds per ounce: 3,400 (120 per g)

Tarragon

Tarragon is a traditional favorite in such French standards as béarnaise sauce and fines herbes (along with chervil, parsley, and thyme). Its delightfully subtle, licoricelike flavor is perfect with chicken and seafood. It's also a great herb for flavoring vinegars. A perennial herb, tarragon is easy to grow and hardy to Zone 4.

PLANTING AND GROWING

"A rose is a rose is a rose" may be true for that fragrant flower, but it isn't for tarragon. The most important thing to remember when you grow tarragon is to purchase the real thing. Lesson number one: Don't purchase tarragon seed. French tarragon, which is the herb you need for cooking, is not propagated by seed but sold as plants. Lesson number two: Purchase the most aromatic plants you can find. When you buy your plants, be sure the leaves are fragrant; don't buy Russian tarragon, which is bland and tasteless.

After you have your plants, set them in slightly acid to slightly alkaline soil. Avoid fertilizing and do not overwater. Tarragon is amazingly drought tolerant. When plants are three to five years old, remove them and replace them with new plants. You can also dig them up and cut off pieces of the roots to replant.

HARVESTING AND STORING

Gather leaves to use fresh as soon as the plants are in full growth, about a month or two after transplanting. The leaves are most flavorful before plants flower. Use them fresh in chicken and fish dishes, as well as with mushrooms, potatoes, or leeks. Or steep tarragon leaves in white wine vinegar (about 1 part tarragon to 2 parts vinegar) for about four weeks.

▲ **Tarragon for the table.** Tarragon's narrow, shiny, dark green leaves pack a punch, with their combination peppery and licoricelike flavor.

Sow & Grow

TARRAGON *(Artemisia dracunculus* var. *sativa)*
Sunflower family *(Compositae)*

SOWING/PLANTING

Seed depth: Not grown from seed
Germination soil temperature: Not grown from seed
Days to germination: Not grown from seed
Sow indoors: Not grown from seed
Transplant outdoors: Spring

GROWING

pH range: 5.5–7.0
Growing soil temperature: 50–80°F (10–27° C)
Spacing in beds: 12–18 inches (30–45 cm)
Watering: Low
Light: Full sun
Nutrient requirements: N=low; P=low; K=low
Rotation considerations: Avoid rotating with sunflower family plants.
Good companion: Basil
Bad companions: Artichokes, sunflower
Seed longevity: Not applicable
Seeds per ounce: Not applicable

Horseradish

Some people claim to grow horseradish, but this vegetable is so easy it really grows itself. Like asparagus, it's a perennial plant. Rather than growing from seeds, it develops from pieces of roots called root cuttings. You just plant the cuttings and stand back. The first season, let the plants grow and develop a strong root system. Harvest the following fall after the first hard frost.

PLANTING AND GROWING

Although it demands little care, planting horseradish in well-drained, rich soil will provide a better yield. In spring, add some compost or well-rotted manure to the spot where you plan to grow horseradish. Loosen the soil with a fork to a depth of about a foot (30 cm) as you mix in the compost or manure. After raking the bed smooth, dig a furrow about 6 inches (15 cm) deep. Set horseradish root cuttings along the side of the trench so the buds are toward the soil surface. Cover roots with about 2 inches (5 cm) of soil and water well.

The shoots should appear in about a week or two. After the first few leaves have completely unfolded, fertilize once a month with an organic fertilizer such as fish emulsion. Don't overdo it; horseradish doesn't need much help to grow quite vigorously. Water during dry spells.

HARVESTING AND STORING

After the first hard frost, loosen the soil around the plants with a garden fork. Lift the plants gently from the soil with the fork, trim off the tops, and brush the roots with a clean scrub brush to remove most of the soil. Remove some of the side shoots to replant. Store roots in the root cellar like carrots or in plastic vegetable bags in the refrigerator. Roots remain fresh for about three months.

▲ **Caution: hot!** A beautiful plant in the garden, horseradish is one of the few vegetables that comes with safety precautions. Like hot peppers, it can be irritating to both your skin and eyes. When preparing horseradish sauce, work in a well-ventilated room or outdoors.

Sow & Grow

HORSERADISH *(Armoracia rusticana)*
Cabbage family *(Cruciferae)*

SOWING/PLANTING

Root cutting depth: 4" (10 cm)
Soil temperature: 40–60°F (4–16°C)
Days to germination: Not applicable
Sow indoors: Not applicable
Transplant outdoors: Early spring

GROWING

pH range: 5.5–7.5
Soil temperature: 50–70°F (10–21°C)
Spacing in beds: 12–18" (30–45 cm)
Watering: Low to moderate
Light: Shade to full sun
Nutrient requirements: N=low; P=low; K=low
Rotation considerations: Don't rotate.
Good companions: Don't grow with other crops
Bad companions: Don't grow with other crops
Seed longevity: Not applicable
Seeds per ounce: Not applicable

Jerusalem Artichokes

Because they spread rapidly, our 6-foot-tall (1.8 m) Jerusalem artichokes grow in a special bed. Once shoots appears a week or two after planting, the plants need little care.

PLANTING AND GROWING

Jerusalem artichokes grow from tubers rather than seeds. Each tuber (a swollen, knotty section of root) contains eyes, much like a potato's. To prepare for planting, cut the tubers into sections; each piece must have at least two eyes. Don't allow the tubers to dry out.

Dig a trench about 6 inches (15 cm) deep and sprinkle in an inch or two (2.5 to 5 cm) of compost. Set the tubers onto the compost, spacing them 12 to 18 inches (30 to 45 cm) apart. Cover and water well.

Keep weeds under control and water during dry periods. Apply an organic fertilizer once a month only in soils lacking organic matter.

HARVESTING AND STORING

Although you can gather Jerusalem artichokes anytime from late summer to early winter, they taste best after a few hard frosts. After the plants have turned brown, cut back the stalks and loosen the ground with a fork. Use the fork to sift through the soil, gathering only as many tubers as you will use in the next couple of weeks.

Mulch the bed with a thick layer of straw or salt hay to keep the soil from freezing so that you can dig tubers for many more weeks. Whatever is left in the ground will come up in spring and provide next year's crop.

BEST VARIETIES

Stampede produces large, white-fleshed tubers.
Boston Red produces flavorful red-skinned tubers.

▲ **Above and below.** Jerusalem artichokes produce small yellow sunflowers to lighten the spirit as well as flavorful tubers that make dinner a feast.

Sow & Grow

JERUSALEM ARTICHOKES *(Helianthus tuberosus)*
Sunflower family *(Compositae)*

SOWING/PLANTING
Tuber depth: 4" (10 cm)
Soil temperature: 50–60°F (10–16°C)
Days to germination: 7–14
Sow indoors: Not applicable
Plant outdoors: After last frost

GROWING
pH range: 6.0–6.7
Soil temperature: 60–70°F (16–21°C)
Spacing in beds: 12–18" (30–45 cm)
Watering: Moderate to heavy
Light: Full sun
Nutrient requirements: N=moderate; P=moderate; K=moderate
Rotation considerations: Don't rotate.
Good companions: Don't grow with other crops
Bad companions: Don't grow with other crops
Seed longevity: Not applicable
Seeds per ounce: Not applicable

Kale

Gardeners, like parents, aren't supposed to have favorites among their vegetables, and I generally follow that rule faithfully. But if I did have a favorite vegetable, it would probably be kale. Kale is easy to grow and hardy enough to harvest from under the snow. It even survives most winters without protection.

SOWING AND GROWING

Kale tastes best when it grows fast, so enrich the soil with compost at least a month before sowing. It needs cool, moist soil, so be sure to keep the soil well watered from germination through the growing season. For better-flavored leaves and less frost damage, stop watering after the first frost.

Though kale, like its cabbage relatives, is a heavy feeder, too much fertilizer is as detrimental to this plant as too little. Fertilize the planting every two or three weeks with a complete organic fertilizer such as fish emulsion. Keep plants weeded.

HARVESTING AND STORING

The flavor of kale improves after the leaves are nipped by frost, but you can begin to harvest individual leaves as soon as they are large enough to toss in a salad. To avoid tearing the stems, use scissors or a sharp knife to gather the leaves. Harvest entire plants by cutting the stems about an inch (2.5 cm) above the ground. Leaves stored in the refrigerator in a vegetable storage bag keep for two weeks to about a month.

BEST VARIETIES

Low-growing varieties, such as *Vates*, are more frost-hardy than tall ones, such as *Lancinato*. But both types are equally delicious.

▲ **Almost perfect.** Kale has just about everything — good looks, good flavor, and high vitamin and mineral content.

Sow & Grow

KALE *(Brassica oleracea)* Acephala group
Cabbage family *(Cruciferae)*

SOWING

Seed depth: ½" (13 mm)
Germination soil temperature: 45–95°F (7–35°C)
Days to germination: 5–7
Sow indoors: 6 weeks before last frost
Sow outdoors: *In cool climates,* late spring or early summer; *in warm climates,* early spring and, for overwintering, late summer or early fall

GROWING

pH range: 6.0–7.0
Growing soil temperature: 60–65°F (16–18°C)
Spacing in beds: 16" (40 cm), staggered
Watering: Heavy during growing season, light after first frost
Light: Best yields in full sun, but tolerates partial shade
Nutrient requirements: N=moderate; P=moderate; K=moderate
Rotation considerations: Avoid following cabbage family crops.
Good companions: Bush bean, beet, celery, cucumber, lettuce, onion, potato
Bad companions: Pole bean, tomato
Seed longevity: 4 years
Seeds per ounce: 10,000 (353 seeds per g)

Kohlrabi

This fast-growing cousin of cabbage and broccoli is a very good vegetable to plant in late fall, when garden spaces start opening up that would otherwise go to waste. The edible part of the kohlrabi plant is a swollen portion of the stem. It stores well in the root cellar and can be eaten raw or cooked in a variety of delicious recipes.

SOWING AND GROWING

If it is to be tender and tasty, kohlrabi must grow fast and without interruption. That means making sure it has rich, evenly moist soil and cool temperatures. Kohlrabi thrives on plenty of compost and benefits from leaf mold as a sidedressing. Start seeds indoors if you like, but best results come from direct-sowing. If you're growing kohlrabi as a late-season crop, start the plants elsewhere and transplant them as a succession crop when space is freed.

Once kohlrabi is off and growing, just fertilize the plants every two to three weeks with a complete organic fertilizer, such as fish emulsion, and keep the soil moist. As the stems begin to swell, add a layer of compost or well-rotted manure to the rows.

HARVESTING AND STORING

To use fresh. Begin harvesting when stems are about 2 inches (5 cm) in diameter. Pull the entire plant and trim the leaves and roots. Store plants in the refrigerator for a month or two.

For winter storage. Harvest 3- to 4-inch (7.5 to 10 cm) stems after a few frosts. Trim the leaves and store in a root cellar for about three months. In Zone 6 and farther south, kohlrabi can stay right in the garden through fall and be harvested as needed. If a cold snap is forecast, mulch plants with straw.

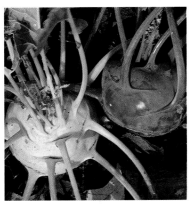

◀ **The Eagle has landed.** Kohlrabi's unique growth habit makes the garden look like a moon landing site.

Sow & Grow

KOHLRABI *(Brassica oleracea)* Gongylodes group
Cabbage family *(Cruciferae)*

SOWING

Seed depth: ¼–½" (6–13 mm)

Soil temperature: 50–70°F (10–21°C)

Days to germination: 5–7

Sow indoors: Not recommended

Sow outdoors: *In cool climates,* from one month before the last frost for spring crops and early summer for fall crops; *in warm climates,* in late winter for spring crops and fall for early winter crops

GROWING

pH range: 6.0–7.0

Soil temperature: 50–65°F (10–18°C)

Spacing in beds: 6–8" (15–20 cm), staggered pattern, 4 rows to a wide bed

Watering: Moderate and even

Light: Best yield in full sun; tolerates light shade

Nutrient requirements: N=moderate; P=moderate; K=moderate

Rotation considerations: Avoid following cabbage family crops.

Good companions: Bush bean, beet, celery, cucumber, lettuce, nasturtium, onion, potato, tomato

Bad companions: Pole bean

Seed longevity: 3 years

Seeds per ounce: 9,000 (318 seeds per g)

Leeks

A bowl of leek and potato soup on a chilly fall evening is all the reason I need to grow leeks in the garden. I know it's frowned on to personify vegetables, but leeks always seem friendly to me. They are gentle on the digestive system and they taste good, in addition to being easy to grow and frost hardy. They also stay fresh all winter long under a thick blanket of mulch. I know some people who don't have that many good attributes.

▲ **The short and long of it.** You can choose between short- and long-season leeks. Short-seasons have a thinner stem and don't keep as well as the hardier long-season types. I grow only long-season varieties like these, with their thick, cylindrical stems carrying a fan of dark green leaves.

Sowing and Growing

Start long-season leeks indoors in late winter. Sow seeds in flats, and when the seedlings are about 2 inches (5 cm) tall, transplant them to individual growing cells. Fertilize once every two weeks with fish emulsion.

Sow & Grow

Leeks
(Allium ampeloprasum) Porrum group
Onion family *(Liliaceae)*

Sowing

Seed depth: ¼" (6 mm)
Soil temperature: 75°F (24°C)
Days to germination: 5–7
Sow indoors: 4 weeks before last frost
Sow outdoors: Not recommended

Growing

pH range: 6.0–7.5
Soil temperature: 60°F (16°C)
Spacing in beds: 6" (15 cm) in rows, 3 rows to a bed
Watering: Moderate
Light: Full sun gives best yields, but tolerates partial shade
Nutrient requirements: N=moderate; P=moderate; K=moderate
Rotation considerations: Avoid following onions, shallots, garlic, chives.
Good companions: Bush bean, beet, carrot, celeriac, celery, garlic, onion, parsley, tomato
Bad companions: Bean, pea
Seed longevity: 2 years
Seeds per ounce: 10,000 (353 seeds per g)

When they're ready for transplanting to the garden, about a week after the last frost, the plants should be as big around as a pencil and 6 to 12 inches (15 to 30 cm) tall. Don't worry if they're bigger than that. With leeks, bigger transplants means bigger yields.

Leeks grow best in very fertile, well-drained soil, so add plenty of compost to the bed. Set the transplants as shown in the photos below.

Water transplants and then water regularly throughout the growing season to keep the stems tender. Fertilize them every two weeks with a complete organic fertilizer such as fish emulsion.

HARVESTING AND STORING

Harvest short-season leeks during the summer and long-season varieties from late summer through winter. To harvest, loosen the soil gently with a garden fork and pull the plants from the ground. Leeks don't store very long — about a week in the refrigerator — so harvest only as much as you need. In early fall, but before the first hard freeze, mulch the bed with a thick layer of straw. This will keep the soil workable through most of winter, allowing you to harvest fresh leeks from the garden anytime a craving for leek and potato soup strikes.

Transplanting Leek Seedlings

1 Remove the leek seedlings from the growing flat, gently teasing the roots apart with your fingers.

2 Trim the roots to about 2 inches (5 cm).

3 Use a hoe to dig a trench about 8 inches (20 cm) deep. Set the leeks in the trench, spacing them about 6 inches (15 cm) apart. Fill the trench with soil and press it firmly but gently in place.

4 Mulch the planting with grass clippings.

5 As the leeks grow, hill the soil up around their base. This traditional technique bleaches, and sweetens, the stems.

Lettuce

People who aren't excited about growing let-
tuce should take a look at a garden full of
today's vibrant cultivars or taste a salad made
from the most flavorful varieties. You can choose
among hundreds of different varieties of lettuce
in a wide range of shapes, colors, and forms, not
to mention tastes. Some of the different types
include leaf lettuces, oakleaf lettuces, summer
crisps, icebergs, romaines (cos), butterheads,
and bibbs. Grow a nice selection of lettuces, and
your garden will be prettier and your salads
taste better than you ever imagined. The secret
to the sweetest lettuce is to keep it growing fast.

▲ **Lovely lettuce.** This leaf lettuce called
North Pole flourished in our unheated greenhouse over winter, surviving outside temperatures of –20°F (–29°C)

Sow & Grow

LETTUCE
(Lactuca sativa)
Sunflower family *(Compositae)*

SOWING

Seed depth: ¼–½" (6–13 mm)
Soil temperature: 40–60°F (4–16°C); germination
rates decline above 68°F (20°C)
Days to germination: 7–14
Sow indoors: 4 weeks before transplanting
Sow outdoors: When soil can be worked

GROWING

pH range: 6.5–7.0
Soil temperature: 55–65°F (13–18°C)

Spacing in beds: *Leaf lettuce for continuous har-*
vest, ½" (1.3 cm) in bands; *leaf lettuce to form*
heads, 8" (20 cm); *summer crisp types,* 8–12";
iceberg, 8–12" (20–30 cm); *romaine (cos),* 10"
(25 cm); *butterhead,* 8–10" (20–25 cm); *bibb,*
6–8" (15–20 cm)
Watering: Light to moderate
Light: Full sun for best yields, but will tolerate
partial shade
Nutrient requirements: N=high; P=high; K=high
Rotation considerations: Avoid following radicchio, endive, escarole, or artichoke.
Good companions: Everything, but especially
carrot, garlic, onion, and radish
Bad companions: None
Seed longevity: 1 year
Seeds per ounce: 26,000 (918 seeds per g)

SOWING

All lettuces are easy to grow and have similar needs — with some important differences. Lettuces that form a head, including romaines, need more space than leaf types. Some types, particularly romaine lettuces, tolerate warm weather better and are less likely to bolt.

You can start lettuce indoors or in a cold frame, or direct-sow it. If you start plants indoors or in a cold frame, sow seeds about four weeks before setting out. In cool climates, direct-sow seeds beginning in early spring and continuing through late summer. In mild climates, sow seeds from fall through early spring.

Succession Success

Lettuce is a good crop for succession planting. To have a continuous supply of lettuce over the season, make successive plantings every 10 days to two weeks. As the weather warms, grow varieties that tolerate hot weather and resist bolting, such as crisphead varieties.

▲ **Getting big-headed.** Given the space, butterhead lettuce, forms a graceful, impressive head.

Lettuce seeds need light to germinate. Sow them on top of the soil and cover very lightly with soil. Keep the seedbed evenly moist. Lettuce germinates and grows best in cool weather. Although it's tolerant of light frosts, provide protection, such as a floating row cover, if temperatures dip below 30°F (–1°C). In warm soil (above about 75°F [24°C]), the seeds become temporarily dormant.

GROWING

The key to tender and tasty lettuce is rapid growth, but lettuce has a relatively shallow, compact root system that doesn't absorb nutrients and moisture from the soil very efficiently, which can slow growth. To encourage fast growth, add plenty of finished compost before planting and again as a sidedressing a week or so after seedlings appear or transplants are planted. Give supplemental feedings of compost tea every few weeks until harvest.

Lettuce doesn't require a *lot* of water, but it needs some water all the time. Lack of moisture causes plant growth to stop, which can also produce a slightly bitter flavor in the leaves. In warm weather, lettuce likes a little shade, which you can provide by growing it under shade cloth or next to taller companion plants, such as vining crops.

HARVESTING

Lettuce goes from seeds to salad in about a month in many regions, and only a little longer in others. Once it has grown to the size you prefer, there are three ways you can harvest the bounty.

Gather outer leaves. With all except iceberg types, start gathering the outer leaves as soon as they're big enough for the salad bowl. The harvest is over when a central stem starts to form. This signals that the plant is getting ready to bolt, and the leaves will start to have a bitter taste.

▲ **A leaf at a time.** Enjoy a continuous harvest of large outer leaves until the bitter center core develops.

▲ **A second chance.** If you cut leaf lettuce about 1 inch (2.5 cm) above the soil, it will regrow one or two more heads.

Cut-and-come-again. Cut leaf lettuces about an inch (2.5 cm) above the soil as soon as most of the leaves are salad sized. The plant will continue to grow and provide a second and sometimes a third harvest.

Harvest the entire plant. This method is for all lettuce types. Wait until the plant is mature, but still young and tender, and harvest the whole thing.

STORING

If a crop doesn't store well in the refrigerator, that's usually viewed as a deficit, but I actually prefer lettuce right from the garden. To get the lettuce for a dinner salad, I like to take an empty wooden salad bowl out to the garden and enjoy the moments I spend gathering lettuce. When I'm done, I have a bowl of salad instead of just a salad bowl.

If circumstances prevent you from making daily jaunts to the lettuce patch, lettuce will keep for about a week in the fridge. Harvest in early morning and store in a plastic vegetable bag.

BEST VARIETIES

Leaf lettuce. In four to six weeks, leaf lettuce usually forms a loose rosette of tender, sweet-tasting leaves. Popular varieties include *Black Seeded Simpson, Simpson Elite, Red Sails, Red Salad Bowl, Impuls, Royal Oakleaf, Cocarde,* and *Galactic.*

Romaine (cos). Romaine lettuce has oblong leaves that form fairly loose, upright, conical heads. The leaves have a crisp, slightly tart flavor and come in shades of green and red. Varieties include *Freckles, Romance, Rubens Romaine, Little Gem, Winter Density, Integrata Red, Rouge d'Hiver,* and *Rosalita.*

Butterhead and bibb. This very special class of lettuce bears broad rosettes of tender, wavy leaves. Leaves have a delicate flavor and creamy texture. Varieties include *Sangria, Tom Thumb, Audran, Deer Tongue,* and *Buttercrunch.*

Summer crisp. This blend of some of the best features of leaf and head types results in a loose head of large, crisp leaves with good flavor. Varieties include *Loma, Vanity, Sierra,* and *Cerise.*

Crisphead. Looking a little like an iceberg type and a little like romaine crisphead, Crisphead produces large, crinkly leaves that have a crunchy texture and pleasingly sharp flavor. All are very heat tolerant. Varieties include *Nevada, Micha, Cardinale,* and *Canasta.*

Melons

I think everyone who gardens has a pleasant memory about melons. Maybe this is because melons do best in hot summer weather — the kind of weather when outdoor picnics and get-togethers happen. Good times, good company, and good food topped off with slices of juicy melon! For me, every melon growing in the garden today carries something of all those summers from long ago inside it. All I have to do is cut a slice, take a bite, and the pleasant memories come back again.

There are lots of different kinds of melons — from muskmelons to watermelons. They are grown in very similar ways, but each has its own unique, enticing personality.

▲ **Passport to summer.** A Galia-type melon, this Passport has sweet green flesh — a darker green near the rind fading to white-green at the center. Because it's an early melon, it's a good one to raise in cool-summer regions.

Sow & Grow

MELONS
Cucumis melo and *Citrullus lanatus*
Cucumber family *(Cucurbitaceae)*

SOWING

Seed depth: ½" (13 mm)
Soil temperature: 80–90°F (27–32°C)
Days to germination: 3–5
Sow indoors: 3 weeks before last frost
Sow outdoors: When soil reaches 70°F (21°C) and after last frost

GROWING

pH range: 6.0–7.0 (6.0 is the absolute minimum; production drops below this)

Soil temperature: 70–85°F (21–29°C)
Spacing in beds: 16" (40 cm)
Watering: Moderate and even from germination to hardening off; low for one week prior to transplanting; moderate again from transplanting until fruit is full sized; low or none during ripening of fruit
Light: Full sun
Nutrient requirements: N=low; P=high; K=high
Rotation considerations: Avoid following cucumber, pumpkin, and summer and winter squash.
Good companions: Corn
Bad companions: Potato
Seed longevity: 4–5 years
Seeds per ounce: 300–1,000 (11–35 seeds per g)

THE SITE

Melons are heat lovers. They really need more heat than they can get in northern regions, but they can grow there with some help from plastic mulch and row covers. Melons are also a bit particular about pH, and their water needs fluctuate during the growth cycle. If you give melons the attention they need, however, they'll give you taste and sweetness you'll never get in a store-bought fruit.

At the same time you start the seeds indoors, work plenty of compost and some seaweed or rotted manure into their bed and then cover the soil with a sheet of IRT plastic to get it good and warm.

SOWING

Start melons indoors in a seed-starting mix, three weeks before the last frost date. Sow three seeds each in 3-inch (7.5 cm) pots. Germinate at a steady 80° to 90°F (27 to 32°C). Once the seedlings appear, lower the temperature to 75°F (24°C) for about a week until the first true leaves begin to emerge. Thin to one plant per pot with scissors. Lower the temperature to 65° to 70°F (18 to 21°C) and reduce watering for another week.

Inside or Out?

In warm climates you can direct-sow melons, but starting plants indoors is preferred, both because the melon plants can grow well in soil 10° to 20°F (6 to 11°C) cooler than that needed for best germination of seed, and because the seeds germinate more slowly in cooler soil. Wherever you live, transplanting will probably give the best yields.

GROWING

Make sure the soil temperature is at least 70°F (21°C) before transplanting. Plant 16 inches (40 cm) apart, one row in the middle of a narrow (30-inch; 76 cm) bed. To avoid transplant shock, be very careful not to disturb the roots while planting. In many regions, melons need every day of the growing season to ripen fruit and cannot afford any setbacks. After planting, cover the beds with floating row covers to increase warmth and provide a barrier to pests. Remove the row covers when the plants begin to bloom.

A Cantaloupe by Another Name

"Why can't melons get married? — Because they can't elope." As common as this melon is, in some places what is called a cantaloupe is really something else entirely. In North America muskmelons are often called cantaloupes, but the two are completely different plants. A cantaloupe has a hard, warty rind, while a muskmelon, like the one pictured here, has a soft rind covered with netting. In addition, cantaloupes are rarely grown outside Europe.

Melons are sensitive to drought throughout the season, but especially from transplanting to fruit set. To get fruits of the proper size, water evenly, but not too much, as excess moisture when fruits are enlarging can diminish flavor. Check soil moisture frequently. Fruits grow quickly and sometimes outgrow the nutrient reserve in the soil. Pale green leaves result. To correct this, use a complete organic fertilizer, such as fish emulsion or kelp, from transplanting to fruit set.

▲ **Fertilizer-wise tips.** From transplanting until flowers appear, use a fertilizer with more nitrogen than phosphorus or potassium, such as a 5-2-2. Later, from flowering until fruit reaches mature size, use a fertilizer with more phosphorus and potassium than nitrogen, such as 3-5-5.

Bitter Relatives

Grow melons far enough from cucumbers and winter squash so the vines cannot intertwine. The melons will be bitter if their blossoms are pollinated by either of these related plants.

HARVESTING

It's pretty easy to tell when most vegetables are ripe, but melons require a little more practice to get it absolutely right. A nice tip to know is that all the fruits on any individual melon plant will ripen over a short period of time. If one melon is ripe, the remaining melons won't be far behind.

Most melons. With the exception of watermelons and French Charentais, melons are ripe when the rind changes from gray-green to yellow-buff. The fruit is still firm, but gentle thumb pressure easily separates the stem from the vine.

Charentais melons. When the leaf nearest the fruit of these melons fades from green to pale yellow, you'll know they're ripe. Harvest charentais melons by cutting the stem (which is still firmly attached to the fruit) with scissors or shears.

Watermelon. Gauging when to pick a watermelon is bathed in tradition as much as science. Find the method that works in your garden and stick with it. Here are the most popular ways to determine when a watermelon is ripe:

▶ The tendril nearest to the fruit turns from green to brown.
▶ The underside of the melon, where it sits on the ground, is yellow.
▶ When you rap it lightly, you hear a low-pitched "thunk" or "thump" instead of a high-pitched "ping." Try a few that aren't ripe to tune your ear to the sound.

STORING

Store melons? Homegrown melons are too good to store. It's like asking children to save their Halloween candy for later. At harvesttime the melons are lucky to make it from the garden to the house unscathed. But if you must pick and eat on separate days, all melons will store in the refrigerator for a week or so. Many melons taste even better chilled. It's your choice!

BEST VARIETIES

Charentais. These produce medium-sized fruit with a grayish green rind. The flesh is bright orange, intoxicatingly aromatic, and sweet. Charentais melons are very popular in Europe, especially France, and are becoming increasingly available in North America. Some nice varieties include *Charmel, Alienor, Honey Girl Hybrid Charentais,* and *Savor.*

Galias. Galias bear medium to large fruits with greenish rinds covered with beige netting. The flesh is a translucent green that looks as refreshing as it tastes. The flavor is rich, sweet, and spicy. Some popular varieties include *Galia Perfume Melon* and *Passport.*

Honeydews. Medium melons with smooth yellowish white rinds, honeydews have flesh ranging from icy white to orange depending on the variety. Very juicy and nicely sweet. Some popular varieties include *Earlidew, Hon-I-Dew,* and *Honey Ice.*

Crenshaws. Similar to honeydews, Crenshaws produce medium to large fruits with a yellowish rind. The flesh is usually pale green, but some varieties have an orange tone. Crenshaw varieties include *Burpee Early Hybrid, Honeyshaw,* and *Early Crenshaw.*

Muskmelons. Medium to large, often ribbed, fruits have rinds covered with tan netting. The flesh is sunset orange, juicy, and sweet. Some varieties are also nicely aromatic. Muskmelons are the most popular garden-grown melon. The many varieties to choose from include *Honey Bun Hybrid, Burpee Hybrid, Sweet 'n Early, Earlysweet, Ambrosia, Alaska,* and *Earligold.*

Watermelons. Popular everywhere, watermelons bear large to very large fruits with smooth rinds colored from pale green to almost black. The fruit is so juicy it could come in a bottle, and it has that sweet, summery flavor that is, well, watermelon. There are many varieties, from the little icebox types favored by cool-climate gardeners to the large arks grown in warm regions. Here are some of the most popular: *Yellow Doll, Sugar Baby, New Queen, Moon and Stars, Tiger Baby, Crimson Sweet, Sweet Favorite,* and *Fordhook Hybrid.*

▲ **What a doll!** Watermelon doesn't have to be red. This Yellow Doll watermelon is even sweeter than the more common reds.

Okra

Okra is one of those plants that is as attractive as it is tasty. But beauty is much more than skin deep in the case of okra. In the South, where preparing and consuming the pods is an art, okra can be boiled, cooked slowly with tomatoes and spices, or dipped in batter, breaded, and fried.

SOWING AND GROWING

In cool climates or for early crops in warm regions, warm the soil with black plastic for about three to four weeks before transplanting okra. At the same time, sow seeds indoors in individual pots. After all danger of frost has passed, set plants 1 foot (30 cm) apart, being careful not to disturb the roots. In warm climates, you can also direct-sow okra.

Water plants during dry periods and fertilize once a month with a natural fertilizer such as fish emulsion or seaweed.

HARVESTING AND STORING

Some folks harvest okra pods when they are 3 inches (8 cm) long, but the pods are probably most flavorful and tender if gathered when 2 inches (5 cm) long. Okra, like beans, is best when it's eaten the day it's picked. If this isn't possible, you can store it for a day or so in the refrigerator.

BEST VARIETIES

In recent years, dwarf, spineless, and early-maturing varieties have brought okra to short-season gardens where it couldn't be grown before.
Cajun Delight is high yielding and early, making it the natural choice for cool-season gardeners.
Burgundy reaches 4 feet (1.2 m) tall with very attractive, deep wine-colored stems and pods, as pretty on the plate as in the garden. The pods are equally tender picked large or small.

▲ **Okra is more than OK.** Wherever you garden, from Zone 4 to Zone 11, easy-to-grow okra can add delicious variety to your garden and dinner plate.

Sow & Grow

OKRA *(Abelmoschus esculentus)*
Mallow family *(Malvaceae)*

SOWING
Seed depth: ¾" (19 mm)
Germination soil temperature: 80–95°F (27–35°C)
Days to germination: 5–14
Sow indoors: 5 weeks before last frost
Sow outdoors: After last frost (only in warm climates)

GROWING
pH range: 6.0–8.0
Growing soil temperature: 70–90°F (21–32°C)
Spacing in beds: 12" (30 cm)
Watering: Low
Light: Full sun
Nutrient requirements: N=moderate; P=moderate; K=moderate
Rotation considerations: Can be rotated with any other crop.
Good companions: Basil, eggplant, pepper
Bad companions: None
Seed longevity: 2 years
Seeds per ounce: 500 (18 per g)

Onions

There's a story about a fellow who bought a dog in hopes of training her to watch over the house. But this dog had an independent personality, and training went poorly. The more upset the owner got, the worse things became. Finally, he just gave up and let the dog do what she wanted to. As it turned out, the house suited the dog very well, and she became the best watchdog that fellow ever had.

Onions are a lot like that dog. To grow good onions, give them just what they need, and then don't bother them. Come harvesttime, you'll have a crop that will bring tears to your eyes.

▲ **A harvest to cry for.** With good soil preparation but little through-the-season care, onions are a satisfying crop to grow. These Stockton Reds are a beautiful and colorful red onion suitable for northern regions.

Sow & Grow

ONIONS
(Allium cepa)
Onion family *(Liliaceae)*

SOWING

Seed depth: *For transplants,* ½" (1.3 cm); *for sets,* 1" (2.5 cm); *for seeds,* ¼–½" (.65–1.3 cm)
Soil temperature: 65–85°F (18–29°C)
Days to germination: 4–5
Sow indoors: 2 months before last frost
Sow outdoors: Spring

GROWING

pH range: 6.0–7.5
Soil temperature: 55–75°F (13–24°C)

Spacing in beds: 3–4" (7.5–10 cm); 1" (2.5 cm) if grown like scallions
Watering: Medium and even
Light: Full sun for best yield, tolerates light shade
Nutrient requirements: N=moderate; P=moderate; K=moderate
Rotation considerations: Follow squash or lettuce; do not follow any onion family crop or legume.
Good companions: Beet, cabbage family, carrot, kohlrabi, early lettuce (in good soil), parsnip, pepper, spinach, strawberry, tomato, turnip
Bad companions: Asparagus, bean, pea, sage
Seed longevity: 1 year
Seeds per ounce: 8,500 (300 seeds per g)

10

THE SITE

Onions are picky about certain things, and the soil they call home is one of them. The plants prefer fertile, loose, friable soil that is well drained with lots of organic matter. Sandy loams are just about ideal. Before planting, turn in good amounts of compost or well-rotted manure no matter what kind of soil you have.

SOWING AND PLANTING

You can grow onions from seeds sown indoors, direct-seed them in the garden, grow them from purchased plants, or grow them from sets.

Growing onions from seeds indoors. Onion plants grow very slowly and need a good head start on the growing season. About 8 to 10 weeks before the last frost date, sow seeds indoors ¼ inch (6 mm) deep, ½ inch (13 mm) apart in flats or four or five seeds per cell. Provide bottom heat and keep the soil moist. When the seedlings are tall enough for the tops to droop, give the plants a haircut (see photo below).

Direct-seeding onions. Because direct-seeding involves the least disturbance in the growth cycle, onions grown this way are less susceptible to stress and disease, less likely to bolt, and store better. Many onion varieties take a long time to mature,

however, so direct-seeding is not always practical in northern regions.

In spring, when the soil temperature reaches 50°F (10°C), sow one to three seeds per inch (2.5 cm), ¼ to ½ inch (6–13 mm) deep, in rows 4 inches (10 cm) apart. When the seedlings are about 2 inches (5 cm) tall, begin thinning. To produce onions to be used as scallions, thin to 1 inch (2.5 cm) apart. For the best overall yield, thin to 2 inches (5 cm) apart. And for the largest bulbs, thin to 4 inches (10 cm) apart. The thinnings can be tossed into spring salads or transplanted.

Growing onions from purchased plants. Transplant purchased plants (as well as those you started indoors) to the garden four weeks before the last expected frost. For the best yield per square foot, set plants about 3 to 4 inches (7.5–10 cm) apart in staggered rows. If purchased plants have long leaves, trim them back by about a third. Interplanting with a companion, such as beets, can help control weeds.

Planting onion sets. Commercial growers produce onion sets by sowing seeds very thickly and then growing the plants very close together. These crowded conditions make the plants mature rapidly, while keeping the bulbs small. This is important because by the time you buy the onion set, it is already one year old and ready to flower (bolt), which you don't want it to do.

▲ **Need a trim?** When seedling tops begin to droop, use shears to cut the plants back to about 3 inches (7.5 cm) high. This stimulates additional root growth. Use the clippings in soups or salads.

▲ **Smaller is better.** Small onion sets are less likely to bolt, so look for bulbs about the size of a dime when you choose sets.

Plant sets 1 inch (2.5 cm) deep, in a staggered spacing about 3 to 4 inches (7.5–10 cm) apart, or in rows 6 to 8 inches (15–20 cm) apart. If you grow both plants and sets, put them in different parts of the garden, as the sets are sometimes more prone to disease.

GROWING

Onions don't compete well with weeds and are easily damaged by many weeding tools. Use careful, regular, shallow cultivation to nip weeds early while avoiding damaging roots.

Watering. Their shallow root systems makes onions sensitive to fluctuations in soil moisture. Though plants don't need a whole lot of water, they like regular watering each week. Mulch to maintain soil moisture and control weeds.

Fertilizing. Onions don't require large amounts of nutrients, but their root systems are so small and shallow they need to grow in highly fertile soil just to absorb what they do need. Sidedress with compost in late spring. If needed, apply an organic fertilizer such as fish emulsion once a month. Be stingy. Too much nitrogen will produce lots of leaves and small bulbs.

HARVESTING

Onions are ready to harvest when most of the tops fall over. Just how many tops have to fall over before you begin to harvest depends on where you live. In cool, humid areas, wait until almost all the tops fall over. In cool, dry areas, harvest when about half the tops have fallen over. And in warm regions, begin harvesting when about a quarter to a third of the tops fall over.

Gently pull onions from the ground, and then leave them to cure in the sun for at least a week. When the tops and papery skin on the bulbs are dry and crinkly, clip the tops about an inch (2.5 cm) from the bulbs and store in onion bags in a cool, dry place.

What Is a Scallion?

A scallion is any onion that produces a bulb no larger than the width of the base of the leaves. In garden catalogs, these are often called bunching onions. Some good varieties of scallions include Parade, Long White Tokyo, White Lisbon, and Deep Purple.

Onions that are pulled before the bulb forms are also often called scallions, although that's not what they really are. Scallions have a softer, less penetrating flavor than onions, even if the onions are pulled when small.

◀ **Give your onions a sunbath.** When it's time to harvest onions, try to anticipate a warm, dry, sunny spell so the bulbs can sun-cure for at least a week. If it rains, move the bulbs to an open shed, porch, or other covered but airy spot.

STORING

Not all onions store equally well. Sweet onions, such as Walla Walla, should be used within a few weeks of harvest. Storage onions, such as Copra and Prince, keep well for months. Use storage onions grown from sets first, because they don't store as well as the ones grown from seed or plants.

Keep stored onions away from apples or tomatoes, which give off ethylene gas that causes onions to sprout.

BEST VARIETIES

First Edition. This onion gives cool-season gardeners all they want — full, rich flavor, long storage, and full-sized bulbs. The bulbs are tightly wrapped in bronze-copper skins that protect the pungent, juicy flesh. An excellent all-around onion.

Yellow Granex. The sweet, mild onion grown in Vidalia, Georgia. Yellow Granex is very juicy but can be peeled with only a hint of a tear. It's an excellent onion for all warm regions, though your crop will probably be slightly more pungent than those grown in Georgia.

Stockton Red. Medium-sized, deep red bulbs hold flesh that is mild enough for polite fresh eating, while still having real onion flavor. Stores well.

Walla Walla Sweet. This is a sweet, mild-flavored onion that has been popular for over a century. It bears juicy white flesh that is excellent in fresh recipes. It does not store well.

Buffalo. If you prefer growing your onions from seed rather than plants, this one's for you. It produces medium-sized bulbs that have good onion flavor. Bulbs store for a few months.

Alisa Craig Exhibition. These onions are big — very big. The large bulbs can be over 4 inches (10 cm) in diameter, with ice white flesh and just enough kick to let you know it's an onion. Best if used fresh but can be stored for a few months.

The Long and the Short of It

Onions are divided into two types, long day and short day.

Short-day varieties, which need about equal amounts of darkness and light to set bulbs, grow best in southern regions. An example of a short-day onion is Yellow Granex, often called Vidalia.

Long-day varieties, which need about 14 hours of light and 10 of darkness, are favored in the North. Long-day onions include First Edition and Baby Borettana.

▲ **Practical and decorative.** If you braid your onion tops before they dry out, they'll store well and be a pleasure to look at as well.

Parsnips

Some people invest in the stock market; I invest in parsnips. This pale cousin of the carrot is like a bank certificate of deposit. I deposit some seeds and labor during the warm months, and my investment matures early the next spring, when my vegetable reserves are at their yearly low. An early-April meal of parsnips fresh from the still-slumbering garden renews my energy and restores my faith that summer is just ahead.

▲ **Spring tonic.** To me, a true sign of spring is parsnips, sliced thinly and sautéed in a little butter over a low flame until they're tender.

SOWING AND GROWING

Parsnips can take even longer to germinate than carrots (about two to three weeks). Plant seeds ½ inch (1.3 cm) deep and 1 inch (2.5 cm) apart in rows 4 to 6 inches (10–15 cm) apart across a bed. Keep the soil evenly moist during the germination period.

When the parsnips are 4 to 6 inches (10–15 cm) high, thin them to 3 to 4 inches (7.5–10 cm) apart, apply a layer of leaf mold around the plants, and mulch with straw. That's it. Your part is done until harvest next spring.

HARVESTING AND STORING

You can harvest parsnips at the end of the growing season, but they don't develop their sweet, almost nutty flavor until after they've been through some hard frosts and preferably through a hard winter. Store in the fridge or root cellar.

BEST VARIETIES

Harris Model. The snowy white flesh makes these parsnips attractive, but its smooth texture and exquisite flavor are what make it exceptional.

Lancer. A Harris type with uniform roots, disease resistance, and excellent flavor.

Sow & Grow

PARSNIPS *(Pastinaca sativa)*
Carrot family *(Umbelliferae)*

SOWING

Seed depth: ½" (13 mm)
Soil temperature: 65–75°F (18–24°C)
Days to germination: 12–14
Sow indoors: Not recommended
Sow outdoors: As soon as soil can be worked

GROWING

pH range: 6.0–7.0
Soil temperature: 60–65°F (16–18°C)
Spacing in beds: 4" (10 cm), in rows 4" apart
Watering: Moderate
Light: Best yields in full sun; tolerates light shade
Nutrient requirements: N=high; P=low; K=low
Rotation considerations: Avoid following carrots, parsley, or celery.
Good companions: Bush bean, garlic, onion, pea, pepper, potato, radish
Bad companions: Caraway, carrot, celery
Seed longevity: 1 year
Seeds per ounce: 6,800 (240 seeds per g)

Peanuts

Up here in Vermont, we love peanuts. The trouble is that the only peanuts we have are the ones for sale in the grocery store. Peanuts don't like cool climates, but in warm climates these relatives of peas and alfalfa are a standard part of the vegetable garden. You can choose from among four peanut types: Runner, a commercial type; Virginia, which has large kernels; Spanish, which are early maturers and therefore good in cooler climates; and Valencia, with sweet, small kernels.

SOWING AND GROWING

Before planting, work some compost or well-rotted manure into the soil. Peanuts do best in soils rich in calcium, so add limestone (which also raises pH) or gypsum (which does not raise pH).

Sow seed peanuts in a hole 4 inches (10 cm) deep or in a furrow about 2 inches (5 cm) deep. As the seedlings grow, fill in around the base of the plants with loose soil. About a month after the stems emerge from the soil, blossoms develop near the bottom of the plant. When the petals fall off, the peg (the flower stem and peanut embryo), bends downward and grows into the loose soil. After all the pegs have buried themselves in the soil, mulch around the plants with a layer of straw.

HARVESTING

Two months after the plants bloom, test for ripeness by lifting a plant with a garden fork. A ripe peanut will feel firm, with dry, papery outer skin. When peanuts are ripe, lift plants from the ground with a fork and shake off excess soil. Cure plants by laying them on a screen in the sun for two or three days. Next, separate the peanuts from the plants, return the nuts to the screen, and place the screen in a warm, dry location for about three weeks.

◀ **Surprise!** Growing peanuts is great fun. They grow underground, so you don't see your harvest until you dig them up. It's like waiting to open a present.

Sow & Grow

PEANUTS *(Arachis hypogaea)*
Pea family *(Leguminosae)*

SOWING
Seed depth: 3–4" (7.5–10 cm)
Germination soil temperature: 70°F (21°C)
Days to germination: 7–14
Sow indoors: 3 weeks before last frost, but difficult to transplant
Sow outdoors: After last frost

GROWING
pH range: 6.0–7.0
Growing soil temperature: 70–85°F (21–29°C)
Spacing in beds: 18" (45 cm)
Watering: Heavy until peg enters soil; moderate thereafter
Light: Full sun
Nutrient requirements: N=low; P=moderate; K=moderate
Rotation considerations: Follow root crops such as carrots; avoid following legumes.
Good companions: Beets, carrots
Bad companions: None
Seed longevity: 1–3 years
Seeds per ounce: Not applicable

Peas

One of the nicest things about gardening is getting to know the vegetables you grow. Living in a world where most of our food is frozen or canned, we risk losing touch with what food looks like when it's growing. Vine-ripened tomatoes, fresh sweet corn, and tender mouthwatering peas fresh from the garden are the three best reasons for having a garden.

SOWING

Tradition holds that you plant peas "as soon as the soil can be worked," but peas actually germinate much more slowly in cold soil. And the colder the soil, the more slowly they germinate: from 9 days in 60°F (16°C) soil, to 36 days in 40°F (4°C) soil. Let the soil warm up a little, or use dark plastic mulch to warm the soil, so the seeds spend less time in the ground. Peas planted a bit later catch up very quickly with those planted earlier.

▲ **Plan in fall for next summer's crop of peas.** Since peas are one of the first crops to be sown in spring, you'll get the most from your pea crop if you get the soil ready for the spring planting in fall by turning in lots of compost or rotted manure.

Ask a bunch of gardeners about how far apart to space pea seeds, and you'll hear everything from ½ inch to 4 inches (1.3–10 cm). I've had good results with very close spacing, about 1 inch (2.5 cm), staggered in narrow bands on both sides

Sow & Grow

PEAS
(Pisum sativum, P. s. var. *macrocarpon)*
Pea family *(Leguminosae)*

SOWING

Seed depth: 1" (2.5 cm)

Soil temperature: 40–75°F (4–24°C), the optimum is 75°F (24°C)

Days to germination: 14

Sow indoors: Not recommended

Sow outdoors: As soon as soil can be worked, late summer for fall crop

GROWING

pH range: 6.0–7.0

Soil temperature: 60–65°F (16–18°C)

Spacing in beds: 1" (2.5 cm) in a staggered pattern

Watering: Moderate until blossoming, then low

Light: Best yield in full sun; tolerates partial shade

Nutrient requirements: N=low; P=low; K=low

Rotation considerations: Follow with kale.

Good companions: Carrot, celery, chicory, corn, cucumber, eggplant, parsley, early potato, radish, spinach, strawberry, sweet pepper, turnip

Bad companions: Onion, late potato

Seed longevity: 3 years

Seeds per ounce: 200 (7 seeds per g)

of a trellis. Dip the seeds in an inoculative solution before sowing to be sure that nitrogen-fixing bacteria will be present in the soil.

GROWING

You may hear that you needn't fertilize peas because they can get nitrogen right from the air. As with much garden wisdom, this is *almost* correct. The truth is that the bacteria that provide peas with nitrogen don't do this trick at the drop of a hat. It takes a few weeks before the plant actually gets any nitrogen from the bacteria. Meanwhile, the plant has to get its nitrogen from the soil like any other plant. To help them along, when seedlings are 2 to 4 inches (5–10 cm) tall, fertilize them lightly with a complete organic fertilizer.

HARVESTING AND STORING

Like corn, peas are delightfully sweet if you pick them at the right time, but they turn starchy if you don't.

Snow peas. Pick snow peas as soon as the pod reaches mature length but before the peas in the pod are very much developed. Check often: The just-right stage doesn't last more than a day or so.

Sugar peas. These are best when both the pods and the peas are plump and the pods snap like a bean pod. If the pod is stringy, remove the "string" by breaking off the tip and then pulling the string up the inside curve and down the outside.

Garden peas. For best flavor and texture, pick garden peas when pods have filled out but aren't bulging around the peas. Pick all the large ones you missed earlier. Pods left too long on the vine signal the plant to stop producing more peas.

BEST VARIETIES

Garden peas, also called English peas. Flavorful varieties include *Knight*, with plentiful, very early pods on 2½-foot-tall (76 cm) vines; *Lincoln*,

Trellising Tricks

Peas are healthier and easier to harvest when they grow on a trellis (see pages 72-73). If a vine strays from the netting, just direct it back. If the whole mass bulges out too far, attach some garden twine to one end of the trellis, and then weave the twine in and out of the netting strings. Pull the twine taut, and tie the twine to the post at the opposite end of the trellis.

▲ **Mind your peas.** Picked at just the right time, before the peas in the pod have developed very much, snow peas are tender and sweet, but over-large pods are tough and stringy.

a reliable heirloom, bearing long, slender pods filled with sweet peas; *Green Arrow*, a high-yield variety with flavorful peas on 3- to 4-foot-tall (0.9–1.2 m) vines.

Snow peas. Some popular varieties include *Corgi*, with thin, sweet pods that taste great in stir-fries; *Oregon Giant*, with very large pods around sweet, tiny peas; and *Norli*, with early, very high yields of flavorful, sweet pods.

Sugar peas, also called snap peas. Thick, succulent pods hold a host of sweet peas. Look for *Super Sugar Mel*, the best of the sugar peas, with disease resistance, early and heavy yields, and long, sweet pods and *Super Sugar Snap*, a tall (6 feet; 1.8 m) variety bearing loads of sweet, tasty peas.

Peppers

Peppers are a vegetable that can warm you right to your bones, with flavors from sweet to very, very hot. They come in many colors, including green, red, yellow, brown, orange, and even lavender and purple. Peppers also come in different shapes, from squarish blocks to long thin cones and cherrylike balls. Regardless of flavor, color, or size, all peppers are grown pretty much the same.

SOWING

Most of peppers' special needs have something to do with temperature: They are very sensitive to frost at either end of the growing cycle. They like relatively high temperatures for germination and for growth outdoors. But oddly, they benefit greatly from a jolt of cold early in life after they germinate.

▲ **Pick a pint for pickled peppers.** If you've never eaten green peppers fresh from the garden, you'll be surprised at how crisp and tender this common vegetable can really be. Fresh, frozen, or pickled, garden peppers earn their garden space over and over.

Sow & Grow

PEPPERS
(Capsicum annuum)
Tomato family *(Solanaceae)*

SOWING

Seed depth: ¼" (6 mm)
Soil temperature: 80–85°F (27–29°C)
Days to germination: 6–8
Sow indoors: 8 weeks before last frost
Sow outdoors: Not recommended

GROWING

pH range: 5.5–7.0 (best results may occur at the acid end of this range)

Soil temperature: 70–85°F (21–29°C)
Spacing in beds: 12" (30 cm)
Watering: Moderate and even until fruit set; less as fruit matures
Light: Full sun
Nutrient requirements: N=high; P=high; K=high
Rotation considerations: Do not follow with tomatoes, eggplant, potatoes.
Good companions: Carrot, onion, parsnip, pea
Bad companions: Fennel, kohlrabi
Seed longevity: 2 years
Seeds per ounce: 4,500 (160 seeds per g)

About eight weeks before the last frost date, fill flats or growing cells with seed-starter mix or screened potting mix. Sow the seeds ¼ inch (6 mm) deep and water well. Keep the soil warm, between 80° and 85°F (27–29°C). Warm temperatures are very important for quick germination. Temperatures below 80°F slow germination, and slow germination gets the plants off to a poor start.

For increased flower and fruit production, try to provide your peppers the following temperatures: As soon as the first true leaves appear, transplant into 4-inch (10 cm) pots and lower the soil temperature to 70°F (21°C), 60°F (16°C) at night. When the third set of true leaves appears, lower the night temperature to 55°F (13°C) for four weeks. Moving plants from the house to a cold frame will likely accomplish this. At the end of four weeks, grow the plants at 70°F

▲ **A bit of a shiver does peppers good.** After a warm germination period, peppers benefit from about a month in the cold before spending the rest of their pre-garden stage in more moderate temperatures.

(21°C) day and night until it's time to put them in the garden.

Light is also important after the true leaves appear and while strong root systems are developing. Sunlight, especially in northern latitudes, isn't sufficient. Use artificial light — grow lights if you have them — to provide up to 16 hours per day.

Sometimes pepper plants begin to form flower buds before the root system is large enough to support a large crop. Remove any blossoms that appear before transplanting time and for about a week afterward.

GROWING

Peppers love heat, so don't rush them into the garden before the soil is thoroughly warm. Use plastic mulch (either black or IRT) to warm the soil and floating row covers to warm the plants once you've put them out.

Plant in a staggered pattern, 1 foot (30 cm) apart, three wide in a 36-inch (90 cm) bed. Peppers like each other's company and grow best when close enough so the leaves of the mature plants are barely touching. As my mother used to say, "Peppers like to hold hands."

Keep the soil evenly moist and remove the row covers when flower buds appear or the air temperature exceeds 85°F (29°C).

HARVESTING AND STORING

You can harvest peppers when they're green, but most are completely ripe when they turn red. When you harvest is largely a matter of personal preference. Red sweet peppers (bell peppers) are sweeter than green sweet peppers. And red hot peppers are hotter than most green hot peppers. People who prefer green peppers do get a slight advantage over those favoring red: As long as you pick the fruits at the green stage instead of letting them ripen to red, the plant goes right on setting new fruits.

Peppers keep in the refrigerator for about two weeks. We like to freeze them for spaghetti sauce or soups by slicing them and putting them in a plastic pint freezer container. It's easy to dry red peppers. Just lay them on a screen or string them and hang them in a dry, airy spot. Dried peppers remain flavorful for about a year when stored in clean glass jars.

Best Varieties of Sweet Peppers

Ace. A bell type and undemanding, Ace produces bountiful, early crops of large, slightly conical fruits.

Ariane. Sunset on a pepper plant! Dutch-style peppers turn stunning orange when ripe.

Early Sunsation. This bright yellow bell pepper has excellent flavor.

Hungarian Sweet Banana. Long and thin-walled, this pepper bears yellow to orange, very tasty fruits.

Islander. A bell type that's as colorful as a pepper can get, Islander bears large, delicious, lavender-purple fruits.

Sweet Chocolate. If only it were true! Named for its deep brown skin color, Sweet Chocolate is more tolerant of cool weather than most varieties and bears reliably large crops.

Yankee Bell. Bred for cooler climates, this pepper bears nice, big, blocky fruits.

▲ **How sweet it is.** Peppers are delicious when green or red or in between, but red ones are sweetest.

Best Varieties of Hot Peppers

Anaheim. A hot pepper with manners, this variety bears long fruit that is pleasingly mild, with only a suggestion of its hot pepper heritage.

Bulgarian Carrot. Bearing 4-inch (10 cm) long, bright orange fruits, Bulgarian Carrot peppers add warmth to any recipe.

Firenza Jalapeño. This is the plant to choose if you want large crops of thick-walled, flavorful hot peppers.

Numex Joe E. Parker. Hot enough to add zip and mild enough to be invited back, Numex Joe E. Parker produces more, and better-tasting, peppers than most hot varieties.

Thai Dragon. One of the best varieties for Asian recipes, Thai Dragon bears lots of 3-inch-long (7.5 cm) peppers that are very hot.

That Warm Feeling Inside

For centuries people knew that not all hot peppers were created equal. Some were much hotter than others. Around 1912, Wilbur Scoville discovered a rather complicated way to measure the "heat" of peppers. Today we know the spiciness of a pepper depends on how much capsaicin it contains. Yet in honor of his contributions to pepper lovers, the heat of peppers is still measured in Scoville units. As a point of reference for understanding the following rankings, pure capsaicin is rated at 15,500,000 Scoville units.

Pepper Name	Scoville Units
Bell Pepper	0
Anaheim	500–2,500
Jalapeño	2,500–4,500
Serrano	7,000–25,000
Cayenne	30,000–50,000
Thai	70,000–100,000
Habañero	100,000–325,000
Red Savina Habañero	350,000–550,000

Potatoes

Commercial growers supply us with so many potatoes that they seem to be everywhere, from our dinner plates to supermarkets to fast-food restaurants. With such abundance, why allocate space in the garden for potatoes? The reason is simple: Homegrown potatoes are delicious — much tastier than store bought. Plus, you can grow potato varieties commercial producers just don't grow.

PLANTING

Time your potato planting according to where you live:

▶ **In warm climates,** plant in fall.
▶ **In warm-temperate areas,** plant in late winter.
▶ **In cool climates,** plant in early to midspring, about the time dandelions and daffodils bloom.

▲ **A rainbow of potatoes.** Not too long ago, garden catalogs carried just a couple of potato varieties. Well, things have changed. Today the selection is so diverse that gardeners can even buy a rainbow of potatoes, from yellow to red to blue — and when you get to the end of the rainbow, gold.

You'll find that some seed potatoes are larger than others. You can plant golf-ball–size tubers directly in the ground without first cutting them; larger ones need to be cut into sections. Whatever their size, seed potatoes need some preparation about two days before planting.

Sow & Grow

POTATOES
(Solanum tuberosum)
Tomato family *(Solanaceae)*

SOWING/PLANTING
Tuber depth: 3–4" (7.5–10 cm)
Soil temperature: At least 45°F (7°C)
Plant tubers outdoors: 3 weeks before last frost

GROWING
pH range: 5.0–6.5
Soil temperature: 60–65°F (16–18°C)
Spacing in beds: 12" (30 cm)

Watering: Moderate, particularly during tuber formation, signaled by the appearance of blossoms
Light: Full sun for best yields; tolerates partial shade
Nutrient requirements: N=high; P=high; K=high
Rotation considerations: Do not follow with tomato family plants.
Good companions: Bush bean, cabbage family, corn, horseradish, marigold, parsnip, pea
Bad companions: Cucumber, pumpkin, rutabaga, squash family, sunflower, tomato, turnip
Seed longevity: Not applicable
Seeds per ounce: Not applicable

Preparing for planting. Cut large tubers into pieces about 1½ inches thick (3.75 cm). Make sure each piece contains at least two "eyes." The eyes should be just beginning to sprout, but not so much that a stem has formed. As a rule of thumb, each piece should weigh between 1½ and 2 ounces (45 and 60 g). To heal the cut potatoes, place them in a well-ventilated area at about 55°F (13°C) for one or two days.

After healing, treat potatoes with a light dusting of agricultural sulfur to guard against fungal diseases and ward off potato beetles (see photos below).

A

B

▲ **Potato prep.** (A) Cut large tubers into 1½-inch-thick (3.75 cm) pieces, and then let them heal in a cool place for a couple of days. (B) Toss the potatoes in a paper bag with a handful of agricultural sulfur before planting.

Traditional planting method. It's usual to plant potatoes about 1 foot (30 cm) apart in a shallow trench about 3 inches (7.5 cm) deep. When the plants are about a foot (30 cm) tall, "hill" them by drawing soil up around them with a hoe until just the top few inches of the plant poke out from the soil. Some gardeners hill a second time two or three weeks later. This method keeps the potatoes from turning green, but it's time consuming and increases the likelihood of problems with high soil temperature and low moisture.

▲ **This amounts to a hill of potatoes.** When the plants are 12 inches (30 cm) tall, hill the soil around them so that just a few inches of the plants show above the soil.

A Pound of Prevention

Get your crop off to the right start with a couple of simple precautions that should help prevent disease:

▶ "Seed potatoes" are potatoes grown specifically for planting. To avoid potato diseases, purchase only certified tubers. Avoid planting supermarket potatoes, which can carry diseases and are often treated with a chemical to inhibit sprouting.

▶ Enrich the soil with compost not manure, which can increase the incidence of potato scab. Potatoes can tolerate a higher pH without forming scab in a well-balanced, fertile soil.

Mulch planting method. Growing potatoes under mulch regulates soil moisture and temperature, makes the potatoes easier to harvest, and is less work all around than the traditional method. Plant in trenches 3 inches (7.5 cm) deep and 1 foot (30 cm) apart. When plants are a few inches tall, apply 1 inch (2.5 cm) of compost topped by a layer of straw so that about a half to two-thirds of each plant is covered. As the plants grow, add more straw, keeping the mulch at least 6 inches (15 cm) deep.

Potatoes have shallow roots (12–15 inches; 30–37.5 cm) and are very sensitive to changes in soil moisture during certain periods in their growth cycle. Be sure to keep the plants well watered from the time they flower until two weeks before harvest.

HARVESTING AND STORING

You can harvest some tender "new" potatoes a couple of months after planting, either by pulling a plant or by feeling around and snitching one or two from each plant, leaving the rest undisturbed.

Harvest the main crop when the foliage dies back. With a garden fork or broadfork, gently loosen the soil and feel around for the tubers. This is easier on the hands and better for the potatoes if you let the soil dry out a bit before the harvest.

Brush dry soil gently from the tubers, but don't wash them. Cure for about two weeks at around 55°F (13°C) in humid conditions, and then store at about 40°F (4°C) in a root cellar. Do not store potatoes with apples.

BEST VARIETIES

Kennebec. One of the most versatile varieties, with well-formed, yellowish tubers that are very flavorful, Kennebec is disease resistant and stores well.

Yukon Gold. Vigorous plants produce large, flavorful tubers that have yellow flesh and store well.

Red Sun. Smooth texture and full flavor make these bright red potatoes very special indeed; they have excellent yields.

▲ **Straw mulch technique.** Instead of hilling potatoes with soil, some gardeners maintain a thick (6 inches; 15 cm) straw mulch around their potato plants.

▲ **Hunting for treasure.** Harvesting vegetables is a joy whether you're picking sweet corn or pulling carrots. But letting your hands swim around in the soil feeling for potatoes is just plain fun.

All Blue. Colorful and flavorful, All Blue bears lots of potatoes, which feature indigo skin and blue and white flesh.

Giant Peanut Fingerling. If you want a change from fluffy, bland potatoes, try these fingerlings, which bear 4-inch-long (10 cm), pale tubers with firm, flavorful white flesh.

Gold Rush. One of the best baking potatoes, Gold Rush has a flaky texture and sweet-flavored flesh.

Sweet Potatoes

Few things are as tasty as sweet potato pie — unless, of course, it's sweet potato fries sprinkled with cinnamon and dipped in tangy mustard. Sweet potatoes are a crop identified with warm regions, but with a little gentle persuasion this hearty vegetable will provide even cool-climate gardeners with a large, sweet harvest.

PLANTING

Most vegetables are grown from seeds, but sweet potatoes are grown from rooted cuttings. The cuttings, called slips or draws, are produced from the sprouts of sweet potato roots. You can buy slips at garden centers, by mail order, and on the Internet. It's also easy to make your own slips, and it's so much fun that most folks prefer to do it themselves. (See What a Slip! in the box on the facing page.)

▲ **A welcome vine.** Sweet potatoes will be ready for harvest from this prolific vine three to four months after planting, but they do need to be harvested before the first fall frost.

Sow & Grow

SWEET POTATOES
(Ipomoea batatas)
Morning glory family *(Convolvulaceae)*

SOWING/PLANTING
Seed depth: Not applicable
Germination soil temperature: Not applicable
Days to germination: Not applicable
Sow indoors: Not applicable
Transplant outdoors: 2 weeks after last frost

GROWING
pH range: 5.5–6.5
Growing soil temperature: 65–90°F (18–32°C)
Spacing in beds: 14–18" (35–45 cm)
Watering: Low
Light: Full sun
Nutrient requirements: N=low; P=low; K=low
Rotation considerations: Avoid following root crops.
Good companions: Marigold
Bad companions: Beets, carrots, potatoes
Seed longevity: Not applicable
Seeds per ounce: Not applicable

GROWING

When all danger of frost is past (about two weeks after the average last frost date), set the slips in the garden in loose, fertile soil that has been amended with compost. Fertilize only if the plants do not appear healthy, as too much nitrogen will diminish yield and produce long, thin roots.

HARVESTING AND STORING

You can harvest sweet potatoes anytime they reach usable size, usually a period from about 100 to 140 days after planting, depending on variety. Be sure to harvest sweet potatoes before the first frost. Cold weather can damage the roots. If you can't harvest and a frost is coming, mulch the area heavily with straw before sunset.

To harvest, cut back the vines and lift the roots from the ground with a garden fork. Do this gingerly, as the skins bruise easily. Cure the roots before storage by letting them bask in the sun for a day, and then move them to a shady area that remains at about 80°F (27°C) for 7 to 10 days. The roots should store well for about six months in a root cellar or similar cool, humid environment. If your passion for sweet potatoes is such that your harvest will be eaten in only a few months, full curing isn't needed.

BEST VARIETIES

Beauregard. This sweetheart of a sweet potato has large, dark burgundy-purple roots and pumpkin orange flesh. Meaty, with a smooth, dessertlike texture, Beauregard is excellent for all your sweet potato recipes. Developed at Louisiana State University.

Vardaman. A nice variety for those who love sweet potatoes but are short on space. This bush variety takes up less space than most varieties and out-yields them, too. The roots are large, with deep orange, flavorful flesh.

What a Slip!

To make sweet potato slips, purchase large, firm sweet potatoes about 30 to 40 days before the last frost. You can either set the sweet potatoes in sand in a warm, sunny room or greenhouse, or cut them into sections and place each section in a glass of water with one half immersed and the remaining half above the water. Shoots will then rise from the cut section.

When the shoots are about 4 to 6 inches (10–15 cm) long, gently twist them from the section of potato. Collect the shoots and put them in a container of water so that only their bottom halves are immersed. Slips are ready to plant when roots appear, usually in just a few days. Don't allow the roots to get longer than an inch or two (2.5–5 cm) before planting.

▲ **Preparing sweet potato slips.** These shoots are just about ready to be pulled from the section of rooting potato. We'll put them in water, half submersed, and in a few days roots will appear and the slips will be ready for planting.

Radishes

If your experience with radishes is limited to small red salad radishes, you're in for a pleasant surprise. All told, there are well over 200 varieties, including French radishes, daikon radishes, and other specialties, in a surprising array of colors, including white, purple, black, and even green. Raw, they can be eaten whole, sliced, diced, or grated, or you can cook or pickle them. Most are best eaten fresh, but some can be stored for months in a root cellar. Although growing radishes is very easy, to grow them well you have to grow them fast and harvest them fast.

SOWING AND GROWING

Radishes are particularly sensitive to any interruptions in their growth. Above all, don't allow the soil to dry out. They thrive in cool, moist soil with a lot of organic matter, a pH of about 6.5, and a readily available supply of nutrients. Radishes do nicely where leaves have been worked into the soil the previous fall.

Sow radishes wherever there is an empty space, from early spring until early summer and again in fall. They make useful "row markers" sown among slow-germinating crops like carrots and parsnips. As you harvest the radishes, they leave behind loosened soil and space for other plants to grow.

HARVESTING AND STORING

Radishes are at their best for a very short time. If they're left in the ground too long, they develop a sharp taste and pithy texture, followed a day or so later by split roots. Harvest the whole crop when it matures and store the roots in the refrigerator.

◀ **Radical radishes.** Pulling up the radish variety Easter Egg is as much fun as playing grab bag. Until you harvest this fast-growing, cool-weather crop, you never know which of a rainbow of vibrant colors hides within the moist spring soil.

Sow & Grow

RADISHES *(Raphanus sativus)*
Cabbage family *(Cruciferae)*

SOWING

Seed depth: ½" (13 mm)

Soil temperature: 45–90°F (7–32°C); the optimum is 85°F (29°C)

Days to germination: 4–12

Sow indoors: Not recommended

Sow outdoors: *In cool climates,* early spring and fall; *in warm climates,* winter

GROWING

pH range: 6.0–7.0

Soil temperature: 60–65°F (16–18°C)

Spacing in beds: Small types, 1" (2.5 cm); large (storage), sow 2" (5 cm) apart, thin to 4–6" (10–15 cm)

Watering: Even and moderate to heavy

Light: Best yields in full sun; will tolerate partial shade

Nutrient requirements: N=low; P=low; K=low

Rotation considerations: Precede with a legume cover crop.

Good companions: Flavor is improved by interplanting with lettuce. Also good with bean, beet, carrot, nasturtium, parsnip, pea, spinach.

Bad companions: Fennel

Seed longevity: 4 years

Seeds per ounce: 3,000 (106 seeds per g)

Rhubarb

Some people prefer rhubarb pie, some straw-berry-rhubarb jam. I think both are delicious and excellent reasons why everyone should have a patch of rhubarb in the garden. Usually exiled to the edge of the garden, this perennial can go just about anywhere. Once it finds a place it likes, however, it doesn't like to leave, so plan carefully.

THE SITE

Rhubarb likes rich, slightly acid, fertile soil with lots of organic matter. You can purchase either root divisions or container-grown plants. Select a site in sun or light shade, and plant in early spring, a few weeks before the last frost. Plant divisions 18 to 24 inches (45–60 cm) apart with the buds about 2 inches (5 cm) below the soil surface.

GROWING

Water well after planting and keep the soil moist throughout the growing season. Snip off any flower shoots as they appear. Once established, rhubarb plants grow rapidly and often become crowded within 5 to 10 years. To rejuvenate the plants, divide them in fall by slicing the crown with a sharp shovel. Dig up and remove one portion of the plant, fill the hole with soil, and replant.

HARVESTING AND STORING

Avoid harvesting the first year after planting and take only a few stems the second year. From the third year on, you can harvest just about all you want. Rhubarb's most flavorful in cool spring.

BEST VARIETIES

Valentine and Strawberry are rhubarbs with especially vivid red color.

Cherry Giant likes warmer weather than most other rhubarbs.

▲ **It's time for pie!** To harvest rhubarb, grasp the stem near the base and pull up, giving the stem a twist as you pull. You can also cut the stem from the plant with a sharp knife. Trim away the base of the stem and the leaves.

Sow & Grow

RHUBARB *(Rheum* x *cultorum)*
Buckwheat family *(Polygonaceae)*

SOWING/PLANTING

Root cutting depth: 1–3" (2.5–7.5 cm)
Soil temperature: 40–60°F (4–16°C)
Plant outdoors: Early spring

GROWING

pH range: 5.5–6.5
Soil temperature: 40–75°F (4–24°C)
Spacing in beds: 24–36" (60–90 cm)
Watering: Moderate and even
Light: Partial shade to full sun
Nutrient requirements: N=low; P=low; K=low
Rotation considerations: Perennial crop; don't rotate.
Good companions: Not applicable
Bad companions: Not applicable
Seed longevity: Not applicable
Seeds per ounce: Not applicable

Rutabaga

Many people think a rutabaga is just a big turnip, but turnips and rutabagas are actually completely different vegetables. The flesh of a turnip is white, while that of a rutabaga is usually yellow. Rutabagas have a rich, mellow taste that goes well with hearty autumn meals.

SOWING AND GROWING

Work compost or leaf mold into soil before sowing to enrich and loosen it. Sow seeds in early summer or, in cool regions, midsummer.

Rutabagas need a good supply of potassium and phosphorus, with slightly lower amounts of nitrogen. To meet these needs, fertilize with compost tea throughout the growing season. Boron deficiency can produce a brown discoloration in the center of the roots. Protect plants from most insect pests by growing them under floating row covers for the first few weeks.

HARVESTING AND STORING

To harvest, pull or carefully dig the plants and cut the tops an inch (2.5 cm) from the top of the root. Store in a humid root cellar with the temperature just above freezing or place in a plastic vegetable storage bag and keep in the crisper of the refrigerator. Roots store well for months.

BEST VARIETIES

York. Resistant to clubroot, York stores very well and has a smooth, rich flavor.

Thomson Laurentian. This variety has good flavor and stores very well.

Gilfeather. A New England heirloom, Gilfeather has a white root crowned with a cap of purple. The flesh is very sweet and mild, with just a slight hint of pungency.

Joan. This rutabaga has excellent, sweet flavor.

◀ **Harvest the heartiness of autumn.** It's usual to dig rutabagas in mid- and late fall, after a few frosts but before the ground freezes. The cool weather helps develop the vegetables' characteristic full flavor.

Sow & Grow

RUTABAGA *(Brassica napus)*
Cabbage family *(Cruciferae)*

SOWING

Seed depth: ½" (13 mm)

Soil temperature: 60–85°F (16–29°C); the optimum is 85°F (29°C)

Days to germination: 3–5

Sow indoors: Not recommended

Sow outdoors: Early spring

GROWING

pH range: 6.4–7.2

Soil temperature: 60–65°F (16–18°C)

Spacing in beds: 8" (20 cm)

Watering: Moderate

Light: Best in full sun; will tolerate light shade

Nutrient requirements: N=low; P=moderate; K=moderate

Rotation considerations: Good succession crop after onion or scallions.

Good companions: Nasturtium, onion family, pea

Bad companions: Potatoes

Seed longevity: 4 years

Seeds per ounce: 11,000 (388 seeds per g)

Spinach

In the cartoon universe, Popeye ate a can of spinach and became instantly muscled and strong. In the real world, spinach doesn't work quite that fast, and fresh spinach right from the garden is light-years better than anything in a can. One of the first spring garden greens, spinach is high in vitamins and minerals, has excellent flavor, and is easy to grow. And who knows? It might help if you have any problems with the neighborhood bully.

▲ **Muscles in a can?** Along with being nutritious, spinach is also versatile in the kitchen. It's delicious raw in salads, and it's the basic ingredient in many hot dishes, including lasagna.

SOWING

Spinach is frost tolerant and grows best in the cool weather that comes at the beginning and end of the growing season. Direct-sow it in the garden in spring as soon as the ground can be worked or in the fall, or start it in flats indoors three to four weeks before the last frost in spring. Spinach germinates and grows well in cool weather, so get it into the ground as soon as the soil is workable.

Sow & Grow

SPINACH
(Spinacia oleracea)
Beet family *(Chenopodiaceae)*

SOWING
Seed depth: ½" (13 mm)
Soil temperature: 50–75°F (10–24°C); the optimum is 70°F (21°C)
Days to germination: 7–14
Sow indoors: 3–4 weeks before last frost
Sow outdoors: Early spring

GROWING
pH range: 6.5–7.5
Soil temperature: 60–65°F (16–18°C)
Spacing in beds: 12–18" (30–45 cm)
Watering: Light but even
Light: Full sun to partial shade
Nutrient requirements: N=moderate; P=moderate; K=moderate
Rotation considerations: Benefits all succeeding crops; should not follow legumes.
Good companions: Cabbage family, celery, legumes, lettuce, onion, pea, radish, strawberry
Bad companions: Potatoes
Seed longevity: 3 years
Seeds per ounce: 3,000 (106 seeds per g)

Instead of sowing one large planting, you'll get more and better spinach if you grow a series of small succession plantings spaced a week or 10 days apart. Stop planting when the warm-weather crops go in, about the last expected frost date, and then start sowing spinach again in late summer. Germination is less uniform in warm soil, so sow a bit heavier than in spring.

GROWING

Spinach grows in a wide variety of soils but produces the best crops in those rich in organic matter such as compost. In fertile soil it usually does not require supplemental fertilization, and applications of nitrogen should be considered only if the leaves are pale green in color. Too much nitrogen can give spinach a sharp, metallic flavor.

HARVESTING AND STORING

You can harvest spinach in a variety of ways. Take your pick of any or all:

▶ Begin snitching individual leaves as soon as they're big enough to use.
▶ Cut the entire plant at soil level when leaves are large and meaty.
▶ Cut the entire plant an inch (2.5 cm) above the soil level. This method encourages the plant to regrow another crop of leaves.

In warm weather, the plants form a central stem that rapidly grows into a flower stalk, a process called bolting. When this occurs, harvest what you can (the flavor of the leaves may be sharper) and put the rest in the compost pile.

BEST VARIETIES

Popeye's Choice is slow to bolt and bears large, tender, very flavorful leaves.
Melody is disease resistant and produces large crops of good-flavored leaves.
Indian Summer is a fast-growing, high-yielding variety with excellent flavor.
Tyee is very slow to bolt. It produces large crops of good-flavored leaves.

A Hot-Weather Look-Alike

If you wish you could have spinach during the hot days of summer, this crop is just for you. New Zealand spinach *(Tetragonia tetragonioides)* is actually not a spinach at all. You can grow this vigorous, low-growing plant (from 1 to 2 feet tall; 30–60 cm) on a trellis or allow it to spread over the bed.

Sow this frost-sensitive plant whenever it's safe to plant tomatoes and peppers. Soak seeds overnight before sowing either in hills, like squash, or spaced about 10 inches (25 cm) apart in rows. Harvest the dark green leaves individually as needed.

◀ **Keep the harvest coming.** You'll often get enough spinach for salads by harvesting just the outer leaves (A) and allowing the rest of the plant to continue to develop. You can also cut the plant about 1 inch (2.5 cm) above the soil (B), and the plant will grow another batch of leaves.

Summer Squash

At first glance, advice on how to grow more zucchini seems silly. After all, who in his or her right mind wants to grow more zucchini? But there's more to summer squash than just zucchini. Yellow straightneck squash, crookneck squash, cousa squash, and the delightful pattypan or scallop squash are just starters.

THE SITE

Pretty much the same growing methods work for each of the many types of summer squash. Summer squash is sensitive to cold temperatures and grows best during the long days of summer. If possible, prepare the growing bed in fall by turning in lots of chopped leaves or compost and covering the bed with leaves and straw. In spring

▲ **Squash squad.** Summer squash comes in a surprising variety of shapes and colors, each with subtly different textures and flavors. In almost every case, summer squash is best when picked young and harvested often.

remove the straw or leaf mulch and warm the soil with black or IRT plastic. In warm regions, remove the plastic before sowing or transplanting to avoid overheating the soil later in the season.

Sow & Grow

SUMMER SQUASH
(Cucurbita pepo)
Cucumber family *(Cucurbitaceae)*

SOWING

Seed depth: ½–1" (1.3–2.5 cm)
Soil temperature: 70–95°F (21–35°C); the optimum is 95°F (35°C)
Days to germination: 6–10
Sow indoors: 3–4 weeks before last frost
Sow outdoors: When soil temperature reaches 70°F (21°C); use row covers during cool weather

GROWING

pH range: 6.0–6.5
Soil temperature: 65–75°F (18–24°C)
Spacing in beds: 12–18" (30–45 cm)
Watering: Heavy and even
Light: Full sun
Nutrient requirements: N=high; P=moderate; K=moderate
Rotation considerations: Avoid following winter squash, pumpkins, cucumbers, melons.
Good companions: Celeriac, celery, corn, nasturtium, onion, radish
Bad companions: Potato
Seed longevity: 4 years
Seeds per ounce: 300 (11 seeds per g)

Starting seeds indoors. For an early harvest, start plants indoors three or four weeks before the last frost date. Squash does not transplant well, but if you start the plants in 4-inch (10 cm) pots and transplant carefully to avoid disturbing the roots, they'll be okay. Sow three seeds to a pot and thin to one plant by clipping the extras with scissors. Keep temperatures at about 70°F (21°C). Harden the plants by cutting back on water and gradually lowering the night temperature to about 65°F (18°C) during the week before transplanting.

Direct-seeding. Wait until the soil is 70°F (21°C) or warmer, and then sow three seeds to a hill. Space the hills about 18 inches (45 cm) apart. After seedlings have one true leaf, thin to one plant by cutting the others with scissors.

Ta-Daa!

Most summer squash varieties grow in bush form, but Zucchetta Rampicante, an heirloom zucchini variety from Italy, is a vine — a whole lot of vine. Grow Zucchetta on a trellis, and pick the curvy fruits when they are 12 to 15 inches (30 to 37.5 cm) long. They're firm and flavorful, with few seeds. Unlike bush-type zucchini, this plant will produce prolifically for the whole season and is resistant to squash borer.

Italian trombone squash, Zucchetta Rampicante

GROWING

After transplanting indoor-started plants, or when direct-sown seedlings emerge, cover the plants with floating row covers if night temperatures dip below 65°F (18°C). This also keeps insect pests at bay while the plants are young and most vulnerable.

Squash is a heavy feeder, but when grown in soils rich in organic matter, it rarely needs supplemental fertilizing. If leaves are pale or plants lack vigor, fertilize with seaweed or fish emulsion. Too much fertilizer, especially nitrogen, can limit yields.

HARVESTING AND STORING

The secret to great squash is more in the harvesting than in the growing. You must pick young, pick small, and pick often. Here are some tips on picking the most flavorful squash yet.

Zucchini lives life in the fast lane. It grows so quickly, it seems as if you could sit in the garden and watch it grow. Once fruits begin to appear, visit your zucchini every day or so. Pick the fruits when they are about 4 to 5 inches (10–12.5 cm) long. Zucchini plants bear for a long time if harvested often, but even with the best of picking, zucchini quality and yields start to decline after a month or so. If you're a real zucchini fan, plan on a couple of succession plantings about a month apart.

Yellow summer squash includes both straightneck and crookneck types, and each of these should be harvested a little differently. Straightneck squash should be picked at about 4 to 5 inches (10–12.5 cm). At this stage, they can be sliced and eaten skin and all. Crookneck squash tends to get a thicker skin earlier than straightneck does, so harvest these when they are slightly smaller.

Cousa squash looks like a compromise between a zucchini and a straightneck squash, with pale greenish yellow skin and the classic summer squash shape. Although it has a distinctive flavor, it resembles zucchini. Harvest cousa squash when it's

Costata Romanesca

Seneca Prolific

Sunburst

about 3 inches (7.5 cm) long. The prolific plants will reward frequent harvesting with more fruits.

Scallop or pattypan squash's shape and flavor are unforgettable. The plants bear round, green or yellow fruit with scalloped edges. Pick these when they are small, no larger than 4 inches (10 cm) in diameter. They are at their best when from 2 to 3 inches (5–7.5 cm) across. Harvest often, for when these plants begin bearing they can continue all summer long.

All summer squash keeps in the refrigerator for about two weeks and freezes well.

BEST VARIETIES OF ZUCCHINI

Costata Romanesco. The perfect ingredient in Mediterranean recipes, this zucchini has a clear, distinct flavor. The fruits are pale green and marked with lighter-colored ribs. Harvest when 6 to 10 inches (15–25 cm) long. This variety makes lots of male blossoms that can be picked, dipped in tempura batter, and lightly fried. Spectacular!

Gold Rush is the zucchini that looks like a summer squash, with clear, bright yellow skin. Its flavor is very similar to other good zucchini varieties, but it is more attractive than most.

Spacemaster. A small zucchini, Spacemaster produces lots of fruits on plants a little smaller than standard varieties. Nicely prolific, so be sure to pick often.

Eight Ball. With dark green, nearly ball-shaped fruit, these plants begin bearing earlier than most varieties, and the little fruits are quite tasty.

BEST VARIETIES OF STRAIGHTNECK

Zephyr. An eyecatching squash with a pale yellow top and light green bottom, Zephyr has firm but tender fruits with excellent flavor.

Saffron. This looks and tastes just like a straightneck summer squash should, with rich flavor and clear yellow color. The plants are nicely compact and produce lots of squash.

BEST VARIETIES OF CROOKNECK

Horn of Plenty. Attractive, delicious fruits grow on well-behaved, compact 3-foot-diameter (90 cm) plants. Pick the fruits when small and the plants will continue to produce for months.

BEST VARIETIES OF PATTYPAN

Sunburst. This prolific and reliable variety produces clear yellow fruits with a creamy, flavorful flesh that can be diced and tossed into mixed vegetable dishes or sautéed all by itself.

Starship. It's good to find a squash with a compact, space-saving habit. The green, scallop-shaped fruits look like little spaceships. Pick when small for a taste that is out of this world.

Winter Squash and Pumpkin

Two things can make me feel rich as winter approaches: a big pile of dry firewood and a garden cart heaped with winter squash. With all the harvesting of tomatoes, peppers, and other summer things, during most of the growing season winter squash doesn't get much attention. Yet when the first chilly mornings come, I find myself down in the squash patch thinking of wood smoke, pumpkins, and buttery baked squash. Months ahead when much of the garden harvest has been eaten, there is still plenty of winter squash in storage.

▲ **Winter wonders.** Squash is healthful, with lots of fiber, vitamin A, and beta-carotene. All that and it's delicious, too. Acorn, buttercup, butternut, delicata, hubbard, and spaghetti squash and pumpkin all fit into this category.

Sow & Grow

WINTER SQUASH & PUMPKIN
(*Cucurbita* spp.)
Cucumber family (*Cucurbitaceae*)

SOWING

Seed depth: ½–1" (1.3–2.5 cm)

Soil temperature: 70–90°F (21–32°C); the optimum is 90°F (32°C)

Days to germination: 6–10

Sow indoors: 3–4 weeks before last frost

Sow outdoors: When soil temperature reaches 70°F (21°C); use row covers during cool weather

GROWING

pH range: 5.5–6.5

Soil temperature: 65–75°F (18–24°C)

Spacing in beds: 12–18" (30–45 cm)

Watering: Heavy and even

Light: Full sun

Nutrient requirements: N=high; P=moderate; K=moderate

Rotation considerations: Avoid following summer squash, cucumber, and melon.

Good companions: Celeriac, celery, corn, onion, radish

Bad companions: Potato

Seed longevity: 4 years

Seeds per ounce: 300 (11 seeds per g)

THE SITE

Summer squash and winter squash need the same things to grow well — winter squash just needs more of them. Winter squash plants are bigger than their summertime counterparts, and those plants produce bigger fruits.

Winter squash needs three months or more of frost-free growing time, and it's extremely frost sensitive on both ends of the growing cycle. Like summer squash, it does not germinate well in cool soil.

Before sowing or transplanting, loosen an area at least as deep and as big around as a bushel basket and work in lots of compost or well-rotted manure and some seaweed. Cover a 3-foot-square (90 cm^2) area with black or IRT plastic at least a week before planting. I leave the plastic in place all summer for weed control.

SOWING

In warm areas, direct-seed once the soil has warmed in spring and the danger of frost is past. In cooler regions (generally from Zone 6 north) you can direct-seed if the soil has been pre-warmed with black or IRT plastic and the plants are protected under row covers. Or, you can start plants indoors three weeks before the last frost date. Avoid starting plants earlier than this, as older plants often do not transplant well. Sow three seeds per 4-inch (10 cm) pot and thin to one plant by selecting the strongest plant and cutting the extras with scissors. Maintain a temperature of about 70°F (21°C) for germination and growth. Transplant carefully, being sure not to disturb the roots.

GROWING

Use row covers to maintain proper growth temperatures and protect against insect pests when the plants are small, but remove the covers when blossoms appear.

The Garden Gorilla

Growing great winter squash while growing all your other vegetables too depends, in part, on what I call the Gorilla Corollary:

Q: "Where does a gorilla sit at the opera?"
A: "Anywhere it wants to."

Winter squash are garden gorillas. The vines are so vigorous they will explore and take over vast amounts of the garden if you don't plan ahead. You can't contain these plants once they get growing. Control them by sowing the seed along the edge of the garden. As the vines grow, direct them outward, away from the rest of the garden. Keep pointing them in the direction of something that might look attractive covered in vines. They will run over something, but at least it won't be the rest of the garden.

▲ **Squash likes it hot.** In cool-weather regions, winter squash will perform better if you warm the soil with black or IRT plastic before planting and then leave the plastic in place, not only to maintain soil temperature, but also to control weeds. Cut a circle out of the plastic, dig a hole deep enough so that the plant will be at the same height it grew in the pot, and set the transplant in place, being careful not to disturb the plant roots. Firm the soil gently around the plant.

HARVESTING AND STORING

In theory, two characteristics signal that winter squashes are ripe

▶ The stems begin to shrivel and dry.
▶ The skin is hard enough so you can't cut it with your thumbnail (pumpkin skin, however, remains a little soft even when ripe).

In practice, at least here in Zone 4, I harvest the evening before the first frost and hope they all are ripe. Some experts advise harvesting after the first frost, but before the first *hard* frost. I find that even a light frost can damage winter squash, especially pumpkins, in ways that shorten its storage life. If there's frost on the pumpkins, then somebody didn't get the harvest in on time.

Leave at least an inch (2.5 cm) of vine on the fruits, preferably a little more. And remember that the stems aren't handles. Because they can't support the weight of the fruit, the stems often break off, and stemless squash or pumpkins don't store well.

Winter squash keeps best if it is cured before being placed in storage. I cure winter squash in the sun for 10 days to help harden the skins. Dry, warm days are advantageous, but sunshine is what really cures the skins. If there's any chance of frost, cover the squash well or move them into a shed or garage.

Store at 50°F (10°C) where it is moderately dry (about 60 percent humidity). Eat the acorn, delicata, and spaghetti squash first. The flavor of both butternut and buttercup improves after a few weeks of storage.

BEST ACORN VARIETIES

Acorn squash are small, usually about 2 pounds (0.9 kg), and vaguely acorn shaped. These, like many winter squash, are best baked. Most acorn squash bear dark green fruits, but some are mottled with white and green.

Heart of Gold. Dark green skin is etched with white variegation. The fruits are about 5 inches (12.5 cm) long with firm, well-flavored, pale orange flesh. The compact plants bear high yields.

Heart of Gold

Tuffy. With very dark green (nearly black), thick rinds protecting succulent yellow flesh, these plants are vigorous and productive.

Table Top. A good squash to use soon after harvest, Table Top produces small, space-saving plants that bear medium to small, golden orange, nicely flavored squash.

BEST BUTTERCUP VARIETIES

A buttercup squash looks like an acorn squash that somebody sat on. The dark, blackish green rind protects the sweet, yellowish orange flesh. The fruits, while looking a bit compressed, store very well and are produced abundantly on vigorous vines.

Burgess. A very popular squash with dark green skin and sweet, rich-flavored flesh, Burgess is very productive and vigorous.

Sweet Mama. A hybrid with pleasant-tasting, sweet orange flesh enclosed within a black-green rind, Sweet Mama produces reliably good yields, and the fruits store very well.

Autumn Cup. This full-flavored, sweet-fleshed squash bears medium to small dark green fruits.

BEST BUTTERNUT VARIETIES

Early Butternut. Medium-size, light tan fruits mature about 10 days earlier than most varieties. The orange flesh is smooth and sweet.

Long Island Cheese. This looks more like a small tan pumpkin than a butternut, with deep orange flesh that is excellent for squash pies.

Waltham. One of the most popular butternuts, Waltham has reliable yields of large, tan fruits filled with bright orange, smooth, sweet flesh. They store very well and actually taste best after being stored for a few months.

BEST HUBBARD SQUASH VARIETIES

Blue Hubbard. Often seen at county fairs, these very large aqua-blue fruits have sweet, yellow flesh, a perfect addition to fall dishes.

Blue Ballet. A smaller version of Blue Hubbard, Blue Ballet has cloudy blue skin and orange, nicely sweet flesh.

Warted Green Hubbard. A large squash with dark green skin and flavorful yellowish flesh, Warted Green Hubbard keeps very well in storage.

BEST PUMPKIN VARIETIES

Atlantic Giant. This huge plant is not for the small garden. Individual fruits often weigh hundreds of pounds; the heaviest ever grown weighed in at over 1,000 pounds (454 kg). That's a lot of pumpkin!

The Great Pumpkin. A variety selected for folks who want to grow big pumpkins. Fruits are pinkish orange and often weigh over 100 pounds (45 kg).

Howden. This pumpkin was developed in Sheffield, Massachusetts and is one of the best large pumpkins. Howden bears well-shaped 10- to 20-pound (5–9 kg) fruits, the perfect size for jack o'lanterns.

New England Pie. The standard pie pumpkin for years, New England Pie pumpkin bears small, 5-pound (2 kg), nicely shaped fruits with flavorful, smooth, bright orange flesh.

Wee-B-Little. This miniature pumpkin has the classic round pumpkin shape, rather than the squashed look of many small pumpkins. The round, 3- to 4-inch (7.5–10 cm) diameter fruits are perfect for decorating the holiday table.

OTHER WINTER SQUASH VARIETIES

Lakota. A new variety, Lakota is said to resemble the winter squash used by its namesake tribe on the northern plains. The fruits are teardrop shaped and marked with orange and dark green, with flesh similar to Hubbard types.

Spaghetti. A medium-sized squash with tan skin and yellowish flesh, spaghetti squash is often called vegetable spaghetti. But the flavor is better than any pasta, with a sweet, nutty taste.

Spaghetti squash

▲ **Taking the cure.** After you pull pumpkins and other winter squashes off the vine, let them sit in the sun for 10 days to cure (harden) their skins for better storability.

Personalized Pumpkins

While pumpkins are still small and the skins are soft, scratch a child's name on one. The name will stay and grow along with the pumpkin. It's a nice surprise at harvest.

Alpine Strawberries

Many gardeners have a love-hate relationship with strawberries. They love the juicy, flavorful fruits but hate the weeds and tangles of runners that overrun garden paths and planting areas. The solution to this dilemma comes in the form of a delicious, well-behaved plant called alpine strawberry, or fraise du bois.

HARVESTING AND STORING

Harvest Alpine strawberries when the fruits turn crimson. Although they're much smaller than commercial types, these fruits have a rich, tart strawberry flavor, and they bear from spring to fall. How long they will store is a mystery, as they're always eaten the same day they are picked.

BEST VARIETIES

Among the many fine varieties of Alpine strawberries are **Alexandria**, **Charles V**, and **Pineapple Crush**.

Saving Strawberry Seed

True Alpine strawberries do not produce runners, but it's easy to propagate your own plants from seed. Collect a handful of ripe strawberries and spread them on a sheet of newspaper in a warm, dry, sunny room. When the fruits are dry, work the pieces between your fingers, allowing the seeds to fall onto the newspaper. Dry the seed for another day or two, and then sow in a flat of seed-starter mix. When the seedlings are about ½ inch (1.25 cm) tall, transplant them to individual pots. After they've formed a nice rosette of leaves, you can transplant them into the garden anytime from spring to early fall.

◀ **Three seasons of strawberries.** You can purchase most Alpine strawberries as plants and transplant them to the garden in spring or fall. Once they begin bearing fruit, you can harvest them from spring through summer and into fall.

Sow & Grow

ALPINE STRAWBERRIES *(Fragaria vesca)*
Rose family *(Rosaceae)*

SOWING

Seed depth: ⅛–¼" (3–6 mm)
Germination soil temperature: 65–75°F (18–24°C)
Days to germination: 7–14
Sow indoors: 8 weeks before setting out in early spring (cool climates) or fall (warm climates)
Sow outdoors: Not recommended

GROWING

pH range: 5.5–7.0
Growing soil temperature: 60–80°F (16–27°C)
Spacing in beds: 12" (30 cm)
Watering: Moderate
Light: Full sun to partial shade
Nutrient requirements: N=moderate; P=moderate; K=moderate
Rotation considerations: Avoid following beet, pea, corn, pepper, or tomato.
Good companions: Melon
Bad companions: Broccoli and other cabbage family plants
Seed longevity: 1 year
Seeds per ounce: 70,000 (2,471 seeds per g)

Sunflowers

In addition to lifting spirits, sunflowers attract birds, like goldfinches and chickadees, and pollinators, such as bees and butterflies. Plus, they produce lots of nutritious, flavorful seeds to add to recipes or save for feeding the birds in winter. They're a great choice for a child's garden because they're easy to grow and they don't disappoint.

SOWING AND GROWING

Sow seeds in spring after danger of frost is past. Make two additional sowings spaced three weeks apart, so that you'll have a long season of cheery sunflowers to enjoy. Sow in hills, like corn, or in rows, and then stand back and watch them grow.

HARVESTING

If harvesting sunflowers means gathering big bouquets of beautiful flowers, then it can begin as soon as the buds open. If you're interested in collecting and saving the ripe seed, though, a little patience is in order. Sunflowers generally take from three to four months to produce seed. The seed is ripe when the back of the seedhead turns from green to brown. Cut the head from the stalk and cure it in a warm, dry room for about a week or until the hulls are dry and hard. Rub the seed from the head with your fingers and allow it to drop onto a screen. Store in clean glass jars.

BEST VARIETIES

Of the many sunflowers there are to try, some are perfect for summer bouquets, while others produce bountiful yields of seeds.

For cut flowers. Italian White, Inca Jewels, Music Box, Sunrich Lemon, and Valentine

For seed crops. Russian Mammoth, Big Smile, and Giant Grey Stripe

◀ **You are my sunshine.** If one adjective could describe a sunflower, it would be happy. A sprinkling of sunflowers around the vegetable garden makes the whole place brighter.

Sow & Grow

SUNFLOWERS *(Helianthus annuus)*
Sunflower family *(Compositae)*

SOWING

Seed depth: 1" (2.5 cm)

Germination soil temperature: 75–80°F (24–27°C)

Days to germination: 5–10

Sow indoors: 3 weeks before last frost; does not always transplant well

Sow outdoors: After last frost

GROWING

pH range: 6.0–7.0

Growing soil temperature: 50–80°F (10–27°C)

Spacing in beds: 12–18" (30–45 cm)

Watering: Heavy when small, moderate to low after

Light: Full sun

Nutrient requirements: N=low; P=low; K=low

Rotation considerations: Avoid following artichoke and other members of sunflower family.

Good companions: Cucumber, melons

Bad companions: Pole bean

Seed longevity: 1–3 years

Seeds per ounce: 200–1,000 (7–35 seeds per g)

Swiss Chard

Many years ago, the cartoonist Al Capp conceived a creature called the Schmoo. The Schmoo's mission in life was to become whatever you wanted it to be. I used to think the Schmoo just a fantasy, until I discovered Swiss chard. Swiss chard is the vegetable garden's Schmoo. You want salad? A mess of greens? Some spinach, even though all the spinach has long ago bolted? Asparagus in the middle of August? And you want all this from a single planting that goes on producing until there's a really hard frost, requiring almost no care along the way? And you'd like all this in bright shiny colors? You've got it, if you planted Swiss chard.

▲ **Turn up the lights.** Who says you need to hide vegetables from view? Few ornamental plants can boast the long-season health, vigor, and color of Swiss chard, especially of varieties like this Bright Lights.

SOWING AND GROWING

How close together you grow Swiss chard plants depends on how you plan to harvest them. If you plan to take the whole plant or to cut it off an inch (2.5 cm) above the soil (it will grow a new

Sow & Grow

SWISS CHARD
(Beta vulgaris) Cicla group
Beet family *(Chenopodiaceae)*

SOWING

Seed depth: ½" (13 mm)
Soil temperature: 50–85°F (10–29°C); the optimum is 85°F (29°C)
Days to germination: 5–7
Sow indoors: 1–2 weeks before last frost
Sow outdoors: After last frost

GROWING

pH range: 6.0–7.0
Soil temperature: Anything above 50°F (10°C); the optimum is 60–65°F (16–18°C)

Spacing in beds: If you harvest entire plant, 4–5" (10–12.5 cm) apart in a staggered pattern; if you harvest outer leaves, 8–10" (20–25 cm) apart in a staggered pattern
Watering: Moderate and even
Light: Best in full sun, tolerates light shade
Nutrient requirements: N=low; P=moderate; K=moderate
Rotation considerations: Avoid following beets, spinach, orach; benefits following a legume crop.
Good companions: Cabbage family, legumes, lettuce
Bad companions: Beets, orach, spinach
Seed longevity: 4 years
Seeds per ounce: 1,500 (53 seeds per g)

set of leaves in this case), space plants about 4 to 5 inches (10–12.5 cm) apart. If you plan to harvest the outer stalks continuously throughout the season, space plants about 8 to 10 inches (20–25 cm) apart to accommodate the larger plants.

If you follow the onetime harvest method, be sure to sow succession plantings throughout summer and early fall. Swiss chard can endure light frosts in spring and tolerate moderate freezes in fall.

Whatever spacing you choose, maintain a thin layer of compost on the bed to ensure sufficient nutrients for the plants.

HARVESTING AND STORING

You can begin harvesting the leaves when plants are about 6 to 8 inches (15–20 cm) tall. You have your choice of harvesting methods:

► Harvest the whole plant; the leaves and stems are especially tender.
► Cut the young plants an inch (2.5 cm) above the soil, whereupon they will continue to grow so that you can harvest them again and again.
► Cut stalks from the outside of the plant, leaving the heart, which will continue to grow.

BEST VARIETIES

Charlotte Swiss chard

Charlotte. A truly stunning variety that is as attractive to look at as it is delicious to eat. Charlotte has large, cherry red stalks and savoyed, dark green leaves.

Bright Lights. Like a display of Northern lights in the garden, Bright Lights is a rainbow disguised as a vegetable. The delicious stalks (which taste a bit like asparagus when steamed) come in five colors — white, red, yellow, pink, and orange. The colors fade when cooked, but the flavor does not.

Bright Yellow. The brightest light of Bright Lights has a show of its own. Bright Yellow has lemon yellow stems beneath richly savoyed, dark green leaves. And, of course, it is delicious.

Fordhook Giant. There are many new and colorful varieties of Swiss chard, but this long-time favorite is the standard they must measure up to. Fordhook Giant is sure to satisfy with its large, meaty stems and thick, tasty leaves.

Argentata. A variety popular in Europe, Argentata has crisp leaves and strong, flavorful stems. Excellent.

▲ **Cutups.** (A) If you cut only the outer stalks, a few Swiss chard plants will offer you a continuous supply of food over several months. (B) You can also cut the entire plant about 1 inch (2.5 cm) above the soil; another plant will grow from the crown to provide you a second harvest.

Tomatillos

What I like about meeting new people is that I might be meeting a new friend. So it was with my introduction to tomatillos. My first thought was, What a strange-looking vegetable! — all green and wrapped up in a husk that looks like a small brown paper bag. But this plant's in a league by itself. Tomatillos are an affordable luxury in the garden, and their plump, firm fruits are the key ingredient in salsa verde, as well as many other Mexican dishes. The plants are easy to grow and hardier than tomatoes, while also less likely to be bothered by pests and diseases. I like making new friends.

SOWING AND GROWING

You grow tomatillos in much the same way you grow tomatoes. Start seed indoors in late winter or early spring, and then move the transplants to the garden after the last frost. Set the plants deep in the soil, with only the top few leaves poking above ground. Tomatillos are rangy plants that can spread more than 4 feet (1.2 m), so give them plenty of room. You can support them on tomato cages, but they seem to grow best if allowed to run free. Fertilizing isn't needed.

HARVESTING AND STORING

Harvesting usually begins about two months after transplanting. When a tomatillo is ripe, its husk usually splits. It may also be ripe when the fruit begins to soften and fills out the husk well.

BEST VARIETIES

Purple. Aptly named, this tomatillo has deep purple skin.

De Milpa. A nearly self-reliant heirloom; De Milpa stores well.

Toma Verde. This variety is early and reliable.

◀ **Good taste:** Tomatillos have been a favorite of many people for generations. If you haven't tried them yet, you are sure to be pleasantly surprised.

Sow & Grow

TOMATILLOS *(Physalis ixocarpa)*
Tomato family *(Solanaceae)*

SOWING

Seed depth: ¼" (6 mm)
Germination soil temperature: 70–80°F (21–27°C)
Days to germination: 7–14
Sow indoors: 4 weeks before last frost

GROWING

pH range: 6.0–7.0
Growing soil temperature: 60–80°F (16–27°C)
Spacing in beds: 2½' (75 cm)
Watering: Moderate
Light: Full sun
Nutrient requirements: N=low; P=low; K=low
Rotation considerations: Avoid following eggplant, potatoes, peppers, and tomatoes; should not follow a legume, because there may be too much nitrogen in the soil.
Good companions: Asparagus, basil, bush bean, cabbage family, carrot, celery, chive, cucumber, garlic, head lettuce, marigold, mint, nasturtium, onion, parsley, pepper, pot marigold
Bad companions: Pole bean, dill, fennel, potato
Seed longevity: 3 years
Seeds per ounce: 17,000 (600 seeds per g)

Tomatoes

If there's something more delectable than a fresh tomato sandwich for lunch in late summer, I haven't experienced it. And tomato sandwiches are just the beginning. There's also pasta sauce made from rich sauce tomatoes, flavorful cherry and currant tomatoes tossed in salads, and fried green tomatoes and pickled tomatoes made from fruits gathered at the end of season. Tomatoes have something for everyone, which is probably why they have been the most popular vegetable among gardeners for years.

THE SITE

Tomatoes prefer a light, fertile soil with plenty of organic matter. Soils with high levels of nutrients, especially nitrogen, reduce yields. Turn some

▲ **Queen of the garden.** If gardeners grow only one vegetable, it's often tomatoes. There's no secret to why this is so: You just haven't tasted a tomato until you've picked a ripe one from the vine and eaten it while it's still warm from the sun.

chopped leaves into the soil in fall, or add compost in spring. A few weeks before transplanting, cover the growing beds with black or IRT plastic to warm the soil.

Sow & Grow

TOMATOES
(Lycopersicon lycopersicum)
Tomato family *(Solanaceae)*

SOWING
Seed depth: ½" (13 mm)
Soil temperature: 80°F (27°C)
Days to germination: 6–8
Sow indoors: 6–7 weeks before last frost
Plant outdoors: After all danger of frost is past

GROWING
pH range: 5.8–7.0
Soil temperature: 70°F (21°C)

Spacing in beds: 15" (37.5 cm) supported, 24" (60 cm) unsupported determinates, 36" (90 cm) unsupported indeterminates
Watering: Moderate to high during growth, low during harvest
Light: Full sun
Nutrient requirements: N=high; P=high; K=high
Rotation considerations: Avoid following potatoes, peppers, and eggplant.
Good companions: Asparagus, basil, bush bean, cabbage family, carrot, celery, chive, cucumber, garlic, head lettuce, marigold, mint, nasturtium, onion, parsley, pepper, pot marigold
Bad companions: Pole bean, dill, fennel, potato
Seed longevity: 4 years
Seeds per ounce: 10,000 (353 seeds per g)

SOWING

If you have a sunny window, or better still grow lights, and a bit of patience, you're most likely to end up with the biggest, best, and tastiest tomatoes if you start your own seedlings. You'll have to take a few extra steps, but the technique isn't difficult.

Germinating seeds. Tomato seedlings are especially susceptible to damping-off disease, so be sure to use a soilless starting mix for your seed flats. Six or seven weeks before the expected transplanting date, sow seeds ½ inch (1.25 cm) deep and an inch (2.5 cm) or so apart in flats or two or three to a cell in growing cells. Keep the containers warm (70–90°F, or 21–32°C; the optimum is 85°F, or 29°C). The top of the refrigerator may give just the right amount of heat. Germination is much slower at lower temperatures. Keep soil moist but not wet.

Caring for young seedlings. Once the seeds have germinated, move the seedlings to a sunny windowsill or put them under grow lights. If you use a grow light instead of natural light, keep the bulb an inch or two (2.5–5 cm) above the plants to keep them from becoming thin and leggy.

If you see a purple color develop in the leaves, it's a sign of phosphorus deficiency. Use a high-phosphorus liquid fertilizer, if necessary. Otherwise, fertilize once a month with fish emulsion or liquid seaweed.

Transplanting seedlings into larger containers. Ten days after germination, transplant to 2-inch-wide (5 cm) growing cells or pots. Clip away all the leaves except those within the top inch (2.5 cm) of the stem, and then replant the seedling. Additional roots will grow from the buried stem section, strengthening the root system. Fertilize with fish emulsion and grow in full sun at 60° to 70°F (16–21°C).

Two weeks after this transplanting, replant again, this time into 4-inch (10 cm) pots. Bury all but the top 2 inches (5 cm) of the plant, removing any leaves that would be below the planting mix, as before. Water regularly but lightly, just enough to keep the growing medium from drying out.

Hardening off. At least two weeks before the plants go into the garden, begin to harden them by moving them outdoors to a sheltered place, increasing their time outdoors a little every day. If you've been growing them in a cold frame, simply lift the top of the frame, each day increasing the time it's open.

BUYING TOMATO PLANTS

A good tomato crop begins with vigorous, compact seedlings about six to seven weeks old in 4-inch (10 cm) pots. Many gardeners like to start their own plants, not only because they can ensure the cost and quality, but also because many tomato varieties, including some of the best-tasting ones, are not commercially available as started plants. But this is changing as more nurseries offer heirloom varieties, so it's worth checking around to see what's available near you. If you decide to buy plants from a greenhouse or garden center, buy early, buy young, and buy plants that are already growing in 4-inch (10 cm) pots.

▲ **Nursery tales.** Your local greenhouse or garden center often carries a wide choice of varieties that will do well in your area. Be sure to visit early in the season for the best selection.

Buy early. You'll have the best selection at the garden center if you get there early, and you'll have more control over how the plants are fed, watered, and hardened off during their early development. Most of the problems that can lower yield and decrease fruit size happen right at the beginning. If you buy young seedlings, you are over that hump and into smoother cruising.

Buy young. The larger and older a plant is when it goes into the ground, the more likely it is to be stressed and set back. Tomatoes should be transplanted to the garden at roughly the last frost date and should be no more than six to eight weeks old at that time. Try to find out when the seeds were sown. Many nurseries start plants too early for the region's climate. Above all, avoid tall, leggy plants or those with open flowers or fruits.

Buy 4-inch (10 cm) pots. Seedlings grown in anything smaller than a 4-inch (10 cm) pot are likely to be potbound, and a potbound plant is already severely stressed. At this stage in the plant's development, a good root system is much more important than luxuriant top growth. This is why "bargain" plants grown in small cells or six to a flat are not bargains at all. Turn the pot over and check to be sure no roots are beginning to creep out of the drainage hole. If the nursery owner allows it, gently remove the plant from the pot to see that roots have not started to develop around the sides of the rootball.

TRANSPLANTING

The usual advice about when to put tomato seedlings in the garden is "after the last frost date," but that's a little vague, especially because the

Brush the plants lightly with your hand twice a day to promote short, stocky plants. The back-and-forth movement of the stem helps promote a hormone called cytokinin, which creates plants with thicker, stronger stems. Outdoors, gentle breezes make this happen naturally.

crucial variables are soil temperature and night air temperature. Soil temperature should be at least 55° to 60°F (13–16°C), and night air temperatures should not go below 45°F (7°C) unless you protect the plants with row covers. You can guess, or you can measure the temperatures with soil and air thermometers.

Set supported plants 15 inches (37.5 cm) apart in a single row down the middle of a 30-inch (76 cm) bed. If you aren't using any kind of supports, allow 2 feet (60 cm) for determinate varieties and 3 feet (90 cm) for indeterminate. Determinate varieties are sensitive to transplant shock, so be very careful not to disturb their roots.

Tomatoes are native to South America, where they get longer and warmer growing seasons than they can get in most of the continental United States. Growing good tomato crops consistently involves setting out well-started plants and then using some tricks to convince them that the growing season is longer and warmer than it really is.

Transplanting Tomatoes into the Garden

1 Dig a hole at least 6 inches (15 cm) in diameter and deep enough so that only about 4 inches (10 cm) of the plant will be above the soil. Use scissors to clip off any leaves that will be buried.

2 Set the plant in the prepared hole. Fill with soil and firm the soil gently around the plant. Water well. This deep planting method encourages a deep root system, which especially benefits tomatoes during prolonged drought and/or hot weather.

Alternative Tomato-Planting Method

This planting method encourages a shallow root system, which can work well in cool regions, but the technique also leaves plants more susceptible to drought and root damage from cultivation.

Dig a trench 2 or 3 inches (5–7.5 cm) deep and long enough for all but about 4 inches (10 cm) of the plant. Lay the plant in the trench, gently turning the top upward and packing soil against the stem to support it. Cover with soil and water well.

GROWING

Fertilizing. Water newly planted plants with a dilute solution of fish emulsion or compost tea. Because tomatoes can grow quite large, they need plenty of nutrients; plan on supplemental feedings every two or three weeks with compost tea, fish emulsion, or another natural fertilizer.

Warming and discouraging insect pests. Row covers help maintain warmth and deter insects, but remove them when blossoms appear or when daytime temperatures reach 85°F (29°C).

Mulching. Studies have shown that tomatoes produce earlier and set more fruit when mulched with red plastic, which both warms the soil and reflects certain wavelengths of sunlight. Red plastic does not suppress weeds as well as black plastic or IRT. I have found that plants do not get enough water through the planting holes in the plastic. I deal with both problems by making the plastic removable (see page 65) and checking periodically to monitor weed growth and soil moisture.

If you don't use plastic mulch, you may want to mulch with grass clippings or straw to keep the soil moist. Make sure the soil is well warmed up before you apply the mulch. In cool regions, most gardeners don't use any organic mulch and even avoid companion planting, so that nothing interferes with maximum soil warming. In warm climates, however, things can get too hot even for tomatoes. In these conditions, organic mulch or "living mulch" companion plantings can be a big help.

Pruning. Optional for determinate tomatoes, pruning is highly recommended for indeterminate varieties, particularly if you grow them on a trellis or stake. Don't do any pruning until the plant has been growing in the garden for a week or so. From then on, remove all suckers — the nonflowering stems that grow between the main stem and the leaf crotches. Pruning directs the growth to a single main stem. Repeat the process once a week.

◀ **Seeing red.** Red plastic mulch has characteristics that lead to earlier and larger tomato harvests. Lay the plastic on the bed in the same way you put down other plastic mulches and cut a circle into the plastic where you can set the plant.

▲ **Don't be a sucker.** Pinch or cut out all of the nonflowering stems that grow between the main stem and the leaf crotches (A). These are aptly called "suckers," because they take up nutrients that are better used by the developing fruits. When the plant reaches the top of the support, prune the tip to stop further top growth (B).

Training. There are many ways to train tomatoes, and all work reasonably well. You can use "cages" for supports, or you can train the vines to a stake by tying the main stem loosely to the support with twist-ties, twine, or torn strips of fabric. Some people think old nylon stockings are best. Be sure to set the stake at the same time you plant the tomatoes, to avoid damage to a developing root system.

My favorite method is to train tomatoes around taut twine suspended from a trellis (see page 72–73). Whichever method you choose, be sure to train or tie the plants to the support weekly, at the same time that you prune them.

▲ **A lot at stake.** Staking is one traditional method for keeping indeterminate tomatoes under control. Continue to tie up the main stem once a week, when you prune. This should be enough to ensure a well-maintained crop of tomatoes.

▲ **Doing the twist.** My favorite method for growing tomatoes is to train them around twine suspended from a trellis and securely staked into soil beneath. Like other methods, once-a-week attention is all that's required. Just gently flip the growing end of the plant around the twine. If you like, you can allow a second stem to develop near the base of the plant and add another length of twine a few inches away from the first one to support it.

A Determined Plant

Various kinds of tomatoes differ in size, color, disease resistance, and the time they take to ripen, but the most important difference for the gardener is growth habit: Some tomatoes are determinate, some indeterminate.

Determinate plants, better described as bushes than as vines, reach a certain size, flower, set fruit, and then pretty much stop growing. You can grow determinate tomatoes without any support at all, allowing them to sprawl along the ground, but they'll do better if you surround them with a low cage-type support. Either way, they don't have to be pruned.

Indeterminate plants are true vines. They grow and set fruit continuously, resulting in much larger plants with a higher foliage-to-fruit ratio. And the bigger plant, the better the fruit. This means that most of the tomato varieties reputed to be most flavorful are indeterminates. Although they take more work to grow, because they should be grown on a trellis and kept pruned, for tomato lovers the reward is worth the investment. Not only is the flavor of indeterminates better, but you'll get more and bigger fruits, you'll get them sooner, and you'll lose fewer to rot, insects, and slugs. You'll also get a whole lot more yield per square foot of garden: Untrained indeterminate tomatoes take up a lot of space.

HARVESTING

As the fall frost date approaches, remove the bottom leaves, flowers, and any fruits that will not ripen before the end of the growing season. These are the small, solid green, hard-as-a-rock ones. Removing this material helps direct all the energy of the plant toward ripening the rest of the fruits.

The best tomatoes are vine ripened, but don't leave them on the vine too long. Pick the fruit when the skin of the tomato yields slightly to finger pressure. The shoulder of the fruit is the last part to change color. Some varieties can be completely ripe and still have yellowish shoulders. You can extend the ripening season through light frosts by draping the trellis with a sheet of clear plastic and closing the ends with clothespins.

Before a hard frost, pick any tomatoes that show a light yellowing at the shoulders. Most of them will ripen indoors. Don't toss out the green ones; they make delicious green-tomato pickles.

BEST VARIETIES OF TOMATOES FOR WARM CLIMATES

Floramerica. An award-winning tomato, Floramerica bears large, evenly red fruit and is disease resistant to boot.

Solar Set. Developed at the University of Florida, this variety produces large crops of big red tomatoes in temperatures where other varieties wilt.

Duke. The large red fruit and reliable crops of Duke have made this disease-resistant variety a favorite in warm-region gardens for years.

▲ **Diversity in tomatoes.** If you have room, try growing many different kinds of tomatoes. One year certain varieties do better; another year you'll find a different batch more successful. From left to right, in this group are (top row) Amish Paste, Rose, and Brandywine; (second row) Roma, Rutgers, Orange Dust, and Moskvich; (bottom row) three Sungolds and Glacier.

BEST VARIETIES OF TOMATOES FOR COOL CLIMATES

Moskvich. Originally from Siberia, Moskvich produces round, medium-size, red fruit with full flavor.

Oregon Spring. Gardeners with short seasons will get bountiful crops of large, flavorful fruits in about two months from transplanting Oregon Spring.

Moskvich

BEST VARIETIES OF HEIRLOOM TOMATOES

Rose. This Amish heirloom (as is Brandywine) might steal your heart. Plants bear large, deep red fruit with high shoulders, good shape, and flavor as good as any tomato out there, bar none.

German. These very large beefsteak-type tomatoes have a full, rich flavor. Their fruits are medium red, with irregular yellow ribs on the shoulders.

Brandywine. This large, ribbed fruit is noted for its rich, aromatic flavor. A yellow form, aptly called Yellow Brandy-

Rose

Shumway German

wine, produces large, though sometimes irregularly shaped, fruit, with a slightly softer flavor than Brandywine's.

BEST VARIETIES OF SMALL-FRUITED TOMATOES

Sweet 100 Plus. Easy to grow, Sweet 100 Plus bears more crack-resistant fruit than regular Sweet 100 and produces abundant clusters of small, cherry-sized tomatoes with a sweet tomatoey taste.

Sun Gold. These small, juicy fruits with a clear, golden yellow skin are mild-flavored and a nice addition to summer salads.

Matt's Wild Cherry. With a flavor that rivals larger main-crop varieties, Matt's bears buckets of very small, ruby-red fruit.

Sun Gold

BEST SAUCE TOMATOES

Juliet. A sauce tomato that is at home anywhere — from the salad bowl to fresh salsa to pasta sauce.

Tuscany. These medium-sized, firm red fruits are excellent dried or used in sauce.

Milano. An early Italian hybrid, Milano is disease resistant with large yields of deep red fruit.

Amish Paste. This heirloom variety is versatile. Its fruits can be used for sauce or sliced and eaten fresh.

San Remo. A very large sauce tomato with Jack-in-the-beanstalk vigor. The fruit is tangy-sweet with few seeds, making it perfect for drying or sauce.

BEST MAIN SEASON TOMATOES

Big Beef. An award-winning, deliciously large tomato, Big Beef bursts with juicy tomato flavor. Disease-resistant plants produce heavy yields earlier than other large-fruited tomatoes.

Celebrity. A long-time favorite, Celebrity has medium-size, deep red fruit. Each tomato is round and nicely shaped with excellent flavor. It's disease resistant, vigorous, and very reliable.

Turnips

Turnips are one of those vegetables with a split personality. In some regions turnips are grown as greens, and in other areas they are grown for their roots. The truth is that turnip greens and turnip roots are both delicious, and each year I look forward to enjoying both.

SOWING AND GROWING

Turnips like cool weather, so they're an excellent spring crop — especially when sown with peas. Some folks think that the peas actually help the turnips grow.

Fertilizing. Turnips' large root systems need deep, loose soil with lots of organic matter to grow their best. Given these conditions, they usually don't need supplemental fertilizing.

Watering. Turnips need only a moderate amount of water. To prevent foliar diseases, be sure to avoid wetting the tops.

HARVESTING AND STORING

Greens. Begin harvesting turnip greens when the plants are young (don't take too many, or root growth will slow down), and continue when you pull the roots. Either cook the roots with the greens or use the greens raw in salads.

Roots. Harvest the roots when they are between 1 inch (2.5 cm) and 3 inches (7.5 cm) in diameter. Larger turnips develop a strong, unappealing flavor. Although you can store roots in the refrigerator for a short time, they are best eaten fresh.

BEST VARIETIES

De Milan. A favorite in Europe, where its tender roots are prized in recipes, De Milan matures early and is easy to grow.

Purple Top White Globe. The most popular garden turnip for many years, Purple Top White Globe produces flavorful roots and tender greens.

◄ **Look what turned up!** Turnips taste best when you harvest them in cool weather. Plant a crop in midsummer and enjoy these sweet root vegetables all fall.

Sow & Grow

TURNIPS *(Brassica rapa)*
Cabbage family *(Cruciferae)*

SOWING

Seed depth: ¼–½" (6–13 mm)
Soil temperature: 50–95°F (10–35°C); the optimum is 85°F (29°C)
Days to germination: 2–5
Sow indoors: Not recommended
Sow outdoors: Early spring to midsummer

GROWING

pH range: 5.5–6.8
Soil temperature: 40–75°F (4–24°C); the optimum is 60°F (16°C)
Spacing in beds: 4" (10 cm)
Watering: Moderate
Light: Best in full sun; tolerates light shade
Nutrient requirements: N=low; P=low; K=low
Rotation considerations: Avoid following cabbage family crops.
Good companions: Onion family, pea
Bad companions: Potato
Seed longevity: 4 years
Seeds per ounce: 14,000 (494 seeds per g)

Many catalogs and references use both the USDA and AHS maps to help consumers evaluate plants for their gardens. Four numbers describe the hardiness of a plant. The first two numbers, such as "5-8," indicate the USDA zones where that plant will grow. The last two numbers, such as "7-3," indicate the range of zones where it will grow using the AHS data. This means that if your garden is in USDA zone 6 and in AHS zone 7, then the plant will be hardy in your garden.

USDA PLANT HARDINESS ZONE MAP

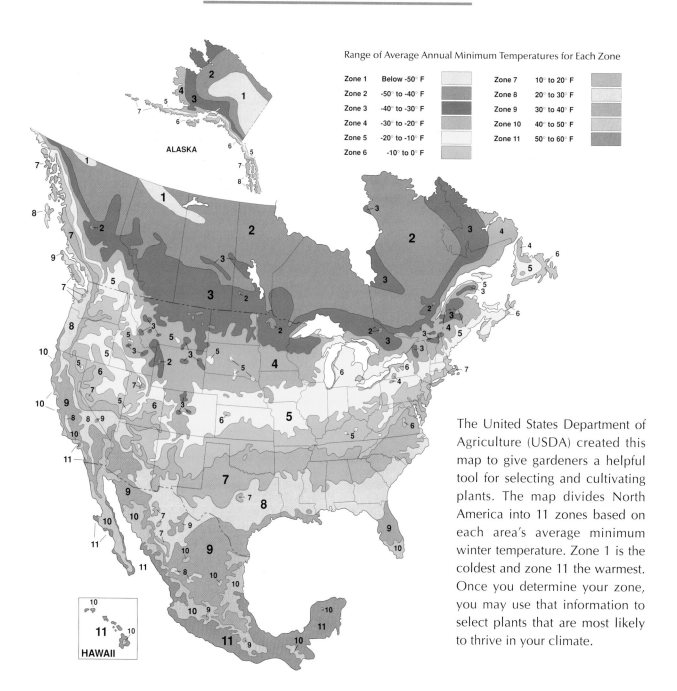

Range of Average Annual Minimum Temperatures for Each Zone

Zone 1	Below -50° F		Zone 7	10° to 20° F	
Zone 2	-50° to -40° F		Zone 8	20° to 30° F	
Zone 3	-40° to -30° F		Zone 9	30° to 40° F	
Zone 4	-30° to -20° F		Zone 10	40° to 50° F	
Zone 5	-20° to -10° F		Zone 11	50° to 60° F	
Zone 6	-10° to 0° F				

ALASKA

HAWAII

The United States Department of Agriculture (USDA) created this map to give gardeners a helpful tool for selecting and cultivating plants. The map divides North America into 11 zones based on each area's average minimum winter temperature. Zone 1 is the coldest and zone 11 the warmest. Once you determine your zone, you may use that information to select plants that are most likely to thrive in your climate.

AMERICAN HORTICULTURAL SOCIETY
PLANT HEAT ZONE MAP

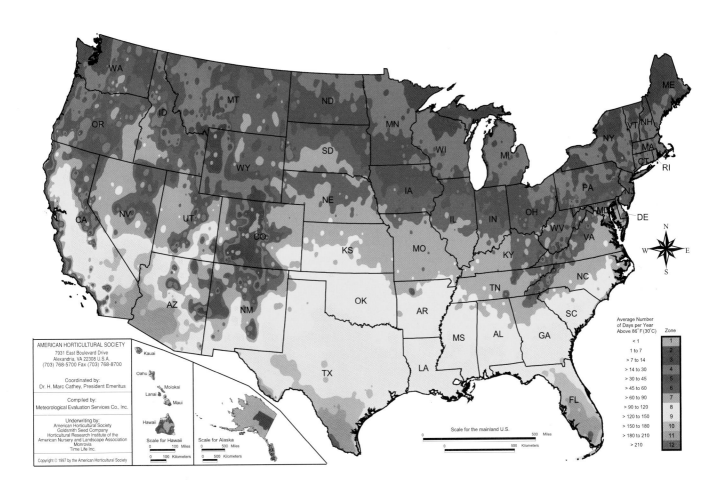

American Horticultural Society
7931 East Boulevard Drive
Alexandria, VA 22308 U.S.A.
(703) 768-5700 Fax (703) 768-8700

Coordinated by:
Dr. H. Marc Cathey, President Emeritus

Compiled by:
Meteorological Evaluation Services Co., Inc.

Underwriting by:
American Horticultural Society
Goldsmith Seed Company
Horticultural Research Institute of the
American Nursery and Landscape Association
Monrovia
Time Life Inc.

Copyright © 1997 by the American Horticultural Society

Average Number of Days per Year Above 86°F (30°C)	Zone
< 1	1
1 to 7	2
> 7 to 14	3
> 14 to 30	4
> 30 to 45	5
> 45 to 60	6
> 60 to 90	7
> 90 to 120	8
> 120 to 150	9
> 150 to 180	10
> 180 to 210	11
> 210	12

For more than 30 years, the USDA Plant Hardiness Zone Map (opposite) has been the preferred reference for determining the ability of plants to survive in different regions. That map bases hardiness on minimum winter temperatures. But, while these are significant, they are not the only factors in determining a plant's hardiness.

Based on the assumption that maximum temperatures are also important, the AHS Plant Heat Zone Map divides North America into 12 heat zones. Each zone indicates the average number of days the temperature exceeds 86°F (30°C) each year. This value was chosen because temperatures in excess of 86°F (30°C) can damage plants.

APPENDIX: SUPPLIERS

A. M. Leonard
P.O. Box 816
Piqua, OH 45356
Phone: (800) 543-8955
Fax: (800) 433-0633
E-mail: sales@amleo.com
Web site: www.amleo.com
General gardening supplies: tool, watering, row covers, thermometers, etc.

Bountiful Gardens
18001 Shafer Ranch Road
Willits, CA 95490
Phone and Fax: (707) 459-6410
E-mail: bountiful@zapcom.net
Seeds, organic gardening supplies, publications

Burpee Seeds & Plants
300 Park Avenue
Warminster, PA 18974-0565
Phone: (800) 888-1447
Fax: (800) 487-5530
Web site: www.burpee.com
Seeds, plants, gardening supplies and decorative accents

The Cook's Garden
P.O. Box 5010
Hodges, SC 29653-5010
Phone: (800) 457-9703
Fax: (800) 457-9705
E-mail: orders@cooksgarden.com
Web site: www.cooksgarden.com
Seeds, some tools and garden supplies

Fedco Seeds
P.O. Box 520
Waterville, ME 04903-0520
Phone: (207) 873-7333
Fax: (207) 872-8317
Seeds, some tools and garden supplies. Very good prices on seeds.

Gardener's Supply Company
128 Intervale Road
Burlington, VT 05401-2850
Phone: (800) 863-1700
Fax: (802) 660-3501
E-mail: info@gardeners.com
Web site: www.gardeners.com
Gardening supplies, greenhouses

Gardens Alive
5100 Schenley Place
Lawrenceburg, IN 47025
Phone: (812) 537-8650
Fax: (812) 537-5108
Web site: www.gardens-alive.com
Organic gardening supplies

Harris Seeds
P.O. Box 22960
Rochester, NY 14692-2960
Phone: (800) 514-4441
Fax: (716) 442-9386
Web site: www.harrisseeds.com
Seeds, tools, gardening supplies, cold frames, compost bins

Heirloom Seeds
P.O. Box 245
West Elizabeth, PA 15088-0245
Phone and Fax: (412) 384-0852
E-mail: mail@heirloomseeds.com
Web site: www.heirloomseeds.com
Nice selection of seeds, tools, and books

Johnny's Selected Seeds
1 Foss Hill Road
RR 1, Box 2580
Albion, ME 04910-9731
Phone: (207) 437-4301
Fax: (800) 437-4290
E-mail: customerservice@johnny-seeds.com
Web site: www.johnnyseeds.com
Seeds, tools, gardening supplies, cold frames, compost bins

J.W. Jung Seed Co.
335 South High Street
Randolph, WI 53957-0001
Phone: (800) 247-5864
Fax: (800) 692-5864
E-mail: info@jungseed.com
Web site: www.jungseed.com
Vegetable seeds

Lee Valley Tools
US orders: P.O. Box 1780
Ogdensburg, NY 13669-6780
Phone: (800) 871-8158
Fax: (800) 513-7885
E-mail: customerservice@ leevalley.com
Web site: www.leevalley.com
or
P.O. Box 6295, Stn. J
Ottawa, ON
Canada K2A 124
Phone: (800) 267-8767
Fax: (800) 668-1807
(E-mail and web site same as above)
Woodworking and gardening tools, home and garden supplies

Liberty Seed Company
P.O. Box 806
New Philadelphia, OH 44663
Phone: (330) 364-1611
Fax: (330) 364-6415
E-mail: info@libertyseed.com
Web site: www.libertyseed.com
Vegetable seeds and more

Nichols Garden Nursery
1190 North Pacific Highway
Albany, OR 97321-4580
Phone: (541) 928-9280
Fax: (541) 967-8406
E-mail: info@gardennursery.com
Web site: www.gardennursery.com
Tools, seeds

Park Seed
1 Parkton Avenue
Greenwood, SC 29647-0001
Phone: (800) 845-3369
E-mail: info@parkseed.com
Web site: www.parkseed.com
Seeds, some gardening supplies and decorative accents

Pinetree Garden Seeds
Box 300
New Glouster, ME 04260
Phone: (207) 926-3400
Fax: (888) 52-SEEDS
E-mail: superseeds@worldnet.
   att.net
Web site: www.superseeds.com
Wide selection of interesting vegetables

Seed Savers Exchange
3076 North Winn Road
Decorah, IA 52101
Phone: (319) 382-5990
Fax: (319) 382-5872
Heirloom vegetable and flower seed collections

Seeds of Change
P.O. Box 15700
Santa Fe, NM 87506-5700
Phone: (888) 762-7333
Fax: (888) 329-4762
E-mail: gardener@seedsofchange.
   com
Web site: www.seedsofchange.com
Organically grown seeds

Seeds Unique
1125 Barboa Ct.
Belen, NM 87002
Phone: (505) 861-0146
E-mail: info@seedsonline.com
Web site: www.seedsonline.com
Unique selection of seeds, including vegetables

Shepherd's Garden Seeds
30 Irene Street
Torrington, CT 06790-6658
Phone: (860) 482-3638
Fax: (860) 482-0532
E-mail: custsrv@shepherdseeds.
   com
Web site: www.shepherdseeds.com
Seeds, tools, garden supplies

Smith & Hawken
Two Arvor Lane, Box 6900
Florence, KY 41022-6900
Phone: (800) 776-3336
E-mail: SmithandHawkenCustom-
   erService@discovery.com
Web site: www.SmithandHawken.
   com
Tools, watering equipment, containers, decorative accessories

Snow Pond Farm Supply
53 Mason Street, Suite 104
Salem, MA 01970
Phone: (978) 745-0716
Fax: (978) 745-0905
E-mail: office@snow-pond.com
Web site: www.snow-pond.com
Seeds (including cover crops), garden supplies, tools, broadfork

Stokes Seeds
P.O. Box 548
Buffalo, NY 14240-0548
Phone: (716) 695-6980
Fax: (888) 834-3334
E-mail: stokes@stokeseed.com
Web site: www.stokeseeds.com
or
P.O. Box 10
St. Catharines, ON
Canada L2R 6R6
Phone: (905) 688-4300
(Fax, e-mail, and web site same as above)
Vegetable, herb, flower, and perennial seeds

Tender Seed Company
4027-C Rucker Avenue #771
Everett, WA 98201
Phone: (425) 257-0866
Fax: (425) 317-0630
E-mail: jeichman@premier1.net
Web site: www.tenderseedcom-
   pany.com
Seeds, some heirloom vegetables

Totally Tomatoes
P.O. Box 1626
Augusta, GA 30903-1626
Phone: (803) 663-0016
Fax: (888) 477-7333
Seeds — lots and lots of tomatoes and peppers

Union Tools
390 Dublin Avenue
Columbus, OH 43216-1930
Phone: (614) 222-4400
E-mail: info.ut@uniontools.com
Web site: www.uniontools.com
Razor-back brand and other heavy duty garden tools

Vesey's Seeds Ltd.
P.O. Box 9000
Calais, ME 04619-6102
Phone: (800) 363-7333
Fax: (800) 686-0329
E-mail: order@veseys.com
Web site: www.veseys.com
or
York, Prince Edward Island
Canada C0A 1P0
Phone: (902) 368-7333
(Fax, e-mail, and web site same as above)
Specialize in seeds for short growing seasons

Virtual Seeds Company
Box 684
Selma, OR 97538-0684
Phone: (530) 686-9735
Fax: (530) 239-3480
E-mail: virtualseeds@yahoo.com
Web site: www.virtualseeds.com
Full line of seeds, including vegetables

Coleman, Eliot. *The New Organic Grower's Four-Season Harvest.* Chelsea Green Publishing Company, 1992. This book is full of useful tips and written in a warm and friendly style. Although its focus is on season-extension, *Four-Season Harvest* is also an excellent source of general gardening help.

Denckla, Tanya. *The Organic Gardener's Home Reference.* Storey Books, 1994. Full of the specific details (germination and growth temperatures, planting dates, and so on) that can make a big difference in garden success. A good reference book.

Editors of Garden Way Publishing. *Just the Facts: Dozens of Garden Charts, Thousands of Garden Answers.* Storey Books, 1994. As the title describes, this book contains valuable information in chart form on everything from compost to frost dates.

Foster, Catherine Osgood. *The Organic Gardener.* Vintage Books, 1972. A pleasant and informative read from an organic gardening pioneer.

Gershuny, Grace. *Start With the Soil.* Rodale Press, 1993. Much of what you need to know about garden soil and how to create the best growing conditions in your garden.

Hart, Rhonda Massingham. *Bugs, Slugs, and Other Thugs.* Storey Books, 1991. The tool you need to help indentify and deal with garden pests.

Hopp, Henry. *What Every Gardener Should Know About Earthworms.* Country Wisdom Bulletin A-21, Storey Publishing, 1978. This concise booklet does just what the title says it will.

Jeavons, John. *How to Grow More Vegetables.* Ten Speed Press, 1982. This book is worth reading, even if you don't end up following all of its rules.

Riotte, Louise. *Carrots Love Tomatoes,* rev. ed. Storey Books, 1998. The best one-stop reference for companion planting.

Smith, Charles W. G. *The Big Book of Gardening Secrets.* Storey Books, 1998. An excellent and easy-to-use general gardening reference. Covers not only vegetables, but also flowers, berries, and common shrubs.

Stell, Elizabeth P. Stell. *Secrets to Great Soil.* Storey Books, 1998. An excellent reference on how to understand soil and create better soil in your garden.

A NOTE OF SPECIAL THANKS:

A number of companies went out of their way to help in the production of this book and deserve special recognition.

Shepherd's Garden Seeds has been a dream come true. Not only did they graciously send loads of vegetable and herb seeds for us to grow, but they also opened their doors to our photographer and editors. We were allowed to wander and photograph the lush trial gardens, where we saw many of the best varieties offered today, as well as a hint of what is to come in future seasons. Thank you, Eliot Wadsworth III, Renee Beaulieu, and Vincent Lawrence.

Gardener's Supply Company took a special interest in the book and did much to help us from beginning to end. The items they supplied, from tools to raised cedar beds, were instrumental in making the book look as good as possible. They are nice people doing what they like to do. Thank you, Meg Smith and Fred Cummings.

L.L. Bean, Inc. helped the author look his best supplying well-made, comfortable clothes that not only looked good, but held up beautifully all season long.

Lee Valley Tools Ltd. sent us some of the nicest hand gardening tools we've seen. Strong, attractive, easy-to-use, and just about indestructible

The Cook's Garden provided vegetable seeds and the seed-starter mix to get them off to a great start.

Harris Seeds was very generous to the project and sent us enough vegetable seeds to grow many gardens. They also supplied deer netting, hot kaps, and a pH meter. All of these made our jobs a lot easier.

Union Tools sent us an array of gardening tools, from manure forks and trowels to shovels and rakes. They're attractive enough for photo shoots and tough as nails.

Mount Greylock Greenhouses. These very generous people allowed us to photograph their sales and production houses, even though we tended to get in the way.

ABOUT THIS BOOK

When you come to the end of a very special project it's nice to look back and see how all the pieces fit neatly together. With *The Vegetable Gardener's Bible*, the satisfaction that hindsight allows has its counterpoint in the trepidation and excitement of the project's early stages. The concept was to create a vegetable gardening book that was truly different from everything else out there. We formed the book team and found an author with techniques both innovative and unique. Then, on an early spring morning, we drove up to Ed Smith's home to become familiar with his garden, where we planned to do the photography for the book.

Although it was early spring, we saw gardens with rich, dark soil and almost palpable potential. We admired neat domes of wide, raised beds, still slumbering against the cold. In the center of the garden was a small miracle: a greenhouse with a warm earthy smell, thriving greens and vegetables. We left with the confidence that the project would come together well, but also a desire to try the techniques ourselves in many different growing conditions. We were going to do some experimenting of our own.

In order to demonstrate the possibilities of small supported raised beds, the whole book team, along with Storey family members, pitched in to build beds in John and Martha Storey's backyard (pages 26–29). We constructed another, smaller raised bed garden in the courtyard of our Williamstown office. The latter became the unofficial salad bar for the staff's summer lunches (page 9).

Charly Smith, horticultural editor and Ed's brother, had the biggest challenge. His own gardens contained rich soil, but they were shaded by pine trees. It is generally accepted that the phrase "shady vegetable garden" is an oxymoron. Could Ed's techniques give plants that needed boost to produce well even in partial shade? In a word, yes. Charly's garden yielded very nice crops of potatoes, onions, tomatoes, squash, and peas.

Gwen Steege, the book's editor, used Ed's techniques to get her best garden ever, even with a

▲ **Candid camera.** Staff photographer Giles Prett went to great heights to photograph every inch of the garden throughout the whole season.

drought in July and August. She harvested huge tomatoes from trellised twines at least two or three weeks earlier than usual, in spite of initial skepticism about whether the method would work.

Storey's staff photographer, Giles Prett, initially was not very fond of the vegetables he was photographing. But Ed's garden turned Giles into a bit of a plantsman. As he photographed the various techniques and began to experience how well they worked, even this nongardener was clearly hooked. He and his wife grew an impressive first garden, with enough tomatoes and pumpkins to supply a small town.

The book is completed, but the project continues. This spring, and for many springs to come, we will reach for our copies of *The Vegetable Gardener's Bible* as we tend our soil and grow our vegetables. Our gardens and our lives have been enriched by the experience of helping to create this book and putting its ideas into action. As you put these ideas to work in your own garden, we hope that you share the same joys and successes.

INDEX

Italic page numbers refer to photos/illustrations; **bold** page numbers refer to tables.

OTHER STOREY TITLES YOU WILL ENJOY

The Big Book of Gardening Secrets, by Charles W. G. Smith. A thorough guide to every aspect of backyard gardening. Step-by-step illustrated instructions and scores of professional secrets for growing better vegetables, herbs, fruits, and flowers. 352 pages. Paperback. ISBN 1-58017-000-5.

Carrots Love Tomatoes, by Louise Riotte. A classic gardening book now available in a revised edition to inspire and instruct a new generation of gardeners. It lists hundreds of plants and their ideal (and not so ideal) companions. 224 pages. Paperback. ISBN 1-58017-027-7.

From Seed to Bloom: How to Grow Over 500 Annuals, Perennials & Herbs, by Eileen Powell. Plant-by-plant chart format includes information on hardiness zones, sowing seeds indoors and out, germination, spacing, light and soil needs, care, and propagation. 320 pages. Paperback. ISBN 0-88266-259-7.

The Lawn and Garden Owner's Manual, by Lewis and Nancy Hill. The ultimate guide to rejuvenating wornout lawns and gardens and keeping them healthy and handsome, from two experienced and highly respected garden authors. 192 pages. Paperback. ISBN 1-58017-214-8.

Secrets to Great Soil, by Elizabeth P. Stell. Readers can create fertile, productive soil anywhere with step-by-step instructions for making compost and fertilizers; fixing problem sites; overcoming drainage, texture, and pH problems; eliminating soilborne fungus; and customizing soil for different purposes. 224 pages. Paperback. ISBN 1-58017-008-0.

Seed Sowing and Saving, by Carole B. Turner. Hands-on instructions for sowing seeds from more than 100 common vegetables, annuals, perennials, herbs, and wildflowers, plus directions for harvesting and storing seeds, creating productive soil, extending the season, and more. 224 pages. Paperback. ISBN 1-58017-001-3.

Storey's Basic Country Skills: A Practical Guide to Self-Reliance. More than 150 of Storey's expert authors in gardening, building, animal raising, and homesteading share their specialized knowledge and experience in this ultimate guide to living a more independent, satisfying life. Step-by-step, illustrated instructions for every aspect of country living. 544 pages. Paperback. ISBN 1-58017-199-0.

These and other Storey titles are available at your bookstore, farm store, garden center, or directly from Storey Books, Schoolhouse Road, Pownal, Vermont 05261, or by calling 1-800-441-5700. Visit our Web site at www.storey.com.